Fundamental QuarkXPress 4

Steve Bain

Osborne **McGraw-Hill**

Berkeley   New York   St. Louis   San
Francisco   Auckland   Bogotá   Hamburg
London   Madrid   Mexico City   Milan
Montreal   New Delhi   Panama City   Paris
São Paulo   Singapore   Sydney   Tokyo
Toronto

Osborne/**McGraw-Hill**
2600 Tenth Street
Berkeley, California 94710
U.S.A.

For information on translations or book distributors outside the U.S.A., or to arrange bulk purchase discounts for sales promotions, premiums, or fund-raisers, please contact Osborne/**McGraw-Hill** at the above address.

Fundamental QuarkXPress 4

1234567890 DOC 901987654321098

ISBN 0-07-882513-X

Publisher: Brandon A. Nordin
Editor-in-Chief: Scott Rogers
Acquisitions Editor: Megg Bonar
Project Editor: Jennifer Wenzel
Editorial Assistant: Stephane Thomas
Technical Editor: Kelly Anton
Copy Editors: Cynthia Putnam, Mark Woodworth
Proofreader: Rhonda Holmes
Indexer: Valerie Robbins
Computer Designer: Patricia Beckwith and Mickey Galicia
Illustrator: Brian Wells
Cover Illustration: Cristina Deh-Lee

Dedication

Without a doubt, writing a book is an enormous task for any individual. However in order for books to be written, doors to the real world must be firmly closed. The first and most significant dedication of *Fundamental QuarkXPress 4* goes to my wife Wendy, not only for helping to close that door, but also for her steadfast encouragement and support. If it were not for her efforts these pages would be blank.

An equal dedication goes to our nearly four-year-old son David, who at times I'm sure must wonder who that stranger is who hovers over the computers making those clickety-clack sounds. Thanks to *Thomas the Tank Engine*, *Franklin the Turtle*, *The Wonderful World of Disney*, and the folks who live in *Busy Busy Town* for helping to put a smile on his face while those sounds were being made.

Finally, this book is also dedicated to you, the reader. Without your inquisitive mind, patronage, and thirst for knowledge, books such as this simply wouldn't exist. It's for you that the high-quality information and creative ideas found in *Fundamental QuarkXPress 4* have been written, designed, and structured—and, for whom the ideas and creativity have been prepared. I trust you'll benefit from the reading adventures you are about to embark on.

About the Author...

Steve Bain is an award-winning technical illustrator, author and writer. He has worked in multimedia, print and related communication fields for nearly two decades, and has been using digital-based software since the early 80s. He was one of the first digital artists to use early Macintosh and Windows-based illustration and publishing software.

Steve is also author of *Special Edition, Using CorelDRAW! 6, Looking Good Online,* and *Fundamental Illustrator 7.* He contributes regularly to various digital illustration and publishing related periodicals including *Corel Magazine (US), Corel Magazine (Germany),* and *The CorelDRAW! Journal.*

CONTENTS AT A GLANCE

PART I

Basic Concepts and Fundamentals

CONTENTS

PART II

Creating Layouts and Documents

PART III

Putting It All Together

PART IV

Beyond XPress Basics

PART V

Reference

I'd like to extend my thanks to the publishing team at Osborne/McGraw-Hill team, whom I can easily attest rank among the most capable publishing group I have worked with. Credit is particularly due to acquisitions editor Megg Bonar—a diamond in the rough and tumble world of book publishing. I'd also like to acknowledge the efforts of project editor Jennifer Wenzel whom I have enjoyed having the privilege of working with, as well as copy editors Cynthia Putnam and Mark Woodworth who have contributed their grammatical expertise and to whom a generous helping of acknowledgment and credit is well due. I'd also like to acknowledge the efforts made by our technical reviewer Kelly Anton (formerly of Quark), for keeping her sanity while offering valuable tips and insights into XPress 4, and checking through possibly thousands of tediously-accurate keyboard shortcuts across both platform versions. All involved have added to the high degree of quality and accuracy you'll see in the pages which follow.

Let me also take this opportunity to thank Quark's public relations manager, Bob Monzel, for his effort and support in providing vital information which make books such as these possible. And, of course let's not forget to acknowledge the efforts of Quark's largely-anonymous software engineers who have put obvious careful thought and consideration into the design of QuarkXPress over the years.

There are many people who provided assistance as we assembled the images found in the pages of the color insert and the Quark In Action elements you'll find in Chapters 1-12. Without the help of this group, the color pages and In Action elements would not have come together. A huge thank you goes to all.

Elaine Chu of Elaine Chu Graphic Design
Malcolm Frouman at *Business Week*
Lourdes Hernandez at *Business Week*
Glenn Munlawin at Osborne/McGraw-Hill
Mary Power Patton at Vantage One Communications Group
Rebecca Rees at *Fast Company*
Brian Wells at Osborne/McGraw-Hill
Jake Widman at *Publish*
Jean Zambelli at *Publish*

Wendy Cotie at Cotie Communications
Thomas Puckett at Intelligent Design Enforcement Agency

Fundamental QuarkXPress 4 is a book for all levels of users who are using (or contemplating using) QuarkXPress 4. Concepts and features of the program have been explained using common, everyday language and many of the creative exercises are easy to follow and quick to perform. *Fundamental QuarkXPress 4* is also supported by a comprehensive glossary and index to help locate and define the not-so-common terms you might encounter. A 16-page color-insert section provides real-word, professionally-produced examples to demonstrate the level of quality and creativity that may be achieved through the use of XPress. The information, reference and examples in this book have been structured and organized in a logical and natural learning progression.

Fundamental QuarkXPress 4 has been written with value for the reader in mind. It has been structured as both a teacher, reference manual and learning tool. Information and step-by-step lessons have been written in everyday terms, and the topics covered, feature complete cross-referencing to related subjects.

Who Should Have This Book

On the creative side of business, *Fundamental QuarkXPress 4* will be of interest to art and design students, digital artists, illustrators, professional designers, Internet artists, art directors, and desktop publishers, regardless of which platform they work on. But, while *Fundamental QuarkXPress 4* is focused toward creative aspects of XPress's use, it will also be invaluable to professionals not entirely familiar with layout techniques such as those working in related industries as technical documentation and commercial publishing or service-based publishing industries such as in-house print shops and service bureaus.

Fundamental QuarkXPress 4 will be a valuable reference and guide for you if you currently use XPress or are upgrading from a previous version, and work in one of the following publishing-related areas:

- Electronic layout artist
- Publishing specialist
- Digital publishing consultant
- Graphic designer

- Technical documentation

- Magazine publisher

- Consumer catalog publisher

- Reference book publisher

- Print shop lithographer

- Service bureau operator

What's So Great About This Book?

Where other electronic layout application books often do well at providing technical information and/or program feature reference they often lack a degree of reader instruction and learning. And, where some how-to layout books often excel in providing techniques, they often fall short when it comes to complete program reference. This is where *Fundamental QuarkXPress 4* has the advantage.

Not only does *Fundamental QuarkXPress 4* provide complete program oper- ational reference and comprehensive feature use, it also fully explores digital-publishing techniques specifically geared toward the use of QuarkXPress 4. Plus, through the inclusion of In Action examples within the chapters, this book provides a wealth of creative stimulation and design and layout ideas to draw on.

While bridging the reference-and-technique gap found in other books, *Fundamental QuarkXPress 4* also delivers in these areas:

- Explains program operation and feature use devoid of technical jargon

- Covers in detail both Macintosh and Windows platforms

- Loaded with tips, tricks, and QuarkXPress 4.02 shortcuts

- Covers comprehensive QuarkXPress 4.02 features

- Fully explains current digital publishing techniques

INTRODUCTION

Conventions Used

In order to cover multi-platform use, you'll encounter command and shortcut notations which may seem confusing at first. Because of the slight differences in keyboard and shortcut identification across Macintosh and Windows platforms, you'll generally see textual reference such as CTRL/CMD and/or ALT/OPTION used to identify certain key combinations. In most cases, the CTRL (short for Control) and ALT (short for Alternate) keys pertain to Windows platform users, while the CMD (short for Command) and OPTION keys pertain to Macintosh users.

Where multiple keys are pressed to accomplish a command, a "+" joins the keystrokes. Where menu and sub-menu access is referred to—all of which are common to all platforms—commands are separated by a vertical stroke in this way: File | Open. The order of these keyboard notations remains constant and consistent throughout *Fundamental QuarkXPress 4*. However, you'll also encounter instances where these platforms deviate from typical commonality. In these instances, both Macintosh and Windows users are addressed separately, and our technical reviewer has ascertained a high degree of accuracy which in many instances surpasses the accuracy of Quark's own documentation.

Tips, Cautions, Notes, and Shortcuts

Fundamental QuarkXPress 4 is fully loaded with relevant *Tips* and *Notes* as they relate to the tools and features being used. The perspective offered by these value-added considerations are combined together in the text with extensive coverage of the keyboard shortcuts implemented in QuarkXPress 4. And, in case you need a complete reference of all available XPress 4 shortcuts (both obvious and hidden), Appendix B covers them all.

Complete Subject Cross-Referencing

As you'll also discover on your exploration of the chapters to come, reference duplication has been avoided by integrating complete subject cross-referencing to optional related ideas and concepts you may wish to explore further. In this unique way, *Fundamental QuarkXPress 4* enables you to focus your reading and learning efforts and avoid the need to hunt-and-pick for related information.

QuarkXPress In Action Examples

Fundamental QuarkXPress 4 includes In Action examples which depict use of certain design and layout techniques in real life situations. The thrust of these *In Action* examples is to demonstrate how to best utilize the features contained in QuarkXPress 4 with a slant toward practical approaches and everyday challenges. You see a portion of these examples reproduced in black and white throughout the chapters as well as color examples in the 16-page color insert.

How This Book Is Organized

Fundamental QuarkXPress 4 has been organized into four parts containing 18 chapters supported by three appendices. While each chapter is designed to guide you through use of XPress 4's tools, the four organized parts have been structured in a sequence logical to learning the program.

Part 1: Basic Concepts and Fundamentals

Whether you're just getting acquainted with QuarkXPress 4 as a first-time user or you're revisiting this latest version, Part 1: Basic Concepts and Fundamentals is designed to cover the basics. **Chapter 1: XPresstrain Quickstart** is designed to have you quickly using the tools and producing layouts.

Chapter 2: After Getting Started provides you with an understanding of XPress 4's basic file operations and tool functionality so that you can begin effectively laying out documents. In an effort to maximize your productivity, you'll get some insight into tackling a layout *before* you actually begin your publishing process in **Chapter 3: Tackling a Layout.**

And, if you're new to working with text and typographic functionality, **Chapter 4: Text Basics and Typography** will introduce you to the world of type and how to work with it specifically in XPress 4. To wrap up basic functionality with a not-so-basic feature, **Chapter 5: Using Drawing Tools** explores the wonderful (and relatively new) world of Bézier drawing tools along with XPress 4's typical item-creation toolset features.

Part 2: Creating Layouts and Documents

After you are familiar with the workings of QuarkXPress 4's text and drawing tools, the next step is to understand XPress' special twist on layout and how to begin assembling the elements on your document pages. The adventure begins with **Chapter 6: Working with Text** where you'll learn to set character and paragraph text properties, work in columns, set styles and generally massage your textual content. **Chapter 7: Adding and Controlling Pictures** takes you into the world of digital photographs and graphics. You'll explore the fundamental techniques you may use in working with pictures and picture boxes including picture formats, picture manipulation, and runaround features. **Chapter 8: Advanced Picture Strategies** looks at the more enthusiastic applications of pictures in XPress by exploring picture color and effects as well as clipping paths. **Chapter 9: Combining Text and Graphics** sets you on your way to marrying text and pictures together by examining text-and-picture runarounds, runaround effects, box-shaping techniques, text-to-box conversions, and anchoring items in text.

Part 3: Putting It All Together

Part 3 has been structured to cover the production of final published documents using XPress 4, including use of long and complex document features available in XPress 4. **Chapter 10: Laying Out Documents** details use of XPress' style sheets, lists and index features while **Chapter 11: Working with Complex Documents** looks at even higher-level publishing features in XPress 4 such as employing the use of Books, working with Chapters and Sections, and managing page content.

   Chapter 12: Fine-tuning XPress, details all the ways you may customize your XPress application and document preferences and the various other ways to work smarter instead of *harder* when producing XPress documents.

Part 4: Beyond XPress Basics

This final part looks at the world beyond your desktop and explores areas such as color, color management, color trapping and offset printing. **Chapter 13: Working with Color** explains how XPress sees and interprets color and details how to set up your document and application for easy and logical use of color. You'll also find out all about the various ways your computer uses color and applies it to real life applications in the outside world. **Chapter 14: The Basics of Trapping** will shed some light on the mysterious world of color trapping for offset reproduction. **Chapter 15: Using Quark's Color Management System** provides you with an understanding of Quark's CMS (color management system) and details steps on how to ensure your color desktop system is telling you what it should.

Perhaps the most referenced section in this book will be **Chapter 16: Printing Your Pages** since XPress is so heavily geared toward offset reproduction. Chapter 16 covers all the aspects of printing, ranging from getting a single page from your desktop printer, though print tiling pages for oversized documents, to getting proper output from a high-resolution imagesetter and working with service bureaus. The printing journey continues with **Chapter 17: Printing Digital Color Separations** where for the most part you'll discover how to understand how digital color images separate into film and efficient ways to achieve this using Quark's DCS (desktop color separation) technology. Finally, **Chapter 18: Beyond QuarkXPress** looks at sticky issues surrounding crossing platforms, and exporting your XPress pages to portable document formats and encapsulated PostScript. And, if you haven't already done so, you'll find out exactly why you should get your hands on the QuarkXPress 4.02 Updater.

Part 5: Reference

Part 5 isn't simply reference but in fact provides a complete insight into the inner workings of XPress by detailing weird and wonderful terms and a universe of keyboard shortcuts. This back-end support defines the more uncommon terminology encountered throughout this book in **Appendix A: Glossary of Terms**, and in a comprehensive and thorough collection, **Appendix B: Summary of Keyboard Shortcuts**, details the extensive shortcuts engineered into QuarkXPress 4.02. Finally, **Appendix C: Color Insert Credits**, provides a reference to all who contributed their talents to the 16-page color insert.

PART I

Basic Concepts and Fundamentals

Athena, Acropolis, Greece

CHAPTER 1

XPress Train Quickstart

If you're a recent updater or convert to XPress 4, you're in for a treat. As far as professional layout applications go, XPress ranks among the very best in achieving control over publishing layouts—whatever your purpose. And, if you've thumbed to this first chapter in search of a fast way to begin working with XPress' most commonly-used tools, congratulations are in order. You've chosen to start at the *very* beginning—always a good choice. This first chapter will get you on your way to installing the program and send you onward to quickly producing your first layout. In this chapter, you'll learn all about XPress' complex installation procedure and how to quickly get up and running. You'll also learn about critical skills such as using XPress' program and document windows, installing auxiliary files, opening and saving documents, and closing and quitting. You'll also get a brief primer on how to get text on the page and print a hard copy quickly. Once your feet are firmly planted, you'll learn where to get help both online and from this book. When you've completed this chapter, you'll be ready to create rudimentary documents to get you started until you move on to the remaining sections of this book.

Installing XPress 4

As far as software goes, XPress is one of the more tricky applications to install. In an effort to protect its intellectual property, Quark has designed a method by which the software itself precisely tracks and limits who installs each copy of the software, on which computer it's installed, and how many times it's done. In order to successfully install a local version of XPress 4, you absolutely *must* have on hand the two 3.5-inch floppy installation disks and the application disc (CD) that come with the program—no way around it.

The two installation disks are both writable, meaning installation data logs created during the installation are stored to memory on the disks. The application disc contains all the compressed data required to build the program on your system, as well as auxiliary files.

Before you attempt an installation, it's worthwhile knowing what you need in terms of your computer hardware and operating system. If you've already installed, feel free to skip ahead in this chapter to *Opening the Program for the First Time.*

Windows Installation Requirements

In order to accommodate XPress 4 in terms of hardware and system resources in a Windows environment, you must be equipped with at least the following:

- Microsoft Windows 95, Windows NT 4.0, or Windows NT 3.51

- 486 or faster system processor

- CD-ROM drive (or access to a CD-ROM drive over a network)

- 3.5-inch high-density (1.44 megabyte) floppy disk drive

- 12 megabytes total RAM (random-access memory)

NOTE *More RAM resources may be required for lengthy or graphic-intensive documents.*

- 12 megabytes of free hard drive space for a minimal installation of XPress; 30 megabytes for XPress Passport and all languages

NOTE *12 megabytes is considered a minimal installation requirement. A typical installation of XPress with XPress Passport (all languages) requires roughly 30 megabytes of available hard drive space.*

- VGA (video graphics adapter—the card in your computer that renders detail to your monitor) or higher resolution display adapter and monitor supported by Windows 95 or Windows NT

TIP *Although XPress operates just fine in VGA, you will definitely want to use a more sophisticated graphics adapter. Most recently-manufactured systems feature graphics adapters capable of at least 256-color SuperVGA or higher.*

■ Windows-compatible mouse or other pointing device

NOTE ───▶ *The above requirements should be considered minimal for installing and using XPress in a Windows environment for rudimentary publishing applications. Having more RAM or a faster processor will certainly speed program operation and operating capacity.*

Along with the preceding requirements, the following items might be considered a potential wish list as far as other resources go. Although having them or not won't affect operation of XPress 4 itself, they may be required for common publishing methods and many of the topics discussed in this book.

■ Windows-compatible PostScript printer with two megabytes of internal RAM (additional printer memory may be required for graphic-intensive documents).

■ Laser, dot matrix, or ink-jet printer supported by Windows 95 or Windows NT.

NOTE ───▶ *If your printer uses RAM and is capable of being upgraded with additional RAM, you may want to add more. Lengthy, font-intensive, graphic-intensive documents and/or higher-resolution printing often require more memory in order to print efficiently.*

■ If you're working with Type 1 fonts, you'll need Adobe Type Manager for them to appear correctly on your screen and print properly.

■ If you're connected to a network and are using it to install XPress in a Microsoft Windows 95, Windows NT 4.0, or Windows NT 3.51 environment, the network must be IPX-compatible (as most are).

Mac OS Installation Requirements

In order to accommodate XPress 4 in terms of hardware and system resources in a Macintosh publishing environment, you must be equipped with at least the following:

■ For a 68K processor-based system, Macintosh system software 7.1 or higher.

1

■   For PowerPC-based systems, Macintosh system software version 7.1.2 or higher.

■   For successful printing of your documents in a Macintosh environment, a LaserWriter driver version 7.0 or higher.

■   In terms of a computer to run XPress on, be sure you are installing on a 68020-based or higher system or a PowerPC-based Macintosh operating system-compatible computer (yes, we have clones now).

■   CD-ROM drive (or access to a CD-ROM drive over a network) for installation.

■   3.5-inch high-density disk drive for installation.

■   At least five megabytes of available RAM for 68K-based systems.

NOTE
Although five megabytes of available RAM is considered the minimum, lengthy or graphic-intensive documents will operate more efficiently with more. Quark recommends eight megabytes for PowerPC-based systems (with virtual memory turned off) and 10 megabytes for font or graphic-intensive documents.

■   To install XPress 4, you'll need roughly 13 megabytes of available hard drive space for Macintosh and 14 megabytes for Power Macintosh.

NOTE
A full installation of XPress Passport and all languages requires roughly 30 megabytes of available hard drive space.

Along with the preceding requirements for installing XPress in a Macintosh environment, it may be wise to have Adobe Type Manager (ATM) for accurate screen display of Type 1 fonts.

NOTE
The preceding requirements should be considered minimal for installing and using XPress in a Macintosh environment for basic publishing tasks. Common sense dictates that having more RAM or a faster processor will speed program operation and operating capacity.

➔ *Before opening the envelopes containing the program disc and installation disks, be sure the version you have is correct for your system. Otherwise, you're stuck with a relatively expensive bookend. Neither Quark nor the dealer you bought the program from will accept returned software once this envelope is opened.*

Following the Installation Procedure

With any new program, you'll want to find out as much information about it as possible before allowing it free rent on your computer. As with most software, Quark lists any "late-breaking" news or problems in a text file located on the installation disk. It's always wise for users to take the time to read this important information. Software companies go to great pains to provide it, and it also seconds as a subtle reminder that software is created by humans. For Windows user, the file is named *Readme.wri* and may be opened with Microsoft's Windows WordPad. For Mac users the file is named *Read Me* and may be opened with SimpleText.

➔ *If for some reason, your program disc or installation disks are damaged or defective, and you require replacements in order to successfully install the program, return the software to the store where you bought it. Or better yet, contact Quark Customer Service at (800) 788-7835 (toll-free in North America) or (303) 344-3491 (Latin America) to arrange for replacements.*

To begin installing XPress 4, insert the 3.5-inch floppy disk labeled *Installer Disk* into your disk drive. For Windows users, the installation disk is labeled *Windows 95/NT*; for Macintosh users the disk is labeled *Mac OS*. The Installer Disk may also feature a bar code sticker, which includes the serial number of the local or network version of the program. Below the bar scan, you'll notice a long list of numbers which comprise your software serial number. Make a note of this number for future reference, or for contacting Quark for technical support should you ever need it.

➔ *Before you proceed with your installation of XPress 4, you'll need to disable any virus protection programs you may have loaded. Some virus protection software can adversely affect the installation process.*

With the disk installed, insert the program disc (CD) into your CD-ROM drive. If the installation *Auto Run* feature is enabled, the installation will begin immediately. If not, you may need to locate the installation program on your own. Windows users can use Explorer to locate the drive and double-click the Install.exe file in the root directory of the disc. For Macintosh users, open the drive folder that appears on your desktop and locate the file named XPress 4 Installer. Both operations launch the installation process scripts. If your Installer Disk is not found after either installer is launched, you will be prompted to provide it. Otherwise, the process comes to a halt until you provide the disk.

TIP

If you have trouble with the installation process and are at your wits' end, you may choose to contact Quark directly by calling (303) 894-8899. No, there's no secret toll-free number to hunt for. And, you'll need to provide your serial number and possibly other sordid details about your specific installation woes, your system, and/or user level.

Registering Your Software

To register XPress, follow these steps:

TIP

Shortly after the initial release of the XPress Windows 95/NT versions, Quark announced certain problems with the installation process (corrected in newly-released versions). The problem involves inserting the XPress 4 program disc after manually launching the installer application from the floppy disk. If the Auto Run feature of Windows is enabled, both the floppy and the Auto Run installation begin to run simultaneously. Clicking OK to the warning message that appears allows the installation process to continue.

1. The registration process begins with entry of your serial number (found on the Installer Disk and on the outside of the envelope originally containing the disks). The registration number is a two-letter prefix followed by an eleven-digit number. Some versions may be preserialized, meaning this number is coded into the installer wizard already. In this case, you won't need to enter the serial number.

2. Enter your user registration information in the Product Registration dialog fields, pressing TAB to jump between fields. Quark uses the information entered here to contact you in the future if necessary.

3. Complete the User Information Survey in the same manner. User information is used by Quark marketing for "future product enhancements."

4. Next, you'll be prompted to insert your User Registration Disk into your floppy drive so the installer can copy an encoded data file containing the information you entered and a detailed profile of your system onto it.

Once ejected, write your name, phone number, and country on the disk, in case Quark is unable to read the information on the file. Mail this disk into Quark using the disk-mailer envelope provided in the packaging. In case you need it, Quark's User Registration department address in the United States is:

User Registration, Post Office Box 480790, Denver, Colorado 80248-0790

5. The next screen that appears asks if you would like a program group created. If you would like the program group created, leave this option selected. If not, deselect it by clicking the check box.

Choosing Installer Options

The installer wizard now continues on to the actual program installation, and displays the screen shown in the following illustration.

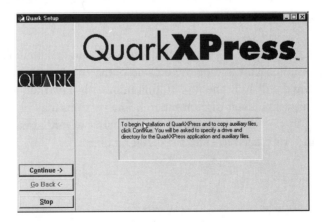

To choose program installation options, follow these steps:

1. If you want a "typical" installation of the program (Quark has determined the most common and minimal features for you already), simply click Continue to proceed to the next screen. The installation wizard also gives you the option of changing the default location where program files are normally copied. To accept the default, click Continue.

2. If you want to pick-and-choose which files you would like to install, click the Customize button shown in the following two illustrations. Here you may change the installation location and select the features you want to install by entering a new path or clicking Browse.

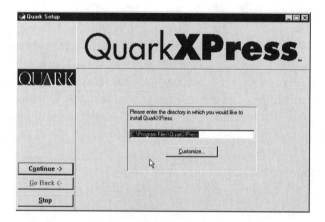

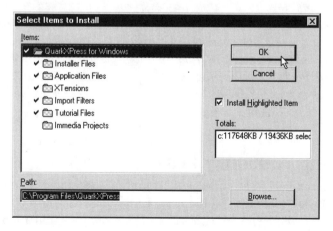

3. Click the Install Highlighted Item option and make your choices. In selecting these options, you may discover that some choices cannot be changed. The choices are organized into folders where double-clicking a folder opens or closes it. The check mark appearing beside a folder or option indicates it is destined for installation. The Totals field indicates the current installation memory required on your system.

TIP *Clicking the Stop button is a quick way to abort the installation. But if the installation process has already begun, then files have been partially copied to your system. If you are reinstalling XPress after a successful installation, clicking Stop is really going to screw things up. It may be wise to wait until the process is complete and files have been copied. If not, your initial installation of XPress may not operate correctly.*

4. Once your choices are complete, click OK to accept the custom installation and return to the preceding screen. There will be no screen indicating that you have chosen a custom installation nor is there a detailed summary of the choices you have made. Clicking the Next button completes the installation choices and installs the program. A prompt will appear to let you know when installation is complete.

TIP *If at some point you change your mind about what you want to install, click the Back button to return to the preceding screen.*

TIP *During the installation process, you'll be asked to insert the User Registration Disk into your floppy drive. The installation program will then create a text file containing all sorts of detailed information about your system as well as the user information you entered when registering XPress with the installation program. Once installed, mail your User Registration Disk to Quark to register your copy of XPress and become eligible for any applicable technical support.*

Installing Auxiliary Files

In XPress, auxiliary files come in the form of XTensions, which are essentially add-on software tools for specific uses. Unfortunately, you can't simply copy an XTension from the XPress program disc to your program folder in order to make it available. Most of the files on the program disc are compressed, meaning they need to be uncompressed to be readable by your XPress application. XTensions not installed with the default installation selection include such tools as Cool Blends, Indexing, and the Kern-Track Editor.

> TIP
>
> *If you decide to install auxiliary files, you will not be able to run the installer while a copy of XPress is currently launched on your system. First quit XPress, and then run the installer.*

If you originally accepted a typical installation and decide at some point you need extra features installed, you must run the installer again and follow the same procedure as the original installation. In other words, insert both the Installer Disk and the XPress program disc into their respective drives. Then, click the Installer on either the Installer Disk or the program disc to launch the installer.

> TIP
>
> *(Windows 95/NT) The Whatsnew.wri file located in the Whatsnew folder on the program disc contains instructions for installing QuarkImmedia viewer and QuickTime. But, it incorrectly states that you should launch a file called QT32inst.EXE to install QuickTime. The actual file name on the Installer Disk is QT16.EXE. To add insult to injury, using this installer under Windows NT 4.0 may cause an illegal program fault (IPF) once the installation process is complete. Luckily, the application still launches successfully. Some experts say installing QuarkImmedia is more trouble than it's worth when weighing the amount of hard drive space it requires against the benefits it provides.*

If XPress is already installed, the installer will proceed to a screen in the usual way. To copy auxiliary files, click Continue until you reach the screen containing the Customize button. Click this button to access the Select Items to Install screen. Once again, items that include a check mark are destined for installation. And unfortunately, what you are viewing is the default installation selection. So, in order to install only the auxiliary files you're looking for, you'll need to review the entire list including all folders in order to narrow your selection to just what you need. Otherwise, the installer will simply install the entire selection all over again. Navigate through the folders and "uncheck" as many selections as the installer will allow.

To program XTensions, double-click the XTensions folder to open it and choose the extensions you want to install. XTensions available with XPress include Cool Blends, CPSI Fixer, Indexing, Kern-Track Editor, and Immedia Project Menu, as shown in the following illustration. To reinstall other files, simply ensure they are selected with a check mark and proceed by navigating the installer screens to the end of the wizard.

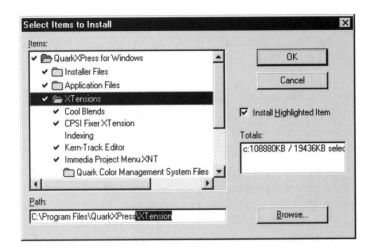

Opening the Program for the First Time

Perhaps the simplest of operations is launching XPress. Mac users double-click the program icon (or alias), while Windows users navigate the Start menu to the XPress program group. On launching, Quark loads application and preference files, XTensions, fonts, and other similar items. If you want, you can watch the status line in the startup screen as these items load (although it moves a little quickly).

Getting Version and User Info

Opening XPress for the first time is like opening it for the hundredth time. No special welcoming banners appear, no congratulations—the program just opens to display what developers call the *splash screen,* as shown in Figure 1-1. This screen identifies the program, its version number (including any maintenance revision numbers), copyright information for third-party licenses, and the name of the entity the software is registered to. Conspicuously missing is the serial number of the software, which is often featured in this screen with other programs.

TIP ➤ *The splash screen may be viewed at any time by choosing Help | About XPress. To make the splash screen disappear, click it with your cursor or press either the ESC or RETURN keys on your keyboard. To see a highly-detailed summary of your version of XPress, including version numbers and other software-specific information, follow these steps: For Windows, hold the CTRL/CMD keys while choosing Help | About XPress. For Mac systems, choose Apple | About XPress. For more information on what this dialog box actually describes and other user information features, see Chapter 12, Fine-tuning XPress.*

XPress' Program Window

If you're looking at the program window for the first time (as shown in Figure 1-2), you'll probably want to familiarize yourself with what you see before going further. The window includes the main menu bars (some of which are grayed out), the program title bar, the main Tool palette displaying some of the tools you'll be using, and an empty Measurements palette.

NOTE ───► *XPress' program window differs slightly between Windows and Mac platforms. Mac users will see their desktop showing through from behind XPress, while Windows users will see a program window that completely covers the screen.*

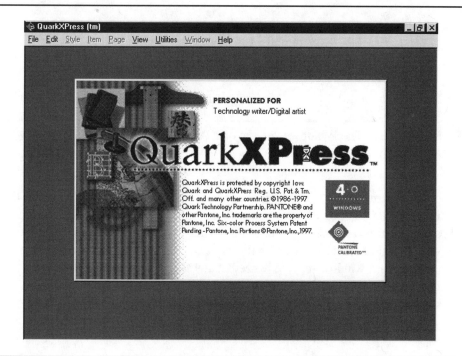

FIGURE 1-1   The splash screen displays user, platform, and version information

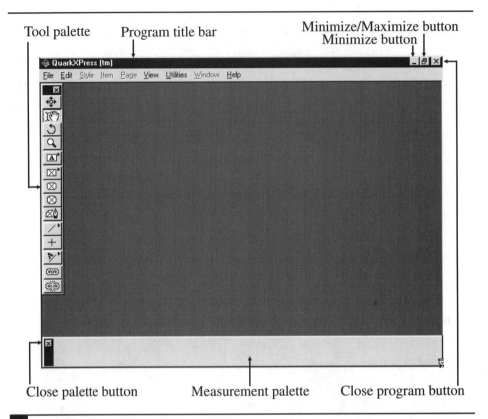

Tool palette   Program title bar   Minimize/Maximize button
                                                        Minimize button

Close palette button   Measurement palette   Close program button

FIGURE 1-2   The Windows version of XPress' program window

If you're familiar with other application window features, you know that the title bar includes the Minimize/Maximize and program Close buttons. The Minimize/Maximize button enables you to control program window size. The Close button quits the program. Windows users will notice that as with any Windows program, XPress' program window may be resized at any time.

The Tool palette contains all the tools you'll be using for the exercises in this book and for all your subsequent layout projects. Because no documents have been opened yet, the Measurements palette has nothing to measure, so it simply sits empty.

1

Both the Tool and Measurements palettes include their own title bars and close buttons, and each may be reopened using commands found under the View menu. For information on working with palettes in general, see *Chapter 2, Working with Palettes*. For more information on working with the Tool palette specifically, refer to Chapters 4 through 7.

Where to Go from Here?

After launching the program, most people want to get started immediately. You're going to want to start either by opening an existing file or creating a brand new one. For either choice, you've turned to the right spot.

Opening Files

Opening new or existing XPress documents, using templates, or setting document or page options requires using File menu functions. Although opening a new or existing document may be a quick and simple operation, there are many types of files you can open and even more that you can create on your own. The following section covers them all.

Creating a New XPress Document

If you're simply looking for a quick way to start your own new file and aren't too concerned about much else, follow this step:

1. Choose File | New | Document and press RETURN in response to the dialog box that appears. A brand new document opens on your screen.

Of course, if you aren't paying attention, you'll miss the details of what exactly you're creating. In essence, what you create is a document set entirely to default values and options. By default, XPress' page settings are set to a portrait-oriented (vertical), U.S. letter-sized (8.5x11-inch) page; the default margin guide values for new documents are set to 0.5 inches on all sides, as shown in the following illustration.

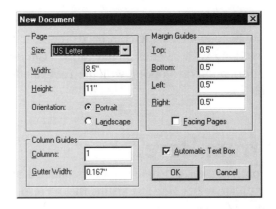

You may also quickly start a new document by using the keyboard shortcut CTRL/CMD+N and pressing RETURN to accept the page options.

The first *new* document you open after launching XPress is automatically numbered *Document 1* in the program title bar. After that, the numbering of new documents is in sequence (*Document 2*, *Document 3*, and so on). You'll also notice a few other things happen automatically. For example, your new document is automatically displayed at 100 percent actual size, the Content tool (second from the top in the Tool palette) is selected already, and your new document window is maximized already.

You won't need to assign a name to your new document until you want to save it using Save or Save As commands, which are discussed later in this chapter.

For details on setting page options for new documents, see *Setting Page Options* a little later in this section.

About Document Windows

The document window contains all the controls related to your open document. In other words, its title bar identifies its name, and page and magnification settings reflect what you are seeing. The document window fits inside (for Windows) or below (for Mac) your XPress program window. XPress supports a multiple- document interface (MDI) so you can have up to 25 document windows open at a time. The document window also features a number of other controls, including the page ruler, scrolling controls, magnification and page options, and Minimize/Maximize and Close boxes, as shown in Figure 1-3. You may also resize the document window vertically or horizontally by dragging its borders.

QuarkXPress 4 IN ACTION

Art Director: Steven Taylor

Photographs: Monica Stevenson

Digital Photo Illustrations: Lisa Knouse Braiman

Description: Magazine feature two-page spread, *Business Week*, March 9, 1997 issue

This two-page spread layout for an editorial feature on McDonald's restaurants integrates process color graphics and digital photographs with text to demonstrate the use of runaround effects in XPress. The layout uses text formatting and drop caps applied in a two-column layout.

NOTE ━━━━▶ *Windows users will notice that XPress documents have a new three-letter extension convention, identifying them as XPress 4 documents. The extension is QXD—an abbreviation for QuarkXPress Document.*

Setting Page Options

Let's back up for a moment to the New Document dialog box. If you're interested in creating a new document to suit exact specifications, this dialog box features

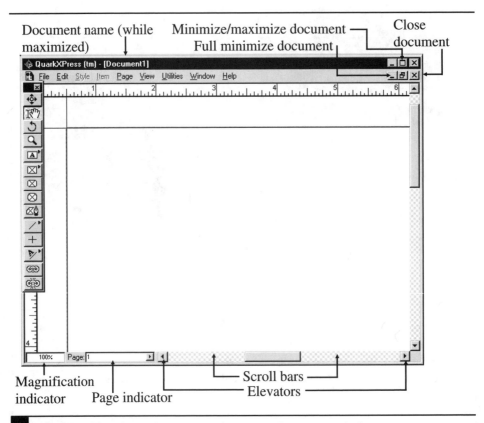

FIGURE 1-3   The various parts of an open document window

1

critical options you'll need to set—some of which can be somewhat involved to change later on.

The New Document dialog box (shown earlier) features page, text column, and page margin settings to control page properties as described in the following sections.

Page Sizes

This set of options enables you to set page sizes for your new document. You may select a preset size from the Page drop-down menu or enter custom widths and heights.

- **Page**   From this drop-down menu, you may select from US Letter, US Legal, A4 Letter, B5 Letter, or Tabloid sizes. After you select the size, the exact page measurements are automatically displayed in the Width and Height boxes.

- **Width and Height boxes**   Use these two boxes to enter exact measurements for your new page. Both vertical and horizontal page dimensions may be set within a range of 1 to 48 inches. Entering custom page dimensions automatically sets the Page size drop-down menu to Custom.

TIP ────────▶ *When entering values that are different from the unit value displayed in any dialog box, you may use the following abbreviations:*

Value	Abbreviation
Inches	In or ″
Inches (decimal)	In or with a decimal
Picas	p
Points	Pt
Millimeters	Mm
Centimeters	Cm
Ciceros	C
Agates	Ag

- **Orientation**   This option sets your page to either Portrait or Landscape. *Orientation* is a term used to describe the direction in which your page is oriented or aligned. A portrait-oriented page's height is larger than its width, while a landscape-oriented page's width is larger than its height. These options are set automatically when custom width and height measurements are entered.

- **Facing pages**   Select this option if you intend the layout you are creating to be in a typical book format where left and right pages exist. Selecting Facing Pages enables you to view pages in pairs within your XPress document window and enables you to set other options such as Section Starts and Book Chapter Starts where left and right page controls are critical.

Setting Columns

XPress enables you to automatically set the number of columns on your page and the space between them using the Columns and Gutter Width options.

- **Column**   The term *column* describes the vertically-oriented rows of text composing your layout. When a column measurement is entered, XPress automatically calculates how many equal-width vertical rows your page can accommodate, and provides onscreen guides for you to follow. So in this box, enter the number of columns you would like in your document. The number can range from 1 to 30.

- **Gutter Width**   The term *gutter* is the traditional name given to the space between page columns. When more than one column is specified, XPress automatically spaces each column according to this value. The Gutter Width value may be between 0.042 and 4 inches.

Setting Page Margins

Page margin values automatically set the space around the area in which you intend to do most of your layout; they are applied to your entire document and to any pages that are added. Page margins also set certain parameters for automatic functions, such as column width measurements. You may independently set the Top, Left, Right, and Bottom margins within a range from zero to the respective maximum width or height of your page. In other words, if your page is 8.5 inches by 11 inches and portrait-oriented, your Top and Bottom margins may be set between zero and 11, and your Left and Right margins may be set between zero and 8.5 inches.

Automatic Text Box

The Automatic Text Box option enables you to add a new, empty container for text when your document is first created and whenever a new page is added. With this option selected, XPress adds one empty text box to align with your page margins; when this option is not selected, you must create the text box yourself.

Creating a New Library

Along with new XPress documents, you may also create other types of files, such as collections of items. These collections are called *Library files*. A Library may contain virtually any item compatible with XPress 4, such as individual text, pictures, or entire layouts. The Libraries appear in your program window as palettes from which items may be interchanged or reorganized. To create a new Library file, follow these steps:

1. Choose File | New | Library (CTRL/CMD+ALT/OPTION+N). The New Library dialog box appears as shown in the following illustration.

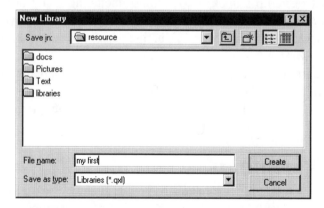

2. Enter a name and set the folder location for your library.

3. Click Create. Your new Library palette appears, as shown in the following illustration.

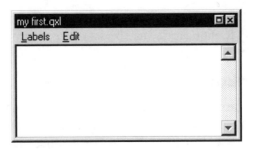

Once a library is created you can drag items into it from your XPress document for later retrieval.

For more information on working with Library files, see *Chapter 11, Working with Complex Layouts*.

Windows users may recognize Libraries by their thumbnail representation in Explorer or by their three-letter extension QXL— *QuarkXPress Library. Mac users will recognize them by their distinctive icon.*

About Book Files

The last type of new file XPress enables you to create is a Book file. The Book feature enables you to manage and organize several large documents (such as the documents that make up a book) at one time—including many of the items and elements they contain. Although the Book feature may be a little beyond what you need to know when just starting out, you can find out all you need to know by turning to *Chapter 11, Working with Complex Layouts*.

The procedure for creating new Book files is similar for creating Libraries. To create a new Book file, choose File | New | Book, set a name and folder location, and click Create. The new Book file opens as a palette in your program window.

Opening Documents

If you need to open existing documents or you're already a seasoned XPress user and are looking for details about opening files, this section describes the procedures. Although opening files is a relatively straightforward operation, some complex issues can crop up if you're working with previous-version or cross-platform files (or combinations of both).

Opening Saved Documents

To open an existing file previously saved in XPress, follow these steps:

1. Choose File | Open (CTRL/CMD+O). The Open dialog box appears on your screen as shown in the following illustration.

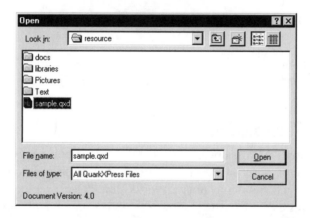

2. Locate the folder containing the saved file you want to open and click the file (in Windows, you can also enter the file name in the File Name box).

3. Click Open or press RETURN. The file opens.

Opening Previous-Version Files

At the bottom-left corner of the Open dialog box is a brief notation describing the version of XPress used to create the selected document before you opened it. If you're curious about where the file came from, you'll want to keep your eye on this area when opening files. For example, when opening an XPress document that has previously been saved in XPress 3.3, the notation will read *Document Version: 3.3*, as shown in the following illustration.

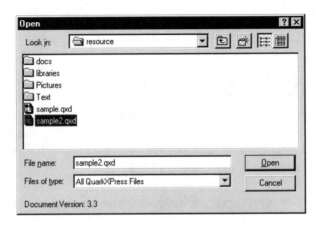

NOTE *XPress only opens and saves files that were saved one version back—in other words, version 3.3 (including 3.31 and 3.32).*

Opening Templates

Along with ordinary XPress documents, you may also open templates. Templates are write-protected files saved from XPress documents. A template may be opened and changed, but it may not be overwritten (at least accidentally). Instead, a template serves as the basis for a new XPress document and may contain text, pictures, colors, style sheets, document preference settings, and most other XPress document-specific properties.

Windows users will notice that templates are given the file extension *QXT,* setting them apart from regular XPress documents. The procedure for opening a template is identical to opening other types of files. Simply locate the folder containing the template, click the file name, and click Open. You may notice that the template opens as an unsaved document, generically titled *Document 1.*

Porting Files Across Platforms

XPress files may be "seamlessly" exchanged between Mac and Windows platforms. The term *seamless* refers to the capability of the host software to support all features on both platforms. So, if you work in a Windows environment and someone hands

1

you a Macintosh-created XPress document, you'll be able to successfully open it. This platform file-exchanging process has been dubbed *porting*.

This seamless support extends to files that have been created on different platforms and in previous versions—something even PageMaker was incapable of doing until recently. For example, you can use the Windows version of XPress 4 to open a Mac-created version 3.3 file, updating *and* porting the file simultaneously. Nifty.

Procedures for porting may not be obvious to all users. To open a version 3.3 Mac-created XPress file into the Windows version of XPress 4, follow these steps:

1. Copy the file to your Windows-based system's hard drive—either by floppy or network connection. Do not attempt to translate the file—it's not necessary.

2. With XPress launched and open, choose the Open command (CTRL/CMD+O).

3. Set your Files of Type field to Display All Files and locate the folder where your Mac file is. Notice the file appears even if a file extension is not attached.

4. Click the file to select it. Notice the bottom-left corner of the dialog box includes a notation indicating file version *and* platform details.

5. Click Open. The file is opened into XPress 4 for Windows.

Opening files created on other platforms may not always be as straightforward as this. There may be font, preference, or linked-graphic issues to contend with. For more information on porting files, see *Chapter 16, Printing Your Pages.*

Getting Text on the Page

One of the first tasks on your quickstart checklist will be getting legible text onto your page. Text ends up on your page in one of two common ways: You type it yourself directly into XPress, or you copy or import it from another application, such as a word-processing program. Either way, you'll be working with a text box and using the Content tool. To get text onto your page by entering it yourself, follow these steps:

1. Click any one of the text box tools in the Tool palette. Text box tools are all identified by the letter *A*.

2. Create a text box by dragging the tool diagonally from the upper-left corner to the lower-right corner of your page, as shown in Figure 1-4.

3. Once you have finished drawing your text box, choose the Content tool from the Tool palette. Notice a blinking cursor is waiting for you to enter text.

4. Enter the text as you would in any word-processing application.

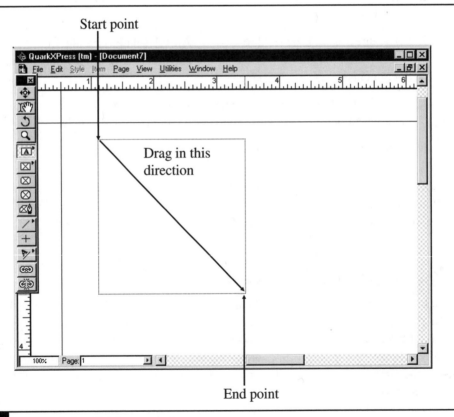

FIGURE 1-4   Getting a text box on your page

5. After entering text, you can resize the text box with the Content tool at any of the eight handles surrounding the text box, as shown in Figure 1-5. Notice the handle changes to a hand-style cursor when the cursor moves over it.

6. To add formatting to the characters you just typed, highlight the text by dragging the cursor across the characters to select them.

7. If the Measurements palette isn't already open, choose View | Show Measurements (F9).

8. Use the buttons and drop-down menus on the Measurements palette to apply font and style changes. For example, click the Font drop-down menu to change fonts or the Size drop-down menu to change sizes, as shown in Figure 1-6. Changes take effect immediately.

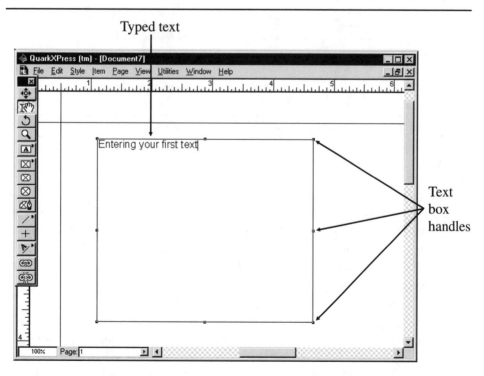

FIGURE 1-5   Resizing your text box

Highlighted text

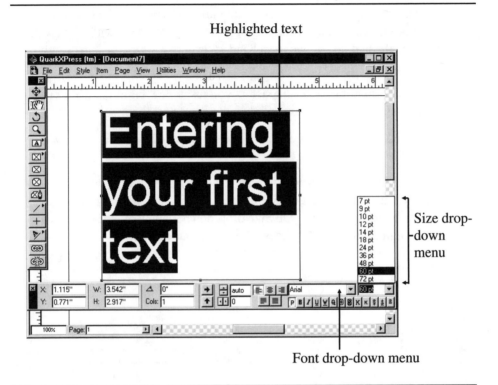

Size drop-
-down
menu

Font drop-down menu

FIGURE 1-6   Changing text formatting using the Measurements palette

NOTE → *There is one slight problem with the initial release of the Windows version of XPress 4. Documentation and menu commands indicate that when the Content tool is selected together with a text box, CTRL/CMD+SHIFT+D selects the Character Attributes dialog box. In reality, when the tool is in this cursor mode, pressing CTRL/CMD temporarily invokes the cursor to become the Item tool.*

Another way to get text on your page is by copying or importing from another application. Copying text directly from another open application involves use of clipboard commands for Copy (CTRL/CMD+C, or, in some Windows programs, CTRL+INSERT) and Paste (CTRL/CMD+V, or, in some Windows programs, SHIFT+INSERT).

The most favored way for getting text onto your page is using the Get Text command. The Get Text command essentially imports text files into a selected text box. To use this command, follow these steps:

1. Create a text box with any of XPress' text box tools (use the same dragging motion described earlier). When you finish drawing your box, choose the Content tool from the Tool palette.

2. Choose File | Get Text (CTRL/CMD+E). The Get Text dialog box appears, as shown in the following illustration.

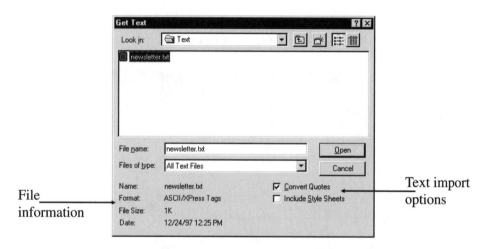

File information

Text import options

3. Locate the folder containing the text file you want to import and click the file to select it. (While XPress is running under Windows, be sure the Files of Type drop-down menu shows the All Text Files option). Information about the file appears in the bottom-left corner of the dialog box, and two options for quote and style sheet handling are available. Leave these options at their defaults for now.

4. Click Open to import the text into your text box. The text box fills with text.

Getting Pictures on the Page

If your first layout involves digital images such as photos or logos, you'll also need to import these onto your page. It might help newcomers to XPress to know that

Quark refers to any image that isn't text as a picture. Pictures include both digital photographs and graphic images such as vector illustrations. Getting a picture onto your page is similar to getting text there and is essentially a file import operation.

As with text, getting pictures onto your page requires that you first create a box. To quickly get a picture onto your page, follow these steps:

1. Create a Picture box anywhere on your page using any of the picture box tools found in the Tool palette. Picture box tools (and picture boxes) feature a diagonal *X*. Picture boxes are created using the same procedure as that for text boxes.

2. Choose File | Get Picture (CTRL/CMD+E). The Get Picture dialog box appears as shown in the following illustration.

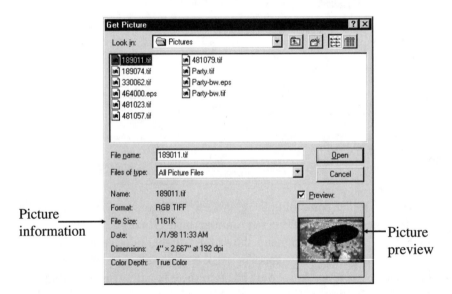

3. Locate the image file you want to import and click to select it. A gamut of information appears in the dialog box. This information provides all sorts of details about your image, including the optional preview for visual reference.

4. Click Open. The picture is imported into your picture box.

5. As with text boxes, picture boxes may also be resized by dragging one of the eight handles. However, as you'll quickly discover, resizing a picture box does not resize the picture inside it. And, as you become familiar with working with pictures and their box properties, you'll discover XPress offers plenty of picture control.

1

Although the preceding exercise is highly simplified, there are many issues to be aware of when working with pictures and picture boxes. This book covers them all in several chapters and across several different topics. For information on manipulating pictures, refer *to Chapter 7, Working with Pictures* and *Chapter 8, Advance Picture Strategies.* For information on creating picture and text box layouts, see *Chapter 9, Combining Pictures and Text.*

A First Quick Print

The next logical question you might be asking yourself is how on earth to get a hard copy of what you just created from the printer on your desk. The quick answer is to select File | Print. But, once you do, you may be overwhelmed by the huge number of options available. To simplify the process, follow these steps:

1. If you haven't already done so, open the file you want to print.

2. Select File | Print (CTRL/CMD+P). The Print dialog box appears and is already opened to the Document tab, as shown in the following illustration.

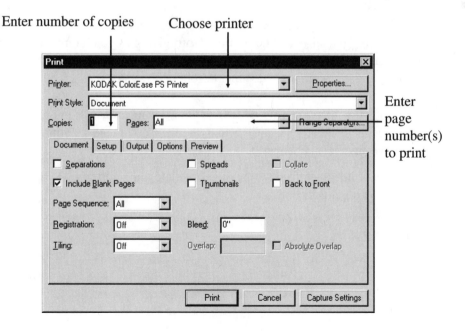

3. Choose the printer you want to use from the Printer drop-down menu. If you are only connected to one printer, it may be selected already.

4. Enter the number of copies you want in the Copies box.

5. If your document is longer than one page, enter the page number(s) you want to print.

6. If necessary, click the Properties button to set your printer to the correct paper size, and then click OK to accept your selection and return to the Print dialog box.

7. Click OK to print your page(s).

Again, these steps are somewhat over-simplified. But in most cases, they'll be just what you're looking for to get a quick hard-copy printout from your local printing device. What if your document is complex and requires a little more user intervention? For that level of detail, check out *Chapter 16, Printing Your Pages.*

Saving Files

Although it's relatively simple, using the Save command is one of the best favors you can do for yourself—and do it often. Unforgiving as your computer is, should you encounter a power interruption (or worse), your work will be lost forever *unless you save it.* To save your open document, follow these steps:

1. Click File | Save (CTRL/CMD+S). If your document has been previously saved and already has a file name, the Save command will immediately save any recent changes.

2. If your document is new, the Save As dialog box appears, as shown in the following illustration.

1

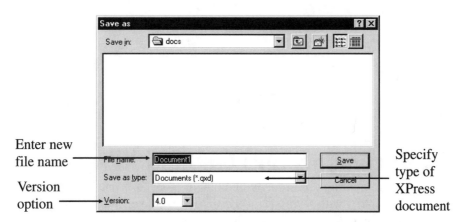

Enter new file name
Version option
Specify type of XPress document

3. Set a location for your new file using conventions specific to your operating system.

4. Enter a name for your new file in the File Name box. By default, all newly created files feature the word *Document* followed by a numeral, but you'll likely want to provide a unique name.

5. For now, accept the default options currently set in the dialog box by clicking Save. Your file and any recent changes are now saved.

XPress enables you to save your document in a number of ways, including as a template and as previous version 3.3 files. To save your file as a template, follow the preceding procedure but choose Template from the Save As Type drop-down menu. Windows files have the QXT extension. To save your file as a version 3.3 file, simply select that option from the Version drop-down menu.

Using Revert

There may be occasions when you have opened a new file and have made changes but later decide to discard the changes (for whatever reason). In these cases, you can choose the File | Revert to Saved command. This command has the effect of closing the file without saving any changes and then reopening it. Any changes you have made since your last save operation will be discarded.

CAUTION
When using the Revert to Saved command, be sure that you don't want to save your recent changes—there is no turning back. There is no Undo command for the Revert to Saved command. Only a single prompt (shown in the following illustration) appears asking if you are sure you want to do this.

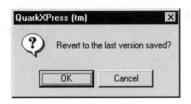

Closing Documents and Quitting XPress

Closing files and quitting XPress may be done in more than one way, and as you progress in familiarity with XPress, you'll eventually settle on the one that suits you. To close a document, do one of the following steps:

- Click the Close box in the upper corner of your document window.

- Choose File | Close

- For Windows users, press CTRL+F4

- For Macintosh users, click CMD+W

TIP
In Windows, you can close all open files by choosing Window | Close All. You will be prompted with the choice to save each file as it closes and eventually you will end up at an empty program window. When using the Macintosh version of XPress, you can close all open files by pressing COMMAND+OPTION+W.

Before closing your document, XPress prompts you to save any recent changes with the message shown in the following illustration. After closing a file, the document window directly beneath your closing document will come to the forefront.

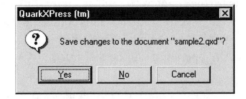

Quitting XPress may also be done in a number of ways. Eventually, you'll come to settle on one of the following choices for quitting XPress:

- Choose File | Quit

- Press CTRL/CMD+Q

- For Windows users, click the Close box in the upper-right corner of the program window or press ALT+F4

If any unsaved files are currently open, XPress prompts you with the choice to save each of them, and will eventually close itself.

Helping Yourself to XPress

Of course, this book is your best source for help while using XPress 4. But, if you need the official company line, you're welcome to use the XPress Help feature. For Windows users, choose Help | Help Topics to access general topics or choose Help | What's This? for context-sensitive help. Mac users can get online help by choosing XPress 4 Help from the Help menu (the question mark icon on the right).

If you need more help than this book provides, or your problem is highly-specific or related to hardware or other software issues, you might need technical support. If you have web access, you can browse the technical support documents online at **www.quark.com/ts001.htm.**

If you need assistance via e-mail, here are some valuable addresses to keep nearby:

QuarkXPress for Mac OS
Internet e-mail: mactech@quark.com
CompuServe: 75140.1137@compuserve.com
America Online: quarktech@aol.com

QuarkXPress for Windows 95/NT
Internet e-mail: wintech@quark.com
CompuServe: 70414.2101@compuserve.com
America Online: winquark@aol.com

If you're looking for general information on Quark itself, or about other products the company develops, check out Quark's web site at **www. quark.com**.

Conclusion

This chapter skims across what could only be considered the surface of XPress 4. Although it provides some roots from which you can quickly get started producing your publishing documents, there's much more for you to sink your teeth into. Although this chapter provides some specific pointers to other parts of the book, you really owe it to yourself to follow along to the next chapter: *After Getting Started.*

CHAPTER 2

After Getting Started

Athena, Acropolis, Greece

If you've just completed Chapter 1, and you want to continue soaking in more of the XPress 4 ambiance, this chapter will take you from the surface to well into the grain of XPress. If you've just upgraded from version 3.3, you'll get a summary on what's new for version 4. You'll learn the fundamental principles behind the interface and critical program features. You'll master document navigation, zoom controls, page commands, and how to use the most common tools, to name only a few skills.

As you'll discover, this book is still in overdrive. As with most chapters in this first section, the goal is for you to quickly grasp XPress concepts while simultaneously learning the tools and features. That's exactly what this chapter continues to do. Along the way, you'll be directed to areas that provide more detail and explanation of the key features being discussed.

The XPress Box Concept

When XPress was first developed about a dozen years ago, nearly all of the graphic and drawing elements you could create or import into the program required that they reside in a box. It was bounding boxes gone mad. It made learning the program difficult for new users at a time when many traditional layout artists accustomed to manual paste-up were still struggling with their new computer skills.

This box concept still largely dominates nearly all the elements that exist in XPress. In order to have something exist on your document page, you first need to create a box for it to live in. And, not only do you have to first create a box, but it also has to be the right *kind* of box, created using a specific tool. In essence, this is the basis on which XPress operates and the working principle that sets it apart from other popular layout programs such as Adobe PageMaker.

What's New in XPress 4?

Quark boasts that there are more than 75 new or improved features in XPress 4. Many of these features have been refined and made more convenient or user friendly from the previous version 3.3. The following list highlights the most significant features for users who have just upgraded.

- **Palettes and tools**   Floating palettes now dominate XPress' new interface, although all of the old dialog boxes they replace are still accessible. You may rearrange the Tool palette to suit your work habits. The Tool palette now includes "pop-out" tool sets to access multiple tools. A new movable Find/Change palette makes text search-and-replace operations more user friendly. And, Windows users may now use the right mouse button to access common clipboard functions. Tool behavior may still be customized individually, or several tools at a time may be customized.

- **Document viewing**   You may now navigate pages quickly using page icons at the lower-left corner of each document window. Screen redraw may now be interrupted or forced to redraw at any time. You may now set your document preferences to more accurately draw items and reflow text as items are being dragged or reshaped. And, the PostScript name for Type 1 fonts may now be viewed by file name, font type, and version number.

- **Page orientation**   Landscape and portrait page orientation may be set automatically instead of swapping width and height measures manually.

- **Drawing tools**   Perhaps the most exciting change to XPress for many users is the introduction of Bézier technology and relatively sophisticated drawing tools. You may now create Bézier *everything*, including picture boxes, text boxes, lines, and text paths. Bézier objects may also be created or edited freely by changing the properties of individual points or line segments. Six new object merge commands now enable you to reshape drawing objects through Intersection, Union, Difference, Reverse Difference, Exclusive Or, and Combine.

You may also automatically create picture boxes whose shape is based on a string of text characters. Any object may be changed to Bézier lines or curves and subsequently edited. And the Measurements palette now enables convenient control over Bézier points.

- **Group control**   You may now resize groups of items with options for scaling the group's contents, and page items may now traverse the seam between facing pages.

- **Dashes, stripes, and fills**   XPress 4 enables you to create your own dash and stripe styles for use with lines (including Béziers) and frames. The dash and stripe feature also now enables you to apply color and shade to gaps *between* the dashes and stripes.

- **Long document features**   A host of new features for working with lengthy documents accompanies this latest release. XPress supports a document length of up to 2,000 bytes (or, two gigabytes) in memory size. The new Index feature enables you to tag words for multilevel indexes, add index entries, create cross-references in documents, and generate a completely-formatted index. A new Lists feature enables you to create formatted tables of contents and style sheets automatically; it also allows you to sort or update lists and indexes. A new Book feature enables you to create book files to manage multiple XPress documents on a local drive or across a network.

- **Text wrap**   You can automatically run text inside pictures while having the text follow the contours of the picture's white area, alpha channels, embedded path, or clipping path. Contours of a text wrap may be edited using Bézier tools.

- **Clipping paths**   You can create new clipping paths without leaving XPress. Clipping paths may be based on white areas, alpha channels, or embedded paths. You can edit or invert clipping paths with Bézier tools.

- **Color**   You can create colors that consist of more than one ink and use user specified percentages of any number of spot or process colors.

Working with XPress' Interface

XPress employs an interface not unlike other newly-released applications, although as with other developers, Quark has put its own unique twist on these program elements. There are the usual menu bars and window controls which, for the most part, operate in keeping with your operating system's standards. And, XPress 4 uses standard directory and dialog box conventions. Palettes are undoubtedly a boon to the interface world, and XPress now employs these interface elements to control many old and new features.

Anatomy of the Document Window

Chapter 1 gave you a general overview of XPress' program and document windows; this section takes a slightly closer look. Document windows feature devices and settings specific to the document in the forefront of your screen, as shown in Figure 2-1.

■ **Title bar**   As mentioned in Chapter 1, the document title bar displays the name of your currently-open XPress document. Under Windows, the Full Minimize button enables you to reduce the document window to nothing more than a short title bar at the bottom of your program window, as shown in Figure 2-2.

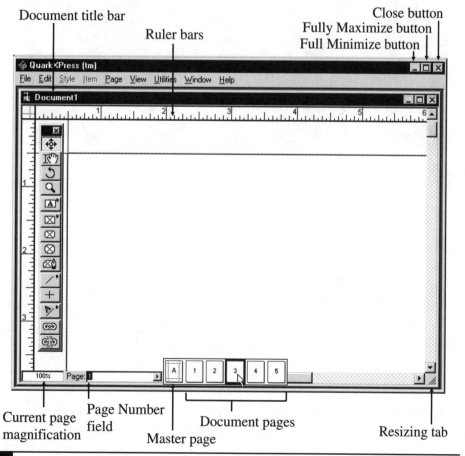

Document title bar
Ruler bars
Close button
Fully Maximize button
Full Minimize button

Current page magnification
Page Number field
Master page
Document pages
Resizing tab

FIGURE 2-1   The document window houses your open layout file and its contents

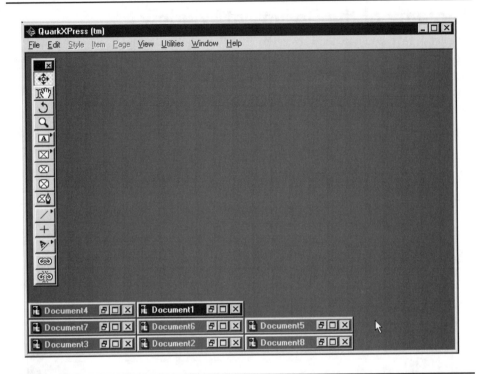

FIGURE 2-2   The Full Minimize button shrinks the document window to a short title bar

- **Full Minimize and Maximize/Minimize buttons under Windows versions**   On the right side of the title bar are the Maximize/Minimize and Close buttons found in all Windows program windows. The Maximize/Minimize button changes appearance depending on whether your document window is maximized or minimized. The term maximize describes the document window opened to envelop the program window, and minimizing the window refers to a manually-adjusted size smaller than the maximum. When toggling between maximize and minimize sizes, your program will recall the manually-adjusted size automatically.

- **Resizing tab**   The resizing tab enables you to resize your document window to any shape that suits your needs. Although the resize tab is a good spot to change the dimensions of your document window, you may resize the window from any part of the document window border.

TIP   *When you use the Windows version of XPress, and you have more than one document open at a time, you may bring any document immediately to the forefront by choosing its name from the Windows menu. The Windows menu also includes commands for closing all documents, cascading and tiling document windows, and selecting to bring open document windows to the forefront when working with multiple documents.*

■ **Page display**   You may quickly move from one page to another in your document either by entering the page number you want to move to in the Page Number field and pressing RETURN, or by clicking the button to the right of this field and selecting the corresponding page by clicking it. Master pages may also be displayed using this feature.

Working with Dialog Boxes and Palettes

In keeping with standard conventions, dialog boxes contain tabs, areas, entry boxes (fields), drop-down lists or pop-up menus, and various other types of check boxes and buttons. Dialog boxes containing large numbers of options are often organized into tabbed areas, which may be selected by clicking the tab's title to bring it forward.

After making selections in a dialog box, pressing the OK button causes the changes to take effect after the dialog box closes. And, nearly all dialog boxes feature an Apply button, which causes the changes to take effect before exiting the dialog box. This way you can preview your changes before actually committing to them. In any case, clicking the Cancel button in the dialog box causes the dialog box to disappear without any changes taking effect.

TIP   *To cancel the settings in a dialog box without actually closing it, press the keyboard shortcut for Undo, CTRL/CMD+Z, to reset all values and controls.*

TIP   *Press TAB to cycle from one field or option of a dialog box to the next, or, press SHIFT+TAB to cycle in the opposite direction. Press CTRL/CMD+TAB to cycle between the tabs.*

Palettes are brief floating dialog boxes that can remain open as you work and can be maximized or minimized. Palettes often replace conventional dialog box functions and are often easier, faster, and more accessible than either menus or dialog boxes. Palette changes often take place immediately after a selection is made instead of having to press an OK or Apply button.

TIP *To minimize or maximize, double-click on the palette's title bar. The display state toggles between the two modes.*

Working with Fields

Fields are the boxes in dialog boxes and palettes that accept numeric values. Field values are often predetermined, such as when entering points to set a font size, or inches to set a page size. But if you want, you may override these values by entering the measurement suffix after your value. The following abbreviations of unit values are accepted by XPress fields.

Inches	*In (or ")*
Inches (decimal)	*In (or with a decimal)*
Picas	*p*
Points	*pt*
Millimeters	*mm*
Centimeters	*cm*
Ciceros	*c*
Agates	*ag*

TIP *You can use fields as if they are tiny calculators. By using operators for addition (+), subtraction (-), multiplication (*), and division (/), you can have XPress calculate the value of a field based on the current measurements. For example, entering the operator /2 after a value of 1.0 in will result in a value of 0.5 in after pressing TAB or moving to the next field. You may use as many operators as you want, such as /2*3+3. Multiplication and division are performed before addition and subtraction. After the calculation is performed, the operators disappear from the field.*

Viewing and Zooming a Layout

What would you do if you couldn't see exactly what you were creating on your screen? Viewing a document is just as essential as having good tools to create one. After all, it is your first method of proofing your layout. And, having a flexible and accurate representation makes all the difference. There are plenty of ways to view your document and zoom around the page, and as far as flexibility goes, XPress is capable of displaying your pages within a range of 10 to 800 percent (to within one decimal place) of their actual size.

Using the Zoom Tool

The magnifying-glass button in your Tool palette represents the Zoom tool and works as your primary method of zooming around your page. Zooming increases or decreases the magnification of your page with either a single click or marquee drag. Zoom views change using your click point, or the area you marquee drag, as the center of reference. Simple clicks with the Zoom tool change the view in set increments, while marquee zooming enables you to zoom to a specific part of your layout.

The Zoom tool has two basic modes: Zoom in or Zoom out, indicated by the + and - symbols in the center of the glass icon. You may choose the Zoom tool in a number of different ways. Selecting it from the main Tool palette is the most straightforward method, but you may also temporarily change your cursor to the Zoom tool (regardless of which tool is selected) by holding certain keys. Using Windows versions, press CTRL/CMD+SPACEBAR and click the mouse button to zoom in, or press CTRL/CMD+ALT/OPTION+SPACEBAR and click the mouse button to zoom out. Using Macintosh versions, press CTRL and click the mouse button to zoom in or press CTRL and click the mouse button to zoom out.

Zoom Tool Settings

If you want, you may change certain settings of your Zoom tool, the most common being the Zoom increment. By default, single clicks change your zoom view by 25 percent of the actual size of your document. You may also change the minimum or maximum view scale. To access the dialog box used for changing these settings, double-click the Zoom tool in the Tool palette. The Document Preferences dialog box appears as shown in the following illustration.

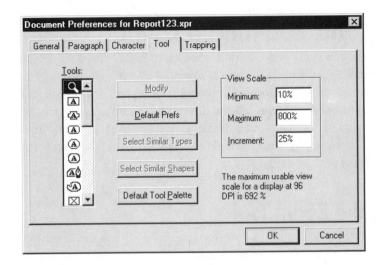

For more information on changing Zoom tool and other tool and document preference settings, see *Chapter 12, Fine-Tuning XPress.*

Changing Zoom Levels

There's usually a slight redundancy in the methods of accomplishing tasks, and perhaps the best example is in zooming. Although the Zoom tool is perhaps the most efficient way to change zoom views, you may also use the menus or shortcut keys, or enter values directly in the View Percent field at the bottom-left corner of your document window.

To quickly select the View Percent field at the bottom-left corner of your document window, press CTRL+ALT+V in Windows, or press Ctrl+V in Macintosh version.

To change your zoom to a preset level, choose one of the zoom levels from the View menu or use one of the following keyboard shortcuts.

To do this	Do this
Fit in window	CTRL/CMD+0 (zero)
Fit largest spread in window	Hold ALT/OPTION and choose View | Fit in Window or press CTRL/CMD+ALT/OPTION+0

To do this	Do this
50 percent	View I 50 percent
75 percent	View I 75 percent
Actual size (100 percent)	CTRL/CMD+1
Toggle between 200 percent and actual size	CTRL/CMD+ALT/OPTION and click on page

Viewing Thumbnails

Thumbnails are the tiny pen-and-paper rough sketches layout artists use to conceptualize their layouts. Thumbnails do not show a high degree of detail and they are not readable. XPress is capable of displaying your entire document in a thumbnail-style view. Choose Thumbnails (SHIFT+F6) from the View menu or enter a *t* in the View Percent field and press RETURN. XPress will display your pages in proper order and proportion enabling you to get a rough impression of the layout, as shown in Figure 2-3.

TIP

Using Thumbnails is a quick way to browse a document for things like overflow symbols at the ends of unlinked text boxes. Overflow symbols indicate text that does not fit into the text box and may be hidden from view. And, while in Thumbnails view, entire single or multiple pages may be selected and moved within your layout or between documents.

Navigating Pages (Page Menu)

If your document is more than one or two pages in length, you'll ultimately want to find a quick way to move between pages. The Page Number field provides a quick way to navigate short documents, but the page icons may only display up to 14 pages at a time under normal screen resolution settings.

For navigating longer documents, you may want to investigate the Page menu, which contains traditional commands for moving through a long document. From here, choose from page commands for Previous (SHIFT+PAGEUP), Next (SHIFT+PAGEDOWN) , First (CTRL/CMD+ HOME), Last (CTRL/CMD+ END), and Go To (CTRL/CMD+J). Although these commands provide rudimentary navigation through your document, they are perhaps the slowest method for changing pages—often even slower than clicking the scroll bars to change your page view (not recommended).

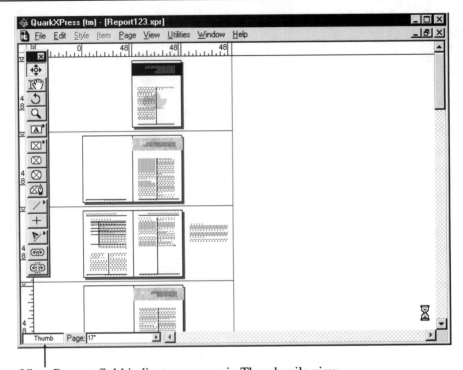

View Percent field indicates you are in Thumbnails view

FIGURE 2-3   Selecting Thumbnails view gives you a bird's-eye view of
your document

Navigating with the Document Layout Palette

A much faster method for traversing your document is through use of the Document
Layout palette. This palette (shown in the following illustration) enables you to control
a number of aspects of your layout—including page navigation. To display the
Document Layout palette, choose View | Show Document Layout (Windows, F4;
Macintosh, F10). The palette is divided into two areas: The top area controls master
pages, and the bottom controls document pages. To display a particular page using these
controls, simply double-click the page icon in the lower half of the palette.

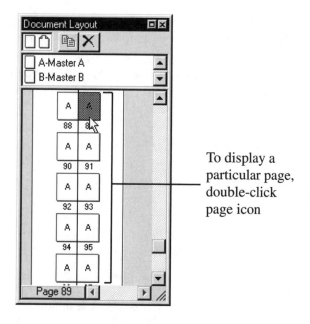

To display a
particular page,
double-click
page icon

NOTE *Don't be confused by the appearance of the pages in the Document Layout palette. Although the icons themselves indicate details about page numbers, master page settings, and left and right facing pages, they don't reflect the actual shape or orientation of your document pages.*

Adding, Deleting, and Moving Pages

While laying out documents more than two or three pages in length, you may add or delete pages manually using the Insert, Delete, or Move Page menu commands. Choosing Page | Insert displays the Insert Pages dialog box, as shown in the following illustration.

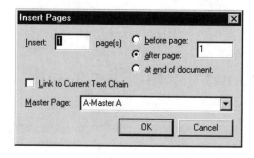

These options enable you to insert multiple pages into specific areas of your document. By default, these options are set to automatically insert one page after the current page, but you may set them according to your needs. You may also choose other options for text linking or use specific master page styles. For more information on text linking, see *Linking Tools* later in this chapter. For information on working with master pages, see *Chapter 3, Tackling a Layout.*

TIP

When importing text with the Get Text command, you may enable XPress to automatically add pages as needed by activating the Auto Page Insertion option. This option adds pages to your document when the text you are importing does not fit into the current text box you are importing it into. Choose Edit | Document Preferences | General tab and select your preferred option from the Auto Page Insertion drop-down menu. For more information on setting document preferences, see Chapter 12, Fine-tuning XPress.

One way to delete pages from your document is to choose the Page | Delete menu command. Choosing this command displays a simple dialog box enabling you to enter the start and finish page number of the pages you want to delete. Any and all objects the pages may contain will be deleted.

The Page menu also includes a command to move pages within your document. Choosing Page | Move generates the dialog box shown in the following illustration and enables you to move one or more pages by entering their page numbers and choosing the destination page number you want to move them to. The Move Pages dialog box operates in much the same manner as the Add Pages dialog box.

Page Commands via the Document Layout Palette

If you're beyond constantly accessing menus to perform page functions, you may lean toward using the Document Layout palette. Among its other capabilities, the

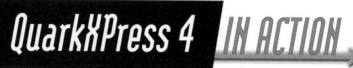

  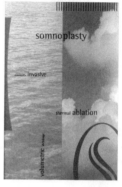

Designers: Elaine Chu, Andrew Fukutome

Design Firm: Chikumura Design, 39 Boardman Place, Loft 101, San Francisco, CA 94103 (Phone) 415/252-9565, (Fax) 415/252-9564, or **www.chikamura.com**

Client: Somnus Medical Technologies, Inc.

Description: Brochure design for Somnus Medical Technologies

Somnus Medical Technologies needed a brochure to explain the common problem of sleep apnea and to introduce their new technology of somnoplasty as a solution.

The brochure was created using four Pantone colors and a combination of stock photography and specific on-site shots which were imported into the Quark layout. The curves were made from ellipses filled with white or a photograph image pasted in the exact same location as the image behind. The vertical stripes, rotated text, and interlocking blocks of copy were also all done in Quark.

Overall, the color palette and images of sky and water were used to convey a sense of calm while the typography suggested a "cutting-edge" company with a new approach.

Document Layout palette is designed specifically for adding, deleting, and moving pages within documents.

To add pages to your document using this palette, hold down ALT/OPTION while dragging a master page from the top portion of the palette into the bottom portion as shown in the following illustration. This action displays the Insert Pages dialog box and enables you to add pages as described earlier.

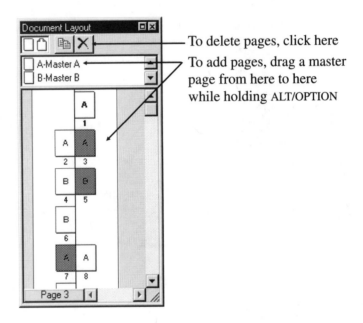

To delete pages, click here

To add pages, drag a master page from here to here while holding ALT/OPTION

TIP   *When adding pages using the Document Layout palette, the point to which you drag the master page determines where the page(s) will be added. For example, dragging it between two pages inserts all new pages between those two and renumbers the pages automatically.*

To delete pages using the Document Layout palette, select the page icon(s) in the palette and click the Delete button (for Windows) as shown in the preceding illustration, or click the trash icon (for Macintosh versions). To move pages, simply select them and drag them to a new location. You may move one or several pages at a time. The point at which you release the pages is critical to where they are moved to.

TIP ───────▶ *You may select pages in sequence when using the Document Layout palette by holding the SHIFT key and selecting the first and last pages you want to select. To select pages not in sequence, hold CTRL/CMD while selecting pages. To deselect pages, click them a second time. To deselect all pages, click anywhere away from the selected pages.*

Moving pages with the Document Layout palette is more interactive than other page commands. Pages may be selected and moved individually or in multiples (in sequence or not).

Controlling Document Appearance

When you consider that your screen is the viewport to how your layout appears to you, it's no surprise many users often desire the ability to control it. For some, this ability is merely a convenience for reducing the time it takes pages to display. For others who work in a fast-paced publishing environment where time is money, it's a necessity. XPress allows you to set how text and pictures appear on your screen and the freedom to interrupt or force the display of your layout.

Setting Text-Greeking

Few experts are sure exactly where the term *greeking* stems from. Perhaps it has something to do with the old saying "it's all greek to me," which has little to do with how greeked text actually looks. In the world of electronic layout, greeking has come to describe the effect of displaying smaller sizes of text as unreadable gray horizontal stripes—a rough representation of your text's appearance, as shown in Figure 2-4. Because font and character detail is omitted, greeked text displays infinitely faster than normal text.

In XPress (as in other layout applications) you have the option to set the text point size at which the text is greeked, referred to as the *greeking limit*. All text below this size limit is greeked. This limit is set using your Document Preferences | General tab dialog box, (shown in the following illustration) which is accessed from the Edit menu (CTRL/CMD+Y).

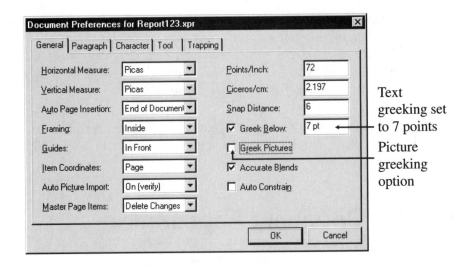

Text greeking set to 7 points

Picture greeking option

Document Preferences for Report123.xpr

General | Paragraph | Character | Tool | Trapping

Horizontal Measure: Picas
Vertical Measure: Picas
Auto Page Insertion: End of Document
Framing: Inside
Guides: In Front
Item Coordinates: Page
Auto Picture Import: On (verify)
Master Page Items: Delete Changes

Points/Inch: 72
Ciceros/cm: 2.197
Snap Distance: 6
☑ Greek Below: 7 pt
☐ Greek Pictures
☑ Accurate Blends
☐ Auto Constrain

OK   Cancel

FIGURE 2-4   Greeked text appears as horizontal stripes

Setting Picture Display

The other layout elements that take significant time to display on your screen are graphic or digital images. Along with text greeking options, you also have the option of setting pictures to greek. Greeked pictures appear more crudely on screen, but they display significantly faster than when greeking is turned off. To set pictures in your layout to greek, select the Greek Pictures option in the Document Preferences window shown in the preceding illustration. Greeked pictures appear as gray-filled boxes until they are selected, as shown in Figure 2-5.

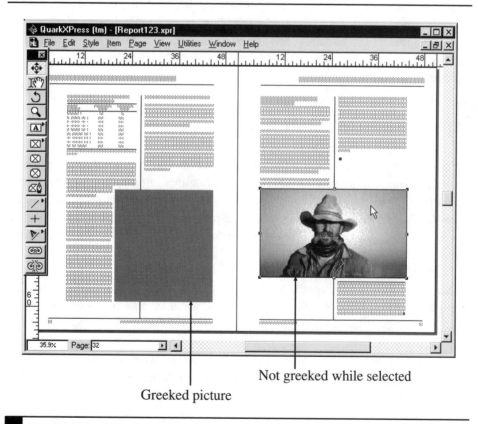

Not greeked while selected

Greeked picture

FIGURE 2-5   Working with picture-greeking options

TIP *If you are viewing a document created by someone else, and you're fairly certain text and pictures should appear better than what you're seeing, you may want to check the greeking options described in this section. Chances are, whoever created the document left the greeking options set to increase screen draw time. Resetting the greeking options will improve the document's onscreen appearance.*

Missing Preview Command

If you've been searching for the Preview command in XPress 4, look no more. This command was removed just prior to the application's release due to technical conflicts connected with screen redraw. Although Quark's manuals refer to the Preview option (formerly found under the View menu), and it may reappear in a subsequent maintenance release, no such command exists at the time of this writing. The shortcut key (CTRL/OPTION+SHIFT+F7) that was historically assigned to this command has no effect.

Screen Redraw Commands

If you've ever become frustrated with the time it takes for your screen to display text or pictures, you may crave a feature that enables you to control screen redraw. You'll be pleased to know that XPress 4 now features *interruptible display*—the capability for you to stop XPress from drawing images in your layout. Screen redraw occurs anytime you change views or pages, or when options are changed or a dialog box blocking your view is closed. Intensive redraw sessions can be maddening if you're not really interested in seeing all the detail of your layout for the hundredth time.

Screen redraw is now interruptible using the shortcuts CMD+PERIOD (for Mac users) or ESC (for Windows users). Screen redraw may also be forced using the shortcut CMD+OPTION+PERIOD (for Mac users) or SHIFT+ESC (for Windows users).

NOTE *Although this section touches only briefly on the key controls for setting page appearance, more information is available in Chapter 12, Fine-tuning XPress.*

Using Common Tools

In any program, there are always one or two commonly-used tools you must absolutely master before becoming even slightly proficient. In XPress 4, these tools are the tools used for selecting, editing, and manipulating your page items. Page items are elements you create on your page to compose your document layout and design. Because page items may be text, pictures, lines, or shapes, there are a number of different types of tools used to work with these elements. Each tool has its own purpose and capabilities.

Key XPress Tools to Master

Whether you're creating XPress documents yourself, or simply editing or browsing through them, the Item and Content tools are the two most critical tools you'll need to know how to use. This quick section is a "must read" for anyone working even occasionally with layouts in XPress.

Item Tool

It's called different things in different programs, but the main tool you'll use in XPress is the Item tool. The Item tool by default is in the first position at the top of the Tool palette for a very good reason—it's your primary tool for selecting, sizing, reshaping, and moving all types of items, and functions for editing text runaround contours and shaping clipping paths.

TIP *Holding CTRL/CMD temporarily changes your pointer to the Item tool, regardless of which tool you have currently selected.*

While the Item tool is selected, clicking any of the objects on your page "selects" them, and places them in a temporary alert state. An object must be selected for you to perform other commands on it such as editing or changing properties.

TIP *XPress provides feedback that objects are currently selected by displaying the eight selection handles at their corners and sides.*

To select more than one object, press SHIFT while clicking additional objects. To deselect a selected object, press SHIFT while clicking the object a second time. To select all objects in a specific area, use a marquee-selection action. Marquee selection involves dragging the Item tool diagonally until a dotted marquee line surrounds the objects, as shown in Figure 2-6. When the mouse button is released, the objects will become selected. Finally, to select only specific objects on your page, press SHIFT and click with the Item tool to select the objects.

Start here

Drag to here

FIGURE 2-6   Marquee selecting with the Item tool

TIP ➤ *When moving objects with the Item tool, holding Shift while moving constrains the vertical or horizontal movement of the object being moved.*

Once an object is selected with the Item tool, it may also be repositioned by dragging it or using one of the UP, DOWN, LEFT, and RIGHT arrow keys on your keyboard. Although dragging enables you to move objects interactively around your screen using visual references, using the arrow keys enables you to move them more accurately by a distance of one point. This action is referred to as *nudging*.

TIP ➤ *Holding the ALT/OPTION key while pressing an arrow key moves a selected object a distance of 0.1 points.*

Finally, the Item tool enables you to resize any selected items by dragging one of the eight corner or side handles. While the Item tool is selected, moving your cursor over one of these handles changes your cursor to a pointing hand. The pointing hand indicates you are about to perform an interactive resizing operation. In the case of the Item tool, resizing usually means changing the size of a box containing text or a picture. Using various keyboard combinations, you may also resize not only the boxes, but also the contents. This action varies depending on the combinations of keys pressed. But resizing is one of those operations learned much more quickly through practice than by simple definition.

For a practical exercise in resizing an object using the Item tool, follow these steps:

1. Create a text box using the Rectangle Text Box tool.

2. Choose the Content tool and enter a short string of sample text when the cursor appears.

3. Leave the text formatting as it is and choose the Item tool again.

4. Select the text box by clicking it once. Notice eight handles appear—one on each side and corner.

5. Move your pointer over one of the corner handles, as shown in the following illustration.

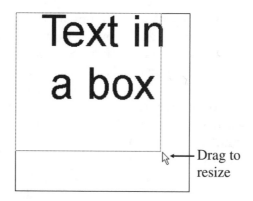

Text in
a box

Drag to resize

6. Drag it in any direction and release the mouse button. The text box has been resized, but the text itself remains unchanged.

7. Now grab the same corner handle and drag it in any direction while holding the SHIFT key. Notice the text box width and height proportions become equal when you click the handle. As you drag, the box shape changes as a constant square, but when you release the mouse the text remains unchanged. Notice also that the box changes shape relative to the center of the corner you drag.

8. Hold CTRL/CMD+SHIFT as you drag the corner handle. When you release the mouse, both the text and the box change size proportionately.

9. Press CTRL/CMD+Z to undo the preceding action. Now, hold only the CTRL/CMD key and perform the action in step 8. As you drag, the box shape changes freely, but when you release the mouse, the text's shape changes either vertically or horizontally depending on your drag direction.

It's extremely important to grasp not only the Item tool's function here, but also the concepts of resizing, constraining, and vertical and horizontal scaling. These are concepts you'll use in other tools as you continue to explore XPress 4.

Content Tool

Next on the list of critically important tools is the Content tool, second from the top of the Tool palette. You may recognize the Content tool by the hand and I-beam symbol on the button. The Content tool enables you to select, edit, and manipulate text and pictures *within* boxes, hence its name. Plus, you might say the Content tool is *content-sensitive*, because the Content tool transforms into a cursor when a text box is selected, and it changes to a "grabber hand" pointer when a picture box is selected.

While editing text, the Content tool conforms to the usual desktop software standards for selecting, highlighting, and clipboard functions associated with editing text. In fact, while in Content tool mode, XPress behaves as if it were a high-end word processor, flowing text within the text box. You may also change text properties while individual characters or words are highlighted by using the Measurements palette (F9) or the Character Attributes dialog box (CTRL/CMD+SHIFT+D).

When a picture box is selected, the Content tool changes to a grabber hand pointer. The grabber hand enables you to interactively move a picture within its picture frame without affecting the position or size of the frame itself or the dimensions of the picture within the frame. When the Content tool is selected, you may also resize picture boxes in the same manner as with the Item tool. SHIFT and CTRL/CMD keyboard combinations for scaling and constraining also apply when using the Content tool on picture boxes. The key principle to keep in mind when working with these tools is that you may manipulate text and picture boxes either together with their content or independently of each other.

For a practical exercise in using the Content tool to manipulate picture boxes within frames, follow these steps:

1. Create a picture box using any of the picture box tools. Picture box tool buttons feature shapes with *Xs* inside them and begin at the sixth tool position down the Tool palette.

2. Select the Content tool and import an image into your picture box by choosing File | Get Picture (CTRL/CMD+E). For the purposes of this exercise, any image will do. Notice your Content tool changes to a grabber hand.

3. Click anywhere on the picture within its frame, drag your cursor, and release. Notice the picture has moved but its frame hasn't.

4. Drag one of the corner handles of the picture box in any direction. Notice the picture remains stationary, but the frame itself changes shape.

5. Hold the SHIFT key while you drag the same handle. Notice the box converts to equal width and height measures and changes shape to match proportionately; again the picture's size remains unchanged.

6. Hold CTRL/CMD+SHIFT and drag the same handle. Notice the picture within the frame changes size while the box size also changes.

7. Hold the CTRL/CMD key and drag the same handle one last time. Notice the handle moves freely in any direction and when you release the mouse the picture becomes nonproportionately resized, as shown in Figure 2-7.

8. With the picture box still selected, press CTRL/CMD+ALT/OPTION+SHIFT+F. Notice the picture changes size to fit within its box. This shortcut key causes your picture to fit to the confines of your picture box while maintaining original proportions.

9. With the picture still selected, press CTRL/CMD+SHIFT+M. Notice the picture becomes centered within the frame, without its size changing. This shortcut key causes your picture to be *centered* within your picture box.

TIP *While using the Content tool for manipulating text and pictures in boxes, a universe of speedy keyboard combinations are available. For more information on using the Content tool to manipulate text, see Chapter 4, Text Basics and Typographic Tools. For more information on using the Content tool to manipulate pictures in boxes, see Chapter 7, Adding and Controlling Pictures.*

NOTE *Many of the capabilities of the Item tool overlap with the Content tool. For example, you may resize text and picture boxes at their handles by dragging or using various keyboard combinations while either tool is selected.*

Resized using a CTRL/CMD and drag action

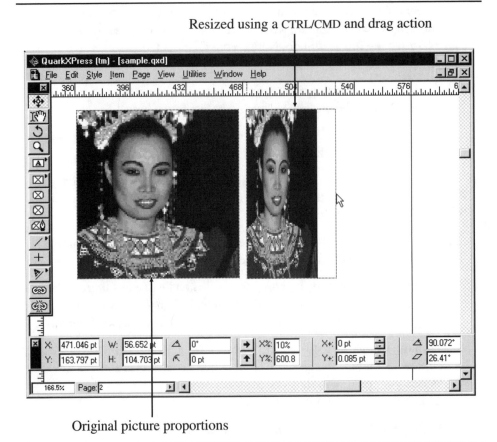

Original picture proportions

![FIGURE 2-7] **FIGURE 2-7** Dragging a picture handle with the CTRL/CMD key changes the proportions of the picture box and the picture

Rotation Tool

The final tool in this first group of three in the Tool palette may not be used as often as the Item and Content tools, but it is no less significant in manipulating objects. The Rotation tool enables you to freely change the angle of objects in relation to your page around 360 degrees. It is completely interactive, visually indicating both the point around which your object is being rotated as well as the angle. Again, getting to know the Rotation tool's behavior is best learned through practical experience.

To rotate an object with the Rotation tool, follow these steps:

1. Create a new object or continue using the picture box from the preceding exercise.

2. Select your object using the Item tool and clicking it once.

3. Select the Rotation tool from the Tool palette. Notice your cursor changes to a circle with crosshairs.

4. Click and drag anywhere on your object, as shown in Figure 2-8; drag in any direction keeping your mouse button pressed. Two key guiding elements appear. One is a crosshair, and the other is a line attached to your cursor. Plus, a representative box appears indicating the new position of your object.

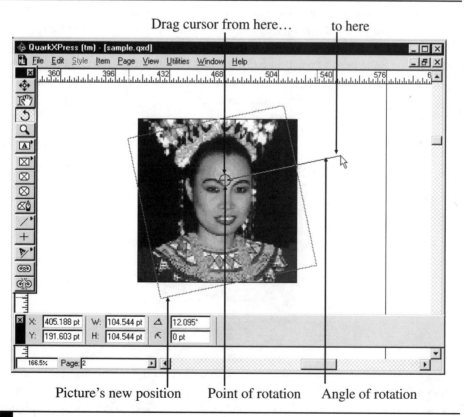

FIGURE 2-8   Rotating a picture with the Rotation tool

The first point at which you click sets the point of rotation; the point to which you drag sets the angle of the rotation, or, slope. The distance you drag has no bearing on the angle of the rotation, but the farther you drag the more rotational control you have.

5. If you haven't already done so, release the mouse button. Your object is rotated to its new angle. Notice that your cursor has changed back to the Item tool. By default, your cursor is set to return automatically to the Item or Content tool, depending on which tool was last in use.

TIP ————▶ *To keep a tool temporarily selected (such as the Rotation tool) instead of allowing it to revert to the last-used tool, hold ALT/OPTION while selecting the tool from the Tool palette.*

6. To go beyond basics for a moment, with your rotated object still selected press F9 to display the Measurements palette. Reselect the Rotation tool from the Tool palette. Notice the Measurements palette's angle field indicates the angle of rotation, as shown in the following illustration. This value indicates the rotation from the original state (or zero), not the most recent rotation. Enter **0** in this field and press RETURN. The object is returned to its original vertical position.

Using the Measurements palette in combination with the Rotation tool enables you to more precisely change the angle of rotating objects. You may enter the angle values directly, or monitor the "live update" in the angle field as you rotate the object.

Entering positive values rotates your object clockwise, and entering negative values rotates the object counterclockwise.

TIP → *To rotate an object without previewing the new position of the object or displaying the stylized crosshair cursor and angle indication line, click and hold for one second before attempting to rotate the object. After the pause, your cursor changes to the free-rotate cursor.*

2

Key Concepts of Linking and Unlinking

If your layout involves flowing text from one area to another, you'll need to use XPress' linking tools. In XPress, *linking* refers to creating a relationship between two text boxes so that they may flow content between them as needed. The simplest—and most likely—scenario involves flowing text from one page to the next. But more complex layouts often involve flowing text within a page layout from one text box to another.

For this, XPress features two separate tools: The Linking tool and the Unlinking tool. Both tools reside at the bottom of the Tool palette. When either tool is selected, links that have already been assigned appear in your layout as patterned lines with start and endpoint arrowheads indicating linked boxes and the direction of text flow, as shown in Figure 2-9.

Links between text boxes may be created manually or automatically. If you're unfamiliar with these Linking or Unlinking tools, or the general concept of linking, the best way to begin understanding them is to create a few manual links yourself.

To create manual links between text boxes, follow these steps:

1. Create several text boxes of any shape or style on your page. For this example, you may want to create the boxes in an arrangement similar to Figure 2-10.

2. Hold the CTRL/CMD key to temporarily set your cursor to the Item tool and click the pasteboard (the area surrounding your page) to ensure no objects are selected.

3. In step 3, you're going to use the Linking tool to create several links. By default, the Linking tool reverts back to the previously-used tool after use. To prevent this from happening, hold the ALT/OPTION key and choose the Linking tool from the Tool palette.

Linked text boxes

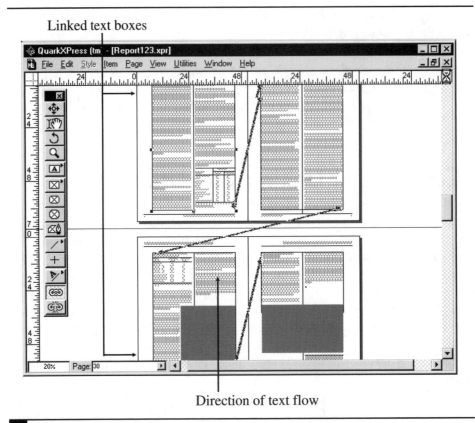

Direction of text flow

■ FIGURE 2-9 Selecting either the Linking or Unlinking tool displays currently-linked text boxes in your layout

4. With the Linking tool selected, your cursor changes to a chain pointer. Click the first text box you would like to flow text from. Notice the frame of the text box displays a marquee, and your cursor shows a chain-link symbol.

5. Click the box you would like text from the first box to flow into. Notice a patterned arrow joins the bottom-right corner of your first text box to the top-left corner of the second, as shown in Figure 2-11.

6. Now click the remaining text boxes in the direction you would like your text to flow. Notice that each time you click a new box, a new link appears, as shown in Figure 2-12.

2

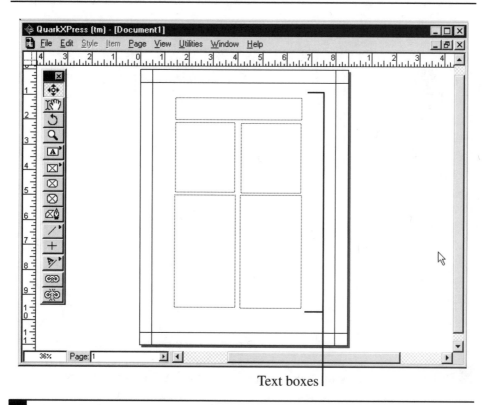

Text boxes

FIGURE 2-10   Create a mock layout of boxes to link manually

Breaking a link between two text boxes eliminates the text flow and the relationship between them. Text will now be flowed between these boxes. To break the links between the boxes you have just created, use the Unlinking tool. To do this, follow these steps:

1. Choose the Unlinking tool from the Tool palette. If you intend to unlink more than one link, hold the ALT/OPTION key while selecting the Unlinking tool.

2. Using the same text box arrangement as in the preceding example, select the first box in the "chain" or story, by clicking it. Notice all the links reappear.

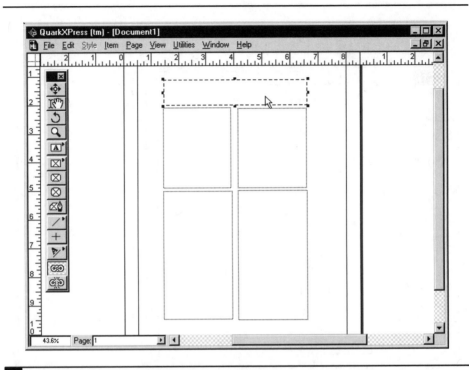

FIGURE 2-11   Click the box you would like the text to flow into

3. Locate the arrow joining the last to the second-to-last text-linked boxes. Using the Unlinking tool, click the arrowhead of this link, as shown in Figure 2-13. The link disappears.

4. Use the same action on each of the links until all boxes are unlinked.

TIP

To break a link, the Unlinking tool requires that you click as close as possible to the pointed end of the linking arrow.

If necessary, continue to practice linking text boxes manually until you have grasped this key concept in XPress. Learning the manual way of linking text boxes in a chain will help for specific layouts; however XPress includes an automated way

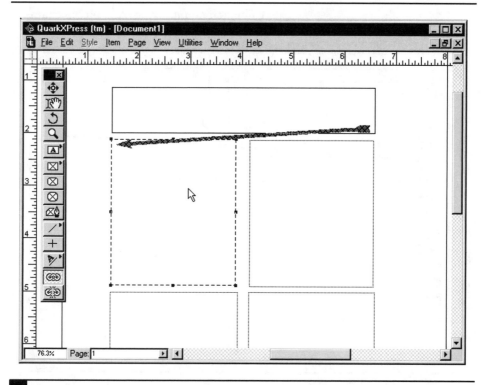

FIGURE 2-12   Each time you link two boxes, a relationship is established

of linking text boxes. In the section on adding pages earlier in this chapter you may have noticed the Link to Current Text Chain option in the Add Pages dialog box. Clicking this option when adding new pages to your document causes the automatic text box added to each new page to be linked to the text box on the preceding page.

Pasteboard and Clipboard Functions

Layouts often involve various types and sizes of visual and textual material destined for assembly on your page. You may find yourself looking for ways to store, copy or transfer this material to various parts of your document. And, there will be times when you want to set something aside for later use—without deleting it. This is where the pasteboard and clipboard come in useful.

Click here to unlink last text box in chain

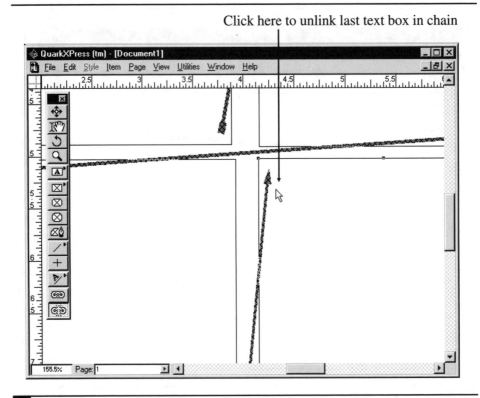

■ **FIGURE 2-13** Unlinking text boxes with the Unlinking tool

If text and picture content gets crowded within your page, you may not be using one of the most useful storage spaces available to you: the pasteboard. The term *pasteboard* is taken from manual layout practices; it refers to the area around an artboard where sticky bits and pieces of text and photographs are temporarily laid until needed. This is exactly what the area around your document page is meant for.

TIP ➤ *Even though items placed on the pasteboard lack a spot in your layout, they are still considered part of your document file, and contribute to its memory size. You may store nearly unlimited material on the pasteboard, but the more items you store there the larger your file becomes. Deleting unused items periodically or storing them in a library may help avoid large file sizes.*

Any content placed on the pasteboard is simply set aside. In other words, content placed on the pasteboard may have assigned link relationships to other elements on your page, but it has no "reserved" space in your layout.

TIP ————→ *The width of your pasteboard may be customized, depending on your needs. For information on changing your pasteboard size, see* Chapter 12, Fine-tuning XPress.

Your clipboard also acts as a temporary storage space, only in a much more limited fashion. Clipboard functionality is actually a characteristic of your operating environment, but XPress supports all characteristics of the clipboard, including the capability to view what's currently on it. Items may be copied (CTRL/CMD+C) or cut (CTRL/CMD+X) *to* your clipboard, or pasted (CTRL/CMD+V) into your document *from* it. Clipboard functions are mostly invisible to the user, and the more you become accustomed to copy, cut, and paste commands the less you'll think about it. The clipboard is capable of only "remembering" one item at a time. Subsequent items copied to the clipboard overwrite the current item.

TIP ————→ *To view what's currently on your clipboard, choose Edit | Show Clipboard. A new window will open revealing the last item that was cut or copied. To close this view, choose Edit | Close Clipboard.*

NOTE ————→ *Macintosh users also enjoy the temporary space found in the Scrapbook— a feature of the Mac operating environment. The Scrapbook is used much the same way as the clipboard, but it is capable of supporting multiple items.*

About Editing

After placing all the various items on your page, there will come a time to change the page (especially if you work in a publishing environment). Because your layout items are varied, so are the procedures for editing them. As a general rule, editing of text and pictures within boxes is accomplished using the Content tool, and editing of the frames and boxes themselves is accomplished using the Item tool. Editing of more advanced items covered in later chapters, such as Béziers, clipping paths, and runarounds may often be done using either tool.

For new users exploring editing functions, two basic commands are found at the bottom of the Item menu: Shape and Content. The Shape submenu includes a collection of preset shapes that you may apply to your currently selected text or picture box. To apply one of these shapes, simply select the box using either the Item or Content tool, choose Item | Shape, and select a preset shape as shown in the following illustration. The current shape selection is indicated by a check mark. Choose from the following shapes: rectangular, rounded corner, concave corner, beveled corner, elliptical, Bézier box, straight line, or Bézier line.

TIP ——————▶ *Bézier-based shape selections are actually conversion scripts in XPress, meaning that a physical conversion takes place rather than a modal conversion. In other words, when you convert a rectangular-shaped box to a Bézier line or box, your box may not be changed to another preset shape automatically. Instead, you must use the drawing tools to edit the new Bézier shape.*

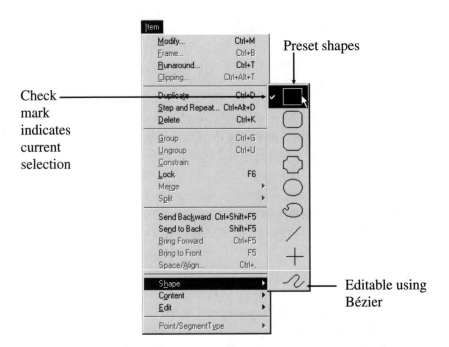

The Content submenu, as shown in the following illustration, enables you to quickly convert text boxes into picture boxes or shapes (and vice versa) so that they may support different types of content.

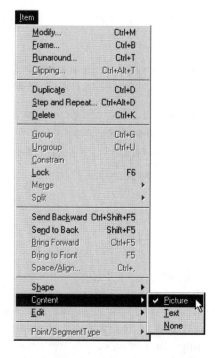

In other words, you may change a text box to a picture box, or a simple Bézier line into a text path and all permutations between. There are some limitations to this conversion process though. The following list defines common limitations.

- An item may support only one of these modes at a time. You can't force a picture box to contain both text and a picture, or vice versa.

- When converting text or picture boxes containing actual content, all text is deleted.

- If more than one item is selected, the Content submenu becomes unavailable—even if the items are the same type.

Because XPress enables you to control so many of the properties of your layout elements, editing functions can often be complex, going beyond the new-user issues this chapter focuses on. The following lists provides some suggested reading for more information on editing basic items in XPress, such as text, pictures, and the boxes that house them.

- For working with text boxes and editing text see *Chapter 4, Text Basics and Typographic Tools* and *Chapter 6, Working with Text.*

- For working with pictures in boxes, see *Chapter 7, Working with Pictures.* For a beyond-the-basics of editing operations, also check out *Chapter 8, Advanced Picture Strategies.*

- For editing items created with drawing tools, see *Chapter 5, Working with Drawing Tools.*

Conclusion

Whether you use XPress for composing layouts, editing content, or simply proofing or browsing documents, this chapter has exposed you to core functionality beyond launching the program. You've seen how to set document appearance and navigate pages and documents, and you've learned key operations such as creating and linking text boxes, and importing content. Some of the concepts covered in this chapter are common across desktop and layout applications and word processors, while others are unique and specific to XPress itself.

Now that you had some exposure you may want to begin laying out pages. Chapter 3 fleshes out more detail on document setup and covers layout planning and XPress' layout conveniences such as master pages, rulers, grids, guides, and measurement controls—all critical to beginning and working with your first layout.

CHAPTER 3

Tackling a Layout

Most desktop layout applications these days claim you can "design" or "create" layouts, illustrations, 3D models, or whatever after purchasing the software. In reality, the software merely provides you with the tools to accomplish your task, instead of making you capable. If you don't know what you're doing, the software certainly isn't going to provide you with the knowledge or creativity (and neither will the program manuals). The *real* capabilities come from your knack for layout or design.

Approaching the construction of a new layout can be a fairly intimidating experience if you're not quite sure where to start, what your document will look like, or what mysterious problems you'll run into along the way. In fact, even the most experienced layout artists face these same questions before starting any layout project.

Laying out any publication or document is a process that is half logic, half creativity, and half plain hard work. The math may be suspect, but my point is still valid. Taken step by step, a layout can be quick and simple, or a challenging and rewarding experience. This chapter explores approaching a layout from the logical perspective, with a little creativity thrown in for good measure. Because XPress is the host for your layout projects, this process will be described using the tools at hand.

TIP
To begin constructing a layout in XPress, you absolutely must have at least a partial understanding of key tools and concepts. This chapter builds on what you have already learned in Chapters 1 and 2. If you haven't yet covered these chapters, you may be lost when it comes to using key tools and following certain steps. Now's a good time to go back and read them.

Planning and Constructing a Layout

When beginning any layout, it's always best to have a plan—or design—to follow before you open the program and plunk down text and pictures. Layout plans are often etched out using good old pen and paper. Often, you'll find gifted layout artists who can conceptualize a layout without the use of paper. These experts are the *Gods of Layout*, capable of accomplishing designs few novices are capable of.

Besides the simple business card or letterhead design, layout usually involves one of two most common project types: brochures and books. This section explores the planning and setup of both, and if you follow closely, you'll see how certain features in XPress can help you save time and accomplish nearly anything in terms of layout formatting.

Planning a Brochure Layout

Brochure layout is a specialized task. Brochures are often packed with a high degree of detail, making the use of paper sketching all the more important. Although smaller than other layouts, brochures can involve enormous amounts of time and thought, so a sketched-out plan will help immensely, as shown in the following illustration.

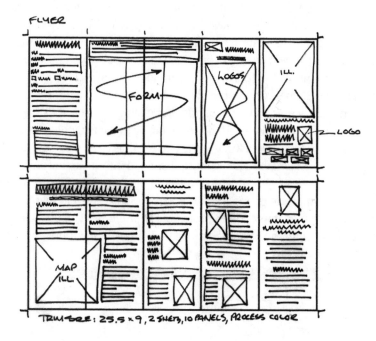

Your layout sketch works as a map to plan where your content will be placed and how it will fit. Your layout should also be created with the following questions in mind:

- What is the size of the material on which your document will be reproduced?

- How big will the margins be?

- How many columns or panels will each page feature?

- What will be the ink colors?

■ Which elements will be in which colors?

■ What are the printers' specifications regarding trim sizes, bleed sizes, and where the material folds?

The sketch will be invaluable for organizing your thoughts and your content. It will also help to answer some of the key questions you'll need answers to before launching XPress and specifying your new document properties. A sketch doesn't need to be an artistic creation. In all likelihood you (or the person following it) will be the only one to see it, and its purpose is merely to guide. Pages may be simply-drawn rectangles in rough proportions to your page size. Text may be etched in with squiggly lines for main heads and straight lines for body copy. And pictures may be merely squares with *Xs* inside to distinguish them from other elements. Based on the information you've collected through your sketching exercise, you may start to format your XPress document. In the following illustration, the layout is a typical brochure format, printed on 25.5x9-inch paper. In technical terms, the format calls for a five-column structure across a five-panel fold. For example's sake, let's set the margins equally at one-quarter (0.25) inch and the space between the text columns (the gutters) at twice the margin (0.5 inches). Because the document is to be printed and folded, it's essentially two pages in length, with each page divided into separate folded panels.

The next step is creating a new document (CTRL/CMD+N). The New Document dialog box asks for information regarding the size, orientation, and margins. With the preceding layout as an example, enter these values in the fields and click the Facing Pages option, as shown in the New Document dialog box in the following illustration.

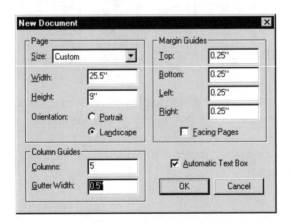

After accepting your page measures, XPress automatically builds the document shell. To add the second page, choose Page I Insert to display the Insert Pages dialog box. Enter **1** in the Insert field, choose the At End of Document option, and click OK. After adding your new page, enter **20** in the View Magnification field and press ENTER to view both pages at approximately 20 percent of their normal size. Your document should appear as shown in Figure 3-1.

If you accepted your document options with the Automatic Text Box option selected, you'll discover you have a single text box added to each page. For a folded-brochure layout, this may not help you very much because the first page of your layout is actually the far-right panel on the first page. Instead, you'll need to create text boxes for each of the panels and if necessary, create text links between them. To do this now, follow these steps:

1. Choose the Item tool from the Tool palette.

2. Select the automatic text box and resize it to occupy the first panel on the far left by dragging the bottom-right corner to the corresponding corner of the first panel. Notice it is still formatted to support five columns.

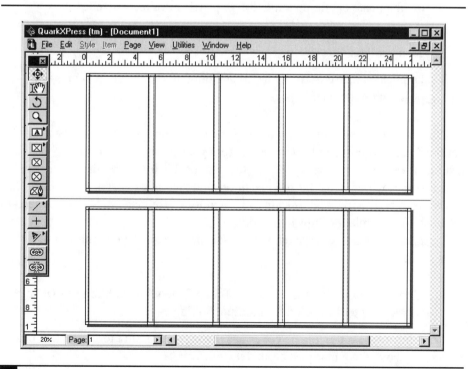

FIGURE 3-1   After creating your first page, insert the second page

3. Double-click on this text box to choose the Modify dialog box (or press CTRL/CMD+M), and then choose the Text tab. Notice the Columns field is set to 5.

4. Enter **1** in the Columns field and click OK.

5. Select the text box on the second page and delete it by pressing the DELETE or BACKSPACE key on your keyboard (or choosing menu command Item| Delete or Edit | Clear).

Now you will create text boxes for the remaining panels.

6. Still using the Item tool, select the text box on the first page by clicking it once.

7. Duplicate the text box by choosing Item | Duplicate (CTRL/CMD+D). A copy of the text box is placed near the original.

8. Drag the copy into position on the second panel of the first page. Repeat the duplicate operation until all five panels have their own text box.

9. Select all the text boxes on the first page by holding SHIFT and clicking each text box once.

10. Duplicate all five (CTRL/CMD+D) and drag all the resulting copies into position on the second page.

Now you have individual text boxes for each of the 10 panels. But, you're still not finished. If you intend to flow text across your panels, you'll need to establish text links—and in the correct order. In the case of this brochure, the cover panel is actually on page one in the far right position, and the back panel is just to the left of it. The remainder of the text links in a counterclockwise fashion. So, you'll need to establish linking relationships in this order.

To quickly link the boxes together to match the example layout, follow these steps:

11. Choose the Linking tool from the Tool palette while holding ALT/OPTION to keep the tool selected for multiple linking.

12. Click the text box on the cover panel with the Linking tool. The text box appears with a marquee around it.

13. Click the first panel on the second page to link to the second panel of your brochure. Notice a linking arrow now joins the two panels, as shown in Figure 3-2.

14. Continue linking the panels until you have linked each of them in the proper order, as shown in Figure 3-3. Notice the back to the left of the cover is the last link in the chain. This is the end of your brochure.

15. Although you haven't begun to lay down text yet, you've done enough work on this document to justify saving it. To save your document choose File | Save (CTRL/CMD+S) and furnish your document with a name and folder location.

According to the layout, several panels will feature pictures in the form of digital photos, logos, or illustrations. For this, you'll need to create picture

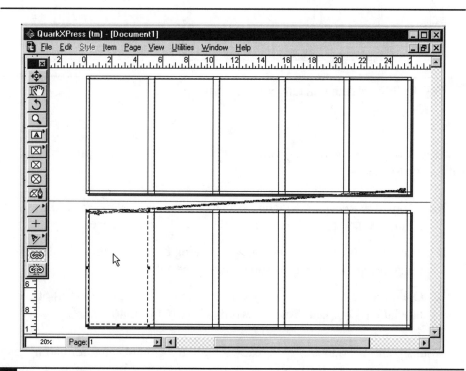

FIGURE 3-2   Linking text boxes in the correct order

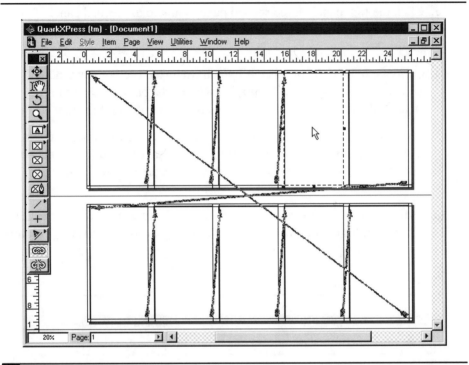

FIGURE 3-3   Adding picture boxes to your layout

boxes and place them in position on the panels. To create picture boxes, follow these steps:

16. Choose the Rectangule Picture Box tool from the Tool palette while holding ALT/OPTION to keep the tool selected for multiple use.

17. Using your layout as a guide, begin creating the picture boxes in their rough position and size, as shown in Figure 3-4.

18. Once you've finished creating your picture boxes, the rough shell of your brochure is complete. And it's worth a save (CTRL/CMD+S).

At this point, your document is ready for you to begin placing, formatting, and fine-tuning the content. But, before we go too much further, there's another type of layout worth investigating—the book-style layout. Book layouts are much more

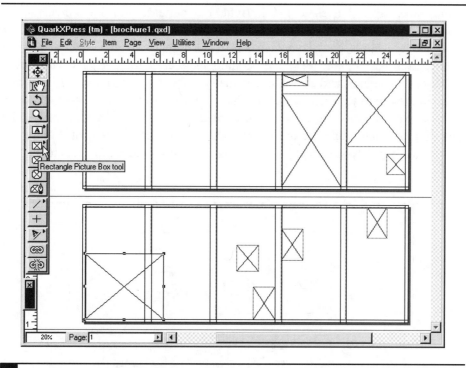

FIGURE 3-4 Text boxes throughout the entire brochure are now linked

simplistic than finicky brochure layouts, but they come with their own set of challenges, most of which involve dealing with the sheer volume of pages.

Planning a Book Layout

A "book" layout doesn't necessarily mean you're going to end up with a printed and bound book. A book layout may be anything from a one-sided photocopied report to a full-color catalog, annual report, or thrifty reference binder. As with the brochure layout, it may help to draw up a sketched plan if your layout involves following a new design, complex color arrangement, or complicated content. If your book layout is going to be quite large and follows a consistent design, it may be helpful to sketch only a single page layout that acts as a guide for all pages. The bottom line is that you need to look at the dynamics of your publication and create a plan for yourself.

It may take several tries to get it right, but at least you'll be investing in groundwork—which almost always saves layout time.

Unlike brochures, book layouts may take more advantage of XPress' automated features such as automatic text boxes, column features, automatic page numbering, master page elements, and so on. In fact, many of the automated features in XPress are geared more toward lengthy books than they are to single-page documents. In this next example, a 16-page book to be printed on 8.5x11-inch paper is etched out indicating a rough guide for the layout, text, and picture placement. Figure 3-5 illustrates a typically-sketched plan showing a rough structure of the content.

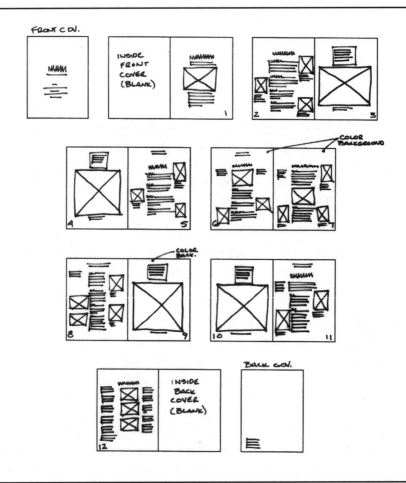

FIGURE 3-5   Typical sketched plan of a 16-page book

With a basic structure and plan in place, you may want to refine the layout slightly more by adding more detail such as color specifications, picture formats, drop caps in text, text alignment, and columns. You needn't go so far as to copy-fit the text—certain text formatting tools in XPress will enable you to do that later when importing your text. And, as long as you plan the typical or most complex page, you can leave the remaining pages to the *actual* layout stage. Figure 3-6 shows a more detailed plan of the preceding book layout.

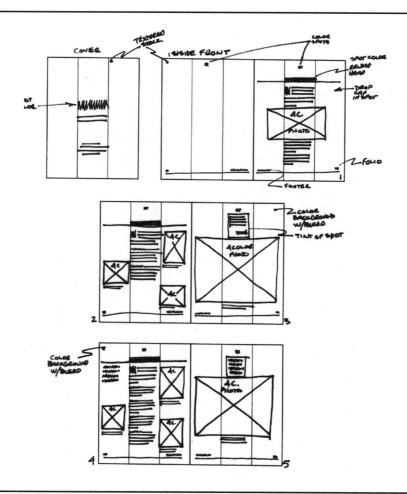

FIGURE 3-6   If time allows, you may want to plan typical or complex pages in more detail

Once your plan is set, you may begin creating your book layout in XPress. The following steps would apply for the preceding book layout:

1. With XPress launched, choose to create a new document (CTRL/CMD+N). The New Document dialog box appears.

2. Choose US Letter from the Size drop-down menu and click the Portrait option for the orientation.

3. Enter **3** in the Columns field and enter **1 p** (picas) for the gutter size.

4. Set the top, bottom, inside, and outside margin measures to **3 p**.

5. Because this is a book format and you'll be working with left and right pages, click the Facing Pages option and choose the Automatic Text Box option to have XPress create the text boxes on each page automatically, as shown in the following illustration.

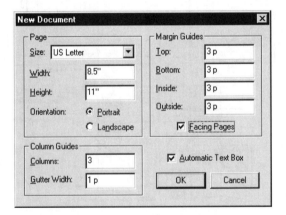

6. Click OK to accept your values and have XPress create the empty shell of your first page, as shown in Figure 3-7. To view the entire page, choose View | Fit in Window (or press CTRL/CMD+0).

7. The next step is to add the remaining pages to your document. First, choose the Item tool and click the text box on your page once. Choose Page | Insert to display the Insert Pages dialog box.

8. For this 16-page layout, enter **15** in the Insert field and choose the At End of Document option.

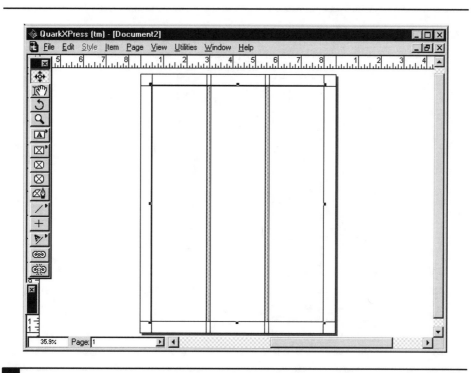

FIGURE 3-7   XPress creates the first page of your book layout

9. To automatically link the text boxes on all pages, choose the Link to
Current Text Chain option.

TIP
> *If the Link to Current Text Chain option is unavailable in the Insert Pages
> dialog box, you must exit the dialog box and reselect the text box on your page.*

10. Click OK to add the pages. XPress creates the remaining pages, complete
with text links.

11. To view more of your document as shown in Figure 3-8, enter **10** in the
View Magnification field and press ENTER. To view Thumbnails of your
document click View | Thumbnails (or press SHIFT+F6).

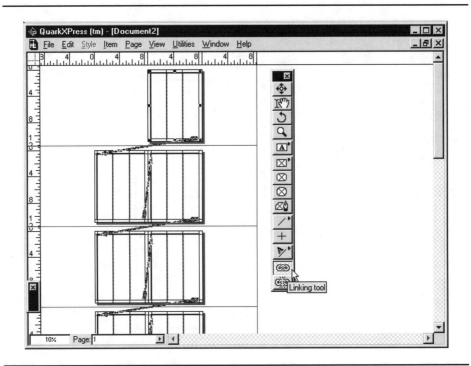

FIGURE 3-8   Remaining pages are inserted with automated text box links

12. Although you've simply created an empty shell for your book layout, you've done enough work to justify saving it (CTRL/CMD+S). Save your document with a unique name and folder location before going too much further. To complete the structure of the shell manually, you'll eventually need to add picture boxes, line rules, and so on throughout your layout.

Using Master Pages

At this point, you've had some time to realize how critical your layout plan is and to build the shell of your book layout in XPress. Going through the manual exercises of creating a document layout provides you with valuable practical experience. But now's the time to take advantage of certain automated features available to you. Through creation and application of "master" page elements, you'll save significant time and allow XPress to perform much of the labor involved in creating common page elements.

What are Master Pages?

As the name implies, master pages enable you to quickly place items common to multiple pages. You may format a master page to include any of the items you can create in XPress, such as line rules, common page headings and footings, design elements, and so on. Guides on master pages are reflected on document pages. Guides are nonprinting lines that indicate column and margin setup on your page.

TIP ——————➤ *One of the most commonly-sought features is the capability to set automatic page numbering for your document. When an automatic page number is placed on a master page and that master page is subsequently applied to specific pages in your layout, the pages are numbered according to their layout order. To create automatic page numbers, create a text box and position it according to your layout plan. With your Content tool selected and the cursor positioned in the text box, press CTRL/CMD+3. The symbol "<#>" appears, indicating an automatic numbering tag. Each of the document pages your master page is applied to will be numbered automatically in sequence according to their layout position. Later, you'll learn how to break a document into sections with different page numbering. Automatic page numbers may be formatted to include any character attributes as with any text in XPress.*

Displaying Master Pages

The display of pages in XPress is subtly divided into two separate worlds: document pages and master pages. The direct way to view a master page is through choosing Page | Display and selecting the master page name from the submenu, as shown in the following illustration.

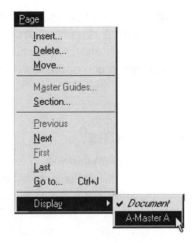

TIP   *To return to the view of your document pages, choose Page | Display | Document.*

By default, whenever a new document is created, a blank master page is automatically created and named. The default master page is named *A-Master A*. In plainer language, the first *A* indicates master page *A*, and what follows is the editable default name *Master A*. In its default condition, the master page contains nothing more than a single text box and margin guides set according to the values you first entered to create your new document.

Perhaps the best way to work with the master page feature is through use of the Document Layout palette (F4). Among other uses, the Document Layout palette enables you to view, duplicate, name, and delete your master pages. It also enables you to quickly apply master pages to specific pages in your document. As a practical exercise in using this feature for working with master pages, follow these steps:

1. With your document open, display your Document Layout palette by choosing View | Document Layout (F4). Notice the palette is divided into two separate areas. The top area displays master pages, and the bottom lists the pages in your actual document.

2. To view a master page, double-click on the page icon adjacent to its name. XPress displays the master page. Notice that the Document Layout palette indicates the name of the master page being viewed in bold type.

3. To rename a master page, double-click its name. The master page name is highlighted and your pointer changes to a cursor enabling you to enter a unique name. Press ENTER or RETURN to accept the new name, shown in the following illustration.

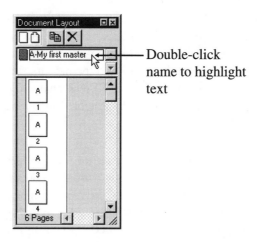

Double-click name to highlight text

4. To quickly create a new master page, drag a new blank single page or blank facing page into the master page list of the palette. A new master page icon appears in the master page list. By default, the new master page is named *B-Master B*. If needed, apply a new name to the second master page.

5. To delete a master page, click its icon once and click the Delete button at the very top of the palette.

TIP

Master pages are identified alphabetically; this feature cannot be changed. The Document Layout palette indicates which master page has been applied to each document page using the corresponding master page letter. When inserting new pages in your document, you may choose which master page properties are applied by making your choice from the Master Page drop-down list in the Insert Pages dialog box.

Multiple Master Pages

If your document layout calls for two or more different styles of layout across several pages, creating a master page for each style will save significant time—especially if your document is lengthy. For example, the book layout example discussed previously includes two unique and different layout styles that apply to several pages in the layout. By creating one master page for each layout style, you may apply master pages to each of the pages according to your layout plan and avoid having to recreate all the elements on those pages.

To add a new master page, click the Duplicate button on the Document Layout palette and double-click its master page icon to view the page. Format the page to include common elements such as text boxes, picture boxes, line rules, page numbers, and so on. Once you have tailored the new master page in the new style, you may apply it to any page you want. XPress enables you to create up to 127 different master pages for each new document. Master pages are alphabetically named AA through DW.

> TIP ═══════▷ *When working with multiple master pages, you may select more than one master page at a time. To select sequential entries, hold SHIFT while clicking the page icons in the top half of the Document Layout palette. To select nonsequential entries, hold CTRL/CMD while clicking the icons. In addition, the master page area is expandable so that you may view more of the master page list. To expand the view, drag the bottom border of the list downwards.*

Applying Master Pages

Once your master page has been tailored to suit your layout needs, you may apply it to specific document pages using the Document Layout palette. Applying a master page is a quick operation. Simply drag the master page icon from the top area of the Document Layout palette directly onto the document page icon in the lower half of the palette. Any item that has been created on your page by a master page transfer is referred to as a *master page item*.

When applying master page formats, XPress simply creates new items according to your master page layout. However, let's suppose you've already created other items on your page from scratch or from another master page. Ultimately, XPress is going to run into a conflict: Keep the original elements, or delete them and apply the new master page elements? The answer depends on how options in your Document Preferences dialog box (CTRL/CMD+Y) have been set.

By choosing Edit | Preferences | Document | General tab, you may set one of two options in the Master Page Items drop-down menu. Choose the Keep Changes option to enable XPress to keep current items intact and unchanged. When this option is selected and new master page items are added to the page, the current items that have already been modified in some way are left as is, but are no longer considered master page items. This option is the default master page option. Choosing the Delete

Changes option enables XPress to replace all items—including those that have already been modified in some way—with the new master page items being applied.

Using the Document Layout palette, you may copy one master page over another by dragging the icons in the top area of the palette. The master page being replaced is deleted from your layout, and the existing master page elements apply to all pages where the deleted master page was applied. In this case, master page items are also replaced according to options set in your Document Preferences dialog box.

3

Working in Sections

If the document you are constructing is only one part of a larger document that you've elected to segregate into individual parts, you may use the Section command to set XPress to number and display pages according to their actual sequence or position in your publication. The Section command also enables you to specify the start of new sections within your document.

You may access the Section command options by choosing Page | Section to open the Section dialog box, as shown in the following illustration. From here, you may set your current page as the start of a new section, which in turn enables you to enter values in the Prefix, Number, and Format fields.

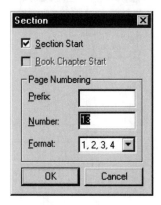

Section command options may be set as follows:

- **Prefix**   The prefix may contain any characters supported by XPress or your operating system, but it must not exceed four characters in length. Prefixes appear before automatic page numbering on your pages and when using XPress' automated page number feature. The prefix also displays when viewing pages in the Page Number field of your document window and in the Document Layout palette.

■ **Number** In this field, enter the page number of the start of your new document section. Pages in your document will automatically appear with whichever page number you specify here. The starting page number of your section must range between 1 and 9,999.

■ **Format** This drop-down menu enables you to choose from one of five page numbering formats. Pages may be numbered using standard numeric, uppercase Roman, lowercase Roman, uppercase alphabetic, or lowercase alphabetic.

Section commands apply to your currently-displayed page. In other words, when you format the start of a new section, the options you set will apply to current and subsequent pages in your document. Section options are best managed and viewed through use of the Document Layout palette. When using this palette, section starts are indicated by asterisks (*) accompanying the page numbers. The Document Layout palette also features a shortcut button to the Section command dialog box. It appears in the lower-left corner whenever a document page is selected, as shown in the following illustration.

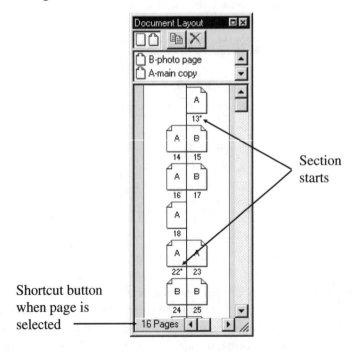

Section starts

Shortcut button when page is selected

TIP *The Section feature keeps track of left and right page usage. If your document setup includes use of left and right pages, and your viewing options are set to view facing pages, the Section command automatically sets even-numbered pages as left-facing pages.*

TIP *The Document Layout palette enables you set section starts without the need to manually navigate to the page. Simply click the start page in the palette, and then click the shortcut button in the palette to apply the Section Start options.*

The Section dialog box also enables you to set the Book Chapter Start option when working with very large documents. For more information on using the Book Chapter Start option, see *Setting a Book Chapter Start* in *Chapter 11, Working with Complex Layouts*.

Rulers, Guides, and Layout Measures

Layout can often involve creating documents with pinpoint accuracy and specific measurements, and positioning items can be finicky business. XPress includes features—in the form of onscreen rulers, repositionable guides, and the display and manipulation of object dimensions—that make accurate layout much easier.

Setting Rulers

Your onscreen rulers have a number of critical functions when laying out your document. They provide a visual reference for measuring and sizing items and enable you to position those items according to your page origin. They also act as an inexhaustible source for pulling guides onto your layout page. Rulers may be customized to display in certain units of measure, and the point from which they measure may be positioned anywhere on or off your page. And, ruler increments change logically depending on your view level magnification.

TIP *Certain standards of measure yield slight differences in equivalent unit measures. XPress enables you to customize equivalent measure values for both picas and points per inch and ciceros per centimeter. For more information on changing the default equivalent measures XPress uses for these units, see* Setting Document Preference Options *in Chapter 12, Customizing XPress.*

To control the display of your document rulers, choose View/Hide | Rulers (CTRL/CMD+R). The rRuler itself is comprised of three essential parts: horizontal ruler, vertical ruler, and the ruler origin. Horizontal and vertical ruler increments may also be set individually to a variety of unit measures, including inches, inches decimal, picas, points, millimeters, centimeters, ciceros, and agates.

TIP

Setting your ruler unit of measure has widespread effects on how you enter unit measures in palettes and dialog boxes. For example, if your rulers are set to a unit measure of millimeters, the default unit measure for item sizes, document dimensions, and positioning items on pages will be measured in millimeters by default—unless you specify differently when entering values. Entering unit abbreviations following the unit values in palettes or dialog box fields enables you to deviate from the default measure as follows:

Inches	in or "
Inches (decimal)	in or with a decimal
Picas	p
Points	pt
Millimeters	mm
Centimeters	cm
Ciceros	c
Agates	ag

As a practical guide to setting up and working with document rulers, follow these steps:

1. With a document open, ensure your rulers are displayed (CTRL/CMD+R), as shown in the following illustration. Ideally, you should be viewing the left and right pages of a two-page spread.

Horizontal ruler   Ruler split

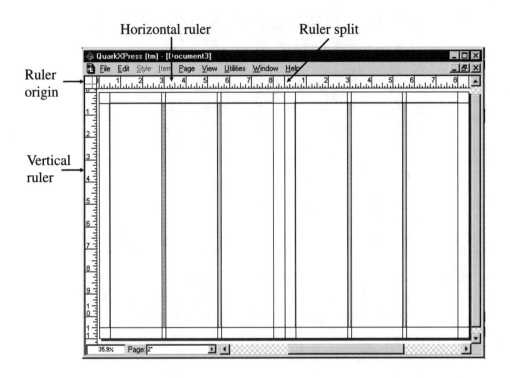

2. Choose View | Fit in Window (CTRL/CMD+0) to completely view two pages.

3. Notice the ruler measures increase as you read left to right and top to bottom from the upper-left corner of each page.

4. Choose Edit | Document | Preferences (CTRL/CMD+Y) and select the General tab, as shown in the following illustration. Notice the first two options in this dialog box control horizontal and vertical measure.

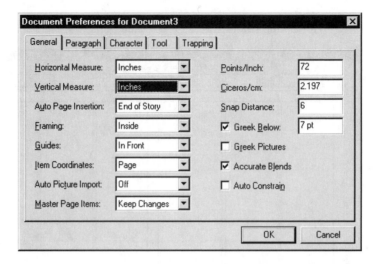

5. Choose the ideal unit measure for the type of layout work you are creating by making a choice from the drop-down list. If you want, you may set each of them to display different unit measures.

6. Select OK to accept your document preference changes and notice the rulers now reflect the new units.

7. To reset the ruler origin, grab the intersection point of the two rulers (upper-left corner) and drag it to a new position on either page. Notice that the ruler resets to measure from the new position, and that this new ruler origin applies to each page.

8. Double-click on the ruler origin (again—the intersection point of your horizontal and vertical rulers). Notice the rulers reset to measure from the upper-left corner of each page.

9. Choose Edit | Document | Preferences (CTRL/CMD+Y) and select the General tab again. Locate the Item Coordinates option, choose Spread from the drop-down menu, and click OK to accept the preference change. Notice now that your rulers measure progressively across *both* pages of your two-page spread.

10. Finally, grab any point on either ruler, and then click-and-drag your cursor to any point on your page. Notice as you drag your cursor a line appears, which you can follow as you drag. When you release the mouse, a line appears on your page. Notice also that this line appears only on the page onto which you dragged it.

Besides setting your unit measure, creating these lines is one of the key functions of the ruler. These lines are called guides; they help in visually or manually aligning items. To delete a guide, click-and-drag it back into the ruler it came from.

TIP *As you use various tools or drag and position items on your page, the horizontal and vertical rulers display dotted reference marks indicating the width, height, and position of the tool cursor, and the position of items. When you need more accuracy than rulers can provide, you can find specific values for guide and item placement in the Measurements palette.*

3

Using Guides

If you're familiar with the use of guidelines—or guides—in other applications, or if you just completed the preceding step-by-step, you may be aware already of how useful they can be. There are essentially three types of guides in XPress, although their differences are subtle: margin, ruler, and column guides.

- **Margin guides** Margin guides appear in blue (by default) on your page and are set when you initially create your new XPress document. After creating your document, these margins may be changed only by applying a new master guide from master pages. For information on changing master page guides, see *Master Guides* further in this section.

- **Ruler guides** These guides are created by dragging from either the horizontal or vertical ruler bars, hence there are vertical ruler guides and horizontal ruler guides. By default, ruler guides appear green on your page.

- **Column guides** Column guides appear within text boxes where more than one column has been specified. Their display changes with the number of columns set in each text box. Display of column guides is not a controllable option in XPress.

TIP *XPress' guide features are easily some of the more useful for positioning and aligning multiple items within your layout. But manually positioning an item close to—but not touching—a guide is nearly impossible. For this, you may want to turn off the snapping feature. To turn the feature off momentarily, choose View | Snap to Guides (SHIFT+F7). If you work with guides often, don't forget to turn the Snap to Guides option back on.*

To control the display of both ruler and margin guides on your page, choose View | Show/Hide Guides (F7). How your guides display may also be controlled through the Document Preferences dialog box by choosing Edit | Document | Preferences (CTRL/CMD+Y) | General tab. The Guides option (shown in the preceding illustration) features a drop-down menu that includes two options to display guides: In Front (the default) or Behind. Selecting to view guides behind your document items causes ruler and margin guides to be hidden behind existing page items.

> **NOTE** *Although margin, ruler, and column guides appear on your screen, they do not print—nor are there options anywhere in XPress to select them to print.*

When items on your page are positioned near or close to margin or ruler guides (and *not* column guides), and the Snap to Guides option is selected, the effect is magnetic, causing items to "snap" to align with the guides. This snapping effect makes it much faster and less tedious to align items along vertical or horizontal points. By default, items will snap to guides when within a distance of 6 pixels. However, the snapping distance may be reduced or enlarged depending on your work habits. To adjust this snapping distance, use the Snap Distance field in the Document Preferences dialog box shown in the preceding illustration. Snap distance may range between 1 and 216 pixels, although larger distances may cause conflicts between several page guides as XPress tries to determine which guide to snap to.

> **TIP** *The display color of your ruler guides may be customized to suit your needs. For more information on setting guide colors, see Setting Application Preferences in Chapter 12, Fine-tuning XPress.*

Setting Master Guides

Although the margin guides on your page may not be moved, you may apply new margin measures based on new master page properties using the Master Guides dialog box. To change your master page margin guides, you must be viewing a master page. Once a master page is displayed (Page | Display | Master Page), the Master Guides dialog box becomes available.

The Master Guides options are identical to the margin options set when creating a new document. There are fields for entering the number of columns, and unit measures for gutter and top, bottom, left, and right page margins, as shown in the following illustration. Changing the master guides on a master page automatically applies the new margin measures to pages that have the master page applied. If you want to have specific margins only for a certain page, you may need to create a new master page, alter the margins to suit your needs, and then apply that master page to your document page.

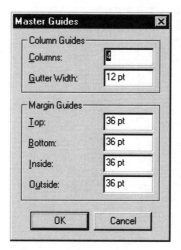

Viewing Baseline Grids

If you're fairly new to working with typographic and layout tools, you may not be familiar with either part of the name of this next feature. Baseline grids are used to ensure that page layouts are neat and tidy and follow standard layout conventions. A *baseline* is the imaginary line on which characters (or strings of characters) appear to rest. In layout terms, a *grid* is an invisible lattice with which all baselines of text align. So, the baseline grid serves as a foundation on which your type aligns. Grids enable you to align headings, body text, rules, and so on so that the layout appears planned and organized.

TIP   *For more information on using baseline grids, see* Working with Baseline Grids in XPress *in* Chapter 11, Working with Complex Layouts.

The baseline grid is a series of horizontal lines that appears by default in magenta (hot pink) on your master and document pages and across your pasteboard, beginning (by default) at the top margin of each page. To control the display of the grid, choose View | Show/Hide Baseline Grid (CTRL/OPTION+F7). When displayed, the baseline grid appears as in Figure 3-9.

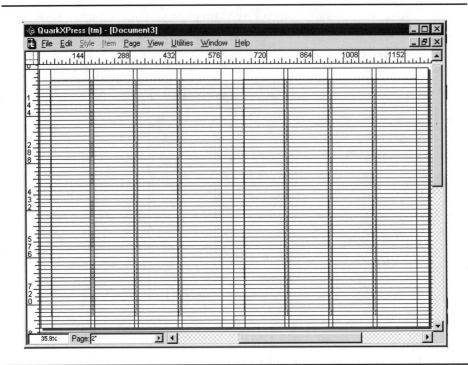

FIGURE 3-9 The baseline grid set to 36 points

Baseline grid spacing is controlled by options set in your Document Preferences dialog box. It is accessed by choosing Edit | Preferences | Document (CTRL/CMD+Y) | Paragraph tab, as shown in the following illustration. Where the grid begins to appear on your pages is set by entering a page position value in the Start field, and the space between the grid lines is set by entering a unit measure in the Increment field. The grid itself may be set to begin anywhere within your pasteboard area, while the Increment value must fall in a range between 1 and 144 points (or two inches).

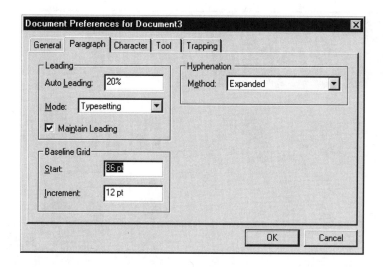

3

Using the Measurements Palette

The Measurements palette could easily be considered the mother of all palettes in XPress 4. Its behavior is chameleon-like, in that it adapts to display relevant values and properties according the selected item or contents. Using the Measurements palette for moving, transforming, scaling, rotating, or skewing items is much more precise than using manual methods.

In certain respects, the Measurements palette replaces editing changes to items normally associated with the Modify dialog box (for text or picture boxes and frames) or the Style menu (for character and paragraph formatting). The palette itself is divided into two separate areas. The left half of the palette displays an item's size and position, and the right side displays content properties.

To control display of the Measurements palette itself, choose View | Show/Hide Measurements (F9). As with other palettes, this palette may be minimized by double-clicking its title bar, or hidden by clicking its Close box.

QuarkXPress 4 IN ACTION

Description: Newsletter design

Design: Thomas Puckett

Firm: Intelligent Design Enforcement Agency (I.D.E.A.)

Client: JW Puckett, Better & Better

QuarkXPress 4 IN ACTION

Better & Better is a self-improvement newsletter that was produced using XPress, Adobe Photoshop, and Adobe Illustrator. Small spot-color illustrations and photography help to provide visual breaks within a fairly text-intensive format. The newsletter is lively but also has a polished look.

The editable properties on the left half of the Measurements palette may include the following fields or options, depending on the type of item selected:

- **X and Y**   These symbols represent the coordinates of your selected item in relation to your ruler origin. Increasing the X value moves the item to the right, and increasing the Y value moves the object downwards on your page in parallel with your ruler increments. For two-point lines these values will include X1, X2, Y1, and Y2, where the numerals 1 and 2 identify the endpoint positions respectively. Depending on how the point measure option is set, you may also encounter XC and YC, representing the "center" or midpoint coordinates, when the Midpoints option for displaying line position is selected (see *Line Points,* later in this section).

- **W and H (Width and Height)**   These options enable you to resize the dimensions of boxes.

- **Angle**   This option enables you to enter rotational values for selected items. The values entered map to the 360 degrees in a circle. Entering positive values rotates objects clockwise, and using negative values enacts counterclockwise rotation.

- **Corner Radius**   When boxes are selected, this option enables you to set the corner radius of rounded corners. The corner radius must range between 1 and 144 points.

- **Cols (Columns)**   When text boxes are selected, this field appears on the palette, enabling you to quickly change the number of columns in your text box.

- **Line Points**   This option appears as a drop-down list, enabling you to set the left half of the Measurements palette to display coordinate values for the endpoints, midpoints, first points, or last points of a line.

To change an item's size or position on the left half, enter a new value and press RETURN or ENTER to apply the new value. To select and highlight the first field in the palette, press CTRL/CMD+ALT/OPTION+M.

NOTE   *When either picture or text boxes are selected with the Item tool, two buttons in the center of the Measurements palette enable you to flip your selected item's contents horizontally (upper button) or vertically (lower button).*

The right half of the Measurements palette displays details about the selected item's content (for example, pictures in boxes, text in boxes, or character and paragraph formatting). When picture boxes are selected and either the Item or Content tool is in use, the right half of the Measurements palette includes the following options, shown in the following illustration:

3

- **X% and Y%**   These abbreviations for horizontal and vertical picture scale respectively measure the percentage of enlargement or reduction in relation to the image's original dimensions. The enlargement or reduction value entered must range between 10 and 1,000 percent of the original's size. Each of the picture scale values may be set independent of each other.

- **X+ and Y+**   These symbols stand for horizontal and vertical picture offset respectively and enable you to reposition the picture within its box. Each of the offset values may be set independent of each other.

- **Rotation**   This option enables you to rotate the picture within its picture box around 360 degrees. Negative values rotate counterclockwise.

- **Skew**   This option enables you to skew the picture right or left within the picture box. Skew values must be between 75 and -75 degrees, with negative values skewing the picture left.

When characters are selected, the right half of the Measurements palette includes the following options, as shown in the following illustration:

- **Leading**   Enter the leading for your selected paragraph, or click the up or down spinners to change leading in one-point increments. Holding the ALT/OPTION key while clicking the spinners changes leading in 0.1-point increments.

- **Tracking**   Enter the tracking value for your selected text, or click the left or right spinners to change tracking in one-tenth em increments. Holding the ALT/OPTION key while clicking the spinners changes tracking in one-hundredth em increments.

- **Alignment**   Choose from left, right, centered, justified, or forced alignment for your selected paragraph.

- **Font Name**   This drop-down list includes all the fonts currently available on your system and enables you to apply the fonts to your selected text.

- **Style**   Choose the style of your selected text from the Plain, Bold, Italic, Underline, Word Underline, Strikethrough, Outline, Shadow, All Caps, Small Caps, Superscript, Subscript, or Superior options. Clicking the Plain option resets all the Style buttons to their inactive positions.

- **Size**   Enter a character size or choose from the drop-down menu.

When lines or Béziers are selected, the Measurements palette includes the following options, as shown in the following illustration:

- **L (Length)**   This option allows you to enter a length for your selected line in the displayed unit measure.

- **W (Width)**   Enter a line-width value for your selected line, or choose a preset size from the drop-down menu.

- **Dash and Stripe**   Choose from any of the dash and stripe patterns currently available to your XPress document for your selected line.

- **Arrowhead**   Choose from any of the arrowhead styles in the drop-down list.

To change the properties of an item's content, enter a new value and press TAB or select another field. Changes to item properties on the right side of the Measurements palette take place immediately after leaving the changed field.

Conclusion

Tackling the layout of a document can often be a complex challenge with a multitude of considerations to keep in mind. In this chapter, you've explored the very beginning stages of planning and beginning construction of an XPress document. You've learned about the critical concept of setting master pages and their options and seen how the Layout palette enables you to navigate pages and manage content. You've also used zoom and page-viewing commands and seen how guides and grids may help you in the organization of your document items. In the next chapter, you'll continue this building process by diving into the enormous power and flexibility XPress has when it comes to working with text.

3

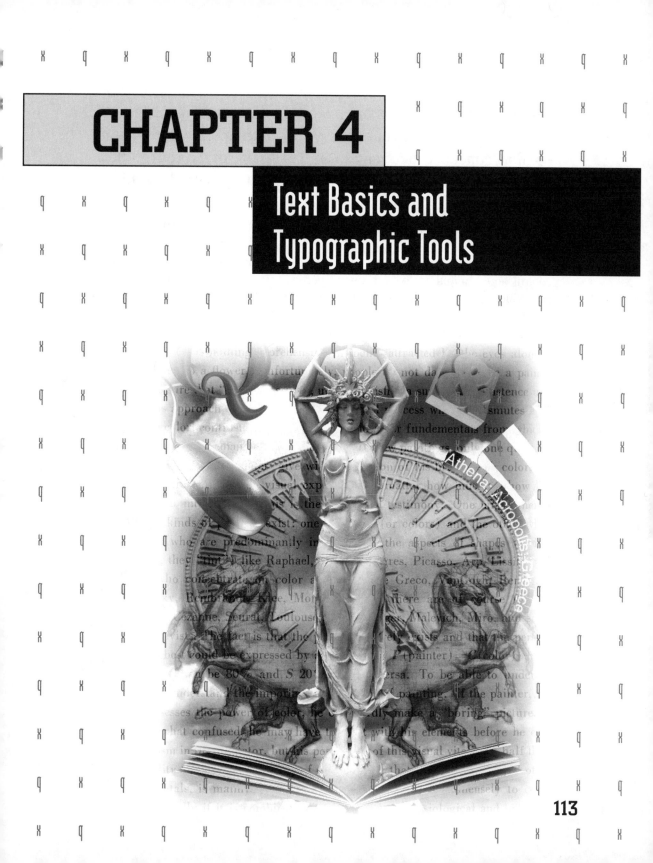

CHAPTER 4

Text Basics and Typographic Tools

Although a picture is often worth a thousands words, it's the text in your layout that will communicate ideas, tone, opinion, concepts, facts, and so on. Text is one of the key resources you have at your disposal for communicating with the audience interpreting your layout. For much of the material published in today's world, text comprises the majority of documents.

How you shape your text greatly determines its legibility. So, knowing how to control and manipulate the various properties of your text content is critical to achieving better layouts. In this chapter, you'll look closely at how XPress sees text. You'll also find out about the available tools for molding it. The more you know about XPress' available text tools and features, the more control you'll have over your layout and the better you'll be able to convey the message in your documents.

Anatomy of Text

For the moment, you're going to forget all about XPress and focus on the anatomy of text. The way most of us have come to know and appreciate text characters stems from our own individual experience reading other publications such as text books, novels, newspapers, and so on. Most people happily read through the text these publications contain, not really caring about how the text characters have been designed or how the publication has shaped the text. But, if you work in an environment where text is your business—such as publishing—you may have come to realize that one character style is not like another.

In typographic design, text characters are based on well-established standards. Without going into a long, rambling (and somewhat boring) history of text design, suffice it to say that characters—in any language—are based on literally centuries of handed-down knowledge and experience. How the text designer interprets or deviates from these standards contributes to the mood and tone of a specific character design. Applications such as XPress enable us to use digital adaptations of these character designs in our document pages. Although you can't change the design of these characters, there are plenty of characteristics you can control.

Character Properties

To understand a little more about how characters behave when manipulated, it may help to have some background on their individual parts. The following illustration indicates some of the basic parts of a typical combination of characters.

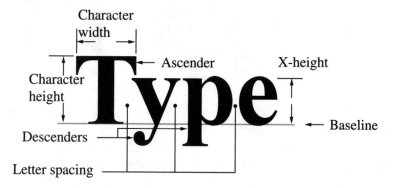

- **Character width**   The physical width of one character, the exact measure of which varies with each character

- **Character height**   The height measured from the baseline to the top of the highest character in the font; as with width, height can also vary with each character

- **Letter spacing**   The physical white space between characters

- **X-height**   The height of one character measured from the baseline and not including ascender or descender measures

- **Baseline**   The imaginary line on which all text appears to rest

- **Ascender**   The top portion of a character that extends above the x-height

- **Descender**   The bottom portion of a character that extends below the baseline of the text

Along with the various parts of the average character, the following illustration depicts one more common feature of text, which categorizes character styles: serif and sans serif. *Serif* is a term that describes the thin lines (often referred to as *tails*) that end the main stroke of a character. *Serif* describes characters that include these strokes, and *sans serif* describes characters that do not have the strokes. Serif type is often used in the main body text of a layout, while sans serif type is often used for headlines (although many designs deviate from this convention).

One of the key factors setting apart typeset-style text from that of typewriters or word processors is the attention given to character pairs. Typewriters and dedicated word processors often leave uniform proportional spacing between characters. In typesetting, certain character pairs appear less distracting if their particular letter spacing is reduced to account for their complementary shapes. Adjusting this space is referred to as *kerning*. Kerning is often applied only to specific combinations of characters.

For example, the spacing between uppercase letters that are open at their lower-right corners (such as the letters T, P, Y and F) may be reduced when they are followed by lowercase characters. The following illustration shows how the spacing between two characters may be kerned so that the space appears less distracting.

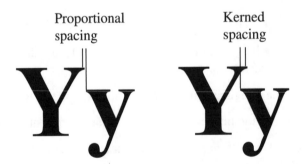

The final characteristic of text to consider is the adjustment of letter spacing. As the name implies, letter spacing is the white space that appears between letters within words. Letter spacing can also be referred to as *tracking*. The tracking of text can be useful for expanding or reducing the line length of text in an effort to force-fit text into a given space. But there is an optimal limit to how much you may increase or reduce the tracking.

Tracking that is set too "tight" or too "loose" can make text extremely difficult to read. And because having your audience read your text is probably a priority, your tracking should be adjusted gingerly. The following illustration depicts the effects of tight and loose tracking of text.

Paragraph Parts

Once you have a grasp of the characteristics of individual characters, it's time to move on to the dynamic properties associated with large quantities of characters we all know as *paragraphs*. A paragraph may be dissected into its individually-controllable parts as shown in the following illustration.

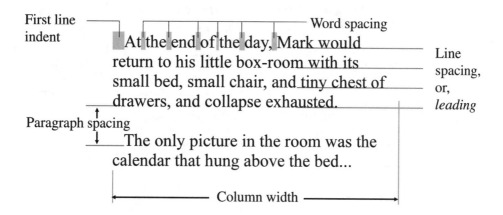

- ■ **First line indent**   An indent of the first line of a paragraph, which makes it easier for readers to identify the start of a new paragraph

- ■ **Word spacing**   The physical spacing between words

- **Line spacing or *leading***   The space between the baselines of text in a paragraph

- **Paragraph spacing**   The space between paragraphs

- **Column width**   The measure of horizontal space your paragraph may occupy

With the exception of actually changing the design of text characters, virtually all the properties of characters and paragraphs discussed so far may be adjusted or controlled in some way by most professional layout applications. Only a handful of lower-end applications lack this level of control.

But once you begin to format the text of your layout, you'll notice subtle differences between XPress and other applications. Many lack XPress' capability to flow text easily and efficiently, or to apply a large number of text styles or text effects such as drop caps and paragraph rules, as shown in the following illustration. In this illustration, you'll notice that applying special text styles and formatting to your paragraph text can improve its impact and legibility.

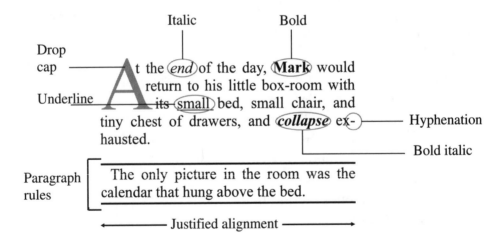

How XPress Sees Text

With a firm understanding now of the various controllable aspects of text characteristics and properties, let's return to the reality of layout in XPress. To

XPress, text is simply the digital matter that happens to be filling your text box. In fact, if your text isn't inside a text box, it can't exist in your XPress document (unless it's been converted to Béziers). The actual characters within text boxes are also fairly unimportant to XPress. To those who know better, this may not come as a great surprise.

When XPress interprets your text box contents, what it's really interested in is the attributes of your text (the actual characters and individual font design information are actually a function of your operating system). Character attributes include the size, style, color, shade, vertical and horizontal scaling, kerning or tracking, and baseline shift of your text. Paragraph attributes include properties such as indents, tabs, paragraph rules, drop caps, leading (line spacing), space between paragraphs, alignment, and hyphenation. Both paragraphs and characters may have extended properties that XPress pays attention to, such as style sheet tags for automated formatting, and index and cross-reference markers for higher text-sorting functions.

Creating a Text Box

As mentioned earlier, unless your characters reside inside a text box, to XPress they simply can't exist on the page. So, if you need to get text on your page, you must create a box first to put the text in. For users used to applications such as PageMaker and Publisher, or most illustration applications, including Adobe Illustrator, Freehand, and CorelDraw, this may be a confusing concept to grasp at first.

Text boxes must be created using text tools. The good news is XPress has seven different types of text tools to choose from, each of which creates text boxes that are editable in various ways and come in preset or custom shapes. Text tools are selected from the Tool palette (F8), and although only one tool displays on the palette at a time (by default), clicking the current tool button displays the remaining six in a pop-out menu. Each time a different text tool is selected, it becomes the default text tool to display in the palette.

To create a text box using one of these tools, follow these steps:

1. With XPress launched, your document open, and the Tool palette displayed (F8), choose any text box tool from the Tool palette. Notice your cursor changes to a crosshair.

2. Position your text box tool on your page and drag in any direction. (Ideally, your dragging action is in a diagonal direction.) Notice a dotted frame appears on the page as you drag.

3. Stop dragging and release your mouse button when the dotted line covers the area where you would like your text box to appear. Once you release the mouse button, a new text box appears in the shape related to the text box tool you are using and features eight sizing handles.

4. To begin entering text in the box, leave the box selected and choose the Content tool from the Tool palette (second from the top). Notice a blinking I-beam cursor appears in your new text box.

5. At this point you have the choice of entering text directly by typing, importing text using the Get Text command (CTRL/CMD+E), or copying text from the clipboard (or the Scrapbook for Mac users).

6. To resize the text box, hold your cursor over one of the eight resizing handles. Notice the cursor changes to a pointing hand. Click and drag the handle and notice a new dotted box frame appears indicating the changing size of your text box. Release the mouse button to accept the new shape.

7. To reposition your text box, click the Item tool or hold the CTRL/CMD key to temporarily select it. Notice your cursor changes to a multiheaded arrow pointer. To move the text box, simply click anywhere on the box and drag it to the new position.

TIP   *For more information on importing text using the Get Text command, see* Importing Text *in* Chapter 6, Working with Text.

Using Text Box Tools

When most text boxes are first created, their state is inherently dynamic, meaning they may be reproportioned without altering their inherent shape properties. For example, the Rectangle text tool creates text boxes with four sides and four corners set at 90 degrees to each other. Resizing the rectangle text box may change the length of its sides, but not the angle of its corners, and not its perpendicular state (unless angle, skew, or rotate values are applied). This is a key concept to keep in mind when creating and manipulating text boxes.

The seven text box tools in XPress 4 are Rectangle, Rounded-corner, Oval, Concave-corner, Beveled-corner, Bézier, and Freehand. The first five tools create new text boxes using simple click-and-drag actions, as shown in Figure 4-1.

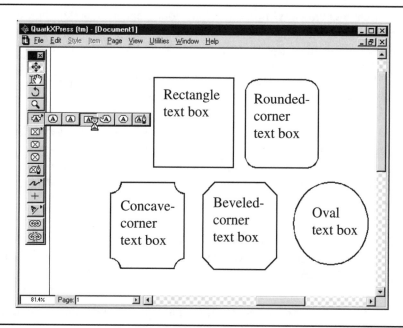

FIGURE 4-1   Text boxes created using the Rectangle, Rounded-corner,
Concave-corner, Oval, and Beveled-corner text tools

- **Rectangle text box tool**   This tool creates a new text box with four sides
  and four corners each set to 90 degrees. Although the rectangle corner
  shape is inherently squared, it may be modified to feature a corner radius
  using Modify (CTRL/CMD+M) | Box tab options.

- **Rounded-corner text box tool**   This tool creates a new text box with
  four sides and symmetrically-rounded corners, the corner radius of
  which may be set to varying degrees of roundness. When creating a
  rounded-corner text box, the default corner radius is applied automatically.

TIP: *To access the Modify dialog box options quickly, double-click any
text box using the Item tool, or double-click while holding CTRL/CMD when
the Content tool is in use.*

- **Concave-corner text box tool** This tool creates a new text box with four sides and concave corners that feature the currently-set default corner radius measure.

- **Oval text box tool** This tool creates a new text box with an elliptical shape.

TIP *To create a text box with sides of equal length using any of the Rectangle, Rounded-corner, Concave-corner, or Beveled-corner text box tools, hold the SHIFT key while creating (or resizing) the text box. To create a perfectly-circular text box, use the Oval text box tool and hold the SHIFT key while creating (or resizing) the new text box.*

- **Beveled-corner text box tool** This tool creates a new text box with symmetric corners with beveled sides, where the corner angle of each bevel is set to 45 degrees.

TIP *To change the shape of a text box, use the Item | Shape command and choose a preset item shape from the pop-out menu.*

With these five tools, text box creation is a relatively straightforward operation. The remaining two text box tools involve slightly more user interaction. Bézier and Freehand text box tools create text boxes that are quite unlike the preceding five. Both Bézier and Freehand text boxes may be any shape you choose.

Bézier objects actually form the basis for most vector-based illustration programs. As is their nature, Bézier shapes involve several points joined by curved or straight-line segments. The points composing the shapes of Bézier and Freehand text boxes affect the shape of the line segments between them. Hence, the Bézier points in these two text box types may be reshaped during their creation. Although the boxes resulting from using these tools are similar, the most significant difference for the user lies in how they are used. As with other highly-interactive tools, the quickest way to learn about their use is through practice.

To create a text box using the Bézier text box tool, follow these steps:

1. Choose the Bézier text box tool from the Tool palette. If the Bézier text box tool isn't currently displayed, click and hold whichever text box tool is showing in the palette, and then select the Bézier text box tool from the pop-out menu that appears, as shown in Figure 4-2. The Bézier text box tool button may be recognized as a pen nib with a nonuniform box shape. Notice your cursor now features a crosshair.

2. Find a clear space to work in, click once on the page and release the mouse button. Notice a tiny blue-outlined square appears where you clicked. This is the first point of your shape.

3. Click a second time on your page a short distance away from the first point and release the mouse. Notice three things happen: the first point changes to a solid black square, a second blue-outlined square appears where you click, and a blue line joining the two squares appears. The square that appears where you click is the second point in your Bézier shape.

4. Continue clicking and adding new points. Each time you click the Bézier text box tool a new point and line segment is created, as shown in Figure 4-2.

4

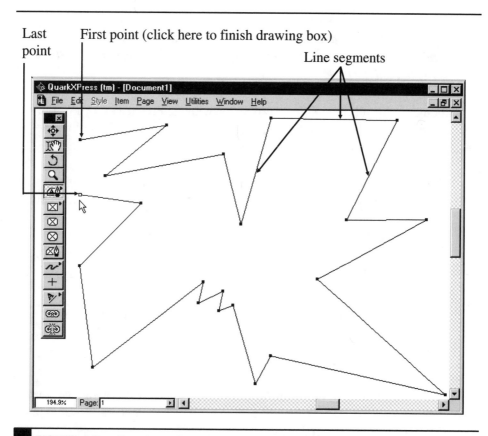

FIGURE 4-2   Creating a Bézier shape with the Bézier text box tool

TIP *Straightforward click actions with the Bézier text box tool create only straight-line segment points. You may also create curved points of varying types. Or, your points may be edited later on to change their shape. For more information on drawing with Bézier tools, see* Drawing with Bézier Tools *in* Chapter 5, Using Drawing Tools.

5. Up until this point, your Bézier shape is merely an incompletely-formed shape. To complete the shape, you need to do one of three things: Hold your Bézier text box tool cursor over the first point until your cursor changes to a rounded square, and then click the first point; double-click the mouse; or select any other tool from the Tool palette. Any of these actions causes your newly-created Bézier shape to be completed automatically.

NOTE *All "box" tools in XPress are set to automatically create "closed" shapes, meaning the first and last points are joined. To create an open shape, you must use a freehand-style drawing tool such as the Freehand Text-Path or Freehand Line tools.*

Although the results of creating a box shape with the Freehand text box tool are similar to that of the Bézier text box tool, its drawing action is slightly different. To create a text box using the Freehand text box tool, follow these steps:

1. Choose the Freehand text box tool from the Tool palette. Again, if the Freehand text box tool isn't currently displayed, click and hold whichever text box tool is showing in the palette and select the Freehand text box tool from the pop-out menu that appears. The Freehand text box tool button may be recognized by an oddly shaped closed-curve symbol. Once selected, your cursor now features a crosshair.

2. Here's where the difference comes in. In a clear space on your page, click and *hold* your cursor on the page. If you're clicking and holding without dragging, you'll notice that very little (if anything) is happening on the screen. The action starts to take place once you begin dragging your cursor.

3. With the mouse button still held, drag the Freehand text box tool to create any shape you want. As you drag, notice a blue line appears to trail your cursor, as shown in Figure 4-3.

Starting point   Line appears behind your cursor as
                               you drag

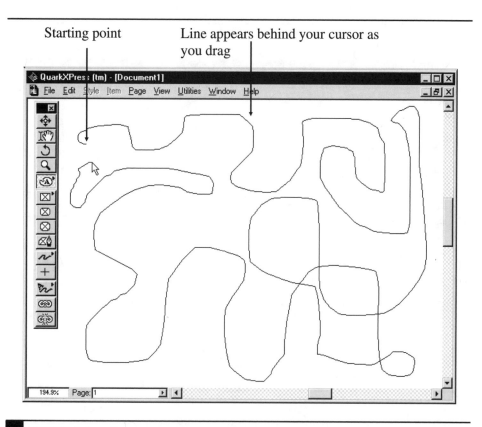

FIGURE 4-3   Creating a shape with the Freehand text box tool

4. Release the mouse once you are satisfied with the shape. Notice the shape automatically closes, and points joining line segments appear where you dragged, as shown in Figure 4-4.

Modifying Text Box Properties

Text boxes have evolved from being simple containers for your text to actual layout elements capable of displaying and printing with certain properties applied. The actual text box frames may have line attributes applied such as thickness, color, pattern, and shade. The inside area of text boxes may also have color, shade, and

Points

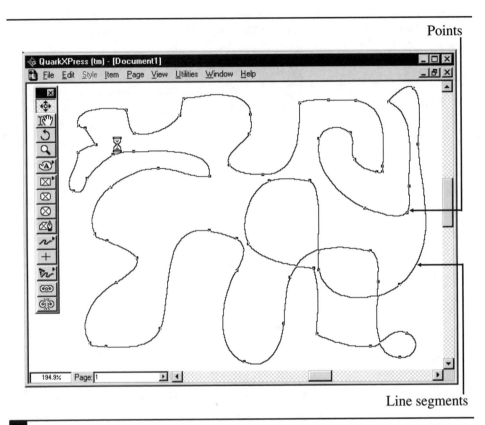

Line segments

FIGURE 4-4   When you release the mouse, your new freehand shape closes, and the new points and line segments appear

various blends applied. And the shape of the text box may be altered, including effects such as changing the height, width, angle, and skew.

In fact, the very capability of XPress to control text box frames and their interiors independently of the text they contain—while still considering the elemental properties as a single unit—is the concept that may be considered an advantage over other layout programs. But the terminology still confuses even long-time users of XPress. You have text boxes that can often be nonrectangular. There are boxes with frames, and there are text properties, text box frame properties, and box properties. If you find yourself confused at times, don't be surprised—you're not alone.

Text Box Frame Properties

The frame of a text box is the actual perimeter that surrounds and encloses it. Given size, color, shade, or a pattern, this frame becomes visible. Otherwise, these boxes are simply the containers that hold your text. Frame properties are set using the Modify | Frame tab (CTRL/CMD+B) dialog box shown in the following illustration. The Frame tab includes options for setting the thickness (width), style, color, and shade of the frame. When using patterned line styles, additional options become available for setting the color and shade of the pattern's gap. The top of the dialog box features the Preview window, which reflects the chosen color and style of your frame and any gap color or shades.

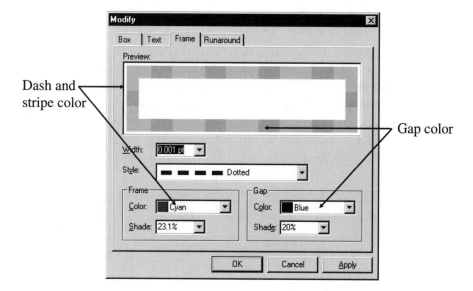

- **Width**   Your frame width may be set in a range between 0 and 864 points (12 inches); the smallest accepted measure is 0.001 points of thickness—although most printers would be incapable of printing such a small measure.

- **Style**   The frame Style field may be set to any of the dash and stripe styles available in your document, including those you may have created yourself.

- **Frame Color**   The Frame Color field may also be set to any color available in your document.

■ **Frame Shade** The Frame Shade value has the effect of limiting your frame color to a screen percentage of the selected frame color. The value may be set within a range between 0 and 100 percent to an accuracy of one decimal point.

■ **Gap Color and Shade** If you have applied a dash and stripe style to your text box frame, the Gap Color and Gap Shade options become available. The "gap" of your frame pattern includes the white or "negative" spaces between the black or "positive" spaces. Gap Color and Gap Shade may be set in the same manner as for the default Frame Color and Frame Shade options.

Text Box Shade and Color

The interior of your text box is referred to as the actual text "box"—although as you saw earlier, that doesn't necessarily mean it's limited to a rectangular shape. Think of the box housing your text as the area inside the frame, or, the interior of your text box shape. The text box may be set with a *potpourri* of options such as page position (origin across and down), dimensions, angle and skew, corner radius, box color and shade, and even background blend colors. All options may be set using the Modify (CTRL/CMD+M) | Box tab, as shown in the following illustration.

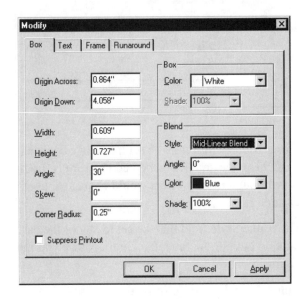

- **Origin Across and Origin Down**   These two origin values enable you to set the vertical and horizontal position of the upper left corner of your text box, measured according to your ruler origin and default unit measure.

- **Width and Height**   These two fields set the dimensions of your text box according to the unit measure of your ruler. The width and height measures remain constant even if the text box is rotated.

- **Angle and Skew**   The Angle field enables you to set a rotation for your text box around a 360-degree rotation. Negative values rotate counterclockwise. Entering a value in the Skew field causes a leaning-style distortion of your text box to the left or right. Skew may be set in a range between 75 and -75 degrees.

- **Corner Radius**   Entering a value in the Corner Radius field causes the corner of the box to become rounded, while leaving the radius at 0 creates a simple right-angle corner. The Corner Radius value must be between 0 and 2 inches.

- **Box Color and Shade**   These two drop-down menus enable you to select from a preset color and shade for the interior area of your text box. Choosing a color other than White or None from the Color drop-down menu enables you to set a Shade value for your color between 0 and 100 percent. Text box color and shade properties appear *behind* the textual content in the text box.

TIP ⟶ *On a white document page where the text box color is set to White, all objects beneath it are hidden from view, and the box color itself is opaque. Choosing a box color of None renders the box color transparent.*

- **Blend Style, Angle, Color, and Shade**   Color blends are essentially gradations from one color to another. The text box Blend feature enables you to create a blended color backgrund for your text box. The Blend Style field may be set to Solid (no blend), Linear, Mid-Linear, Rectangular, Diamond, Circular, and Full Circular. Once a blend style has been selected from the drop-down menu, the Angle, Color, and Shade options for the blend color become available.

■ **Suppress Printout**   Selecting this option enables XPress to ignore any box options and causes your box, its color, and contents to be left as an empty space when your document is printed.

TIP ─────→ *For more information on working with color and blends, see* Exploring XPress Color Blends *in* Chapter 5, Using Drawing Tools.

Text Box Runaround

Not only may you control the characteristics and behavior of the text box frame and the box properties themselves, but XPress also enables you to set how other outside elements, such as the text in adjacent text boxes, react to your text box. The term *runaround* describes the effect of your text box *repelling*—or keeping away—text in other boxes. Text runaround properties may be set according to the type of text box you are currently working with, as shown in the following illustration.

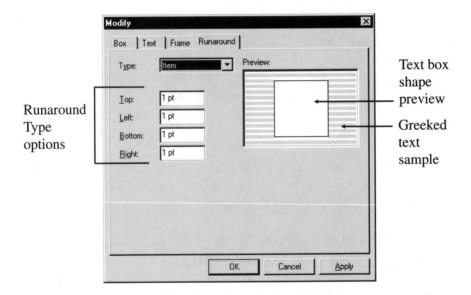

■ **Type**   Two runaround types are available from this drop-down menu: Item and None. Choosing Item (the default) causes text to be repelled from your text box shape according to options set. Selecting None turns off the runaround feature.

- **Top, Left, Bottom, and Right**   The values entered in these four fields enable text adjacent to your text box frame to be repelled individually from each side. The default runaround value is set to 1 point. These options are available only when rectangular text box items are selected. For other text box types, the Outset option is available instead. Runaround values for these four fields and the Outset option may be set within a range between -288 and 288 points (4 inches).

TIP ———————▶ *Setting the runaround value to a negative number enables text in adjacent text boxes to "creep" within your selected text frame.*

4

- **Outset**   When text boxes other than the rectangular type are selected, this option enables you to set a runaround amount uniformly around all sides. Outset may also be set within a range between -288 and 288 points (4 inches).

TIP ———————▶ *For more information on setting runarounds, see* Strategies for Runarounds *in* Chapter 9, Combining Text and Graphics.

As a practical exercise in exploring text box, text frame, and box formatting options, follow these steps (for this example, you may want to have a few paragraphs of sample text prepared):

1. With a new or existing document opened to a blank page, choose the Rectangle tool from the Tool palette and create a text box of any size.

2. Choose the Item tool and double-click the box to open the Modify dialog box.

3. Select the Box tab by clicking its name; enter **4** in the Width field and **4** in the Height field.

4. Choose Black from the Box Color drop-down menu and 40 percent from the Shade drop-down menu.

5. Choose Circular from the Blend Style drop-down menu, choose Blue from the Blend Color drop-down menu, and choose 60 from the Shade drop-down menu.

6. Click OK to accept the new coloring of your box. Notice your box now appears with a gradation of color from 40 percent Black around the edges to 60 percent Blue in the center, as shown in the following illustration.

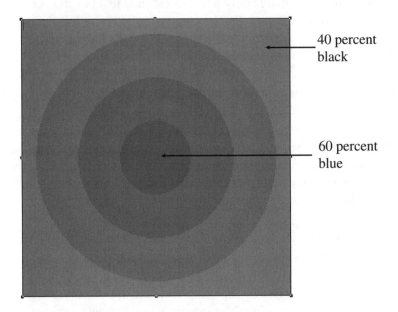

40 percent black

60 percent blue

7. With your box still selected with the Item tool, access the box frame properties by pressing CTRL/CMD+B (or choose Item I Frame from the menus). Notice the Modify dialog box opens specifically to the Frame tab.

8. Choose the following values from the drop-down menus: Width=8 points; Style=Thick Thin; Frame Color=Red; Frame Shade=50 percent; Gap Color=Blue; Gap Shade=60 percent. Notice with each choice you make, the Preview window reflects your new box frame property.

9. Click OK to accept your frame properties. Notice your text box frame now appears with a 50 percent red outline in a Thick Thin style and the gap between the lines appears in 60 percent blue, as shown in the following illustration.

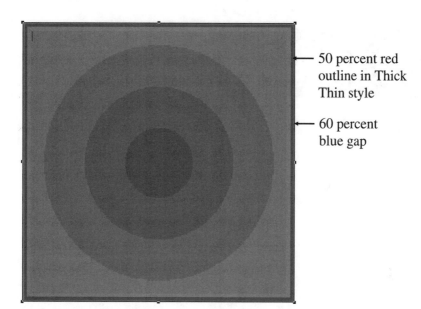

50 percent red outline in Thick Thin style

60 percent blue gap

4

10. Next, insert a text sample into your text box. To enter text directly, choose the Content tool and begin typing. You may also paste your text from another application using clipboard commands or import the text using the Get Text command (CTRL/CMD+E).

11. With characters now in your text box, open the Modify dialog box again and this time select the Text tab.

12. Enter **24 pt** in the Text Inset field and choose Centered from the Type Vertical Alignment drop-down menu. Click OK to accept the changes. Notice the text in your text box now appears centered and indented from all sides, as shown in the following illustration.

QuarkXPress 4 IN ACTION

QuarkXPress 4 IN ACTION

Description: 2-color invitation

Designer: Elaine Chu

Firm: Elaine Chu Graphic Design, 748 Oakland Ave., #302, Oakland, CA 94611
Phone 510/547-7705, Fax 510/597-1087 e-mail egchu@aol.com

Client: USCF Center for Health Professions

To celebrate the 5-year anniversary of UCSF's Center for the Health Professions, this invitation was created for the gala event. Even with the constraints of a low budget, a 2-color piece can be effective using tints and overlapping elements created right in Quark.

The client expressed interest in using irises for the table centerpieces, so I picked up on the visual idea. Using clip art, I made a scan of the flowers and imported it into the Quark layout. I incorporated the circular logo into the anniversary theme by placing it directly on top of the large number 5 and making sure both elements were assigned the same color.

Response to the invitation was great, and the gala event was very successful.

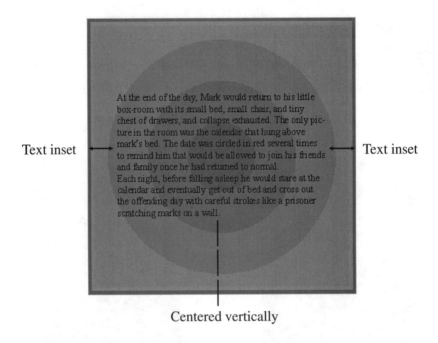

Text inset ← At the end of the day, Mark would return to his little box-room with its small bed, small chair, and tiny chest of drawers, and collapse exhausted. The only picture in the room was the calendar that hung above mark's bed. The date was circled in red several times to remind him that would be allowed to join his friends and family once he had returned to normal.
Each night, before falling asleep he would stare at the calendar and eventually get out of bed and cross out the offending day with careful strokes like a prisoner scratching marks on a wall. → Text inset

Centered vertically

NOTE ➝ *You may want to continue using this sample document in the exercise that follows later in this chapter. To save your sample, choose Save (CTRL/CMD+S) or Save As (CTRL/CMD+ALT/OPTION+S) to open the Save dialog box, and then give your document a unique name and folder location.*

Applying Text Formatting

Text formatting is perhaps the most sought after feature when working with text in your document. The capability to emphasize or de-emphasize text has become an essential feature for nearly all desktop software. For typesetting-capable quality applications such as XPress 4, the capability to apply formatting quickly and easily is the key. So, it's no wonder XPress provides you with a multitude of ways to apply general and specific formatting to your characters and paragraphs.

All text formatting in XPress must be applied while using the Content tool and working in text boxes. Without meeting these two conditions, you simply won't be able to edit the text on your page. Once in text formatting mode though, a universe of formatting methods is available to you. In terms of basic formatting, this section discusses the quickest methods. More complex methods of globally controlling text formatting are covered in subsequent chapters, such as *Chapter 6, Working with Text, Chapter 10, Laying Out Documents,* and *Chapter 11, Working with Complex Layouts.*

Text Selection Methods

As mentioned, to format text you must be working with the Content tool and have a text box selected. While in this state, your Content tool changes to an I-beam cursor, which is used for working with text. To quickly format text with the Content tool, you must first select and highlight the characters or paragraphs to which you want to apply your new formatting. There are several ways to select text within a text box. You may use standard text-selections methods such as dragging your cursor, using shift selection to choose characters in a sequence, or applying various successive cursor clicks to select words or paragraphs.

4

NOTE   *When selecting text characters in XPress 4, you may only select characters and paragraphs that follow in sequence. In other words, you may not select two words in different lines, paragraphs, or text boxes.*

The following guide indicates the various text selection methods available in XPress 4:

Select specific characters	Drag cursor vertically and/or horizontally across characters or lines
Select a word	Double-click the word
Select a word and its period or comma	Double-click between word and punctuation
Select entire line	Triple-click anywhere in the line
Select entire paragraph	Click four times anywhere in the paragraph
Select all text in story	Click five times anywhere in story or press CTRL/CMD+A
Highlight between insertion points	SHIFT+Click insertion points

TIP   *It helps to be working at a magnification level high enough to be able to actually read the text. To zoom into a text box and enlarge your view, use the Zoom tool or keyboard shortcuts.*

In some cases, when navigating the characters in a text box, it may be quicker to use keyboard shortcuts to move your I-beam cursor. In these cases, XPress enables the following quick keys for *moving* your Content tool I-beam cursor:

One character	LEFT or RIGHT ARROW keys
One line (vertically)	UP or DOWN ARROW keys
One word	CTRL/CMD+LEFT or RIGHT ARROW keys
One paragraph	CTRL/CMD+UP or DOWN ARROW keys
Start of line	CTRL/CMD+ALT/OPTION+LEFT (or HOME in Windows)
End of line	CTRL/CMD+ALT/OPTION+RIGHT (or END in Windows)
Start of story	CTRL/CMD+ALT/OPTION+UP (or CTRL+HOME in Windows)
End of story	CTRL/CMD+ALT/OPTION+DOWN (or CTRL+END in Windows)

Once your text is selected, and before you start applying your formatting, it may be helpful to know the various ways you may delete text in XPress 4. The following shortcuts apply for deleting text while the I-beam is inserted in text (with no text selected):

	Windows	Mac
Delete previous character	BACKSPACE	DELETE
Delete next character	DELETE or SHIFT+BACKSPACE	SHIFT+DELETE
Delete previous word	CTRL+BACKSPACE	CMD+DELETE
Delete next word	CTRL+DELETE or CTRL+SHIFT+BACKSPACE	CTRL+SHIFT+DELETE
Delete highlighted text	BACKSPACE or DELETE	DELETE

As a practical exercise in using XPress' basic text-selection methods, follow these steps (for this example, it'll help to have a text sample to work with. This example continues using the text box and frame formatting exercise we used earlier):

1. Create or open a document containing text in a text box of any style and select the Content tool.

2. Place the Content tool text cursor at the very start of the text by clicking just in front of the first character.

3. To familiarize yourself with moving the cursor through your text using keyboard keys, press the RIGHT or LEFT ARROW keys several times each. Notice each time you press the keys the cursor moves by one character.

4. Press CTRL/CMD+ALT/OPTION+LEFT to return to the beginning of your current line, and then press CTRL/CMD+ALT/OPTION+UP to return to the beginning of the text once again.

5. Hold the CTRL/CMD key and press the RIGHT or DOWN ARROW keys again. Notice as you press CTRL/CMD+RIGHT ARROW the cursor moves by whole words, and as you press CTRL/CMD+DOWN ARROW the cursor moves by whole paragraphs.

6. Hold the SHIFT key and click any of the ARROW keys. Notice as your cursor moves, the text appears in negative one character at a time. The negative appearance is XPress' feedback that your text is now highlighted.

7. Now try adding the CTRL/CMD key to the mix—your selected text increases by whole words or whole paragraphs. Practice these keyboard-selection techniques to become familiar with their use—you're bound to be using them.

8. Now we'll try mouse cursor selection. To select text with the mouse, use a click-and-drag action with your Content tool I-beam cursor. Notice as you drag across the text it becomes highlighted as before.

9. Click anywhere in your text to deselect it. Hold the SHIFT key now and click at a different point in the text. Notice all the text from your first insertion point to your second insertion point becomes selected.

Click anywhere in your text to deselect it and click twice in rapid succession on any whole word. Notice the word becomes highlighted and selected. Click three times and the whole line becomes selected. Click four times and the whole paragraph becomes selected, as shown in the following illustration. If you click five times, you select all the text in your story (including text that may not be appearing in your text box).

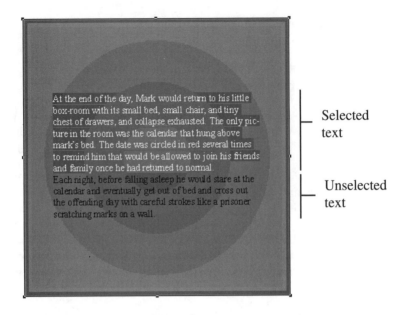

At the end of the day, Mark would return to his little box-room with its small bed, small chair, and tiny chest of drawers, and collapse exhausted. The only picture in the room was the calendar that hung above mark's bed. The date was circled in red several times to remind him that would be allowed to join his friends and family once he had returned to normal.

Each night, before falling asleep he would stare at the calendar and eventually get out of bed and cross out the offending day with careful strokes like a prisoner scratching marks on a wall.

Selected text

Unselected text

Quick Ways to Format Text

Because XPress 4 enables you to control so many of the properties associated with text, there are quite a number of shortcut keys to be aware of. The magnitude of shortcuts available makes it possible for you to become more efficient with the software as you become familiar with using it. Although you may not be interested in memorizing the shortcuts in the following lists, it helps to know these speedy methods are available. Once you're settled in with XPress 4, you'll significantly increase the speed at which you apply text formats.

Character Style Formatting

Plain	CTRL/CMD+SHIFT+P
Bold	CTRL/CMD+SHIFT+B
Italic	CTRL/CMD+SHIFT+I
Underline	CTRL/CMD+SHIFT+U
Word underline	CTRL/CMD+SHIFT+W
Strike through	CTRL/CMD+SHIFT+/

Outline	CTRL/CMD+SHIFT+O
Shadow	CTRL/CMD+SHIFT+S
All caps	CTRL/CMD+SHIFT+K
Small caps	CTRL/CMD+SHIFT+H
Superscript	CTRL/CMD+SHIFT+0 (numeral zero)/+ (plus on Mac)
Subscript	CTRL/CMD+SHIFT+9/– (minus on Mac)
Superior	CTRL/CMD+SHIFT+V

4

Paragraph Alignment

Left	CTRL/CMD+SHIFT+L
Centered	CTRL/CMD+SHIFT+C
Right	CTRL/CMD+SHIFT+R
Justified	CTRL/CMD+SHIFT+J
Forced	CTRL/CMD+ALT/OPTION+SHIFT+J

Character Size

Increase to next largest preset size	CTRL/CMD+SHIFT+>
Increase one point	CTRL/CMD+ALT/OPTION+SHIFT+>
Decrease to next smallest preset size	CTRL/CMD +SHIFT+<
Decrease one point	CTRL/CMD +ALT/OPTION+SHIFT+<
Or, to change character size by using mouse action, press the mouse and keyboard combinations as follows:	
Proportional sizing	CTRL/CMD+ALT/OPTION+SHIFT+Drag text box sizing handle
Constrained sizing	CTRL/CMD+SHIFT+Drag text box sizing handle
Unproportional sizing	CTRL/CMD+Drag text box sizing handle

TIP *To access the* Other *point size field in the Character Attributes dialog box, press CTRL/CMD+SHIFT+\ with the text selected.*

Text Shaping

A text shaping modification could be considered any command that alters the horizontal or vertical measure, or space between individual characters or whole paragraphs. Although leading, tracking, and kerning can change the vertical and horizontal length of text, scaling commands actually distort the appearance of the characters themselves. Adjusting the baseline shift of characters may be considered advanced formatting.

- **Leading**   Changing leading increases the horizontal point measure between lines of text in a paragraph. Changing leading also changes the spacing between paragraphs an equal amount. The following keyboard shortcuts alter leading amounts when applied to selected text:

Increase 1 point	CTRL/CMD+SHIFT+"
Decrease 1 point	CTRL/CMD+SHIFT+:
Increase 0.1 point	CTRL/CMD+ALT/OPTION+SHIFT+"
Decrease 0.1 point	CTRL/CMD+ALT/OPTION+SHIFT+:

TIP *To access the Leading options in the Paragraph Attributes dialog box, press CTRL/CMD+SHIFT+E.*

- **Kerning and tracking**   These values set the horizontal spacing between characters, certain character pairs, and words. Kerning and tracking are measured in em spaces. One em space equals the point size height of one character of the selected text. You may also adjust kerning and tracking settings by inserting your I-beam cursor between characters when using keyboard shortcuts. When changing spacing between certain pairs of text, the command is called kerning; when changing the spacing of selected text, the command is called tracking.

The following kerning and tracking shortcuts apply:

Increase by 1/20 of an em space	CTRL/CMD +SHIFT+}
Decrease by 1/20 of an em space	CTRL/CMD+SHIFT+{
Increase by 1/200 of an em space	CTRL/CMD+ALT/OPTION+SHIFT+}
Decrease by 1/200 of an em space	CTRL/CMD+ALT/OPTION+SHIFT+{

TIP

Although you may set kerning and tracking values to your text without knowing exactly what they are, it may be best to find out as much as you can before making too many adjustments to your text. Customizing kerning and tracking for perfect text appearance is the pride of some advanced users. But the tools and concepts can be quite complex for newer users. For more information on working with kerning and tracking features in XPress 4, see Custom Kerning and Tracking in Chapter 12, Fine-tuning XPress.

4

- **Horizontal and vertical scaling**   Scaling your text actually applies a distortion effect instead of simply applying a style. Nevertheless, it is a quick way of creating certain effects. Adjusting the scaling by keyboard shortcuts is a tricky endeavor because you may only change one scaling direction at a time. The scaling mode by default is set to Horizontal and may only be changed to Vertical mode using the Scale option in the Character Attributes dialog box (CTRL/CMD+SHIFT+D). The following keyboard shortcuts apply:

Increase 5 percent	CTRL/CMD+]
Increase 1 percent	CTRL/CMD+ALT/OPTION+]
Decrease 5 percent	CTRL/CMD+[
Decrease 1 percent	CTRL/CMD+ALT/OPTION+[

- **Baseline shift**   Changing character baseline shift may be applied to individual characters, words, or whole paragraphs. Baseline shifts occur only in 1-point increments by pressing the following shortcut keys:

Raise characters 1-point	CTRL/CMD+ALT/OPTION+SHIFT+) [+ plus on the Mac]
Lower characters 1-point	CTRL/CMD+ALT/OPTION+SHIFT+([– minus/hyphen on the Mac]

TIP

If using keyboard shortcuts remains a mystery while you continue to take in XPress 4 basics, you may want to use the Measurements palette (F9). Even for expert users, the Measurements palette is quicker than using dialog boxes, and it enables you to format the most common text formatting attributes, including leading, tracking, alignment, font name, style, and size. For information on the text tools available in the Measurements palette, refer to Using the Measurements Palette *in* Chapter 3, Tackling a Layout.

As a practical experience in formatting your text characters, follow these steps (for this example, it'll help to have a text sample to work with. This example also continues using the previous text box frame formatting and text selection exercise):

1. With a document open and a text box containing text selected, click the Content tool in the Tool palette.

2. Select all the text by clicking five times anywhere in the text box, or use the Select All command by choosing Edit | Select All (CTRL/CMD+A).

3. With all your text selected, open the Character Attributes dialog box by choosing Style | Character (CTRL/CMD+SHIFT+D). Choose a common and readable text font from the Font drop-down menu, and then choose 14 pt from the Size options and White from the Color options. Click OK to accept the changes and exit the dialog box. Notice your text now features these attributes.

4. Open the Measurements palette (F9) and position it in a convenient spot without blocking the view of your text. (To move a palette, drag its title bar). Notice that the Measurements palette also reflects the character attributes you just applied.

5. By default, your text may still feature automatic leading, which usually suffices for quick formatting but not for professional-looking line spacing. To reduce the leading with your text still highlighted, press CTRL/CMD+SHIFT+: (colon) *two* times. Notice the leading measure in the Measurements palette now reads 15 pt. A leading measure of 1-point more than the point size is usually sufficient to avoid ascenders and descenders touching.

6. Next, you'll use the Measurements palette to apply a few attributes. Click the Centered button in the alignment area and click the Bold and Italic buttons in the style area, as shown in the following illustration. Notice as

you change these attributes using the Measurements palette, the effects are immediate.

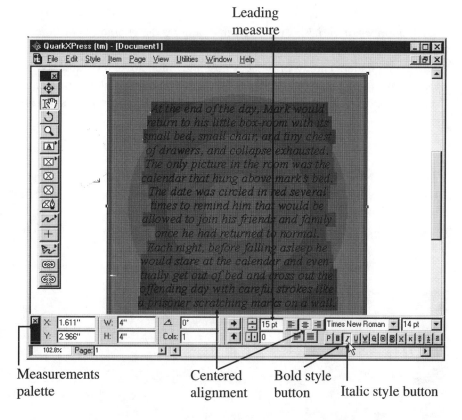

Leading measure

Measurements palette

Centered alignment

Bold style button

Italic style button

7. Next, familiarize yourself with a few common keyboard shortcuts. Minimize the Measurements palette (by double-clicking its title bar) so that you may see more of your text, and then press CTRL/CMD+SHIFT+J. This command sets your paragraph alignment to Justified.

8. Now adjust the kerning and tracking amount. Press CTRL/CMD+SHIFT+{ once only. Notice the text length decreases. You have just decreased the kerning and tracking measure by -10, or, 0.2 ems.

9. Now press CTRL/CMD+ALT/OPTION+SHIFT+} several times. Notice each time you press the shortcut keys, the length of the text increases. This is the shortcut for increasing the kernng and tracking measure by 0.02 ems, applied each time it's pressed.

10. Maximize the Measurements palette by double-clicking its title bar. Notice all the current character attributes are displayed—including changes you just made to the kerning and tracking.

The number of variables involved in changing the character attributes of your text in XPress 4 are seemingly endless, but the preceding exercise provides a fundamental understanding of what is possible, and shows how quickly keyboard shortcuts may apply attribute changes compared to using dialog boxes or palettes. Continue your exploration of these shortcuts using your text sample and the shortcuts listed in the preceding text.

Special-purpose Text Characters

High-end users will appreciate the capability of XPress to accept certain "soft" characters demanded by layout professionals. Soft characters cause effects such as forcing a line feed, hyphen, or indent, and are often required for high-end book publishing.

The following shortcuts create soft characters when working in text boxes:

	Windows	**Mac**
Discretionary hyphen	CTRL+HYPHEN	CMD+HYPHEN
Discretionary new line	CTRL+ENTER	CMD+RETURN
Force indent	CTRL+\	CMD+\
New box	SHIFT+ENTER (on keypad)	SHIFT+ENTER (keypad)
New column	ENTER (keypad)	ENTER (keypad)
Nonbreaking em dash	CTRL+ALT+SHIFT+-	CMD+OPTION+=
Nonbreaking en dash	CTRL+SHIFT+-	OPTION+-
Nonbreaking hyphen	CTRL+=	CMD+=
Right indent tab	SHIFT+TAB	OPTION+TAB
Nonbreaking space	CTRL+5	CMD+5
Breaking en space	CTRL+SHIFT+6	OPTION+SPACE
Nonbreaking en space	CTRL+ALT+SHIFT+6	CMD+OPTION+5

	Windows	Mac
Breaking flexible space	CTRL+SHIFT+5	OPTION+SHIFT+SPACE
Nonbreaking flexible space	CTRL+ALT+SHIFT+5	CMD+OPTION+SHIFT+SPACE
Breaking punctuation space	SHIFT+SPACE or CTRL+6	SHIFT+SPACE
Nonbreaking punctuation space	CTRL+SHIFT+SPACE or CTRL+ALT+6	CMD+SHIFT+SPACE

4

Conclusion

This chapter has taken you on a journey that has ventured from understanding the basics of text characters to applying basic character attributes using keyboard shortcuts—and all the details in between. At this point, you may want to congratulate yourself for coming so far so quickly. But in all likelihood, you still have a million questions about working with other text properties such as those applied to paragraphs. The next chapter takes a short break from text and deals with XPress' drawing tools—another key learning area. But, if you'd like to skip ahead to explore paragraph properties, check out Chapter 6, Working with Text. There, you'll discover that a paragraph can be much more than just a collection of characters strung together.

CHAPTER 5

Using Drawing Tools

There's a certain degree of pressure on today's desktop developers to invent software tools that meet everyone's needs— whether those are layout, illustration, engineering, 3D modeling, or what have you. But often, in trying to please everyone, the developers ultimately disappoint the professionals who demand speed, accuracy, and control from software tools. The one-size-fits-all application rarely pleases everyone. Fortunately, XPress maintains a healthy balance and focus in this regard.

With the discoveries you'll make in this chapter, you'll realize you may not be creating complex illustrations with the drawing tools in XPress 4, but you'll be capable of drawing with Béziers—a new feature for XPress 4. Specifically, the Bézier drawing feature enables you to create various types of vector objects similar to professional illustration programs. Béziers enable you to create boxes and lines of virtually any shape, and then edit, color, and combine these shapes for uses such as design elements, text paths, and clipping paths.

In this chapter, you'll discover that XPress' arsenal of drawing tools has been fine-tuned for the needs of designers and layout artists and is fully capable of enhancing nearly any publishing challenge you can dream up. And although you'll find plenty of information on all available drawing tools, the step-by-step exercises in this chapter assume you have at least a basic understanding of working with Item and Content tools, dialog boxes, certain palettes (such as the Measurements palette) and certain fundamental Modify command options covered in Chapters 1 through 4.

Using Line Tools

Line tools in XPress are used primarily for creating objects which behave independently from text. One of the most confusing issues surrounding lines in XPress is the existence of two nearly identical line applications that operate in completely different ways and are used for different purposes. The confusion revolves around the difference between *drawn* lines, and paragraph lines—or rules. Rules may be formatted directly in your text above and below paragraphs. As your text flows, so do these rules. To make it more confusing, XPress 4 also enables you to anchor lines you draw in text manually.

The behavior and properties associated with drawn lines in XPress is quite different from that of paragraph rules. Drawn lines do not flow with your text and may not be assigned to embellish paragraphs. Drawn lines may be assigned any of the basic properties of text and picture boxes, including the capability to set text runaround. In other words, although text and rules may flow together throughout your columns and layout, text may be set to flow *around* drawn lines.

Lines are also considered "open" paths, meaning they are composed of a start point, an end point, and at least one line segment. Line tools may be selected from the Tool palette positioned just below the picture box tools. They have been separated into three specialized tools: the Line, Bézier, and Freehand tools. Each tool is used slightly differently and creates a different type of line with different properties.

> **NOTE** *When choosing a line tool, newer users may confuse the term "line" to refer to either curved or straight lines. In fact, the Line tool only enables you to create straight lines. If you want, you may convert and edit straight lines to curved lines later on using the Item | Shape command and Bézier editing.*

Drawing Straight Lines

In layout, the capability to quickly and accurately create single or multiple straight lines is critical. Straight lines may be used as design elements or for practical applications such as structure for certain tabular content, forms, and diagram labels. A straight line is considered any line that connects two or more points without wavering. In XPress, straight lines may be created using the Line tool.

Creating a straight line with the Line tool is a quick operation. To create a straight line, follow these steps:

1. With a document opened, choose the Line tool from the Tool palette. The Line tool features the symbol of a diagonal line. If you don't immediately see the tool, it may be hidden in the pop-out menu. You may have to click and hold on whichever line tool is currently displayed to access it. If your intention is to draw multiple lines in succession, hold the ALT/OPTION key while choosing the tool. Notice your cursor changes to a crosshair.

2. Click and hold to define the location of the first point of your straight line.

3. Still holding the mouse button, drag your cursor to the position of your second point. Notice as you drag, a dotted line appears joining the two point locations.

4. When your cursor is in the right spot, release the mouse button to create the second point. Notice a line appears with the start and end points highlighted with black handles.

5. Click and hold the point with the hand cursor, drag it to a new location, and release the mouse. You have just edited the point's position and made the line longer.

When drawing lines with any of XPress' line tools or editing their points, standard constraining conventions apply. Holding the SHIFT key constrains the angle of lines to 45-degree increments and constrains their movement to vertical or horizontal planes when moving points.

Editing a straight line created with the Line tool is a straightforward operation involving selecting the line with the Item tool, holding the cursor over one of its points, and dragging the point to the new location.

Holding SHIFT+ALT/OPTION constrains the editing of a line to its originally-drawn angle.

Drawing Freehand Lines

In Chapter 3, you may have discovered that Freehand text boxes may be created with the Freehand text box tool. If so, you may already be aware of how the Freehand line tool operates. The action involved in creating freehand lines is slightly different compared to other tools. Freehand lines are created by clicking-and-dragging your cursor.

When your mouse button is released, an exact duplicate of your drag path is created in the form of Bézier lines. Bézier lines are made up of various types of points, which in combination can virtually replicate any shape or path in vector format. In fact, that's exactly what's happening when you use the Freehand line tool to create irregularly-shaped paths. The Freehand Line tool may also be used for tracing shapes on screen, or used in combination with electronic drawing tablets for creating images such as signatures or even simplistic line sketches, as shown in the following illustration.

TIP ➤ *Editing a freehand line's shape involves manipulating curved and straight segments and their adjoining points—the same operation as for Bézier lines. For a complete and detailed explanation of editing these types of lines, see* Bézier Lines Unplugged, *later in this chapter.*

5

Creating Bézier Lines

The Bézier line tool is the most complex of all the tools in XPress. But don't let that discourage you from using it. The Bézier line tool is unlike any other tool in layout—on or off the screen. In fact, the Bézier concept of drawing was adapted from features in professional illustration software such as Adobe Illustrator, Macromedia Freehand, and CorelDraw. When you create a Bézier, you're not just replicating your mouse movement or an onscreen path. It's more a controlling of the actual properties that compose and control irregularly-shaped paths.

Béziers may be composed of both curved and straight line segments and various types of points controlling their shape. Although straight lines are fairly straightforward to create with the Bézier line tool, accurate curves can be difficult to achieve the first time around and nearly always need to be reshaped for refinement. So, don't be too upset if you find yourself having to redraw Bézier lines.

The best way to perfect line creation with the Bézier line tool is through practice. For a practical exploration into using this tool, follow these steps:

1. With a document open, find a clear practice space on your page and choose the Bézier line tool from the Tool palette. If you don't immediately see the tool, it may be hidden in the pop-out menu. You may have to click and hold on whichever line tool is currently displayed to access it. If your intention is to draw multiple Bézier lines in succession, hold the ALT/OPTION key while choosing the tool. Notice your cursor changes to a crosshair.

2. Click once on your page to define the location of your first point. Notice a small blue marker appears where you clicked.

3. Move your cursor to a new position and click again. Notice the first marker turns black, and your new click creates another small blue marker. A line segment appears between these two markers. Up to this point, you've simply created a straight line.

4. Define a third point, but this time use a click-and-drag action to define the new point. It may help to change the direction of the line path as you drag. Notice several things happen at once. Your cursor changes to a hand-style pointer and two *curve handles* appear—one of which you are now dragging. A new line segment also appears between your second point and your newly-defined point. As you drag your cursor, the line appears as a curve and a *curve path* is created.

5. If you haven't done so already, release the mouse button to finish defining the curve.

6. Click a fourth time using the same click-and-drag action, but don't release the mouse yet. Notice another pair of curve handles appears, and you're now dragging one of them. Before releasing the mouse button, press the SHIFT key and continue dragging in a circular motion. Notice the curve handle you are dragging is constrained to 45-degree increments.

7. Release the mouse button to define the fourth and final point.

8. To end your Bézier session with the intention of beginning a new line, click the Bézier line tool in the Tool palette again and start a new line, or double-click to your current point to define it as the last point. To end your Bézier drawing session, click any other tool, such as the Item tool.

TIP ━━━━━━▶ *If you want to reposition your entire Bézier line before you have completed drawing it, hold the CTRL/CMD key to temporarily select the Item tool and drag the line to your new position. Once you release the CTRL/CMD key, you will be returned to the Bézier line tool.*

As you may conclude from following this exercise, creating accurate curved lines is tricky business. If you're new to drawing with Béziers, you'll have some practice ahead. The saving grace is that Béziers can easily be edited and reshaped.

If you need more information on drawing and editing Bézier lines right now, skip ahead to *Drawing with Béziers,* which appears later in this chapter.

Orthogonal Lines

The name may seem complicated but its operation is straightforward. The Orthogonal line tool is designed to quickly create perfectly-straight horizontal or vertical lines for use in creating items such as forms or tabular layouts. Using the Orthogonal line tool is quite similar to using XPress' Line tool in combination with the SHIFT key—except the lines are limited to straight up-and-down or side-to-side instead of 45-degree increments.

TIP *When using the Orthogonal line tool for creation of multiple lines, holding the ALT/OPTION key while selecting the tool from the Tool palette keeps it persistently selected, meaning that you can continue to use it without XPress automatically selecting the last-used tool. Plus, it may help your alignment of the lines you create to place guides on your page to define the start and end points of the lines before you begin drawing them. When using guides for alignment, be sure you have the Snap to Guides (SHIFT+F7) feature active. For more information on using guides, see* Using Guides *in* Chapter 3, Tackling a Layout.

To create a vertical or horizontal line when using the Orthogonal line tool, use a click-and-hold action to define the first point, drag your cursor to the second point position, and release the mouse button to complete the line. Your initial vertical or horizontal mouse movement determines whether your new line will be aligned vertically or horizontally with your page. Editing a line created with the Orthogonal line tool is a straightforward operation involving selecting the line with the Item tool, holding the cursor over one of its points, and dragging the point to the new location.

TIP *XPress 4 enables you to set your drawing tools to suit your work style or project type. For more information, see* Changing Tool Behavior *in* Chapter 12, Fine-Tuning XPress.

Setting Line Styles

Once a line is created or selected, the Style menu changes to a series of pop-out menus enabling you to choose various attributes for your line. Pop-out menus include the following:

- **Line Style**   This menu displays the 11 default Dash and Stripe styles that come with XPress, as well as any you have created yourself or appended from other XPress document files.

- **Arrowheads**   You may apply an arrowhead style to your line using the choices in this pop-out menu, which includes two arrow types in either direction and one double-headed arrow style.

- **Width**   From this pop-out menu, you may choose from Hairline (very thin), 1, 2, 4, 6, 8, or 12 point line widths. You may also choose Other (CTRL/CMD+SHIFT+\) to open the Modify dialog box with the Width field already highlighted, and then enter a custom width. The Modify dialog box also contains complete options for setting your line attributes.

TIP   *You may change the width of a selected line using keyboard shortcuts also. To increase or decrease the width of a line by preset increments, press CTRL/CMD+SHIFT+> or CTRL/CMD+SHIFT+< respectively. To increase or decrease the width by a single point, press CTRL/CMD+ALT/OPTION+SHIFT+> or CTRL/CMD+ ALT/OPTION+SHIFT+<, respectively.*

- **Color**   This pop-out menu applies color to your selected line and displays all the colors currently available in your document.

- **Shade**   The Shade pop-out menu works with the color chosen for your line and sets it in 10 percent increments to a specific value ranging from 0 to 100 percent. Choosing Other from this menu opens the Modify dialog box with the Shade field already highlighted, enabling you to enter a custom shade value.

When working with lines, you may find applying attributes to your line is a little faster if you use the Measurements palette (F9). While lines are selected, the Measurements palette contains options for setting the page position of your line (relative to your ruler origin), width and height dimensions for scaling your line, and degree values for rotating your line. You may also quickly set the Width, Arrowheads, and Line Style options for your line from drop-down menus, as shown in the following illustration.

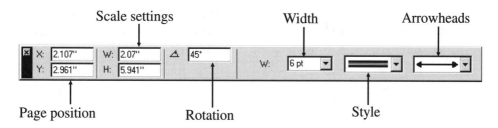

Scale settings   Width   Arrowheads

Page position   Rotation   Style

To set highly-specific line properties, use the Modify dialog box options. In addition to the preceding options, the Modify (CTRL/CMD+M) dialog box allows full control over all line attributes, including gap color and shade, and print suppression.

TIP

XPress enables you to create your own line styles using Dash and Stripe features. For more information on creating custom line styles, see Custom Dashes and Stripes *in* Chapter 12, Fine-tuning XPress.

5

The Modify dialog box also enables you to set other attributes for a line, depending on which type of line you have selected. The options for Freehand and Bézier lines are described in the preceding text. But when selecting regular or orthogonal lines, the options change to enable you to set the position of specific points, the angle of your line, and its length, as shown in the following illustration.

The Mode drop-down menu sets which points to change, and the Angle and Length fields enable you to enter new measures for those points. Mode choices include End Points (both end point positions displayed at the same time), First Point, Mid Point, and Last Point. To change a point position, angle or the line's length, you must first choose which point to apply the new values to.

Select a point mode first, and then enter your new measures

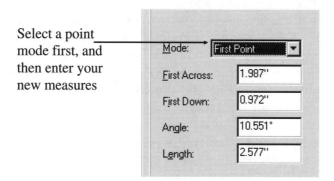

For quick access to these same options when regular or orthogonal lines are selected, the Point Mode, Point Origin, Angle, and Length options are also displayed on the Measurements palette, as shown in the following illustration.

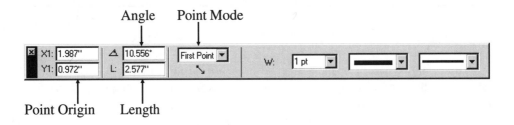

Drawing with Béziers

If you have some experience drawing Bézier lines, you'll have an advantage over most when it comes to creating them. But as with most developers, Quark has put its own little twist on the tools used in creating and editing these items. If you plan on working with Béziers to any degree, this section is a "must read." You'll find out all about the various types of points and discover how to edit and shape Bézier lines to fit your needs.

Bézier Drawing Unplugged

If you've arrived here directly from Creating Bézier Lines earlier in this chapter, you're likely ready to start editing your shape. But before you do that, there are a few things to know that will help you grasp the concept.

In drawing a Bézier line, your mouse movement determines which type of point you are creating; XPress simply fills in the line segment between the points based on the properties of the two points. There are three types of points and two type of lines to be aware of in XPress. Bézier lines may consist of symmetrical points, smooth points, and corner points, which are joined by either curved or straight segments.

■ **Symmetrical point**   This type of point applies an equal curve shape to the line segments on either side of it. Symmetrical point marker symbols are square-shaped and feature curve handles an equal distance from the point position, as shown in the following illustration.

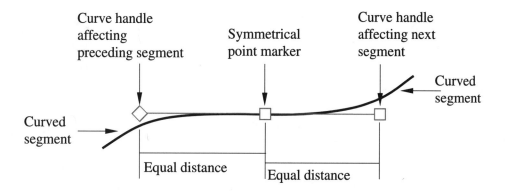

- **Smooth point**   As the name implies, a smooth point causes line segments on either side of it to be curved, but each curved segment may have a different "slope" or curve value. Smooth point marker symbols are diamond-shaped and feature curve handles of unequal distance from the point, as shown in the following illustration. The shorter the distance from the point to the handle, the less dramatic the curve.

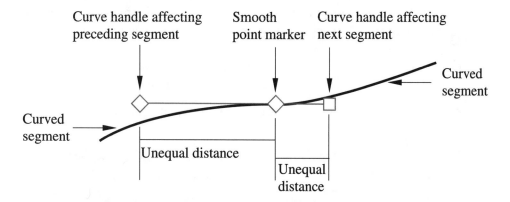

- **Corner point**   This type of point sets the line segments on either side of it to be straight, enabling the line to immediately change direction at the corner point. Corner point marker symbols are triangle-shaped, as shown in the following illustration, and do not feature handles.

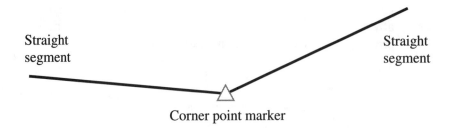

Corner point marker

- **Curved segment** A curved segment is simply a line that has either a symmetrical or smooth point at one end or the other, causing it to be curved.

- **Straight segment** In order to be defined as exactly straight, straight segments must have corner points on either end, causing them to be straight lines.

It may seem like over-complication of a simple subject, but when you see how these elements behave in combination with each other, you'll begin to grasp how significant their differences are. The properties of each point affect the shape of the line segments before and after them. And although line segments are shaped by the points they separate, changing a line segment's state can also change the properties of the points on either side of it. With these principles in mind, let's try quickly creating a Bézier line complete with curved and straight segments by following these steps:

1. With your document open to a practice spot on your page, choose the Bézier line tool from the Tool palette. Your cursor changes to a crosshair.

2. At the left side of your screen, click to define the position of your first point.

3. Move the cursor to the right slightly and upwards slightly, and then click and hold.

4. Still holding, drag to a position level with your first point and an equal distance from the first point to define the curve of your second point, and then release the mouse button. As you drag, you are actually dragging one of the curve handles of your second point; the point at which you just clicked the cursor defines the second point's page position.

5. To define the third point, click and hold to the right and downwards an equal distance again as between the first and second points.

6. Still holding the mouse button, drag upwards and to the right another equal distance until your cursor is level with your second point's marker. Then release the mouse button.

7. To define the fourth point, click once (without holding or dragging anywhere) to the right of the third point.

8. To define the final point, click again (without holding or dragging) downwards and to the right of the fourth point.

9. To complete the Bézier line drawing session, choose the Item tool from the Tool palette. Notice your new Bézier line is selected already.

5

10. To increase the visibility of the line, press CTRL/CMD+SHIFT+> three times. Your new line should appear somewhat similar to Figure 5-1.

In the preceding steps, as you clicked-and-dragged you were actually defining curved segments by dragging the curve handles. The distance and direction you dragged the curve handles determined how dramatic the curved segments before and after the point would be. Then, when you simply clicked the mouse to define the fourth and fifth points, you were creating a straight segment with corner points on either end.

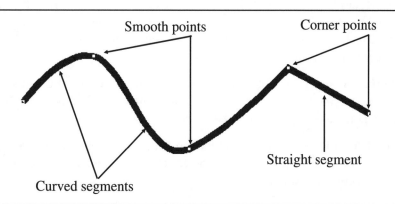

FIGURE 5-1   Drawing a Bézier line with both curved and straight line segments

Selecting and Editing Points and Curves

To select single or multiple points on a Bézier line, you must have completed drawing the line and have either the Content or Item tool selected and ready to edit points and curve handles. Ideally, you'll have selected the Item tool, and you'll have clicked your Bézier line to select and highlight it. Whether you have just drawn a Bézier line or you've converted a box, shape, or text to Béziers, knowing how the points and line segments will react to manipulation is critical to guiding its new shape.

Nearly any type of object may be changed to a Bézier state, including text and picture boxes, all line types, and even text. Once in Bézier state, individual points and the line segments that join them may be reshaped by dragging either a line segment, a point, or the curve handle controlling a point. Before doing any reshaping though, you must first select the point (or points) you want to edit. In other words, it's a three-step operation. For a quick hands-on experience editing Bézier points and lines, follow these steps:

1. Start by converting a shape to Bézier lines. As an example, choose the Oval picture box or the Oval text box tools and create a wide oval on your page.

2. Choose Item | Shape and select the very bottom choice from the Shape pop-out menu—the Freehand shape. Notice the oval shape is now a Bézier composed of 7 points joined by curved segments.

3. Select any point on the oval shape by clicking directly on one of the black point markers. Notice when selected, the point now includes two curve handles joined by a blue line with a symmetrical point (small blue square) marker in the center.

4. Move the point by dragging it in any direction and releasing the mouse. Notice as you drag, a blue line indicates the new curve shape of the line based on the new position of the point.

5. Hold the SHIFT key to constrain the movement of the point, and drag it either vertically or horizontally. The effect is the same, but the point's movement is constrained.

6. Grab one of the curve handles and drag it in any direction. Notice the new shape of the segments is indicated in blue until you release your mouse button, and both curve handles maintain an equal distance from the symmetrical point.

7. With the point still selected, choose Item | Point/Segment Type | Smooth Point (CTRL/ OPTION+F2) to change the point to a smooth point, as shown in the following illustration. Notice the shape of the point changes to a small diamond.

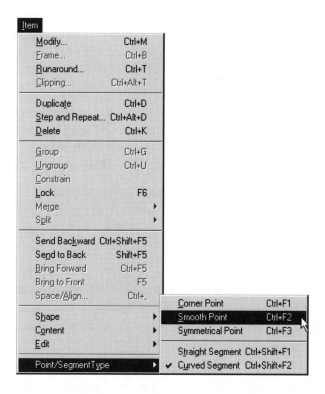

8. Drag one of the point's curve handles in any direction. Notice the two points still move together to shape the curved segments on either side of the point, but they no longer maintain an equal distance from the point.

9. With the same point still selected, choose Item | Point/Segment Type | Corner Point (CTRL/OPTION+F1) to change the point to a corner point. Notice the shape of the point changes to a small triangle.

10. Grab one of the handles again and drag it in any direction. Notice the two handles no longer move in unison but independently. You have just discovered the practical difference between the three point types.

11. Hold the SHIFT key again and click once on any other point. Notice both points are now highlighted and each includes its own curve handles.

12. Click directly on one of the points and drag in any direction. Notice both points move at the same time, altering the shape of the oval accordingly.

13. Deselect all the points by clicking the Item tool on the page and reselect what used to be an oval by clicking it once. Click one of the curved segments to select it. Notice the entire line segment momentarily turns blue indicating it is selected, and the two points on either side of it become highlighted and have their curve handles showing.

14. Grab the segment by clicking and holding it, and then drag it to a point parallel to its current position. Notice as you drag, the two points remain stationary, the shape of the curve changes, and the curve handles of the two points change position to match the curve shape.

15. Choose Item | Point/Segment Type | Straight Segment (CTRL/OPTION+SHIFT+ F1) to change the segment from a curved to a straight segment. Notice the shape of the segment changes and the two points change states—one to a corner point and the other to a smooth point.

16. Grab your new straight segment by clicking it, and then change its path position by dragging it. Notice the points move with your straight segment, and their curve handles remain in fixed relative positions.

17. Deselect all by clicking on the background, and then reselect the shape by clicking it once. Hold the ALT/OPTION key and click anywhere on a curved or straight segment. Notice a new point appears and remains highlighted. The segment also remains in its current shape.

18. Position your cursor over one of the other points, hold the ALT/OPTION key, and click the point. The point is deleted. These two actions enable you to add and delete points as needed when shaping any Bézier shape.

TIP ➤ *To select all the points in a path, double-click any of its points. To select all the line segments in a path, double-click any of its segments.*

If you've followed the preceding exercise closely, you may have noticed a number of different cursor styles appeared as you selected and moved points, segments, and curve handles, and added and deleted points. These cursors let you know you are in various states of editing when working with Bézier elements.

The following list may serve as a useful guide to shortcuts when editing and manipulating points, segments, and their curve handles:

Selection Shortcuts

Select multiple segments or points	SHIFT+Click
Select all points or segments in a path	Double-click any point or segment

Reshaping Shortcuts

Set point to corner point	CTRL/OPTION+F1
Set point to smooth point	CTRL/OPTION+F2
Set point to symmetrical point	CTRL/OPTION+F3
Set segment to straight line	CTRL/OPTION+ SHIFT+F1
Set segment to curved line	CTRL/ CMD + SHIFT+F2
Delete point	ALT/OPTION+Click point or BACKSPACE/DELETE
Add point	ALT/OPTION+Click segment
Convert symmetrical point to smooth point	CTRL +SHIFT+Click point
Constrain point and handle moves to 45 degrees	SHIFT+DRAG point or segment
Delete one curve handle (and change to corner)	ALT/OPTION+Click curve handle
Drag one curve handle out	ALT/OPTION+Drag handle from point
Drag both curve handles out symmetrically	CTRL+SHIFT+Drag handles from point
Retract curve handles (but leave as same type)	CTRL+SHIFT+Click point

5

Reshaping Shortcuts (continued)

Nudge point or segment exactly 1 point	Select point or segment and use any ARROW key
Nudge point or segment exactly 0.1 points	Select point or segment and press ALT/OPTION+any ARROW key
Specify corner point while drawing Béziers	Hold F1 while defining point
Specify smooth point while drawing Béziers	Hold F2 while defining point
Specify symmetrical point while drawing Béziers	Hold F3 while defining point

The Measurements Palette and Béziers

If you intend to work with Béziers a lot, becoming familiar with—or even memorizing—the tiny symbols that identify points, segments, and their curve handles will help your work a great deal. Knowing the preceding manipulation shortcuts will also help. But it may also be convenient to use the Measurements palette when first working with Béziers or when you need to move Bézier elements exact distances.

The context-sensitive Measurements palette displays properties of segments, points, and their curve handles, and includes convenient buttons for displaying and converting types of points and segments. The following illustration indicates which fields control specific Bézier options.

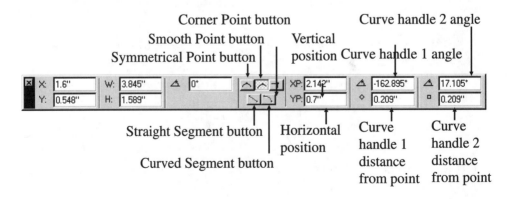

NOTE *If multiple points are selected, the XP, YP, and Handle Angle and Position fields are left empty, enabling you to change only the type of point using the Corner Point, Smooth Point, or Symmetrical Point buttons. While a segment is selected, these fields are also left blank, leaving only the Curved Segment and Straight Segment buttons available.*

Creating Complex Shapes with Merge

As you work further with Béziers, you're bound to run into a situation where you would like to create an object slightly more complicated than a simple line or enclosed shape. For this, you'll need to enter an area of XPress where you can work with shapes in various ways in order to create new, more complex shapes. You also have a choice in creating your shapes—you may draw the shapes freehand or work with preset existing shapes. Ultimately, you'll end up with a complex series of points on either *open* or *closed* paths. An *open path* is any path whose end points are not joined, while a closed path's end points are joined to create an enclosed shape. You may also end up working with something called *a compound path*—or, a single object composed of more than one open or closed paths. This section explores XPress' Merge functions, which enable you to combine objects in various ways to form new objects. The resulting objects may be open, closed, or compound paths. If this sounds complicated, you're right—it's vector drawing in all its glory.

About Compounds Paths

Before you suddenly end up with one on your page, it may be nice to know exactly what a compound path is. As described, a compound path is any single object composed of more than one path. In other words, a line and a circle may be joined to form a compound path resulting in a single object. Any attributes applied to the object apply to both the sub paths in the object. But, you may be thinking to yourself, any group of selected objects behaves this way.

Here's the difference. Let's say you have two different-sized circles—one inside the other (as in the letter *O*). One circle represents the interior, and the other represents the exterior. While selected or grouped, the objects actually overlap, and each shape may still retain its own properties. But as compound paths, these two circles don't overlap each other—they actually compose a single compound object, whereby each path composes the complete shape. Figure 5-2 depicts the difference between two circles behaving as two separate objects and two circles behaving as a single compound path.

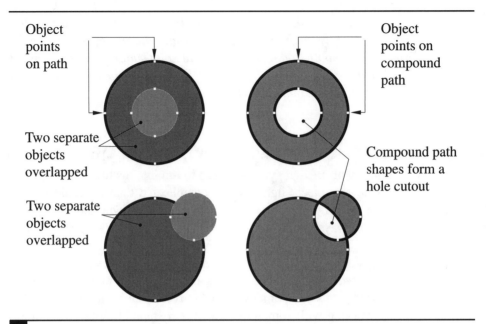

Object points on path

Object points on compound path

Two separate objects overlapped

Compound path shapes form a hole cutout

Two separate objects overlapped

FIGURE 5-2   The difference between multiple objects and a single compound path

Now with a firm understanding of the basic difference between single and compound paths, you can begin your adventure merging objects with the Merge commands. The Merge commands become available when two separate objects are selected with the Item tool. The objects may be any type including text, lines, shapes, or boxes as either open or closed paths. XPress' Merge commands are Intersection, Union, Difference, Reverse Difference, Exclusive Or, Combine, and Join Endpoints, as shown in the following illustration. Their functions are described as follows:

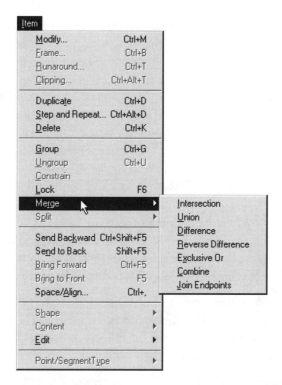

■ **Intersection**   This Merge command has the effect of creating a new
object based on where the two or more selected objects overlap.

NOTE   *When using Merge commands on objects, the original objects are deleted
when the new object is created.*

■ **Union**   As the name implies, performing a Union merge on objects has
the effect of uniting their shapes into a single shape, essentially creating
an outline of the combined objects. If the selected objects do not overlap,
a union still takes place, but the objects' outside shapes remain separate.

When two or more objects are selected for merging, the resulting object takes on the properties of the object farthest in back of the selected arrangement of objects. For example, if one black picture box is merged with two red text boxes, and the objects are arranged so that the black picture box is behind the other two, the resulting new object is a black picture box. The ordering of objects may be layered using the Send Backward (CTRL/OPTION+SHIFT+F5), Send to Back (SHIFT+F5), Bring Forward (CTRL/OPTION+ F5), and Bring to Front (F5) commands found under the Item menu. For more information on using these commands, see Working with Overlapping Items *in* Chapter 11, Working with Complex Layouts.

- **Difference**   When overlapping objects are selected, this Merge command has the effect of creating a new object based on the shape of the object in the back of the stack arrangement and removing the shapes of the other overlapping objects. The other objects are deleted.

- **Reverse Difference**   As you might guess, this Merge command has the opposite effect of the Difference Merge command. The new object created is based on the shape of the objects in front of the arrangement, andthe shape of the object farthest back is deleted.

- **Exclusive Or**   This Merge command creates a new object based on the overall shape of the arrangement. Where the objects originally overlapped, a hole remains. When using this command, the paths of objects influence the resulting shape. So, where two objects overlap, two separate outline paths result.

- **Combine**   The Combine Merge command is perhaps the most common, simply combining two or more objects' paths into a single compound path. Where the objects overlap, a hole remains. Unlike Exclusive Or, the line paths of the objects remain as single paths.

- **Join Endpoints**   This Merge command is available only when the selected objects are open paths. It has the effect of joining the end points together to form a single open path. When two or more items are merged using this command, their end points must be close enough (usually overlapping) for the Merge command to successfully locate and join the points. Unlike other Merge commands, which result in Bézier boxes or closed paths, this Merge command results in an open Bézier path. The point at which the paths are joined is, by default, a corner point. The distance between the points to be joined must be closer to each other than the snap distance set in the General tab of the Document Preferences dialog box. For more information on using this option, see *Setting Document Preference Options* in Chapter 12, Fine-Tuning XPress.

NOTE ⟶ *When joining end points, ensure the points are closely overlapping before attempting the Join Endpoints Merge command. If it makes it easier for you, do this by creating horizontal and vertical guides at the exact point you want them to join. If two points are not precisely overlapping, the Join Endpoints Merge command may not be successful.*

For a practical exercise in merging shapes, follow these steps:

1. In a clear area on your document page, create two rectangular text boxes that are roughly 1-inch square, and an oval picture box of the same dimensions.

2. In the first text box enter an uppercase *A* and format it to Times 72 point (or equivalent). Leave the second text box empty but assign a box color of Black set to a shade of 20 percent.

3. Leave the oval picture box empty, but assign a box color of Black set to a shade of 60 percent.

4. Because you'll be working with one object that is a text character, you must convert it to a box shape first. To do this quickly, choose the Content tool, highlight the character, and choose Style | Text to Box. The character is now converted to a shape. Choose the Item tool, open the Modify dialog box (CTRL/CMD+M), and assign a box color of Black at the default shade of 100 percent.

5. Arrange the three objects in a layout similar to the following illustration, with the empty text box at the bottom of the stack and the text shape in front. To position the text box at the bottom, select it with the Item tool and choose Item | Send to Back (SHIFT+F5). To position the *A* at the top of the stack, choose Item | Bring to Front (F5).

TIP ⟶ *To move the A-shaped box without selecting its Bézier points for editing, hold the CTRL/CMD key to access the mover pointer.*

5

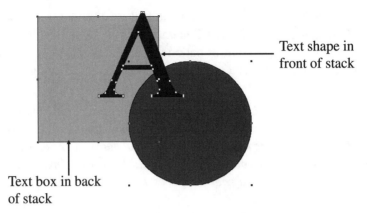

Text shape in front of stack

Text box in back of stack

6. With your objects arranged, choose the Item tool and press SHIFT while clicking the objects to select them. Choose Item | Merge | Intersection. Notice what remains is a new object representing the shape where the three objects overlapped, as shown in the following illustration. The original objects are now deleted, and what remains is a text box shape set to 20 percent Black—the same properties as the text box at the back of the stack. Immediately undo your Merge command by choosing Edit | Undo (CTRL/CMD+Z).

7. With your objects still selected, choose Item | Merge | Union. Notice what remains is a new object representing an *outline* shape of all three objects, as shown in the following illustration. Immediately undo your merge (CTRL/CMD+Z).

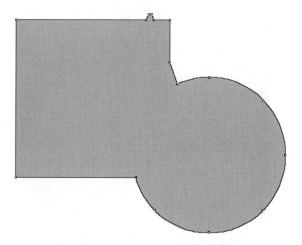

8. Next, choose Item | Merge | Difference. Notice the text box that was originally at the back of the stack remains, and the shapes of the other objects have been cut out of it, as shown in the following illustration. Undo your merge once again (CTRL/CMD+Z).

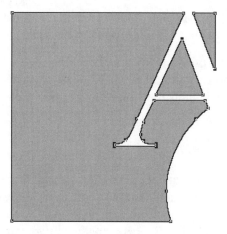

5

9. Finally, choose Item | Merge | Combine. Notice a shape composed of all the paths of the original objects remains. Because the paths cross each other, open holes are created, as shown in the following illustration.

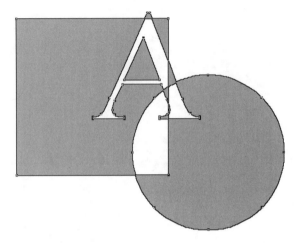

10. Delete the new merge object by pressing the BACKSPACE/DELETE key, and choose the Line tool from the Tool palette. Click the ALT/OPTION key while selecting the Line tool to persistently select it.

11. Create two new lines of any length and angle by click-dragging the Line tool.

12. Choose the Item tool (or Content tool) from the Tool palette and position the lines so that two ends are overlapping each other.

13. Select both lines by pressing SHIFT and clicking each of them, and then choose Item | Merge | Join Endpoints. Notice a new single object is created with the end points now joined as a corner point.

Splitting Objects

Now that you have a firm understanding of how to merge multiple shapes into single or compound paths, it's time to examine some of the tools XPress has to enable you to rip them apart. The Split command comes in the form of a pop-out menu available in the Item menu and enables you to separate paths in two ways. You may use the Outside Paths command to split apart an object composed of two separate paths that don't overlap. Or, you may split apart all the paths in a compound object, overlapping

QuarkXPress 4 *IN ACTION*

Who among the S&P 500 has the most on the ball? Our growth rankings offer surprising insights into America's most closely watched companies

IN THIS REPORT:

76 THE TOP 50 performers cut a wide swath across Corporate America

78 HOW WE crunched the data to find the winners

82 THE NEW stars you may not know about

88 HOW TODAY'S numbers can point investors to tomorrow's gains

91 REPORT CARD on all 500 companies

123 PERFORMANCE by industry

150 INDEX of companies

THE BUSINESS WEEK 50

In a period marred by slowing computer sales growth, allegations of antitrust, Capitol Hill hostility, and even a pie in the face, there is one thing William H. Gates III hasn't had to worry about: corporate performance. Whether you think Microsoft Corp. anticompetitive or simply ultracompetitive, under Gates's leadership it has racked up a record of annual profit and revenue increases that is the envy of Corporate America. "We've been cruising for 23 years," says Gates, Microsoft's chairman.

It sure looks like full speed ahead to the rest of us. With earnings galloping ahead 57% last year, the Redmond (Wash.) software giant turned in an eye-popping 76.3% gain for Intel Corp. out of the No. 1 spot in BUSINESS WEEK's second annual performance ranking of the 500 companies in the Standard & Poor's Index. And getting there was no easy ride: To earn the highest honors, Microsoft blew past staunch competition from such top 10 sizzlers as Dell Com-

puter, Cisco Systems, credit-card dynamo MBNA, and Morgan Stanley Dean Witter & Co.

Ask Gates what's behind the success that has kept his company several steps ahead of such a crowd, and he credits being in the right business at the right time. "It's the Information Age, and we're giving people great tools for getting at and handling information," he says. There's certainly more to it than that. Thanks to the legendary aggressiveness Gates fosters, 90% of the 80 million PCs shipped last year were loaded with one version or another of Microsoft's Windows operating systems. But what's really impressive about Microsoft in its obsession with efficiency and gradually improving products.

From every dollar in sales, Microsoft pulls out 29.7¢ in profits—a margin that grew by 13% over the year before. That's almost four times the average for its industry, and better than all but four other companies in all the 500. Moreover, between fiscal 1995 and 1997, the company's share of revenues going into research and development climbed from 14% to 17%—without denting profits. "How do we do it? We watch costs like a hawk," says Microsoft President and Chief Operating Officer Robert J. Herbold. Given the phenomenal growth that the PC industry has seen

THE BEST PERFORMERS

78 BUSINESS WEEK / MARCH 20, 1998

1 MICROSOFT
2 DELL COMPUTER
3 CISCO SYSTEMS
4 INTEL
5 COMPAQ COMPUTER
6 MBNA
7 TELLABS
8 EMC
9 COMPUTER ASSOCIATES INT.
10 MORGAN STANLEY DEAN WITTER
11 SCHERING-PLOUGH
12 PFIZER
13 APPLIED MATERIALS
14 US AIRWAYS GROUP
15 MERCK
16 TRAVELERS GROUP
17 GAP
18 SCHLUMBERGER
19 MERRILL LYNCH
20 SUN MICROSYSTEMS
21 TJX
22 BRISTOL-MYERS SQUIBB
23 HBO
24 CHASE MANHATTAN
25 CONSECO
26 MGIC INVESTMENT
27 COUNTRYWIDE CREDIT INDUSTRIES
28 GUIDANT
29 PACCAR
30 OMNICOM GROUP
31 NORTHERN TELECOM
32 CHARLES SCHWAB
33 PROGRESSIVE
34 BANKAMERICA
35 STATE STREET
36 LEHMAN BROTHERS HOLDINGS
37 PARAMETRIC TECHNOLOGY
38 GILLETTE
39 COBESTATES FINANCIAL
40 NORWEST
41 GENERAL ELECTRIC
42 FANNIE MAE
43 HALLIBURTON
44 HOME DEPOT
45 FREDDIE MAC
46 HEALTHSOUTH
47 CLEAR CHANNEL COMMUNICATIONS
48 RITE AID
49 ALLSTATE
50 NATIONSBANK

5

Design: Malcolm Frouman

Description: Magazine feature, *Business Week*, March 24, 1997 issue

This two-page spread layout for an editorial feature on top-performing Standard & Poor 500 companies uses process color applied in layers to demonstrate the use of text box runaround effects in XPress. The layout is basic but effective, using staggered columns in a symmetrical format across the two-page spread.

or not, using the All Paths command. These commands will work well for you only if you have a solid understanding of how they operate and can accurately anticipate the results. In order for an object to be eligible for either Split command, it must contain more than one path.

Splitting Outside Paths

The Item | Split | Outside Paths command separates multiple closed paths in a single object without splitting the closed paths within their shapes. For instance, suppose you had used the Merge command to combine two separate boxes that weren't overlapping to form a single compound-path object. Using the Split | Outside Paths command would have the effect of separating the two shapes into individual shapes—or separate boxes independent of each other. Let's suppose again that one of those boxes already had a hole cut out of it—for example, from a previous merge. The Outside Paths command would still separate the two boxes, but the box with the hole would remain intact—a box with a hole. So, only paths that do not touch or overlap are affected.

All Paths

The Item | Split | All paths command is slightly more destructive than its Outside Paths cousin. Instead of simply splitting enclosed objects from each other, this command separates *all* the paths. So, in the above example, where a box with a hole was combined with another box, the Split | All Paths command would result in three separate boxes: the paths representing the two boxes and the path for the hole.

Changing Text into Boxes

As you saw in previous exercise steps, you may change any type of object in XPress into boxes by using the Item | Shape | Freehand command. And, you may also change *text* into boxes—opening the doors for seemingly limitless creative opportunity. The capability to convert text to boxes enables you to use character shapes as picture boxes or clipping paths, reshape the characters, and combine them into illustrative elements.

There are a few key limitations to watch for though. For example, you can't convert text that occupies more than one line—even if the line change is a line feed. In order to be eligible for conversion, your text characters must be on a single line before a conversion. You may also want to keep the number of characters to a minimum. Changing large numbers of characters to box shapes may result in a path so complex you won't be able to print it easily.

To convert text to boxes, your process begins with the Style | Text to Box command. By default, the Text to Box command converts selected text to XPress' Freehand picture box format with all color and frame attributes set to White and a line width of 0 points respectively. You may import a picture directly into the shape using the Get Picture command (CTRL/CMD+E). The choice is yours, but as a practical exercise in converting text to a box and working with it any way you choose, follow these steps:

1. In an open space on your document page, create two text boxes of any variety by selecting one of the text box tools from the Tools palette.

2. Type **Real** in one box and **Power** in the other using the Content tool, and then apply your favorite font. Illustrations in this example use Arial/Helvetica. Set the type size of each word to roughly 48 points. If guides are not showing, choose View | Show Guides so you'll be able to see the new boxes you create.

3. Select the text box containing the word *Real*, and select all the characters with the Content tool (CTRL/CMD+A), and then choose Style | Text to Box. Notice a new shape is created on your page representing the text characters of the word.

4. Select the Item tool, double-click the new shape, choose the Box tab and set the Box Color option to Black.

5. Perform the same steps on the word *Power* to create a black shape representing the word. The result is two separate picture boxes, as shown in the following illustration.

Text boxes containing characters

Text converted to boxes

5

6. Select one of the shapes and choose Item | Shape. Notice the Freehand selection is highlighted. Choose Item | Content and notice the Picture selection is highlighted. Leave these selections as they are, but make a mental note that XPress enables you to change any character or word into either a picture or text box through use of the Text to Box command.

7. Next, reposition the word *Power* so that it is centered with and below the word *Real,* as shown in the following illustration. Overlap the bottom of the *R* and the top of the *P.*

Overlap here

8. Let's take the process a little further toward a practical application. Use the Item tool in combination with the SHIFT key to select both shapes, and choose Item | Merge | Union. Your two shapes are now a single picture box. If you want, choose Get Picture to import a picture into the shape.

NOTE   *When using the Text to Box command, the font in use must be either an Adobe Type 1 or TrueType font.*

Once your text has been converted to a picture box, you may use it for whatever purpose you choose. If you followed the steps in the preceding exercise, you may realize the full potential of having this capability to embellish a layout or create special picture-cropping effects using characters.

TIP   *Pressing ALT/OPTION while choosing Style | Text to Box automatically anchors the character, which can be useful when creating effects such as manually-created drop caps.*

Looking for Blends?

If you've arrived here looking for a drawing feature named *blend,* you may have fallen victim to some confusion associated with the term. In many illustration applications, the term *blend* describes the action of blending one object to another, creating a wonderful collection of intermediary shapes as one object is transformed into the shape of another.

Although XPress now features a multitude of drawing tools, its use of the term *blend* refers to something entirely different. Instead, this term refers to the effect of blending colors within a single shape, making this feature more a function of color than of drawing. XPress 4 enables you to use the Modify | (CTRL/CMD+M) Box command to apply two-color gradations—or blends—to boxes. Blend styles include Linear Blends, Mid-Linear Blends, Rectangle Blends, Diamond Blends, Circular Blends, and Full-Circular Blends. But, as mentioned, assigning blend styles and colors is more a function of color than it is of specific drawing tools. For more information on working with color blends, see *Exploring XPress Color Blends* in *Chapter 13, Working in Color.*

5

Conclusion

As in previous chapters, you've covered plenty of ground in a short period and you deserve some credit for your perseverance. Drawing tools and the objects they create can be a complicated subject to grasp if you're new to the tools. You've learned how to create a straight line, discovered how to edit and apply various properties to it, and have had hands-on experience using Béziers—one of the most complex drawing concepts in illustration. You've also seen how you can create interesting shapes for your layout from simple characters.

You've also reached the end of the basics section of this book, which means you're more than ready to progress to *Part II: Creating Layouts and Documents*, where you'll learn how to work with text in layouts, control all the properties of imported digital images, and integrate all these elements into comprehensive layouts.

PART II

Creating Layouts and Documents

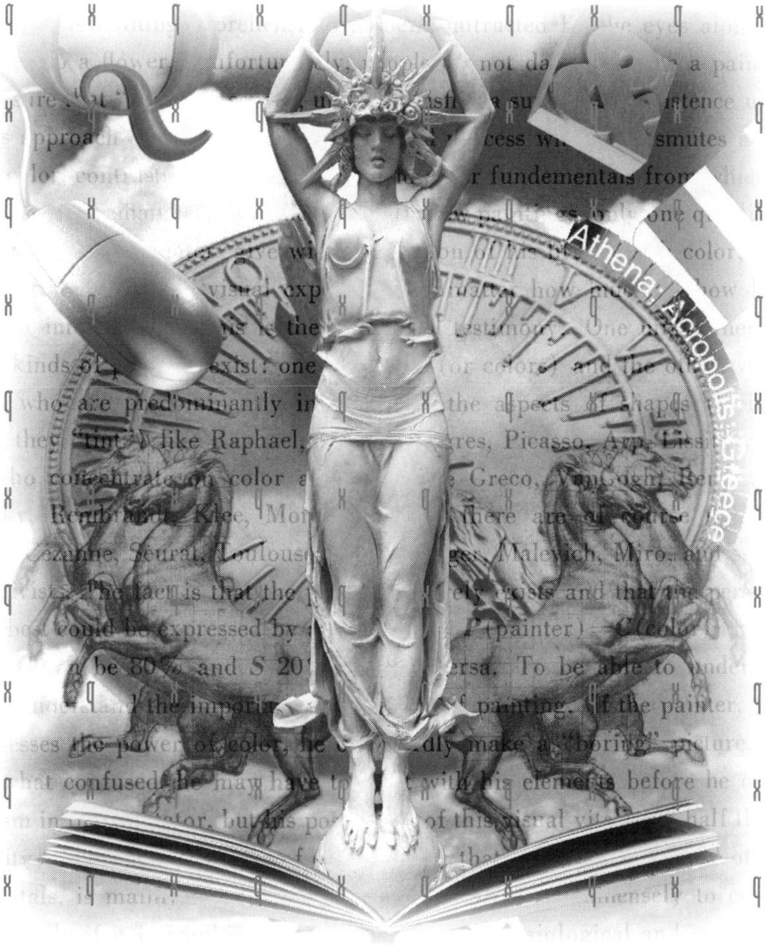

CHAPTER 6

Working with Text

If you're new to the world of layout and design and have already been exposed to XPress on a flirtatious level, Part II is especially designed for you. These next four chapters build on the fact that you know a bit about the tools and some fundamentals of working with text, and that you are at least familiar with the concept of getting text and pictures onto your page. You'll follow a staggered progression between working with text and pictures in your layouts, and you'll often encounter tips and techniques on slightly more advanced issues.

If you've come here looking for some direction on using the fundamentals or basics of text tools and boxes, you may be getting slightly ahead of yourself. Although this chapter isn't reserved for those who might consider themselves experts, it does assume you have grasped the concept of using XPress' core collection of text-related tools such as the Content tool and the various text box tools. You'll also need to have an understanding of applying the very basics of character attributes such as size, style, and so on.

As you begin this chapter, you're about to discover how sophisticated XPress is when it comes to working with text and how this sets the program apart from others. You'll learn about columns and paragraph formatting issues such as tabbing and drop caps. And you'll learn to work with styles, hyphenation and justification, and document checking utilities such as dictionaries and Find/Change tools. By learning how to work with text in paragraphs, you'll be well on your way to creating very readable and effective layouts.

Your Critical Words

Imagine trying to read a document where the text is difficult to follow because it is too small or too large, the layout is confusing, or words are misspelled. In fact, we've all seen these types of documents, and with the onslaught of hasty desktop publishing (which seems to be more abundant with each passing year), you're bound to see more.

In today's publishing world, though, the very fact that a published document may have errors, is poorly laid out, or contains poor grammar is *inexcusable* only if the tools used in creating it lacked the necessary capabilities to correct errors. In these cases, whatever slips through simply boils down to human error. For XPress users though, there are plenty of tools for molding, manipulating, and checking your text. In other words, you now have no excuse for allowing spelling mistakes to live in your final published documents.

Getting Text on the Page

If you visited Chapter 1, you may have noticed already that XPress is one of the few layout programs that doesn't include an import command. Unfamiliar users may find themselves searching hopelessly trying to find it. Instead of an obvious import command, Quark maintains a separation between imported picture and text document types, forcing users to look specifically for text or picture files while text boxes or picture boxes are selected. You may also enter text directly into a text box as you would with any word processor, and many users do just that. XPress' text entry tools are fast and efficient enough to enable you to do this.

The Automatic Text Box Option

When you first create a new document, the New Document dialog box, shown in the following illustration, offers the Automatic Text Box option, which enables you to automatically create a rectangular text box. With this option selected, the automatic text box is created to work within the parameters of other options in the dialog box.

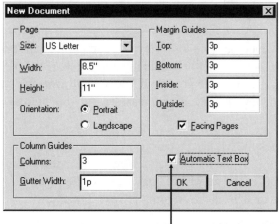

Check box indicates option is selected

For example, as shown in the preceding illustration, setting your new document column guides to three columns with a gutter width of 1 pica, and margin guides to 3 picas at the top, bottom, inside, and outside allows XPress to create and display the guides at these measures. And, choosing the Automatic Text Box option creates a single text box on your first page that is flush with the margins and formatted to three columns with a 1-pica gutter.

You may change these properties of your automatically-created text box later by double-clicking the text box with the Item tool to open the Modify dialog box, and then changing settings in the Text tab. If you do not select the Automatic Text Box option, your column and margin guides are created and displayed, but no text box is created.

TIP   *If importing or text entry is your first and foremost task, creating an automatic text box saves you the time of creating your own page text boxes.*

The automatic text box is also a function of your master page. When you create a new document, your first master page is created for you, and its properties are applied to your first page. By default, your first master page takes on the properties set in the New Document dialog box. You may create up to 127 master pages, each with its own page column and margin properties. You may turn the Automatic Text Box feature on or off for each of the different master pages, causing each subsequent new page based on the chosen master page to be created with or without the automatic text box. If your document will be dozens or even hundreds of pages in length, this option is going to save you hours of text box creation. To deactivate the Automatic Text Box option on a master page, follow these steps:

1. In an open document, choose View| Document Layout (F4/F10) to open the Document Layout palette. Notice the upper half of the palette lists the master pages in your document. If you are still working with defaults applied to a new document, you may see only one master page listed and named *A-Master-A*.

2. Double-click the Master Page icon to the left of its name (not the name itself), to display the master page. Notice your view changes to show the master page. In the upper-left corner of the page, you'll notice a large text chain symbol. This is the Automatic Text Box control.

3. Choose the Unlinking tool from the Tool palette and click the symbol.

4. Next, click the text box on the page. Notice the text chain-link symbol changes to a *broken* text chain-link symbol, as shown in Figure 6-1.

TIP

If your master page does not have a text box on it (meaning it may have been deleted), the chain-link symbol will already display as a broken text chain-link symbol.

5. To reactivate the Automatic Text box option, click the Linking tool in the Tool palette.

Click here with the Unlinking tool to deactivate the Automatic Text Box option on a master page

6

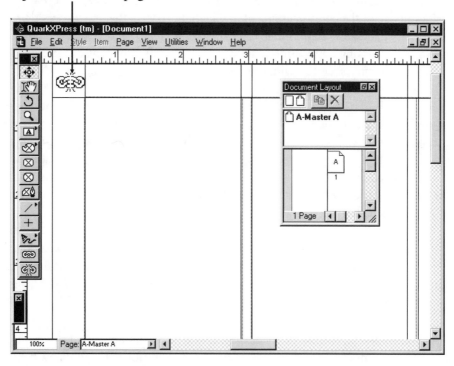

FIGURE 6-1   Deactivating the Automatic Text Box option on a master page

6. Click the chain-link symbol again and immediately click the text box on your master page. Notice a link arrow appears joining the chain-link symbol to the text box. Now your Automatic Text Box option is active once again.

7. If there is no text box on your master page, you'll need to create one in order to create automatic text boxes. You may create a new text box with any properties you want. To do this, create the text box in the usual way and follow the previous two steps.

Entering Text

Regardless of whether or not your text boxes are automatic, you probably want to get started immediately working with content and creating your layout. If the text you need to work with doesn't exist yet, you may be faced with entering it yourself. Or, you may simply be editing an existing document. Text entry could easily be considered one of the core functions of any layout program that most users take for granted. The good news here is that you can enter text into XPress without the need for a word processing application. And, if you're a really fast typist, XPress won't slow your text entry speed as with other cumbersome layout applications.

To enter text directly into an existing text box, you need only select the Content tool from the Tool palette, click the text box you want to enter text into, select a text entry point with the I-beam cursor, and begin typing. If you want to replace text in the box, select the text to be replaced by highlighting it (click-and-drag the characters), and then begin entering your new text. The new text is formatted with the same character attributes as the text you highlighted. For more information on working with text entry and text highlighting procedures, see *Chapter 4, Text Basics and Typographic Tools.*

TIP ⟶ *If the text you are entering is brand new content, you'll need to use one of XPress' text box tools to create a new text box to hold it. For information on using text box creation tools, see* Getting Text on the Page, *in* Chapter 1, XPress Train Quick Start.

As you enter text, XPress flows the new text within your text box. For new users such as editors, this can be both a blessing and a curse. As you enter your new content and the text flows within your text box, the text you are entering may exceed the size limitations the text box is capable of displaying. Or the new content may cause subsequent text to flow beyond your text box. In order to view text beyond the borders of your current text box, you'll need to do one of two things: Extend the existing text box and increase its physical size by dragging one of its sizing handles, or create a new text box and link it to the current box, allowing the text flow to continue into the new box. The appearance of the text overflow symbol at the bottom-right of a box indicates more text exists in the box than that box is capable of displaying, as shown in Figure 6-2. For more information on linking text boxes, see *Linking Text Boxes* in *Chapter 2, After Getting Started.*

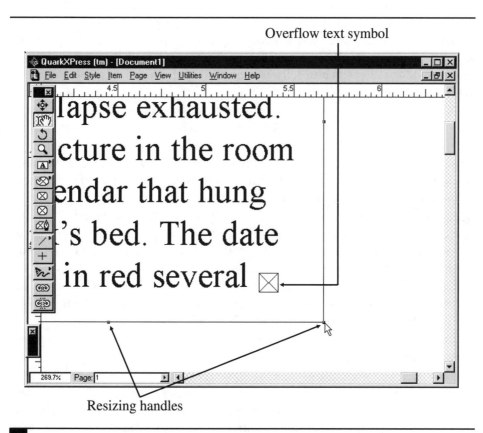

FIGURE 6-2   When entering text, watch for the overflow symbol, which indicates some content may be hidden from view

TIP

If the text box you are entering text into with the Content tool is linked and flowing to another text box somewhere else in your document, and you want to quickly locate the next linked box, position your I-beam cursor after the last character of the text box and press the RIGHT ARROW key. XPress will display the top of the next box where your cursor has gone. If the text box is not linked to any other box, the cursor will simply disappear.

Importing Text

For many designers and layout artists, the job of entering large quantities of text is done by someone else, such as a writer, editor, professional word processor, or researcher. In these cases, text may or may not be prepared to suit your documents' needs. Whatever the case, you'll need to get the text onto your XPress pages somehow, and that somehow is more than likely through importing the file. When working with text and text boxes, the import command is found under the File menu as Get Text (CTRL/CMD+E).

XPress supports most text entry or word processing programs in a number of ways, depending on the source application from which the text is imported. Both Mac and Windows platforms have a large number of popular and competing text-entry applications ranging from extremely basic to quite sophisticated. Basic applications often prepare text simply as unformatted characters, while the more professional applications are capable of advanced formatting such as specific character attributes, specialized punctuation, styles, and character tagging. In many cases, both the Mac and Windows XPress 4 versions support accurate importing of text documents across platforms, but in specialized cases these text files may require specialized file-saving options to be selected.

Compatible Windows text formats include ASCII text (TXT), Rich Text Format (RTF), XPress tags (XTG), Microsoft Word 2.0 and 6.0, Microsoft Write (WRI), and WordPerfect 3.x, 5.x, and 6.x (WPD, DOC, WP, WPT).

Compatible Macintosh text formats include MacWrite, MacWrite II, Microsoft Word, Microsoft Works, WordPerfect, WriteNow, and XPress tags.

TIP

If the text box you are importing your text into is too small to accommodate all the text, the overflow symbol will appear. If the text box is linked to a subsequent text box, the document will continue to flow into the linked box. And, if text is imported into an automatic text box with the Auto Page Insertion option enabled, additional pages containing the flowed text will be created automatically. To enable new pages to be added automatically

when importing text (and even when entering text manually), make sure the
Auto Page Insertion option is active in your Document Preferences dialog
box by choosing Edit\ Document Preferences | General tab (CTRL/CMD+Y).

As a quick practical exercise in importing text into XPress, follow these steps:

1. In an open document, choose the Content tool from the Tool palette
and click the text box into which you want to import the text file. If no
text box exists, choose one of the text box tools from the Tool palette
and draw a box. If needed, you may also want to define other text box
properties such as the number of columns, gutter size, and so on by using
the Modify dialog box (CTRL/CMD+M).

2. With the Content tool and your text box selected, choose File | Get
Text (CTRL/CMD+E) to open the Get Text dialog box shown in the
following illustration.

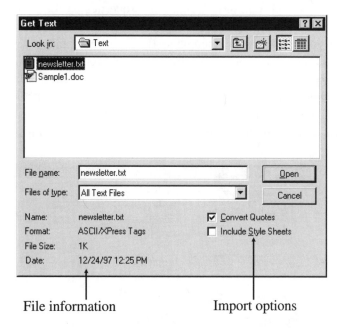

File information   Import options

3. Use the dialog box controls to locate the folder containing the file you
want to import and select the file name by clicking it once.

4. Before clicking the Open button, notice the information that appears in the dialog box concerning the file's name, format, size, and date. Notice the Convert Quotes and Include Style Sheets options and choose these accordingly.

5. Now, click Open to import the file. Your file is imported into your text box.

The import options in the dialog box determine how your file is imported. The Convert Quotes option converts straight quotes (") to curly open and close quotes (" "). The Include Style Sheets option enables XPress to interpret, load, and apply any styles that are currently formatted with the document. Include Style Sheets applies only to documents from Microsoft Word and WordPerfect applications.

Advanced Character Attributes

The ability to set such common formatting properties as font, size, and style is available in most desktop applications and often translates directly into your text boxes when you import your document. But there are quite a large number of character attributes that other applications aren't capable of setting and XPress handles with ease. All of these "advanced" character attributes may be applied through the Style menu or options in the Character Attributes (CTRL/CMD+SHIFT+D) dialog box shown in the following illustration. But as you'll soon discover, there are quicker ways of applying these properties spread throughout XPress.

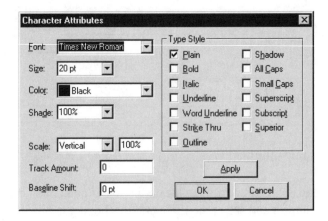

If you've come here to discover how to apply some of the more common attributes, or if some of the terminology appears like a foreign language to you, you may want to flip back to an earlier chapter. For more information on identifying a character's various parts, see Anatomy of Text *in Chapter 4, Text Basics and Typographic Tools. As you continue beyond the anatomy section, you'll discover how to apply common character formatting attributes.*

Setting Font Color and Shade

Font colors and shades may be set only if your text is in XPress. The quickest way to apply font colors and shades is through use of the Colors palette shown in the following illustration. Among its other uses, this palette enables you to apply any of the colors available in your XPress document to your text, and sets these colors to display and print based on a given shade percentage. The Shade value is accurate to a tenth of a percentage point. Even if you intend to use only a single color in your document (including black—which is also considered a color), the Colors palette is the most convenient and efficient feature with which to do this.

6

Text mode button

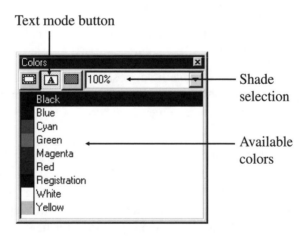

Shade selection

Available colors

Although certain character properties may be applied only if your text characters are in XPress, you may use XPress tags to precode some of these properties before the text ever reaches XPress. For more information on preparing documents with tags, see Working with Tags *later in this chapter.*

Before you apply colors or shades to your text using the Colors palette, your text must be selected using the Content tool. If all the text in your text box is to be the same color, you may do this quickly using the Select All command (CTRL/CMD+A) while your cursor is positioned anywhere in the text box. Once your text is selected, you may instantly apply the color and shade properties. For some hands-on experience, follow these steps:

1. Select a text box containing text and choose the Content tool from the Tool palette.

2. Select the characters to which you want to apply the color using your usual text selection method.

3. With the text highlighted, open the Colors palette and choose View | Show Colors (F12). Notice three buttons in the upper-left corner of the palette and a field/drop-down menu at the upper-right. The first button sets the palette to control frame color, the second controls text, and the third controls your text box background color. The drop-down menu sets the shade.

4. Click the second button to set the palette to control your text.

5. Choose a color from the Colors list. Notice your text changes color immediately.

6. Enter a shade in the Shade field, or select a preset percentage from the drop-down menu. Notice the color of your text is immediately altered based on the percentage you enter.

NOTE *If the shade you are applying is entered as a typed value, you must press RETURN (or click anywhere on your page) before the Shade value is applied.*

Although the preceding exercise demonstrates generic steps to apply color and shade to text, one of the most common questions for new users is how to create "reverse" text, or, white text in a color box. Although white isn't considered a color and cannot be shaded, it's one of most common properties applied to text. So, to take this a little further and create reverse text, follow these steps:

1. Create a text box of any shape or size using any of the text box tools available in the Tool palette.

2. Choose the Content tool, enter the words **White text** in the text box, and apply any font, size, or style attributes, or simply leave the text at default settings.

3. Highlight the text using your usual text selection method (or use CTRL/CMD+A to select all the text).

4. Open the Colors palette (F12) and click the Text Color button.

5. Click White in the Colors list. Notice choosing White does not enable you to apply a shade percentage, and now that White is applied, your text characters seem to have disappeared (don't worry—they're still there).

6. Click the Background button and click Black (or any other color). For the purposes of this exercise, leave the Shade value set to 100 percent. Notice your text reappears.

7. You won't be able to see an accurate display of your reverse text while the text is highlighted, so click anywhere off the text box to deselect the text. Notice your text is now white on a black background, as shown in the following illustration.

As you browse the list of available colors in the Colors palette, you may notice a color named Registration. Choosing Registration for your text color has the effect of making the text display in black on your screen, even though the text color will print in all *the colors used in your document. The Registration color is designed as a method for registering different ink layers when your document is printed using XPress' color separation feature. For more information on using registration and printing color separations, see* Chapter 16, Printing Your Pages.

Scaling Fonts

If you're a type designer, you're going to sneer at this next feature of XPress. Scaling fonts has the effect of distorting their shape either vertically or horizontally. The sneering is due to the fact that type designers spend their creative efforts fine-tuning characters based on a specific design—without consideration for distortion. Many designers believe that if you need a wider or narrower font, you should pick a different font entirely instead of distorting an existing design.

Having stated that little disclaimer, XPress 4 enables you to freely distort fonts to your heart's content either one character at a time, or throughout your entire document, without much care or consideration for the original design of your particular font. Scaling a font can result in either terrible or useful and interesting effects on the characters themselves, and slightly scaling large amounts of text can often be useful for helping your text fit a given space.

Vertical and horizontal scaling of fonts are interrelated functions, with one type of scaling affecting the other. Applying these effects is much easier than trying to understand what's happening in terms of scaling. Suffice it to say that a vertical scale value greater than 100 percent has the effect of making fonts appear taller, and a vertical scale value less than 100 percent essentially widens the fonts. Horizontal scaling works in the opposite manner; applying a horizontal scale value greater than 100 percent expands the font, and applying a horizontal scale value less than 100 percent compresses the font. Scaling must be set within a range between 25 and 400 percent. The following illustration demonstrates the results of exaggerated scaling using the Scale effect.

TIP ────────> *Setting either the vertical or horizontal scaling of your font to 100 percent reverts the font to its original state.*

Vertical and horizontal scaling are more easily understood by using the keyboard shortcuts that apply it; the feedback your screen provides tells you exactly how much of the effect you need. Keyboard shortcuts for both scaling effects are as follows:

Increase vertical/horizontal scaling by 5 percent	CTRL/CMD+]
Increase vertical/horizontal scaling by 1 percent	CTRL/CMD+ALT/OPTION+]
Decrease vertical/horizontal scaling by 5 percent	CTRL/CMD+[
Decrease vertical/horizontal scaling by 1 percent	CTRL/CMD+ALT/OPTION+[

NOTE ────────> *Keyboard commands scale text vertically or horizontally according to the current Scale options set in the Character Attributes dialog box.*

Tracking Amount

If you've visited Chapter 4, you may already be aware of how tracking adjustments affect your text. Tracking is a value associated with combinations of both letter and word spacing of text. Using XPress, you can change tracking between characters and words to improve the readability of text. Tracking changes are usually required for text that is poorly justified or poorly hyphenated, or for justified columns that are long on words but short on space or line length. Tracking may also be applied where text must expand or reduce in length to fit a given space. The following illustration demonstrates the results of "loose," or, expanded tracking and "tight," or, reduced tracking; neither is very readable or acceptable for layout.

At the end of the
day, Mark would
return to his little
box-room with its
small bed, small
chair, and tiny
chest of drawers,
and collapse
exhausted. The
only picture in the
room was the cal-
endar that hung

At the end of the day,
Mark would return to his
little box-room with its
small bed, small chair,
and tiny chest of drawers,
and collapse exhausted.
The only picture in the
room was the calendar
that hung above Mark's
bed. The date was circled
in red several times to
remind him that would

Loose tracking   Tight tracking

As with other character attributes, the characters for which you want to adjust the tracking must first be selected with the Content tool. Tracking amounts are measured in em spaces and may be adjusted in either 1/20th or 1/200th em increments. The following keyboard shortcuts apply when adjusting track amounts:

Increase tracking amount by 1/20 of an em space	CTRL/CMD +SHIFT+{
Decrease tracking amount by 1/20 of an em space	CTRL/CMD+SHIFT+}
Increase tracking amount by 1/200 of an em space	CTRL/CMD+ALT/OPTION+SHIFT+{
Decrease tracking amount by 1/200 of an em space	CTRL/CMD+ALT/OPTION+SHIFT+}

TIP

Tracking amount is set by the size of em spaces. You may set the method by which em spaces are measured by using the Document Preferences (CTRL/CMD+Y) | Character tab. A standard em space equals the point size of the text. The width of nonstandard ems is set according to the width of two numeral 0s of the font in use. For more information on using these features, see Setting Document Preference Options *in Chapter 12, Fine-tuning XPress.*

QuarkXPress 4 *IN ACTION*

Design: Malcolm Frouman

Description: Cover design, *Business Week*, March 24, 1997 issue

This *Business Week* cover design uses text characters for graphic appeal while using line rules to provide a simple background effect and visual impact. The numerals "50" are printed in spot color (gold) to increase emphasis while the remaining layout uses process color.

Shifting Text Baselines

The baseline of a line of text is the imaginary line on which all type appears to rest. The capability to shift baselines of text for special formatting or effects was a useful feature when first introduced, and in many cases it is still used in designing documents that require fine-tuning or tailoring to fit tight spaces. A baseline shift is measured in points and may be set using the Character Attributes (CTRL/CMD+SHIFT+D) dialog box or keyboard commands.

As with other character attributes, to adjust the baseline shift of characters, the characters must first be selected with the Content tool. Applying positive baseline shift values has the effect of raising the selected text above the original baseline, while negative values lower the text below its original baseline. A baseline shift may be applied in a negative or positive amount up to three times the font size. For example, 12-point text may be shifted within a range between -36 to +36 points.

The following illustration shows a practical application of using a baseline shift to emphasize text.

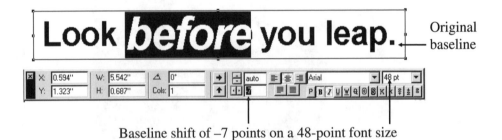

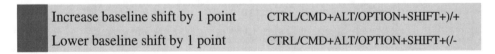

Baseline shift of –7 points on a 48-point font size

When applying a baseline shift using keyboard commands, the following shortcuts apply:

Increase baseline shift by 1 point	CTRL/CMD+ALT/OPTION+SHIFT+)/+
Lower baseline shift by 1 point	CTRL/CMD+ALT/OPTION+SHIFT+(/-

Setting Paragraph Attributes

Up until now, you've been discovering mostly how to set individual character attributes. If you're new to typography or working with the finer details of text, it helps immensely to know a little about applying character attributes before making the leap to controlling the properties of entire paragraphs.

TIP

Although certain paragraph properties may be applied only if your text characters are in XPress, you may use XPress tags to precode some of these properties before the text ever reaches XPress. For more information on preparing documents with tags, see Working with Tags *later in this chapter.*

In XPress, a paragraph is defined as any text sandwiched between two full paragraph returns. Between these returns, paragraphs may be molded and shaped in a number of ways, depending on the design of your publication or document. All paragraph properties may be controlled, including alignment, first and subsequent line indents, spacing, tabs, rules, leading, and even drop cap effects. And, as you'll see later on in this chapter, learning how to control paragraph properties will enable you to define paragraph styles using XPress' style commands. Many of the properties associated with paragraph formats may be set using the Paragraph Attributes |Formats tab (CTRL/CMD+SHIFT+F) dialog box options shown in the following illustration.

6

For more information on identifying a paragraph's parts, see *Anatomy of Text* in *Chapter 4, Text Basics and Typographic Tools.*

Setting Indents and Alignment

The capability to control paragraph indent values enables you to identify to your reading audience the start and end of paragraphs. New paragraphs usually indicate a change in the topic, subject, or voice of your textual content. Alignment is often merely a function of layout. Indent and alignment options may be set using the Paragraph Attributes | Formats tab (CTRL/CMD+SHIFT+F) dialog box shown in the preceding illustration.

___TIP___ → *In order for the Formats tab options to be available, you must be working with the Content tool. To apply formatting to a specific paragraph you must also have your cursor positioned in the paragraph to which you want to apply the indents.*

- **Left Indent and Right Indent**   These two options enable you to set the lines of your paragraph text to begin and end at specific points within your text box. The positions of your left and right indents must fall within the column itself and are measured according to the width of your column. Indent values must fall within a range between 0 and the maximum width of your column.

- **First Line**   This indent option enables you to control where the first line of your text begins in relation to the (read this slowly) *left indent of your paragraph*—not the left edge of your text box. For example, a first line indent of 0.25 inches sets the first line of your paragraph one-quarter inch from the left indent of your selected paragraph. Entering negative values for the First Line measure causes XPress to format a *hanging indent* for your paragraph, where the first line is closer to the left edge of your text box than the remaining lines in your paragraph.

___NOTE___ → *If you're finding it impossible to set the paragraph indents of your text to align with the left or right edges of your text box, it may be because the text box already has an* inset value *applied to it. Inset values are a function of the text box itself and work in combination with applied indent measures. Insets are applied using the Modify (CTRL/CMD+M) | Text tab. When applied, insets recess the text within a text box uniformly around the inside of the box. For more information on insetting text within a text box, see* Working in Columns *in the next section.*

As a throw-back from the days of typing, many users entering text in basic word processing applications—or directly into a XPress text box—commonly enter tabs at the beginning of each paragraph as a manual way of inserting a first line indent. Most layout applications and many word processing applications have the capability to control first line indents of paragraphs, so using this tab is unnecessary. If the text you are working with contains tabs at the beginning of each paragraph, it may be wise to delete them and instead rely on the First Line indent option.

TIP *First line indents are a function of paragraph formatting, while tab characters may only be controlled using tabbing options. For more details on working with tabs, see* Working with Tabs *later in this section. For information on searching for and replacing unwanted characters such as extra tabs or paragraph returns, see* Using Find/Change Tools *later in this chapter.*

When using the Paragraph Attributes dialog box, a small ruler appears just above and aligned with the text in your text box. It includes options to interactively set left, right, and first line indents for your selected text, as shown in Figure 6-3. To apply values (or sometimes even to see the ruler itself), you may have to reposition the Paragraph Attributes dialog box on your screen by dragging its title bar. To use this small ruler to change values, simply drag the markers to align with your chosen measure using the ruler markings for reference. First Line and Right Indent markers may be positioned independently, while dragging the Left Indent marker moves both the Left Indent and First Line markers together.

- **Alignment** When aligning paragraph text, you may choose from Left, Right, Centered, Justified, or Forced. Justified alignment justifies all but the last line of a paragraph. Forced alignment justifies all the lines in a paragraph, including the last line, even if it's only one or two words. Alignment is a paragraph attribute rather than a character attribute; this means you may align all the characters between two full paragraph returns using one of these alignment styles, but you may not apply alignment to a single word in a paragraph.

Working with Tabs

XPress' tabbing feature is both sophisticated and simple to use. You may format any number of tab positions per paragraph to accommodate the most complex tab

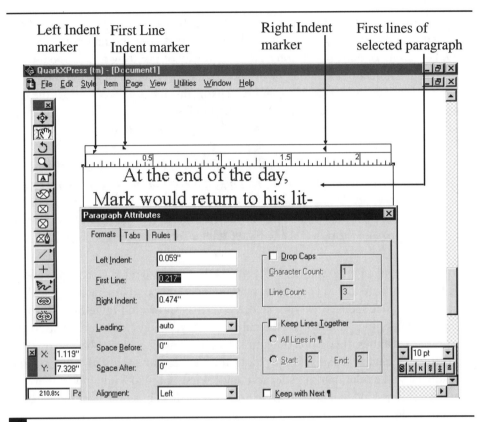

Left Indent marker   First Line Indent marker   Right Indent marker   First lines of selected paragraph

FIGURE 6-3   Left Indent, First Line, and Right Indent markers may be set interactively using this small ruler, which appears when the Paragraph Attributes dialog box is open

formatting. There are several types of tab styles to choose from. You may also set leaders to appear between tabs using any character you want. *Leaders* are repeating characters between text and tab positions in your paragraph. They are used for visual alignment of tabbed text in cramped or lengthy spaces. Tabbing is a function of the Paragraph Attributes | Tabs dialog box (CTRL/CMD+SHIFT+T) shown in the following illustration. It is available only when using the Content tool in a text box.

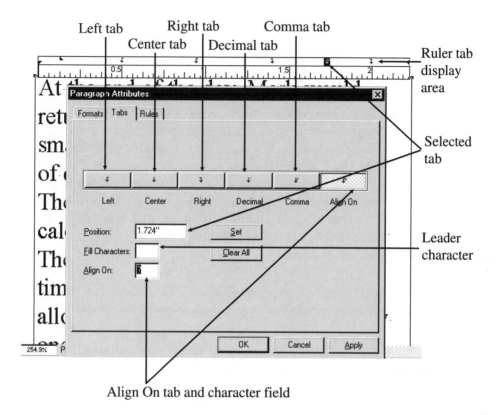

Align On tab and character field

- **Type** Choose from six types of tabs including Left, Right, Centered, Decimal, Comma, and a wildcard style named Align On. The Align On style enables you to align text on a specific character in your text in the same manner as a Decimal tab. While a tab set using the Align On style is selected, the Align On field becomes available, enabling you to specify an alignment character.

- **Position** The Position field enables you to set the exact position of tabs numerically or select tabs by entering their ruler position.

- **Fill Characters** When specifying leaders, you may enter any single character in this field.

TIP *You may set tabs anywhere on the ruler including between the First Line and Left Indent markers and within the Left Indent and Right Indent markers. You may also set tabs beyond the Right Indent marker, but not to the left of the Left Indent marker.*

When setting tabs in text, you must be working with the Content tool and have your cursor positioned somewhere in the paragraph to which you want to apply tab properties. Once the Tabs dialog box is open, click your tab type and click a ruler position to create the tab. You may also enter a numeric value in the Position field and click the Set button. To delete a tab, select it by clicking directly on it in the top half of the ruler, and then press DELETE or BACKSPACE (or drag the tab off the ruler). To delete all tabs, click the Clear All button. To change a tab type, click it once to select it, and then click a different tab type. To move a tab, click the tab to select it, and then drag it to a new position.

TIP *When working with rulers in the Formats | Tabs dialog box, clicking the ruler while holding ALT/OPTION clears all currently-set tabs.*

NOTE *A minor "hiccup" in the operation of XPress' tab and paragraph indent features causes your view to display the beginning of the paragraph ruler at zero. In close-up views where the width of your text box may not completely fit on your screen, you will not be able to scroll to the right side of the text box while the Paragraph Attributes dialog box is open. This may cause some inconvenience for creating, deleting, or changing tabs beyond your view. You may have to zoom out to see the tabs applied to text at the far right of your paragraph.*

Paragraph Spacing

Applying additional space between paragraphs can be used as an alternative to indenting text in an effort to identify where the topic or subject of your textual content changes. Spacing between paragraphs may also be used to fit text to a given layout. XPress enables you to insert additional spacing both before and after paragraphs using the Space Before and Space After fields in the Paragraph Attributes | Formats tab (CTRL/CMD+SHIFT+F) dialog box. Paragraph spacing must fall within a range between 0 and 15 inches.

NOTE *You may not apply paragraph space before the very first paragraph in a text box nor may you apply space after the very last paragraph. In addition, any paragraph spacing applied to text on a path is ignored.*

Paragraph Rules

If a portion of the body text of your document calls for line rules to be added above or below your paragraphs, this next feature will be appealing. Because of the capability of text to flow throughout columns and text boxes, adding manual lines may not be very efficient. Manually-drawn line rules do not flow with text unless they have been specifically anchored with text. And drawing lines manually to align with your text is time consuming.

XPress' Rules features helps you avoid much of this tedium. Rules may be set using the Paragraph Attributes | Rules (CTRL/CMD+SHIFT+N) dialog box options shown in the following illustration. Clicking the Rule Above and Rule Below check boxes enables the remaining options where you can set the following rule properties:

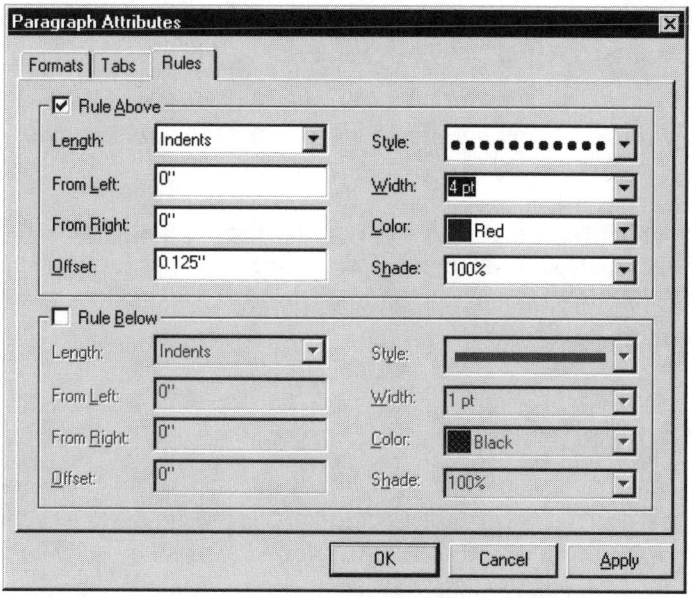

6

- **Length**   The Length drop-down menu lists two options: Indents and Text. Setting the length of your rule to Indents enables the maximum rule to extend to the indents formatted to your paragraph. Choosing Text limits the maximum length of your rule to the beginning and ending points of the first and last characters of the first line of text in your paragraph.

- **From Left**   This field option enables you to indent the left end point of your paragraph rule by a given amount. The value you enter determines the starting point of the rule measured from either the left indent or the left edge of the first text character as set by the Length option.

- **From Right**   This field option enables you to indent the right end point of your paragraph rule by a specified amount. The value you enter determines the end point of the rule measured from either the right indent or the right edge of the last text character as set by the Length option.

- **Offset**   The position of your paragraph rules is set according to the baseline of your text. So, the Rule Above Offset option is set to 0 by default; this means the bottom edge of the rule you create will rest on the baseline of the first line of your paragraph—*and directly underneath your text*. Unless this is your design intention, you may want to change this value. Enter an offset equal to *at least* the leading size of your text. For example, if your text is 12 points set with 13 points of leading, set the Offset value to 13 points. The Offset value must be within a range between −0.007 and 14.993 inches.

NOTE   → *The Rule Below options are identical to the Rule Above options.*

Along with the preceding options to specify the position of your rule, the right half of the Rules dialog box enables you to set line attributes for your rule including Dash and Stripe Style, Width, Color, and Shade. These options are identical to XPress' line attribute options.

Adjusting Leading

The term *leading* refers to the point spacing between the baselines of your paragraph text. Leading is nearly always measured in points in the same way as your text's font size. Setting the leading of text to zero is referred to as *leading set solid*, meaning there is little or no breathing room between the letters. A single extra point of leading is usually enough to ensure the ascenders and descenders of your text don't touch and are at a comfortable reading distance. In traditional text terminology, text size and leading were referred to as a unit, such as "12-on-13," or "12/13," which meant 12-point type set on 13 points of leading. In many circles, text size and leading are still referred to in this way.

The leading of your type is one of the more critical yet forgiving properties. Leading may be slightly adjusted to enable a column of text to fit a vertical space. Where letter and word spacing are critical to the readability of text, leading may be tinkered with and tuned without significantly distracting your readers, as shown in the following illustration.

At the end of the day, Mark would return to his little box-room with its small bed, small chair, and tiny chest of drawers, and collapse exhausted. The only picture in the room was the calendar that hung above mark's bed. The date was circled in red several times to remind him that would be allowed to join his friends and family once he had returned to normal.
Each night, before falling asleep he would stare at the calendar and eventually get out of bed and cross out the offending day with careful strokes like a prisoner scratching marks on a wall.

12-point text with no leading

At the end of the day, Mark would return to his little box-room with its small bed, small chair, and tiny chest of drawers, and collapse exhausted. The only picture in the room was the calendar that hung above mark's bed. The date was circled in red several times to remind him that would be allowed to join his friends and family once he had returned to normal.
Each night, before falling asleep he would stare at the calendar and eventually get out of bed and cross out the offending day with careful strokes like a prisoner scratching marks on a wall.

12-point text with automatic leading

At the end of the day, Mark would return to his little box-room with its small bed, small chair, and tiny chest of drawers, and collapse exhausted. The only picture in the room was the calendar that hung above mark's bed. The date was circled in red several times to remind him that would be allowed to join his friends and family once he had returned to normal.
Each night, before falling asleep he would stare at the calendar and eventually get out of bed and cross out the offending day with careful strokes like a prisoner scratching marks on a wall.

12-point text with 1point of leading

Leading may be left at the default of Auto—often the safest setting when frequently changing type sizes. Automatic leading has the effect of setting the baseline-to-baseline spacing between your lines of text to 20 percent of the text size. You may change the leading of your text using the Paragraph Attributes dialog box (CTRL/CMD+SHIFT+E selects the Leading option) or the Measurements palette (F9), but the most efficient way of setting leading is through keyboard shortcuts. The following shortcuts apply when adjusting leading:

Increase leading by 1 point	CTRL/CMD+SHIFT+"
Decrease leading by 1 point	CTRL/CMD+SHIFT+:
Increase leading by 0.1 point	CTRL/CMD+ALT/OPTION+SHIFT+"
Decrease leading by 0.1 point	CTRL/CMD+ALT/OPTION+SHIFT+:

Creating Drop Caps

Around two thousand years ago, the implementation of drop caps in text indicated where to begin reading text. To a great extent, drop caps still do the same thing today. Drop caps in history began as simple characters that were larger than the rest of the body text.

In the early days of publishing, elaborately-drawn drop caps were usually used at the very beginning of fictional or historical books. In the most lavish examples, drop caps were used to set the tone of each particular chapter. Drop caps of ancient history often involved detailed drawings of coats of arms, battle gear, folk lore, royalty, and heroes, and they were usually rich with flourishes and other artistic embellishments. In this way, they provided visual interest where none existed before and acted as descriptive illustrations. In fact, in many cases the drop caps themselves served as the illustrations for the content of the books. Today, designers tend to break tradition, opting for mostly austere-looking drop caps tossed into text to break up the monotony of long documents.

XPress enables you to format drop caps at the beginning of your paragraph text automatically with two variables. Applying automatic drop caps is a function of the Paragraph Attributes| Formats dialog box (CTRL/CMD+SHIFT+F). By default, the Drop Caps option applies properties using the same font used in your paragraph text. Applied drop caps align with the top ascender of your existing first line of text and the bottom baseline of the selected line of characters, and your remaining text flows within the text box.

Selecting the Drop Caps option enables you to set Character Count and Line Count options, which are defined as follows:

- **Character Count**   Entering a number in this field sets how many characters at the beginning of your paragraph will be used for the drop cap effect.

- **Line Count**   Entering a number in this field sets how many lines of depth your drop cap occupies at the beginning of your paragraph.

Once your Character Count and Line Count options have been set and applied, XPress automatically formats the characters, as shown in Figure 6-4. Once a drop cap effect is applied, you may customize it using either options in the Character Attributes (CTRL/CMD+SHIFT+D) dialog box or the Measurements palette (F9). When you do, however, you'll notice that the size is no longer based on points, but is measured and set based on a percentage of the drop cap's space. For example, a freshly-created drop cap is set to a size of 100 percent by default. To increase its size, choose a percentage higher than 100 percent; to decrease its size, choose a percentage less than 100 percent. Drop cap size may be set within a range between 25 and 400 percent of its original size.

6

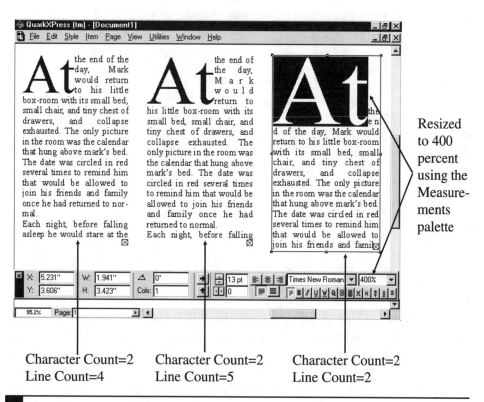

Character Count=2   Character Count=2   Character Count=2
Line Count=4   Line Count=5   Line Count=2

FIGURE 6-4   Applying and sizing automatic drop caps

By default, drop caps automatically align with the baseline of the last line specified in the Line Count option. As their size is increased or decreased, they are reformatted in size but still rest on the specified baseline.

Working in Columns

As you build your layout, you'll ultimately use XPress' column feature—even if your text box features only one column. Columns enable you to flow textual content within a text box in vertical rows. Columns flow text from right to left, top to bottom, in each of the columns set, with the spaces between the columns set uniformly. Column formatting serves as the very core of layout in XPress, and grasping the concept is critical to planning how your layout will be executed. Column formats are set using Modify (CTRL/CMD+M) | Text tab dialog box options for selected text boxes, as shown in the following illustration.

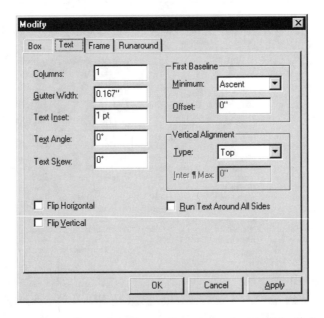

Column properties are based on the options you select in this dialog box and the dimensions of your text box. Column width is an automatic function. In other words, you may not enter a specific column measure. Instead, XPress calculates the column size based on the width of your text box, the number of columns set, and the space value—or gutter—you define between your columns. Column width is a constant measure and is recalculated any time your text box is resized. XPress does not enable you to set different column widths within a single text box.

- **Columns**   This field enables you to enter the number of columns in your selected text box. XPress enables you to set up to 30 columns, the size of which is automatically calculated. The minimum number of columns is 1.

- **Gutter Width**   The term *gutter* refers to the space between your columns of text. This value may be set within a range between 0.042 and 4 inches. Gutter space is automatic and constant, meaning all gutter space is equal within a single text box.

- **Text Inset**   This field allows you to inset the text within your column uniformly from the top, bottom, left, and right edges of your text box. Insets are often necessary if your text box features a frame—or line attribute—around its perimeter. The inset value you enter must fall within a range between 0 and 288 points; the default is set to 1 point. Inset values applied to columns work in combination with *indent* values set in paragraph text.

- **First Baseline Minimum**   Specifying the first baseline of your text could be considered fine-tuning or the ultimate in controlling where your first line of text aligns at the top of your text box. The first line of text in your text box may be set using two options: Minimum and Offset. The Minimum drop-down menu offers three choices for setting the first line in your text box: Cap Height, Cap+Accent, and Ascent. The Cap Height option aligns the highest uppercase character in your first line of text flush against the text inset. The Cap+Accent option sets the highest character including any accent marks (such as those found in nonEnglish-language characters) flush against the text inset. The Ascent option (not to be confused with Accent) aligns the first line of text using an overall value set by the font's original designer. Ascent values take into account all spacing required for uppercase and accent characters, regardless of whether they are present in your first line of text.

- **First Baseline Offset**   This setting enables you to insert space between the text inset of your text box and the first line of text. It works in combination with the Minimum option set. The offset value you enter must fall within a range between 0 and 48 inches.

6

Vertical Column Alignment

When working with columns of text, XPress enables you to align the text in your text box in much the same manner as the horizontal alignment for paragraphs. Among other uses, the capability to align text vertically enables you to automatically center or fit the columns of text in your layout within a given space, which in the long run saves the tedium of positioning text boxes with vertical spaces, or applying extra leading or paragraph spaces in order to stretch text to fit a vertical space. The Vertical Alignment feature is also a function of the Modify | Text tab dialog box and includes a drop-down menu containing four Type options as follows:

- **Top and Bottom**   Each of these options sets the text in your text box to align to the top or bottom edge of the text box or an applied text inset value. Alignment is applied to all columns within the text box.

- **Centered**   This option has the effect of automatically centering your text within the vertical space—or height value—of your text box, if columns don't fill the text box completely.

- **Justified**   This option is perhaps the main reason the Vertical Alignment feature exists. The Justified option enables you to spread the text in your text box to align with both the top and bottom edges of your text box (or applied text inset). The spacing between the paragraphs is set automatically, and it is limited by the value entered in the Inter-Paragraph Maximum field, which becomes available when Justified is chosen from the drop-down menu. If XPress can't justify your paragraphs vertically without exceeding this value, the text is left unjustified. The additional spacing required to vertically justify the paragraphs in a column is only added to those columns that do not completely fill the height of your text box.

Using Styles and Style Sheets

The capability to formulate and apply styles to text has long been a boon to the automation of the publishing industry and remains one of the most powerful capabilities of character and paragraph formatting. Styles are essentially formatting recipes for the text in your document.

Style formatting may be set and applied to any or all formatting attributes in XPress. Styles may end up in your document a few different ways—by importing the text from another application that supports styles, by appending styles from other XPress documents, or by being user-defined directly in XPress. Styles may be edited, renamed, customized, or deleted as you require in the production of your document.

Style formatting is a function of several features in XPress. There are two basic types of styles: character styles, which define properties set in the Character Attributes dialog box, and paragraph properties, which are specified in the Paragraph Attributes dialog box. You may manage and apply styles using the Style Sheets dialog box (SHIFT+F11) for both characters and paragraphs or through use of the Style Sheets dialog box shown in Figure 6-5.

Defining Styles

Styles may be defined and based on either existing styles, selected text, or XPress' default style. If you currently have text selected with the Content tool, the Style

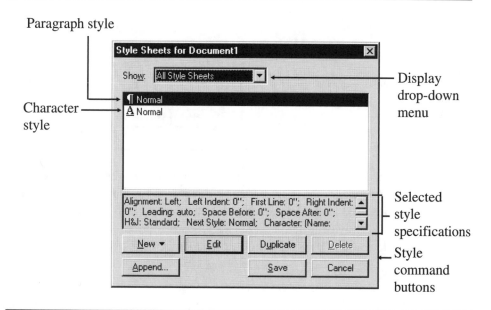

FIGURE 6-5   Styles may be managed through use of the Style Sheets dialog box

Sheet dialog box automatically sets character and paragraph attributes to match the selected text. To define a new character style, follow these steps:

1. With your document open, choose Edit | Style Sheets (SHIFT+F11) to open the Style Sheets dialog box. Notice a listing of preset styles appears.

2. Click the New button and select Character from the drop-down menu that appears. Notice the Edit Character Style Sheet dialog box appears, as shown in the following illustration, and contains two separate areas.

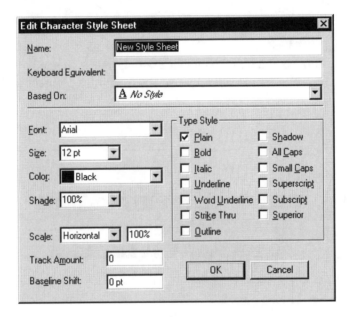

The top area of the dialog box features three fields that enable you to identify your style; the bottom area is identical to the Character Attributes dialog box. The Name field enables you to enter a new style name, the Keyboard Equivalent field accepts a keyboard shortcut for applying your new style, and the Based On drop-down menu enables you to set the character attributes in the lower area of the dialog box to an existing style to serve as a starting point for selecting your new style attributes.

TIP
To enter the keyboard command, simply highlight the Keyboard Equivalent field and press the actual *shortcut keys you want to apply. Keyboard equivalents must be pressed—rather than typed.*

3. To define your new character style, change the properties in the lower area of the dialog box as you would normally, and then click the OK button to create the style and return to the Style Sheets dialog box. Notice your new style name now appears as a character style in the list of styles.

4. To complete the operation, click the Save button to save your style with your document and close the dialog box.

TIP
When opening the Style Sheets dialog box, you may notice that XPress features two default styles already. Although both are named Normal, *one is the default paragraph style and the other is the default character style. You may create your own default styles by closing all documents and opening the Style Sheets dialog box and creating a new style. By doing this, the style(s) you create are saved with XPress' default styles instead of being associated with a specific document.*

6

The procedures for creating a new paragraph style are slightly more involved than for creating a character style because the paragraph style also includes character attributes. To define a new paragraph style, follow these steps:

1. In an open document, choose Edit | Style Sheets (SHIFT+F11) to open the Style Sheets dialog box.

2. In Windows versions, click the New button and choose Paragraph from the drop-down menu. Notice the Edit Paragraph Style Sheet dialog box appears, as shown in the following illustration. In Macintosh versions, simply click New and bypass the menu to create a new paragraph style.

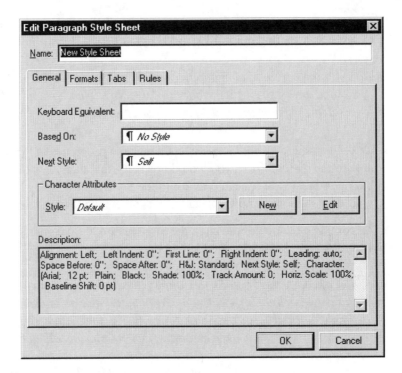

The Edit Paragraph Style Sheet dialog box includes access to all of the properties associated with paragraphs covering the Formats, Tabs, and Rules options, as well as access to the Character Attributes dialog box options.

3. Choose an existing style from the Style drop-down menu. If you need to change character properties for your new paragraph style, click the New button to create a new style, or the Edit button to change the properties of an existing style. Clicking either of these buttons gives you access to all the Character Attributes dialog box options.

4. If you want, select the Keyboard Equivalent field and press a shortcut key.

5. If you want, choose an existing style upon which to base your new style from the Based On drop-down menu

6. Choose the paragraph properties you require in the Formats, Tabs, and Rules dialog box tabs as you would normally.

7. Choosing a Next Style option applies a subsequent style to text while content is being entered directly into your text box in XPress. If this doesn't apply, choose Self from the drop-down menu.

8. Enter a unique name for your new paragraph style in the Name field.

9. Before accepting your new paragraph style, examine the summary of the style in the Description field.

10. If you are satisfied the description is accurate, click OK to return to the Style Sheets dialog box, and then click Save to save the new paragraph style and close the dialog box.

TIP

If setting character or paragraph attributes by choosing options alone is confusing or impossible for you until you see the text itself, you may use already-formatted text. To do this, use the Content tool to select the text, apply the character and paragraph attributes you require, and then press SHIFT+F11 to open the Style Sheets dialog box. When you choose to create a new character or paragraph style, the selected text will serve as the sample and will be listed in the Description field when the dialog box is opened.

6

Applying Styles

Once your character or paragraph style has been created, applying a style is a quick operation. Styles may be applied in a number of ways—according to whichever method suits the way you work. To apply a style using program menus, select the text to apply the style to and choose Style | Character Style Sheet or Style | Paragraph Style Sheet and select the style name from the pop-out list. The new style is applied to your selected text immediately following your style choice.

You may also apply a style using the Style Sheets palette shown in the following illustration. The Style Sheets palette enables you to view and apply all of the character and paragraph styles currently saved with your document. The palette itself is separated into two lists. The top lists paragraph styles and the bottom lists character styles. To open the Style Sheets palette, choose View | Show Style Sheets (F11). To apply styles using this palette, select the text to apply the style to and click the style's name in the palette. You may also press the Keyboard Equivalent key if one has been applied to your style choice. Keyboard equivalents enable you to apply styles even more quickly than using the palette.

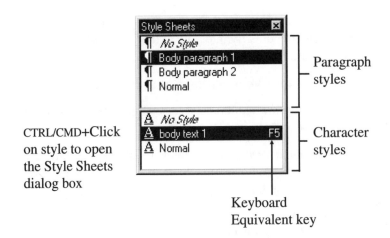

CTRL/CMD+Click on style to open the Style Sheets dialog box

Paragraph styles

Character styles

Keyboard Equivalent key

TIP *If you need to get to the Style Sheets dialog box quickly to revise existing styles or create new ones, hold the CTRL/CMD key while clicking a style in the Style Sheets palette.*

Using Styles from Other Documents

If you find yourself using the same styles over again for various documents or periodicals, you may copy styles from one document to another using the Append command. Append enables you to copy a number of document-specific properties in general, but specifically styles in the Style Sheets dialog box. When styles are appended, they are simply copied from another XPress document file to your existing document, leaving the original document unaffected. To append styles from another document into your current document, follow these steps:

1. With your document open, choose Edit | Style Sheets (SHIFT+F11) to open the Style Sheets dialog box.

2. Click the Append button to open the Append Style Sheets dialog box.

3. Locate the document containing the style sheets you want to copy into your current document and click Open. A second Append Style Sheets dialog box appears, as shown in the following illustration. This dialog box is separated into two halves. The styles contained in the Available list in the source document are shown on the left, while the right side lists the styles you have chosen to include with your current document.

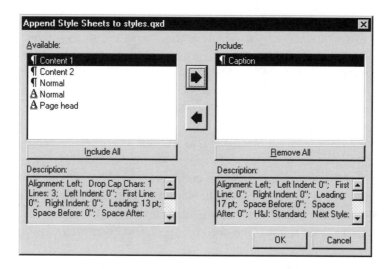

4. To copy a style from the source document, click the style name in the list on the left half of the dialog box, and then click the right-pointing arrow to copy it. Notice the style name now appears on the right side of the dialog box. Notice also that when you selected the style, a description appeared in the Description field below the listing. Review the description to ensure you have chosen the correct style.

5. Include as many styles as you require or click Include All. Clicking the OK button in this dialog box returns you to the Style Sheets dialog box, where you may now click Save to save the newly-copied styles to your document and close the dialog box.

Working with Tags

Although many of the properties of characters and paragraphs may be applied only if your text resides in XPress, you may want to consider precoding text if you find yourself constantly having to reformat text coming from the same source. This precoding operation is referred to as *tagging;* the codes themselves are called *tags.*

If you are at all familiar with HTML (hypertext markup language) in web page design, you may already be familiar with tagging procedures. XPress includes its own twist on these tags, which may be saved with text in ASCII text format and imported directly into XPress through a tags filter.

The tags feature uses no dialog box, nor is it very high-tech. It simply involves preceding text characters in the ASCII text document with a tag code whenever character or paragraph attributes are required. Tagging is actually done in the text entry program used to save text destined for your XPress document. Tagging information may be used to define any of the formatting available in XPress 4, including all character and paragraph style sheets, colors, and H&Js (short for hyphenation and justification).

Applying tags can be tricky business and involves understanding the nomenclature involved in codes and symbols that set various text parameters. For users who prepare text in this way, the codes are a blessing—they enable users to apply XPress text properties without having to own or use the program, and they enable users to save XPress text in a generic text format that may be saved and archived in a database without the need for specialized interpreting programs.

How Tags Work

When an XPress tags document is imported into XPress, it flows through a filter capable of interpreting and converting the information it sees. Filters operate in a linear manner, interpreting information from beginning to end. Imagine the codes and characters of your XPress tags document being fed into the filter one character at a time as if through a funnel. First comes the tag specifying the character or paragraph style sheet or attributes, followed directly by the text it applies to, followed by another tag, and more text, and so on. If the coding is in an incorrect format, tag characters are missing, or information has been saved incorrectly, the whole process can be a wasted effort.

All tags in a document are contained within pointed parentheses (< >), and tags always precede the text they apply to until the filter interprets another tag and changes the character or paragraph attributes.

When coding a text document with tags, consider these guidelines:

■ Always use pointed parentheses (< >) to contain and specify tags. Do not include spaces between parentheses and the codes, or between the codes and the text they apply to. Tags may contain multiple style codes. For example, whereas <B> sets text in bold only, <BIU> sets it using bold (B), italic (I), and underline (U) styles.When importing XPress tag documents, select the Include Style Sheets option in the Get Text dialog box to have XPress apply the specified properties to your imported text. If this option is not selected, the actual tags will appear in your document instead of being interpreted by the XPress filter.

■ Each version of XPress uses a different tags filter version capable of interpreting the features the program supports. XPress 3.1 uses XPress tags filter version 1.5, and XPress versions 3.2 and 3.3 use filter version 1.7. XPress 4.0 uses version 2.0. The filter version is critical and must be the first code contained in the XPress tags document.

The information in a document saved with XPress tags must follow a specific order. First comes the filter version followed by the definitions of character and paragraph style sheets. Once the style sheets are loaded, they may be referred to by their name instead of by specifying character attributes. Once the styles are loaded, the document precedes each paragraph with tags specifying or modifying those styles. Perhaps the best way to familiarize yourself with the structure and use of tags is to examine a typical tagged document line by line. The following is an example of the beginning of a tagged document:

```
<v2.00><e1>
@Normal=<Ps100t0h100z12k0b0cKf"ArialMT">
@body text 1=[S"","","","Normal"]<f"TimesNewRomanPSMT">
@Normal=[S"","Normal","Normal"]<*L*h"Standard"*kn0*kt0*ra0*rb0*d0*p(0,0,0
,0,0,0,g,"U.S. English")>
@Body paragraph 2=[S"","Body
 paragraph1"]<*J*h"Standard"*kn0*kt0*ra0*rb0*d0*p(0,0,0,13,0,0,g,"U.S.
 English")Ps100t0y100z10k0b0cKf"TimesNewRomanPSMT">
@Body paragraph 1=[S"","Body paragraph 2","body text
1"]<*J*h"Standard"*kn0*kt0*ra(2,4,"Red",100,0,0,14.4)*rb0*d(1,7)*p(0,0,0,
13,0,0,g,"U.S. English")>
@Body paragraph 1:<c"Red">A<c$>t the end of the day, Mark would return
to his little box-room with its small bed, small chair, and tiny chest
of drawers, and collapse exhausted. The only picture in the room was
the calendar that hung above Mark's bed. The date was circled in red
several times to remind him that would ...
```

6

When digested line by line, the following information is being specified through the filter:

```
<v2.00><e1>
```

This information specifies the filter and operating system character set. In this case, the tags are set to be interpreted by XPress 4, using the Windows characters set.

```
@Normal=<Ps100t0h100z12k0b0cKf"ArialMT">
```

The document begins by loading styles. Since Normal is the default style, it's loaded first. The symbol *@Normal=* defines the style's name, and *Ps100t0h100z12k0b0cKf"ArialMT"* is the font specification as follows:

Plain text (*P*)
At a shade of 100 percent (*s100*)
With a tracking amount of 0 (*t0*)
And a horizontal scale of 100 percent (*h100*)
A size of 12 points (*z12*)
No kerning (*k0*)
No baseline shift (*b0*)
Color is black (*cK*)
Font name is Arial (*f"ArialMT"*)

Notice the style name is not in parentheses although the character attributes are.

```
@body text 1=[S"","","","Normal"]<f"TimesNewRomanPSMT">
```

Another style sheet is being loaded here. The symbol *@body text 1=* defines the character style sheet, based on the Normal style *[S"","","","Normal"]* with TimesNewRomanPSMT as the font name.

```
@Normal=[S"","Normal","Normal"]<*L*h"Standard"*kn0*kt0*ra0*rb0*d0
*p(0,0,0,0,0,0,g,"U.S. English")>
```

Another paragraph style sheet is being loaded. This is the default paragraph style called Normal, and it is based on the character style also called Normal. It is followed by another listing of paragraph attributes as follows:

*L specifies a left alignment
*h"Standard" specifies the Standard H&J style

kn0 sets the Keep with Next Paragraph option to Off

kt0 sets the Keep Together option to Off

ra0 sets the Rule Above option to Off

rb0 sets the Rule Below option to Off

d0 sets the Drop Cap option to Off

p(0,0,0,0,0,0,g,"U.S. English") sets paragraph attributes for Left Indent, First Line Indent, Right Indent, Leading, Space Before, Space After, and Lock to Baseline to Off. The dictionary specification is for U.S. English.

```
@Body paragraph 2=[S"","Body paragraph
1"]<*J*h"Standard"*kn0*kt0*ra0*rb0*d0*p(0,0,0,13,0,0,g,"U.S.
English")Ps100t0y100z10k0b0cKf"TimesNewRomanPSMT">
@Body paragraph 1=[S"","Body paragraph 2","body text
1"]<*J*h"Standard"*kn0*kt0*ra(2,4,"Red",100,0,0,14.4)*rb0*d(1,7)*
p(0,0,0,13,0
,0,g,"U.S. English")>
```

Two more style sheets are specified as Body Paragraph 2 and Body Paragraph 1.

```
@Body paragraph 1:<c"Red">A<c$>t the end of the day, Mark would
return to his little box-room with its small bed, small chair,
and tiny chest of drawers, and collapse exhausted. The only
picture in the room was the calendar that hung above Mark's
bed. The date was circled in red several times to remind him
that would
```

The preceding codes are placed before the text and refer to the style sheets that have just been loaded.

Tag Codes

When entering and interpreting codes you'll discover that there's a specific protocol that is followed, often matching the order in which options are organized and listed in dialog boxes. The following is the full list of tagging codes that may be interpreted by XPress 4.0.

NOTE *For the purposes of clarity in identifying tag formats, these conventions apply: # represents a wildcard number; italic text specifies an entry name specific to your document or one of its elements; a 0 (zero) turns off an option, and a 1 (one) turns it on; all codes are case-sensitive.*

Character Attributes	Code
Plain	<P>
Bold	<B>
Italic	<I>
Outline	<O>
Shadow	<S>
Underline	<U>
Word underline	<W>
Strike through	</>
All caps	<K>
Small caps	<H>
Superscript	<+>
Subscript	<->
Superior	<V>
Type style of current style sheet	<$>
Change font	<f"*fontname*">
Change font size	<z###.##> (measured in points)

Character Attributes	Code
Change color	<c"colorname"> or <cC###,M###,Y###,K###,cW###>
Change shade	<s###>
Horizontal scale	<h###>
Kern the next two characters	<k###.##>
Track	<t###.##>
Set baseline shift	<b###.##>
Vertical scale	<y###.##>

Paragraph Attributes	Code
Left-align paragraph	<*L>
Center-align paragraph	<*C>
Right-align paragraph	<*R>
Justify paragraph	<*J>
Force justify	<*F>
Set tab stops	<*t(##.#, #,"fillcharacter"> where *t* sets the tab stop, and information within parentheses indicates tab stop, tab type (*0*=left, *1*=center, *2*=right, *3*=decimal, *4*=comma or align on character), and leader character.
Set paragraph attributes	<*p##.#,##.#,##.#,##.#,##.#,##.#,g *or* G> where the first 6 values set Left Indent, First Line, Right Indent, Leading, Space Before, Space After, and Lock to Baseline options to On (G) or Off (g).
H&J (hyphenation and justification)	<*h"H&Jstylename">

6

Paragraph Attributes	Code
Rule above	<*ra(##,#,*"colorname"*,#,##,##,##*> where items within parentheses represent Line Width, Line Style, Color, Shade, From Left, From Right, and Offset values. The style number corresponds to the order in which line styles appear in the Rules Style drop-down menu, beginning at 1. The Rules Offset value may be specified in points or a percentage, as in *##%,* and including a *T* before the left indent sets the option to the width of actual characters in the first line of text of the paragraph text to follow.
Rule below	Same as above but preceded by <*rb.*
Drop cap	<*d(*charactercount,linecount*)>
Keep with next	<*kn1> turns on the feature ;, <*kn0> turns it off.
Keep together	<kt(A)> set the feature to Keep All lines together, while <kt(#,#)> sets it to begin and end on specific lines.

Style Sheet Definition	Code
Apply normal style sheet	@$:*paragraph text*
Apply no style sheet	@:*paragraph text*
Define a style sheet	@*stylesheetname*=<*paragraphattributes*>
Base a style sheet on another	@*stylesheetname*=[s*"based-onname"*] <*paragraphattributes*>
Apply a defined style sheet	@*stylesheetname:paragraph text*
Style definition	@*stylesheetname [s]* <*paragraphattributes*>

Special Characters	Code
New line (soft return)	<\n>
Discretionary return	<\d>
Hyphen	<\->
Indent here	<\i>
Right indent tab	<\t>
Standard space	<\s>
Figure space	<\f>
Punctuation space	<\p>
1/4-em space	<\q>
Discretionary hyphen	<\h>
Previous text box number character	<\2>
Current text box number character	<\3>
Next page text box number character	<\4>
New column	<\c>
New box	<\b>
Decimal ASCII code for character	<\#*decimalvalue*>
Indicator for Mac OS character set	<e0>
Indicator for Windows OS character set	<e1>
ISO Latin 1 character set	<e2>
@ symbol	<\@>
< symbol	<\<>
\ symbol	<\\>

6

TIP *The best way to generate sample tags to work with is by using your own example. Use the File | Save Text command to export your sample text as a XPress tags (XTG) document and examine the tags it creates.*

Text Management Tools

During the production and layout of your XPress documents, you may find it necessary to fine-tune the content or the appearance of text on your pages. For these types of tasks, XPress includes a powerful spell-checking engine, hyphenation tools, and Find/Change commands. Although the three features may at first seem only remotely connected, both dictionaries and H&J tables have a profound effect on how your text is read, and both may be customized for your particular document. Although Find/Change commands may not be customizable, they remain a critical tool set for managing and performing global changes to textual content and character properties in your document.

Using Dictionaries

It's shocking that many people using desktop publishing tools simply never check their document's spelling for accuracy. There's nothing worse than finding a spelling error in a document after it's been reproduced *en masse*. Equally shocking are the cases where a document is checked, but specialized words or spellings are missed. Both of these hazards may be overcome using spell-checking and custom dictionary features in XPress.

Spell-checking

XPress enables you to check your document in three ways. You may check either a selected word, your current story, or the entire document. If no type or text box is selected, the only option available is to check the entire document. To check a single word, select the word using the Content tool and choose Utilities | Spelling | Check Word (CTRL/CMD+W/L). To check all the text in your currently-selected text box, choose Utilities | Spelling | Check Story (CTRL/CMD+ALT/OPTION+W/L). To check all the text in each and every text box included in your XPress document, choose Utilities | Spelling | Check Document (CTRL/CMD+SHIFT+ALT/OPTION+W/L).

After spell-checking your text, XPress displays the results in the Word Count dialog box, as shown in the following illustration. The Word Count dialog box summarizes the number of characters and unique words in your document and indicates the number of words that are "suspect" and not found in the dictionary.

The purpose of the Word Count dialog box is to provide information only, and your choice for accepting this information is merely to press the OK button. If no suspect words are found, the dialog box simply closes and nothing further appears. But, if more than one suspect word is found, XPress opens the Check Story or Check Document dialog box, depending on the extent of your spell-check, as shown in the following illustration. Both dialog boxes include tools for looking up misspelled words and replacing or skipping the instance. When using the Replace button to replace misspelled words with Lookup results or entered characters, all instances of the word(s) are automatically replaced with your selection.

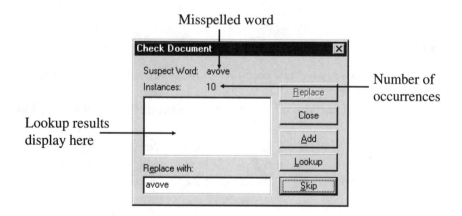

When reviewing the results of a spell-check, using the following keyboard shortcuts may speed your spell-checking operation:

To look up a suspect word	*ALT/CMD+L*
To skip a suspect word	*ALT/CMD+S*
To add a suspect word to your auxiliary dictionary	*ALT/CMD+A*

Auxiliary Dictionaries

If you have an auxiliary dictionary loaded and are reviewing the results of a spell-check in the Check Word | Story | Document dialog box, the Add button also becomes available. The Add button enables you to store the instance of the word in your own private dictionary file, which is called an auxiliary dictionary. If your Add button is unavailable, you have not yet specified an auxiliary dictionary. The auxiliary dictionary stores all words not found in the default dictionary, which is nonwritable. When XPress performs a spell-check and an auxiliary dictionary has been specified, the main dictionary is used in combination with the auxiliary dictionary to located misspelled words.

To specify an auxiliary dictionary, follow these steps:

1. With your document open, choose Utilities | Auxiliary Dictionary.

2. Locate the auxiliary dictionary you want to use by navigating to it and selecting it. Clicking OK loads the dictionary for use.

3. If you want to create a new dictionary, enter your new dictionary name in the File Name field and click the New button. The new dictionary is automatically created and loaded, although it currently contains no entries.

TIP ──────▶ *If you want XPress to check a document without using an auxiliary dictionary, but one is already loaded, choose Utilities | Auxiliary Dictionary to view the current dictionary in use and click the Close button.*

4. To add words to your auxiliary dictionary during a spell-check, simply click the Add button. XPress automatically adds the instance of your word in the case in which it appears.

5. To change or review the instances of words stored in your auxiliary dictionary, choose Utilities | Edit Auxiliary to open the Edit Auxiliary Dictionary dialog box shown in the following illustration.

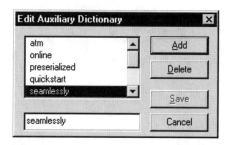

6. To add a word to the auxiliary dictionary, enter the new word in the field at the bottom-left of the dialog box and click the Add button.

7. Once you have finished your editing, click Save to save your dictionary changes and close the dialog box.

6

TIP *Spell-checking your document using the Utilities | Check Spelling | Check Document command will not check the text placed on master pages, nor will it check master page items on the pages of your document should they happen to be text. For this, you'll need to navigate to any master page and use the Utilities | Check Spelling | Masters (CTRL/CMD+ALT/OPTION+SHIFT+W/L) command. The Masters command automatically checks the spelling of all words in all text boxes on all master pages of your document, including those pages that contain text generated as master page items.*

Hyphenating Rules and Exceptions

When working in text, you may at some point need to hyphenate a word manually either to improve spacing or the readability of your text. If you happen to have a dictionary at your side, you probably have all the information you need, but looking up words repeatedly can be time-consuming. XPress includes a nifty little feature for suggesting the hyphenation of words. The feature is included in both its main and auxiliary dictionaries through use of the Suggested Hyphenation command. To use this command, click anywhere in the word you would like to look up and choose Utilities | Suggested Hyphenation (CTRL/CMD+H). XPress will display a dialog box containing the word including optional placement of hyphens, as shown in the following illustration.

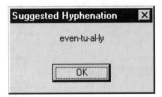

You may add your own hyphenation instances to XPress' hyphenation dictionary using the Hyphenation Exception feature. Adding hyphenated words to your hyphenation list is a similar operation to adding words to your auxiliary dictionary, as shown in the Hyphenation Exceptions dialog box in the following illustration. To open this dialog box, choose Utilities | Hyphenation Exceptions. Once you have added a word or two, click the Save button to store your changes and close the dialog box.

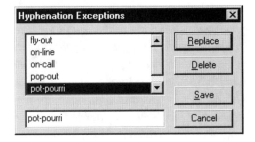

Using Find/Change Tools

XPress enables you to search for nearly anything in your text and change it to anything else. You won't find a search-and-replace feature more flexible than that. The Find/Change palette enables you to search for instances of character strings and replace them with other characters, as shown in the following illustration. A character string is any collection of characters in a sequence.

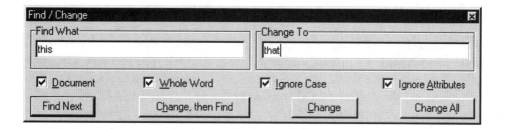

To open the Find/Change palette, choose Edit | Find/Change (CTRL/CMD+F). When open, the palette behaves much the same way as other palettes and floats on top of your document. You may still access your document and items on your page, and you may minimize or maximize the Find/Change palette by double-clicking its title bar. In brief state, the palette includes a field for entering Find What characters and a field for replacing them with Change To characters using the Find Next (or Find First when holding the ALT/OPTION key), Change Then Find, Change, or Change All command buttons. There are also options to search the entire document, search for whole words only, and ignore case.

The one option that changes the palette from a simple text search tool to a highly-complex search-and-replace tool is the Ignore Attributes option. Selecting *not* to ignore the attributes of the text you are searching for (or the text you want to change it to) causes the Find/Change palette to expand to encompass many text properties. Once expanded, as shown in the following illustration, you may choose any or all character attributes for Find What and Change To parameters.

To define the parameters for a search, enter your text in both the Find What and Change To sides of the palette. Choose the parameters you want to search for by clicking the check boxes opposite Text, Style Sheet, Font, Size, and Type Style. The Style Sheet drop-down menu contains only the styles that your document currently uses. The Find What side of the Font drop-down menu contains only a list of the fonts used in your document. Other than these two limitations, the sky's the limit. The Text fields on both the Find What and Change To sides of the palette are capable of searching for and replacing up to 80 characters at a time.

Behind the scenes, XPress searches for combinations of text strings, and character and paragraph attributes in the form of tags. Once the text is located, the tags are examined to match the selected options. The only properties that may not be specified individually are color and shade for character attributes, although these are also attributes of the styles you may choose to search for.

Text Searches

You may search for and replace any character in your document. Each time you enter text in the Find What side of the palette, you limit your search parameters to the characters themselves and not their attributes. Each time you select an additional attribute, the search becomes more specific.

For example, to search and replace text in your document, simply enter existing characters in the Find What Text field, enter the replacement characters in the Change To Text field, and click Find. Once the first instance is found, the remaining command buttons become available, enabling you to proceed either by examining each instance with the Change | Then Find button, or simply changing the text using the Change button. You may also change all instances in the entire document by pressing the Change All button. To close the palette click the Close button in its title bar.

Text and Attributes Searches

When changing text by attributes, you have the option of searching for and replacing identical character strings using different attributes.

For example, search for the term "pot pourri" (which often appears in italic style) and leave the attributes unchecked on the Find What side. Enter the same text on the Change To side or uncheck the Text field on the Change To side, but specify an italic type style by clicking the Italic button in the Type Style options twice (clicking it once makes it indeterminate). Clicking Find First, and then Change All results in each instance of "pot pourri" being changed to italic—no matter what it was previously. You may build on this process by creating a special character style for the Find/Change process and applying color and shade properties if that's what your design calls for.

Find/Change Strategies

It helps to use your imagination when formulating search-and-replace strategies. Some of these strategies may even involve two- to five-step operations when searching for specific instances of text while trying to exclude others. For example, if you want to change all instances of double paragraph returns to single paragraph returns except where four paragraph returns occur, your search operation will involve three steps. The first step is to exclude the four returns. For this, you would need to change them to a unique character string, such as three tildes (~~~). The second step is to change the double returns to single returns, and the last step is to change the three tildes back to four returns, as in the following steps:

	Find What	Change To
Step 1	\p\p\p\p	~~~
Step 2	\p\p	\p
Step 3	~~~	p\p\p\p\

The same type of multistep process applies to any exclusion. To make things easier in this regard, XPress enables you to search for and replace any of the invisible or soft characters that occur in your text. The following list may serve as a guide for searching for and replacing wildcard and soft characters:

Search/Change Character	Press Shortcut	Result/Code
Any character (wildcard, Find only)	CTRL/CMD+?	\?
Tab	CTRL/CMD+TAB	\t
New paragraph	CTRL/CMD+RETURN	\p
New line	CTRL/CMD+SHIFT+RETURN	\n
New column	CTRL/CMD+ENTER	\c

Search/Change Character	Press Shortcut	Result/Code
New text box	CTRL/CMD+SHIFT+ENTER	\b
Previous box page #	CTRL/CMD+2	\2
Current box page #	CTRL/CMD+3	\3
Next box page #	CTRL/CMD+4	\4
Punctuation space	CTRL/CMD+.	\.
Flex space	CTRL/CMD+SHIFT+F	\f
Backslash	CTRL/CMD+\	\\

Conclusion

If working with text is your business and livelihood, you'll appreciate the topics covered in the last few dozen pages. In this chapter you have learned the essentials of working with text in XPress, beginning with getting text on your page to setting paragraph attributes and styles, and on through to using tags and text management tools. If you've followed closely, you're more than ready for putting some of this knowledge to work in XPress.

But before you venture too far into your layouts, there's still the issue of pictures. Although many documents feature text as the only form of communication, design often entails working with graphics or digital photographs. XPress includes some interesting features for importing, manipulating, and managing these pictures. *Chapter 7, Working with Pictures* takes a slight holiday from text for a basic journey into handling pictures in your XPress documents.

CHAPTER 7

Adding and Controlling Pictures

Preparing a layout or design using text only is quickly becoming a thing of the past. Everybody wants pictures on their page, whether they choose to use quick clip art graphics or professional-style photographs. XPress enables you to work with a variety of picture formats, and adjust or control their appearance in various ways. From an editorial standpoint, adding pictures to a layout often stimulates visual interest; from a creative perspective, pictures often open doors to nearly limitless design opportunities.

XPress classifies pictures differently than other layout applications. The properties of your pictures can range greatly depending on how they are prepared. XPress considers a picture to be anything from a single-color graphic to a full-color digital photograph, and all permutations between. Certain options for altering or changing the appearance of pictures can depend on their file format. It's tricky business, especially when you consider that the pictures you are using in your document may originate from a variety of sources, such as your favorite graphic illustration or bitmap editing programs.

In this chapter, you'll begin by discovering how to get pictures on your page. You'll learn to use XPress' picture box tools, and you'll get some hands-on experience in examining, altering, and controlling their properties. You'll also learn the ins and outs of working with the various picture formats, and find out about their strengths and weaknesses.

Get a Picture onto Your Page

Pictures must reside within picture boxes in order to exist on your page. So, getting a picture onto your page requires that you create a picture box first, using any of the seven picture box tools available. As you'll soon discover, these tools each enable you to create different picture box shapes. If deciding which type of picture box to use becomes a barrier to getting started, rest assured you can change your picture box to nearly any shape you want even after you've created it and loaded a picture.

To quickly get a picture onto your page, follow these steps:

1. In an open document, choose any picture box tool from the Tool palette. Picture box tools may be identified by the *X* symbol they contain. After the tool is selected, notice your cursor changes to a crosshair.

2. Using the same action as you would to create a text box, drag diagonally across your page to define the new picture box size, and then release the mouse. Notice a new picture box appears on your page, and when guides are showing (F7) this box contains diagonal lines joining the corners (even if your picture box isn't rectangular).

3. Choose File | Get Picture (CTRL/CMD+E) to open the Get Picture dialog box.

4. Locate the folder containing your picture and click it once to select it. Notice information about the file appears in the lower part of the dialog box, as shown in the following illustration. When using the Windows version of Xpress, you may use the Files of Type drop-down menu to limit the display of picture formats to the specific file format of your picture. Otherwise, leave the selection at the default All Picture Files selection.

7

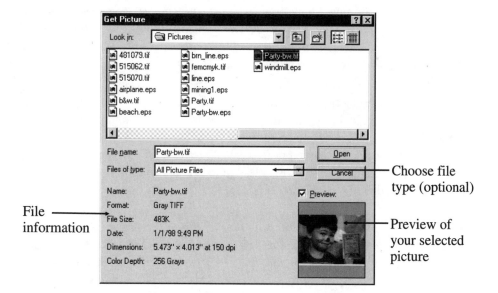

File information

Choose file type (optional)

Preview of your selected picture

5. If the Preview option isn't selected already, choose it now. Notice a small representation of the image appears in the preview window. Using the Preview option is a quick way to check that you are selecting the correct picture.

6. Click Open to import the picture and close the dialog box. Notice your picture now appears in the picture box you created.

7. If you don't see the complete picture in the picture box, don't be alarmed—it's there all right. The dimensions of your picture may simply be larger than the picture box you created. XPress automatically places pictures in their originally-prepared size, and aligns them with the upper-left corner of the picture box. To see the complete picture, choose the Content or Item tool from the Tool palette and with your picture box still selected, press CTRL/CMD+ALT/OPTION+SHIFT+F to resize the picture to automatically fit the picture box.

TIP To delete a picture from a picture box, choose the Content tool, select the picture by clicking it once, and press the BACKSPACE/DELETE key. To replace a picture box's content with a different picture, repeat the import process by selecting the picture box, choosing the Get Picture (CTRL/CMD+E) command, and opening another picture. The new picture simply replaces the preceding one. To delete the picture box and its contents, choose the Item tool, select the picture box, and press the BACKSPACE/DELETE key.

Now that your picture is there, you may want to perform any number of operations next, including sizing the picture or its box, positioning it on your page, and applying properties to integrate it into your layout. All these operations are covered in the pages to follow, but it may help to do a little investigation first into what the other picture box tools enable you to do, and to look more closely at the inherent properties of your picture box content.

TIP When importing a picture using the Get Picture command, you may change the color depth of the picture as it appears in your XPress document without changing the original picture itself by pressing certain command keys while clicking the Open button. For more information on changing a picture's color depth on import, see Changing Picture Color Depth *in Chapter 8, Advanced Picture Strategies.*

Using Picture Box Tools

When you create a picture box, essentially what you are doing is creating a container to house your picture. But there's a more logical way of looking at it. A picture box may also be thought of as a sort of "viewing window" through which you may see the pictures. In XPress, this window can be nearly any shape you want, depending on the requirements of your layout or creative needs. Once the window has been created using picture box tools, it may be altered or transformed later on, but when first creating the window's shape, seven tools offer the convenience of preset shapes or effects, as shown in Figure 7-1.

- **Rectangle** This picture box tool creates a picture box with four straight sides joined by four corners at 90-degree angles. Holding SHIFT while creating or resizing a rectangular picture box creates a perfect square.

- **Rounded-corner** This tool creates a picture box similar to the Rectangle picture box, only with uniformly-rounded corners that may be set to a specific corner radius within a range between 0 and 2 inches. Holding SHIFT while creating or resizing a Rectangle picture box constrains its width and depth to equal dimensions.

7

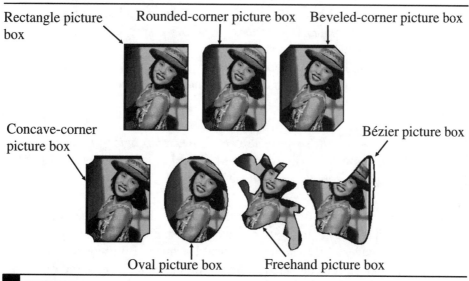

Rectangle picture box

Rounded-corner picture box

Beveled-corner picture box

Concave-corner picture box

Bézier picture box

Oval picture box

Freehand picture box

FIGURE 7-1 Each of the seven picture box tools results in a different shape

■ **Oval**   The Oval picture box tool is used for creating oval or circular-shaped picture boxes. Holding SHIFT while creating or resizing an Oval picture box constrains its width and depth to equal dimensions, resulting in a perfect circle.

■ **Concave-corner**   The Concave-corner picture box tool creates boxes with rounded corners that face inwards, essentially the opposite of rounded-corner boxes. Concave corners may be set to a specific corner radius within a range between 0 and 2 inches. Holding SHIFT while creating or resizing a Concave-corner picture box constrains its width and depth to equal dimensions.

■ **Beveled-corner**   The Beveled-corner picture box tool creates boxes with flattened corners. Beveled corners may be set to a specific corner radius within a range between 0 and 2 inches. Holding SHIFT while creating or resizing a beveled-corner picture box constrains its width and depth to equal dimensions.

■ **Freehand**   Using the Freehand and Bézier picture box tools is unlike using any of XPress' other picture box tools. The Freehand and Bézier picture box shapes must be drawn or traced, as opposed to simply clicking-and-dragging a preset shape. The Freehand picture box tool enables you literally to freehand draw your new picture box directly on your screen. While in Freehand mode, clicking-and-dragging your mouse button creates the contour of the box's shape. Freehand picture boxes must exist as closed shapes, so no matter where you finish drawing your Freehand picture box shape, the result will be a closed box. Beginning and end points are automatically joined when you release the mouse button.

TIP　　　➤ *You may change the shape of a selected picture box quickly from one picture shape to another by choosing Item | Shape, and then selecting one of the preset shapes from the pop-out menu.*

■ **Bézier**   Creating a Bézier picture box is done much the same as creating Bézier lines and points. Bézier picture boxes are created point by point, each joined by either a straight or curved segment. Both segments and points may be controlled using Bézier editing tools. Bézier picture boxes must exist as closed shapes, so the beginning and end points of your Bézier picture box shape are joined automatically. When drawing Bézier picture boxes, holding the SHIFT key while creating points constrains segment angles to 45 and 90 degrees.

NOTE *The shapes created with picture box tools are virtually identical to those created with text box tools, and the same standard constraining conventions also apply. When creating or resizing Rectangle, Rounded-corner, Oval, Beveled-corner, or Concave-corner picture boxes with your mouse, holding the SHIFT key constrains the picture box to an equal width and height.*

TIP *For more information on using Bézier drawing tools, see* Drawing with Béziers *in* Chapter 5, Using Drawing Tools.

Working with Picture Formats

If working with various types of picture formats is completely new to you, you're about to have a crash course in all the different types of graphic and digital formats out there. There is certainly no shortage of format types, the majority of them being bitmap in nature. Although this section defines types of formats, many capabilities of these formats depend on the characteristics of the image in question, the application used to create it, and how it is prepared and saved.

7

Graphics Versus Digital Photos

As mentioned earlier, XPress considers any image that can be placed into a picture box a picture. A picture may be any of the following images:

- A graphic, such as a logo

- An illustration

- A map or diagram

- A fancy separator or border pattern

- A graphical drop cap

- A fancy graphical bullet

- A design icon

- A digital photograph

- A texture background

With this many variables it's no wonder that pictures may come from a variety of programs and be prepared in a variety of conditions or file formats. Certain picture types work well in vector-file formats; others work well as bitmaps. A vector-style picture may be a graphic symbol or illustration that is composed of line and pattern information, while bitmap images usually take the form of digital photographs and textures—although these rules are not hard and fast. Virtually any image may be prepared in bitmap format.

The various file formats influence how the picture may appear or be reproduced, while the picture itself may feature varying degrees of resolution and color. To a large degree, the level of color in your picture will determine how much control you have over it in XPress. You'll have more control with bitmap formats and less with vector illustrations. But before we explore color and its capabilities in XPress, let's look more closely at what bitmap and vector art is, and the file formats compatible with XPress.

Bitmap Formats

A bitmap is a file format that contains dot patterns measured in resolution values. Resolution is the measure of dot detail that displays and prints your digital image.

In the Windows version of Xpress, bitmap image types compatible with XPress are selected using the Get Picture | Files of Type drop-down menu. In Macintosh versions, all picture file types for which necessary import filters are installed are shown. File types include specific import filters for the following files:

- **Bitmap files (BMP, RLE, DIB)**   These three bitmap formats may be imported into Xpress using a single filter, including standard uncompressed bitmaps (BMP), and bitmap images compressed using run-length encoding (RLE) and DIB compression.

- **PCX files (PCX)**   PC Paintbrush is one of the image editing programs developed by Microsoft and is a standard format for preparing bitmap images.

- **GIF files (GIF)**   The graphical interchange format (GIF, sometimes pronounced "giff") was originally developed for CompuServe, the first commercial online service in wide use. GIF files have become a standard format for graphic and digital images in web site design on the World Wide Web. By their nature, GIF files only support up to 256 individual colors.

- **Windows Metafile (WMF)** This file format is still widely supported by illustration and bitmap editing programs. The WMF format is capable of supporting both vector and bitmap images in the same file.

- **TIFF files (TIF)** The tagged image file format (TIFF) bitmap was one of the first formats developed for preparing and printing digital images for desktop applications. It remains one of the most popular and widely supported. TIFF files support a wide range of color and resolution values.

- **Mac PICT files (PCT)** The Mac PICT file format is still one of the standards on the Macintosh platform; it is capable of supporting both bitmap and vector objects in a single file. The PICT format is well known for its compression strengths.

- **Scitex CT files (SCT, CT)** If you're using Scitex CT (continuous tone) image files, you're using one of the first high-end file formats designed for handling a variety of sophisticated, multi-ink image files. Scitex files often include their own built-in color trapping properties prepared using dedicated Scitex *file-RIPping* software and workstations.

- **JPEG files (JPG)** If you work in web design, you may be aware already of the intricacies of the JPEG (pronounced "jay-peg") format. The JPEG format was originally developed and standardized by the Joint Photographers Expert Group. As you might have guessed, it is specifically geared toward reproducing accurate digital picture quality with the smallest possible file size using varying degrees of compression. The JPEG format is prized for its compression capabilities and has become a virtual standard in web page design.

- **Kodak PhotoCD (PCD)** This format is owned by Kodak, which developed it originally for the purposes of compressing high-quality scanned images for viewing on proprietary home video systems. Because of its relatively low cost and highly-controlled image quality, PhotoCD has slowly been adopted as a method for scanning and distributing desktop images and stock or royalty-free digital images.

Each of these picture import formats has its own characteristics and properties. When imported into XPress using the Get Picture command, the import operation is seamless, meaning that no further import options are offered. The color and resolution information in the picture file is interpreted, and then the picture is loaded and displayed in your new picture box in the same format it was saved in. This may not be the case for other types of files, as you'll discover in the next section.

PostScript Formats

If your image is based mostly on vector objects, it's more than likely that the encapsulated PostScript (EPS) file format has been used to prepare it. Adobe, the creator of PostScript language, has continually upgraded and improved the capabilities of PostScript as print technology advances. Over the years, EPS has become a standard for printing and preparing images destined for PostScript-compatible printers. PostScript language supports both bitmap and vector objects. A PostScript file may be a simple graphic or a completely self-contained page with crop and registration marks.

One of the key things to keep in mind when working with EPS files in picture boxes is that what you see on your screen is merely a representation—or *header* image of the EPS file. Incorporating a header into the EPS file enables anyone working with the file to see exactly what it contains. But headers are bitmap format files, meaning they can take any form of bitmap the creator of the image desires. The two main characteristics of previews are resolution measured in dots per inch (DPI) and color.

Headers are often kept crude—or eliminated altogether—in order to reduce the overall size of EPS files. The lower the resolution and the less color depth in the header, the less memory it will require. If you import an EPS file onto your page and all you see is a gray box where the picture should be, the header may have been left off the file, so what you are seeing is the overall bounding box of the image. If you see a crude representation in black and white, the image may be in black and white, grayscale, or even full-color, depending on how the header was originally prepared. The following illustration indicates how various headers appear on your page when imported into picture boxes.

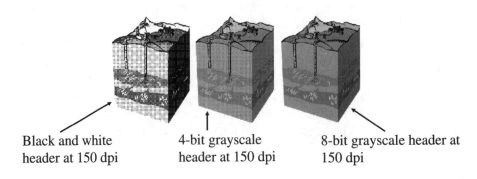

Black and white
header at 150 dpi

4-bit grayscale
header at 150 dpi

8-bit grayscale header at
150 dpi

Bitmap and Vector Color

Bitmaps also come in a variety of levels of color including 1-bit, 2-bit, 4-bit, 8-bit, 24-bit, and 32-bit color levels. When it comes to describing color in bitmaps, black is also considered a color. These color levels range from 1-bit black-and-white images to 32-bit full-color CMYK color. The letters *CMYK* represents the standard four-color process inks—cyan (blue), magenta (red), yellow, and black—used in traditional printing in order to closely reproduce color pictures.

Another level of color you'll encounter in bitmap images is *gray*, or, *grayscale*. Grayscale color divides a single color into 256 individual shades, none of which necessarily is gray. Grayscale color is simply a standardized method of measuring the shades of a single color, and it is commonly used in reproducing single-color digital images in print, such as black-and-white photographs.

The color model on which a picture is based determines the level of color the bitmap is capable of supporting. Color models represent the way in which a bitmap's color is measured. For example, CMYK is a color model because it measures color broken into four ink colors, each of which is based on a percentage of ink. Several color models used in XPress are standards in the digital image world:

- Red, green, blue (RGB)

- Hue, saturation, brightness (HSB)

- Luminescence values A and B (LAB)

The colors in your digital image may have been created and measured using any of the preceding models. Although these color models are mostly used for display and manipulation of color in images, the printing of your images is done using ink colors such as spot and process color. Spot colors are premixed ink printing colors that may reproduce certain parts or all of your digital image. Ink is a product manufactured by several companies around the world, and each ink company has its own catalog of ink colors identified using the manufacturers' own numbering system. XPress supports process and spot color ink specifications and catalogs from Pantone, TOYO, DIC, Trumatch, Focoltone, and Hexachrome. Spot colors are displayed on your screen using standard red, green, blue (RGB) colors, but when printed, they reproduce in the specified ink color.

For more information on colors in pictures and in your document, see *Chapter 13, Working in Color.*

Managing Picture Boxes

Once you have a picture box on your page, you may want to do any number of things first in order to begin fitting the box into your layout. As you'll soon discover, moving a picture box must be done using the correct tools. Picture boxes may be gradually moved around your page or document in a number of ways, or they may be moved instantly using dialog box options or the features on the Measurements palette.

Moving Picture Boxes

Perhaps the most natural way to move a picture box is by grabbing it with the Item tool and dragging it into position. As with other objects, the Item tool is the only tool that enables you to do this interactively. In keeping with standard constrain conventions, holding the SHIFT key while dragging a picture box enables you to constrain it to vertical or horizontal movement.

To move a picture box using the Item tool, follow these steps:

1. With a picture box created on your page, choose the Item tool from the Tool palette, or, to temporarily select the Item tool while using any other tool, hold the CTRL/CMD key.

2. Click-and-drag the picture box in any direction. Notice as you drag the picture box a dotted line appears on your screen to indicate the new picture box position. If your Snap to Guides option (SHIFT+F7) is activated, you may also notice the picture box snaps when it nears a ruler or guideline.

3. Release the mouse button once your picture is in position and the operation is complete.

4. To experience the action of constraining, perform the preceding steps while holding the SHIFT key. Notice your initial mouse movement determines whether the constraining action is horizontal or vertical.

Moving pictures with the Item tool can be a quick way of setting its position, but when you need to move the picture box very short and precise distances, you may also use the nudge keys. Nudge movement is accomplished by pressing the UP, DOWN, LEFT, or RIGHT ARROW keys on your keyboard while both your Item tool and the picture box are selected. Each time a nudge key is pressed while the Item tool is in use, the picture is moved by 1 point. Holding the ALT/OPTION key while pressing a nudge key moves the picture box by 0.1 points, making picture placement with nudge keys highly accurate.

Picture Box Size and Position

The physical width and height of your picture box may be set using the Modify (CTRL/CMD+M) | Box tab dialog box options shown in the following illustraton. The Origin Across and Origin Down fields enable you to enter exact page positions for the upper-left corner of your picture box, and the Width and Height fields enable you to enter the exact dimensions of your picture box, also measured from the upper-left corner.

Origins set your picture box page positions

Width and Height options set picture box dimensions

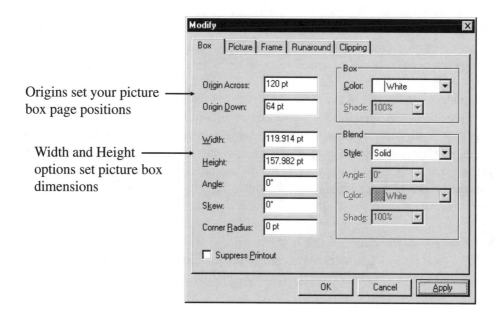

Setting the position and size of Rectangle picture boxes might be considered straightforward, but when working with picture boxes that are not rectangular in shape—such as Oval, Freehand, or Bézier picture boxes—the measurements become a little trickier. In these cases, the upper-left corner of the picture box is measured from the upper-left corner of its bounding box, which is indicated by the top-left picture box handle.

To size a picture and its picture box simultaneously, hold the CTRL/CMD button while resizing the picture box with one of its corner handles.

Picture Box Rotation and Skew

Should your layout or design call for such an effect, XPress enables you to apply rotation and skew effects to picture boxes. Picture boxes may be rotated or skewed using the Angle and Skew options in the Modify | Box tab dialog box. Applying a rotation value in the Angle field rotates the picture box and its contents around the center origin of the picture box within 360 degrees. Entering positive values in the Angle field rotates the box counterclockwise; entering negative values rotates it clockwise. After a rotation has been applied, you may return the picture box to its upright orientation by entering 0 in the Angle field.

A more interactive method of rotating picture boxes is through use of the Rotation tool in the Tool palette. Using the Rotation tool has advantages over simply entering values in the Angle field of the Modify dialog box in that it enables you to freely rotate the picture box around a point anywhere on your document page. For detailed directions on using the Rotation tool, see *Key XPress Tools to Master* in *Chapter 2, After Getting Started.*

The Skew option enables you to apply a horizontal "slant" to picture boxes and their contents. The advantage of applying skew to picture boxes is it avoids the need to convert the boxes to other shapes such as Bézier or freehand in order to distort their shape. And, using Skew values, you may achieve interesting effects by actually distorting the picture's contents. As with rotation, skew effects are reversible, meaning you may return the picture box and its contents to normal.

To edit the shape of a picture box without distorting its contents, use either the Item or Content tool to change the position of the picture box handles. The Item | Shape commands may also be used to change the shape of items without altering their contents.

The Skew value you apply must fall within a range between -75 and 75 degrees, where positive values skew to the right, and negative values skew to the left. Skew values are applied based on the center position of the picture's bounding box. The overall width and height values remain constant, but with skew applied, the bounding box of the picture changes to become wider, as shown in the following example.

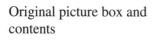 Original picture box and contents

Picture box and contents with 50-degree Skew value applied

7

Picture Box Color and Blend

The Modify | Box tab dialog box also enables you to apply color to the background of your picture boxes in much the same manner as for text boxes. Colors may be chosen from the drop-down menu, and a Shade value may be applied using any value between 0 and 100 percent. Blend styles and colors are applied in the same manner by making a selection from the Style drop-down menu and setting an Angle, Color, and Shade value for the secondary Blend color.

TIP ➡️ *Picture box color may also be applied to your picture's background using the Colors palette (F12). To apply a color background, select the picture, click the Background Color button, and click your desired color and shade. You may also apply a background by dragging a color from the palette directly onto your picture—without selecting it first.*

When setting Color and Blend properties to picture boxes, the color is applied to the actual area of the picture box itself wherever the content leaves a space or gap between the edge of the image and the picture's frame. This area is sometimes referred to as the picture box *background*. For example, if you apply a picture box color of Black at a shade of 20 percent to a square image imported into a circular picture box, the background shows through as 20 percent black wherever the background is visible, as shown in the following illustration.

Edge of picture

Edge of picture frame

20 percent black

Background area of picture box

> TIP   *To make the space or gap between the picture box content and the frame of your picture box transparent, choose None from the Color drop-down menu. Any items behind the picture box will show through the gap between the edges of your image and the picture box frame.*

On the other hand, applying the Color and Blend effects to picture boxes opens up several creative but confusing issues. First and foremost, setting a picture box color does not affect the actual content of a picture box in a straightforward way. How color affects the picture box's content is determined by the color depth of the imported picture. When applying color to the background of a picture box containing a full-color image, the image itself is unaffected by the background color. However, if you import a black-and-white (line art), 4-bit grayscale, or 8-bit grayscale image, the background color will show through and actually affect the image's color.

For an exploration into the effects that can be achieved by applying color backgrounds to black-and-white and grayscale images, see *Color in Picture Boxes* in *Chapter 8, Advanced Picture Strategies,* and in the color insert of this book.

Setting Corner Radius

The Corner Radius option is set through the Modify I Box tab dialog box in much the same way as for text boxes. The value entered in the Corner Radius field must fall within a range between 0 and 2 inches. When Freehand or Bézier picture boxes are selected, the Corner Radius option is unavailable in the Modify dialog box.

Picture Boxes via the Measurements Palette

Although any of the properties associated with picture boxes may be set using the Modify I Box tab dialog box, the Measurements palette (F9) provides more access and convenience for the user, and effectively adopting its use will undoubtedly speed your production time. Only the most commonly-changed picture box properties are included in the palette, including Origin Across, Origin Down, Width, Height, Angle, and Corner Radius options, as shown in the following illustration. The functionality of these options is identical to those in the Modify I Box tab dialog box.

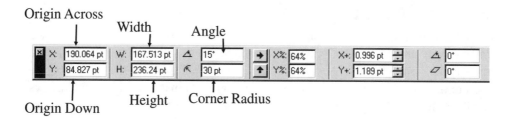

Origin Across   Width   Angle

Origin Down   Height   Corner Radius

Working with Pictures *Inside* Boxes

Now that you understand how the properties of the picture container may be controlled, next comes the important part. Let's examine how XPress enables you to set the properties of your picture box's *content*. You may apply nearly all the same properties to your picture content as you may with the picture box itself—independent of the box it resides in. Once again, there are several ways to apply these properties, but first let's examine the complete set of controls available through the Modify (CTRL/CMD+M) | Picture tab dialog box, shown in the following illustration.

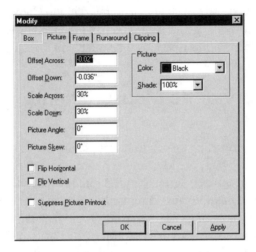

Picture Offset and Scale

Moving your picture around inside of your picture box is perhaps done most interactively and conveniently using the Content tool. With a picture box selected, the Content tool turns to a grabber hand cursor enabling you to grab and drag the picture within its box. You may also move a picture within the box using nudge keys. While both your Content tool and picture box are selected, the UP, DOWN, LEFT, and RIGHT ARROW keys act to nudge the picture within its box. Pressing a nudge key moves your picture 1 point in a given direction, and holding ALT/OPTION and pressing a nudge key moves the picture 0.1 points.

When you drag or nudge a picture within its box, you are actually changing its offset measures, which may be set precisely by entering values in the Offset Across and Offset Down fields of the Modify (CTRL/CMD+M) | Picture tab dialog box. Both the Offset Across and Offset Down measures may only be set to the maximum width and height dimensions of the picture box. In other words, you can make your picture box contents seem to disappear by entering the maximum offset values.

Scaling pictures within picture boxes could easily be considered the most commonly-used command next to sizing picture boxes themselves. Pictures are seldomly digitally prepared in their exact published dimensions and cropping. In fact, because of its visual flexibility, a picture's size and cropping is often used as a technique for tailoring the fit of text into a layout.

QuarkXPress 4 IN ACTION

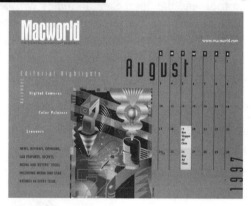

Design: Elaine Chu

Firm: Elaine Chu Graphic Design, 748 Oakland Ave., #302, Oakland, CA 94611 (Phone) 510 547-7705, (Fax) 510 597-1087, e-mail egchu@aol.com

Illustrator: Steve Lyon

Client: *Macworld* magazine

Description: Macworld monthly calendar postcard

Created for Macworld magazine, this monthly calendar postcard was mailed out to Macworld's advertisers to remind them of the close dates and to preview upcoming editorial highlights. The EPS illustration was imported into the Quark layout. The piece printed in process colors. For the background type, I made a color palette in Quark, using CMYK screen builds which supported the illustrator's palette. It was easy to rotate type or reverse it out to white against a strong color background to achieve maximum visual impact. The direct mail piece received positive response both at Macworld, and from their advertisers

7

Getting your picture into the size and cropping you need for your layout is an operation that requires more than one tool or command, and often relies on simple common sense. Ideally, you will have already set your picture box in position on your page and integrated it into your layout. The tool you will work with much of the time is the Content tool, and the quickest commands will be through keyboard shortcuts. The Content tool enables you to control the offset of your picture (its position within the picture box); keyboard commands for fitting, centering, or scaling enable you to control the remaining variables.

The following keyboard shortcuts apply for scaling and positioning pictures in boxes:

Fit picture to box (nonproportionately)	CTRL/CMD+SHIFT+F
Fit picture to box (proportionately)	CTRL/CMD+/ALT/OPTION+SHIFT+F
Center picture within box	CTRL/CMD+SHIFT+M
Increase size by 5 percent	CTRL/CMD+ALT/OPTION+SHIFT+>
Decrease size by 5 percent	CTRL/CMD+ALT/OPTION+SHIFT+<

Picture Rotation and Skew

While your picture is inside its picture box, you may also apply Rotation and Skew effects. These effects may be applied independent of the picture box using Picture Angle and Picture Skew options in the Modify | Picture tab dialog box. The picture's angle may be rotated 360 degrees in either a clockwise or counterclockwise direction, and the picture's skew may be slanted to the left or right within a range between -75 and 75 degrees. The following illustration shows the Rotation and Skew effects applied to a picture.

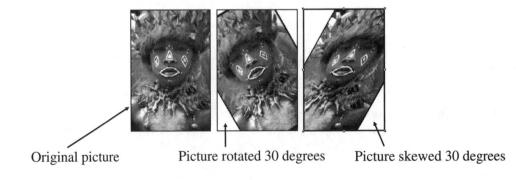

Original picture   Picture rotated 30 degrees   Picture skewed 30 degrees

Picture Color

Applying color to your picture changes the color of the picture itself without affecting the picture box background or frame. The picture you choose to apply the color to must be either in black-and-white or grayscale in order for color options to be available—pictures that already feature inherent color or are in any file format other than bitmap may not be affected by these options.

TIP *Color may also be applied to pictures using the Colors palette (F12). To apply a color, select the picture, click the Picture Color button on the palette, and click your desired color and shade. Color changes are immediate when you use the Colors palette. You may also apply a picture color by dragging a color from the palette directly onto your picture without selecting it first.*

Color is applied using the Color and Shade options in the Modify | Picture tab dialog box. The Color option enables you to set black-and-white or grayscale images to print in a color other than black with any of the colors available to you in XPress. Or, you may simply set the picture to appear in black, but limit its appearance to a shade of black based on a percentage of the original picture's tones. To apply a color, simply choose a color from the Color drop-down menu and apply a shade by selecting a percent value from the Shade drop-down menu. The following illustration shows a grayscale picture set to various shades of black.

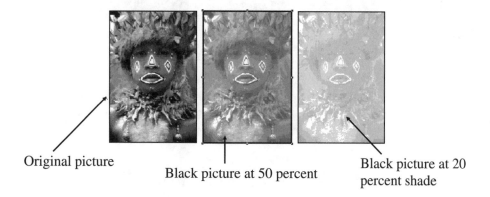

Original picture

Black picture at 50 percent

Black picture at 20 percent shade

Flipping and Flopping Pictures

The terms *flipping* and *flopping* stem from the days when traditional film halftones were assembled by hand during film-stripping operations in the preparation of material to be printed. To flip a picture used to mean the film representing the picture would be turned over vertically, essentially turning the picture upside down. The term *flop* referred to simply turning the film over—without rotating it—and because film was transparent, the result was a mirror image of the picture. To lessen the confusion, these two terms were simplified to simply *flip*.

Pictures are often flipped in order to conform to the layout and design convention that all pictures should ideally face into the textual content they relate to. XPress enables you to flip pictures vertically and horizontally for this and other purposes with the simple selection of an option or click of a button. Flipping options affect the picture itself without affecting the picture box containing the picture. They are set using the Modify | Picture tab dialog box options for Flip Horizontal and Flip Vertical, the effects of which are shown in the following illustration. You may apply one or both of these options to pictures, or return the picture to its normal state by deselecting the options.

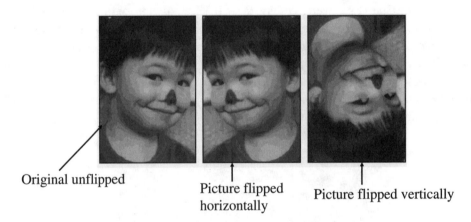

Original unflipped

Picture flipped horizontally

Picture flipped vertically

TIP ➤ *To flip pictures vertically or horizontally without the reader catching on, be sure there are no recognizable features in the picture such as text, landmarks, or characteristic facial features.*

Pictures via the Measurements Palette

Although any of the properties associated with pictures may be set using the Modify | Picture tab dialog box, the Measurements palette (F9) may be more convenient. The palette contains only the most commonly changed picture properties, including the Scale Across, Scale Down, Offset Across, Offset Down, Picture Angle, and

Picture Skew options, as shown in the following illustration. The functionality of these options is identical to those in the Modify | Picture tab dialog box.

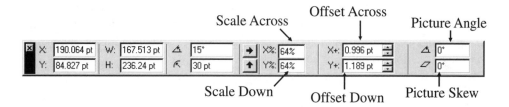

Scale Across   Offset Across   Picture Angle

Scale Down   Offset Down   Picture Skew

Controlling the Picture Frame

The properties you may apply to your picture frame are identical to those found in other frame-related property dialog boxes and may be set using the Modify | Frame tab dialog box, as shown in the following illustration. To access these options quickly, select the picture to which you want to apply frame properties, select the picture, and press CTRL/CMD+B. The Width, Style, Frame Color and Shade, and Gap Color and Shade options may be applied to picture frames.

7

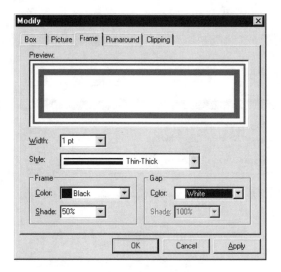

For more information on applying frame options to items such as picture frames, see *Setting Line Styles* in *Chapter 5, Using Drawing Tools.*

Getting Information About Pictures

As you go through the process of importing and integrating pictures into your layout, you may find it useful to know that XPress enables you to obtain a complete report of all the pictures you have used in your document. You may use the Usage command to obtain detailed information about individual pictures and even locate pictures in your layout automatically.

The Usage Command

The Usage command is an invaluable tool for working with documents that contain any number of pictures in any of the formats compatible with XPress. To use the Usage command to obtain a summary of the status of pictures in your document, choose Utilities | Usage to open the Usage dialog box, and then click the Pictures tab (SHIFT+F2/OPTION+F13). As the Usage dialog box opens, it examines each picture in your document and quickly summarizes its status in a table-style window, as shown in the following illustration. The summary includes information on whether the picture is selected to print , the picture's file name and path, the page it is located on, the type of file representing the picture, and its status.

Print drop-down menu

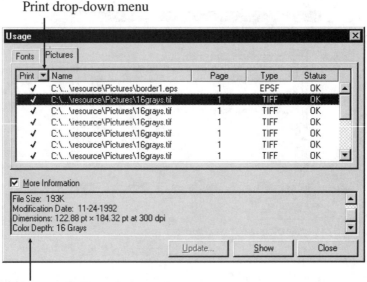

Selected picture information

- **Print** A check mark in the Print column indicates the picture is currently selected to Print. The Print option may be set in the Modify (CTRL/CMD+M) | Picture tab dialog box by choosing the Suppress Picture Printout option when setting other properties for your pictures, but you may also change this option here by clicking the picture listing and selecting either Yes or No from the Print drop-down menu. Turning off the Print option for pictures is often used to reduce printing time when printing text-only proofs of documents.

- **Name** The Name column lists the name and brief path location of the picture when it was first imported into your document. By default, XPress simply links to picture files instead of storing all the data that represents them. Pictures that are embedded or linked to your document are indicated using the terms *embedded object* or *linked object*. Embedded objects are objects whose source information is stored in your XPress document, while linked objects are those that must be accessed externally and referenced by XPress in order to be printed properly. Linking and embedding is a function of OLE (object linking and embedding) commands specific to the Windows operating system. In the Macintosh version of Xpress, the Publish and Subscribe feature performs a similar function.

- **Page** The Page column indicates the page number on which the picture has been imported. The page number corresponds to the page numbers set in your XPress document layout. In the Windows version of Xpress, the abbreviation *PB* in the Page column indicates the picture currently resides on the pasteboard of your document. In the Macintosh version, a dagger symbol next to the page number indicates the item is on the pasteboard.

- **Type** This column indicates the type of file format the picture has been prepared in. For example, TIFF indicates an imported tagged image bitmap file and EPSF/EPS indicates an imported encapsulated PostScript file.

- **Status** The status of the picture file is listed in this column as either OK, Modified, or Missing. A Modified status indicates that something may have changed in the original picture file since it was imported, because the last-modified date on the file has changed. A Missing status indicates that when the Usage command performed an examination of all links to all picture files, the original picture file was not found and may have been moved or deleted.

7

The Usage dialog box features button commands for getting more information, and for updating and locating picture files in your document. Clicking the More Information option expands the dialog box to reveal detailed information about your selected picture, including the file name and its complete path, the memory size of the file, its last modification date, width (first measure) and height (second measure) dimensions, resolution (for bitmap files only), and color depth (again—bitmap files only).

The Update button is only available when files have either Modified or Missing status. Clicking the Update button enables you to reimport selected modified picture files; clicking the Update button when missing pictures are selected opens the Find *filename* dialog box, which allows you to search for and locate the missing picture file. Both commands enable you to automatically update the picture files using the same applied properties.

TIP *The Update command enables you to update multiple selections of mixed modified and missing pictures. To select sequential listings of picture files, hold the SHIFT key while clicking. To select nonsequential picture files, hold CTRL/CMD while clicking. When the Update command button is clicked, file updates are dealt with in the order in which they appear in your document. When more than one copy of the same picture is used throughout a document, all copies of the picture are updated at once.*

Clicking the Show command button when you double-click a picture file instantly displays the picture no matter where it is in your document. When a picture is displayed it automatically appears in the upper-left corner of your XPress document window.

TIP *When performing the Update command on a picture, XPress recalls all properties applied to the picture in your document without the need to reapply them (including offset, scaling, rotation, skew, flipping, and color).*

Conclusion

Incorporating pictures into your document layout can be an integral part of creating an interesting design. This chapter showed you how to get pictures on your page, and exposed you to the properties and capabilities of using pictures and picture boxes in XPress on a fundamental level. But, not all projects are created equally, and there will no doubt come a time when you need to perform a special operation on a picture, such as adjusting its color or tone, or working with its clipping path. All of these subjects and more are covered in the next chapter, *Advanced Picture Strategies*.

CHAPTER 8

Advanced Picture Strategies

Athena, Acropolis, Greece

Working with pictures in your XPress document can be a relatively straightforward exercise that simply involves importing a picture onto your page. But, as you may have guessed from the issues covered in the preceding chapter, pictures can often be complex and feature various formats that are inherently capable of—or limited to—certain effects in XPress. If your design calls for special treatment of pictures, and you've arrived here in need of some direction and detailed information on working with pictures, you've come to the right place.

This chapter explores the finer details of working with some of the more advanced picture commands in XPress 4, whether you're preparing the pictures yourself or using pictures from foreign sources. You'll discover how to change the colors of imported pictures, and work with the Color, Contrast, Halftone, and Negative commands to enhance or alter your pictures. And, you'll learn how to tailor your pictures by using XPress' complex clipping path commands.

Preparing Pictures for XPress

If you happen to have the luxury (or burden, depending on how you view it) of preparing the pictures destined for your XPress document yourself, there are some tricky design issues to ponder before preparing your final image. Most of the time, the images you import into XPress will be prepared using an external application. Bitmap images may be prepared using a variety of software tools ranging from sophisticated applications such as Photoshop or PHOTO-PAINT to basic applications such as Paintshop Pro or MacPaint. Other types of images, such as encapsulated PostScript (EPS) images, which are often composed mostly of vector objects, may be created from an equally-diverse variety of graphic illustration programs ranging from professional-style applications such as Illustrator, Freehand, or CorelDRAW, to basic applications such as MacDraw.

Because these applications rarely have dedicated import filters in host layout applications such as XPress, the files they create are prepared through use of software filters. The files created depend enormously on the sophistication of the filter used to prepare them and the experience of the individual choosing the filter options. Suffice it to say, when you are working with picture files prepared by someone else, you can seldom be sure of what you're getting.

Many professional desktop designers and layout artists deal with this quandary on a daily basis, and it can often be one of the great hazards of working with pictures in your XPress document. For example, one of the biggest problems when exporting EPS files from graphic applications is the issue of embedded fonts. Many older filters lack options for either embedding font information in the exported file or converting the fonts to curves as do most current EPS export filters. This problem isn't restricted to just EPS formats though—it can crop up when preparing picture files with any export file format that supports vector objects. There is no straightforward, generic solution to a problem such as this, beyond examining the file you are preparing for export and determining exactly which filter options you must choose in order for the file to properly display and print when imported into your XPress document.

To properly prepare bitmap images for your XPress document, you may also need to consider a few issues before exporting from your bitmap editing application—the biggest two issues are color and resolution. If your image is destined to be reproduced in print, you'll need to prepare the original picture file with roughly twice the resolution of the final printed document. For example, if the level of detail required by the final output of your XPress document is to be 150 dots per inch (dpi), your bitmap images must be prepared with roughly 300 dpi of resolution when reproduced at their final published size.

TIP   *For more information on printing from XPress 4, see* Chapter 16, Printing Your Pages.

8

The inherent color of your bitmap image is another area for consideration. If your image is to be reproduced in color, it should be saved as a color image *before* it reaches XPress. Grayscale images cannot be converted to color while in XPress. The same issue applies when color pictures are destined to be reproduced in combinations of two or three spot colors. For these images to correctly display and print from XPress, they will need to be specifically prepared as such before being imported onto your document page.

TIP   *For more information on working with color models, see* Chapter 13, Working with Color *and* Chapter 15, Using Quark's Color Management System.

You may also need to be aware that when preparing pictures for use on your XPress document pages, certain effects or properties may be applied only to certain types of picture formats. While on your Xpress page you may apply color, shade, negative, contrast, and halftone properties, which will be discussed later in this chapter. The following table summarizes whether certain picture formats are "modifiable" when applying these properties.

NOTE *Although the Color and Shade options for color pictures may not be available when working with certain picture formats, you may control contrast properties in pictures by using the Contrast command (CTRL/CMD+SHIFT+O).*

The format you choose for your picture will depend largely on how you would like to use it. It may also depend on whether the picture file is to be in color, grayscale, or black and white, and on how it was originally prepared. Although the following table lists the modifiable properties of various picture formats compatible with XPress, you will discover these capabilities when your file is imported onto your page, and you determine that various options are unavailable to you. If you have the capabilities to return to the host application, or if you are providing guidelines to a third party for preparation of picture files, this information will be invaluable.

Setting Picture Color in XPress

Once a picture resides on your page in XPress, a number of limited color avenues are available to you through use of the Color and Shade options. These options enable you to assign a color to your pictures, independent of the picture boxes they reside in, and they enable you to change imported black-and-white or grayscale bitmap images from the black color they were originally prepared in to print and display in an assigned color. The colors you assign may be any of those available to you in XPress.

NOTE *If you're looking for a way to set the color of your picture once it has been imported into XPress, you are no doubt working with a black-and-white or grayscale bitmap picture. If your picture is in full color, or is in PostScript, DCS (desktop color separation), or Scitex format, the Color and Shade options will be unavailable to you.*

Setting Picture Color and Shade

When working with black-and-white or grayscale images, the capability to display and print pictures in color enables a world of color options where before there were

Picture Format	Color	Shade	Negative	Contrast	Halftone
EPS	No	No	No	No	No
DCS	No	No	No	No	No
GIF	No	No	Yes	Yes	No
JPEG (JPG)					
Grayscale	Yes	Yes	Yes	Yes	Yes
Color	No	No	Yes	Yes	No
Mac PICT (PCT)					
1-bit color	Yes	Yes	No	No	Yes
Grayscale bitmap	Yes	Yes	Yes	Yes	Yes
Full color bitmap	No	No	Yes	Yes	No
Object-oriented	No	No	No	No	No
Bitmaps (BMP)					
1-bit color	Yes	Yes	No	No	Yes
Grayscale	Yes	Yes	Yes	Yes	Yes
Color	No	No	Yes	Yes	No
PhotoCD	No	No	Yes	Yes	No
Scitex CT (SCT, CT)					
Grayscale	No	No	Yes	Yes	No
Color	No	No	Yes	Yes	No
TIFF (TIF)					
1-bit color	Yes	Yes	Yes	No	Yes
Grayscale	Yes	Yes	Yes	Yes	Yes
Color	No	No	Yes	Yes	No
Windows bitmap (BMP, PCX)					
1-bit color	Yes	Yes	Yes	No	Yes
Grayscale	Yes	Yes	Yes	Yes	Yes
Color	No	No	Yes	Yes	No
Metafile(WMF)	No	No	No	No	No

TABLE 8-1   Modifiable Picture Format Properties

none. Color has the effect of adding excitement and appeal to graphics and digital images in your layout. But, keep in mind, the color is added to pictures on a global basis. In other words, only one color per customer. By their very nature, black-and-white or grayscale images feature black as a color. When you use the Color and Shade options to assign color, essentially you are forcing the picture to display and print in a color *other* than black. The remaining properties of the picture remain unaffected.

1. The Color and Shade options may be set a number of ways, the most logical of which is through the Modify (CTRL/CMD+M) | Pictures tab dialog box. You may also apply the Color and Shade options through the Style | Color and Style | Shade submenus, or more interactively through the Colors palette (F12). To apply color and shade to a picture, follow these steps: Create a picture box for your picture, and then choose File | Get Picture to import the file.

2. Once located, click the file once. Be sure the file is either 1-bit black and white or grayscale when selected by checking the file information area in the Get Picture dialog box.

3. Click the Open button to import the picture, then size and position the picture as you see fit.

4. With the picture still selected, view the menus and submenus under the Style menu. Notice the Colors submenu includes all the colors available to you in XPress. The Shade menu features a list of shades ranging from 0 to 100 percent in increments of 10 percent and includes a selection for Other to enter your own value.

5. Instead of applying color and shade through these menus though, open the Colors palette by choosing View | Show Colors (F12). The Colors palette appears.

6. Click the Picture Color mode button in the center of the three buttons at the top of the palette. The palette is now in Picture Color mode.

7. Decide on a color for your picture and click it. Color palette changes to your picture are immediate.

8. Click the Shade drop-down menu and select a shade for your picture's color. Once selected, Shade properties are changed immediately.

When used in combination with picture box properties, the graphic appeal and interest of even the simplest images may be greatly enhanced, as shown in the following illustration.

Original imported 1-bit black-and-white image at 150 dpi

A simple reverse image: White picture with solid black picture box

Black picture with 40 percent black picture box

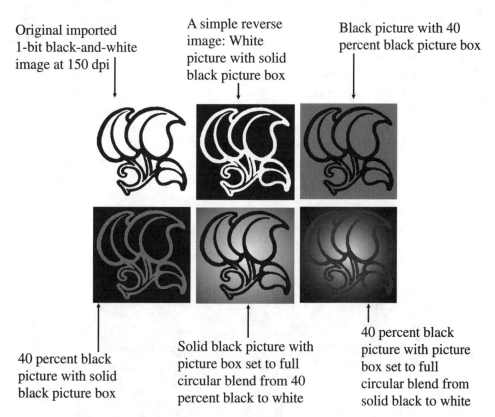

40 percent black picture with solid black picture box

Solid black picture with picture box set to full circular blend from 40 percent black to white

40 percent black picture with picture box set to full circular blend from solid black to white

Although the preceding graphic image has been applied using only black, percentages of black, and white, black is considered a color. You may apply any of the colors available to you in XPress in its place, including process or spot colors. Although the picture and its box are considered a single unit, the colors will separate on individual plates when printed.

TIP → *When blended backgrounds are applied to pictures, only black-and-white images can display the effect inside the boundaries of the image, making the 1-bit image uniquely flexible in contrast to other picture formats.*

Creating "Fake" Duotones

The term *duotone* refers to any single-color grayscale picture reproduced in two colors. There are fake duotones and real—or true—duotones. Fake duotones are essentially single-color grayscale pictures with an additional color placed behind them for added interest and appeal. The duotone has often been considered the poor persons' color picture. For little or no added cost, duotones can add color to an otherwise colorless page, and when colors are chosen carefully, duotones can be an effective and inexpensive way of simulating more than two colors of ink in print.

In XPress, creating a fake duotone effect is done quickly by applying a solid or screened color background to your picture box while leaving the picture itself unchanged. The following illustration (although reproduced here in black and white) shows how a color applied to the background of a single-color picture enables you to add uniform color to the background, independent of your picture's color.

Original grayscale image

Same image with 20 percent color background applied to picture box

Creating True Duotones

As discussed, a duotone is simply a grayscale picture reproduced in more than one color. Although fake duotones add flat color to grayscale images and may be done directly in XPress, creating a true duotone requires the use of a sophisticated image-editing application such as Photoshop or PHOTO-PAINT. True duotones feature a second spot color that shows through the highlights and shadows of the original image's tones. The amount of ink that shows through in the second color is usually a standard function of the image editor being used to create the duotone, but it may be adjusted depending on the desired effect.

In order for duotones to display and print properly, they must adhere to standard display and printing conventions. As a rule, doutones are created as EPS files and usually contain at least one spot color of ink. The display you see on your XPress page is actually an RGB TIFF representation of the data contained in the file. Because data representing the duotone is already prepared in EPS format, it may not be modified or adjusted in any way in XPress. This is simply the nature of duotones.

If you watch closely while importing a duotone image into XPress, you may notice the file information area in the Get Picture dialog box reveals that the image is an EPS file with a TIFF preview, but XPress is unable to determine what the color depth of the image is, as shown in the following illustration. In other words, the two colors used in the duotone image can often be a mystery.

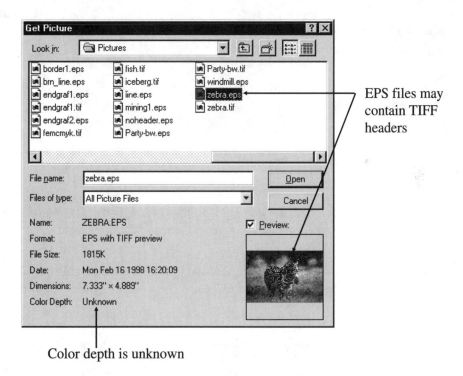

EPS files may contain TIFF headers

Color depth is unknown

Color depth is unknown. Fortunately, when the file is imported into XPress, all of its color separation information gets imported along with it. This particular image has been prepared as a duotone and saved to EPS format using black and an orange-yellow color. The second duotone color was applied using Pantone 3955 CV.

As a result, this Pantone color was automatically added to the current selection of colors in the XPress document, as shown in the following illustration. If the imported colors already exist in your XPress document, the colors simply separate to the corresponding plate as required during separation.

Original image in TIFF grayscale

←EPS image in duotone format

Color palette now includes second EPS color in duotone

TIP ──────▶ *When you select your document to print to separations, the duotone will separate into two colors—in this case, black and Pantone 3955 CV.*

TIP ──────▶ *There are automatic safeguards against colors used in PostScript picture files being deleted from your document's color selection, as shown in the following alert message.*

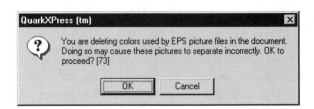

Controlling a Picture's Look

If the picture on your screen does not look like the final image you intend to print, there may be a number of things you need to adjust. XPress enables you to control how your picture appears on your screen as well as how it prints. You may also adjust the associated properties of pictures themselves through the Contrast and Negative options.

Changing Picture Color Models

If the picture you are importing into your document is in color, and you need a grayscale image, XPress enables you to quickly convert the image when you import it through the Get Picture dialog box. In actuality, XPress does not alter or change the image file represented by what you see on your screen. Rather, XPress does two things. First, it builds a new preview based on the image's inherent picture data. Then, XPress applies a tag which performs a quick bitmap conversion when your document is printed or exported.

There are any number of reasons why you may want to convert an image when it's imported into your document. Converting color images to grayscale is the most obvious example. But, you may also want to change a grayscale image to black and white for a quickly-created visual effect, (as shown in the following illustration), or change the crude preview of a black-and-white image to grayscale to enable you to see more detail (as seen in the Illustration at the top of the next page). The more detail a preview can render, the more accurately the image will be integrated into your layout should you need to tailor a graphic image to fit a text shape, for example.

8

Original grayscale image

Image converted to black-and-white on import

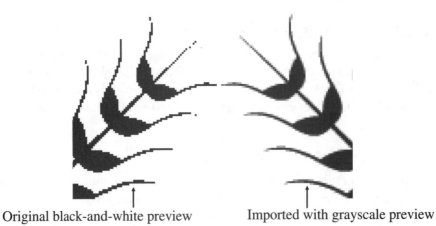

Original black-and-white preview   Imported with grayscale preview

When working with images that are large in width and height on your document page, you may want to decrease the resolution of the preview in order to reduce the time it takes your preview to be drawn on the screen. The higher a preview's resolution, the longer it will take to render to your screen. Reducing the resolution for larger images enables you to work much faster. When XPress converts the preview of the picture from its default of 72 dpi to low resolution, the detail is halved and the resulting preview is displayed at a screen resolution of 36 dpi, as shown in the following illustration.

TIP *Using low resolution previews for your picture files also reduces the file size of your XPress document.*

Original image preview   Preview converted to low resolution

The following keyboard combinations perform bitmap conversions when importing bitmap images into XPress through the Get Picture command.

Bitmap conversions can only be applied to bitmap-based picture files. These conversions don't apply to EPS files containing TIFF previews.

Convert full color to grayscale	Hold CTRL/CMD while clicking Open
Convert grayscale to black and white	Hold CTRL/CMD while clicking Open
Change black-and-white preview to grayscale preview	Hold ALT/OPTION while clicking Open
Change preview to display in low resolution	Hold SHIFT while clicking Open

Keep in mind that when a picture is converted, the original remains intact, and the conversion only affects how the picture displays and prints in XPress. And, although converting color to grayscale or grayscale to black and white affects how the picture displays and prints, changing the preview affects the display only—leaving the printing quality unaffected.

These keyboard combinations may be used in combination with each other when importing pictures through the Get Picture dialog box. For example, when selecting to import a color TIFF picture, holding CTRL/CMD+SHIFT converts the picture to grayscale and displays it at a low resolution simultaneously.

Changing a Picture's Screen Display

The picture you see on your screen is merely a reflection of the actual data contained in the picture file linked to your document. Large pictures that feature high-resolution previews can be critical to productivity due to the added time it takes XPress to render the previews to your screen. On the other hand, pictures that feature crude previews with reduced detail can be equally frustrating to work with. Crude

8

previews often disguise poorly prepared pictures, the quality of which becomes obvious only at print time.

You can control how your pictures appear on screen by using the preference commands. These commands are accessed by choosing Edit | Preferences | Application (CTRL/CMD+ALT/OPTION+SHIFT+Y) to open the Application Preferences dialog box, and then clicking the Display tab, as shown in the following illustration.

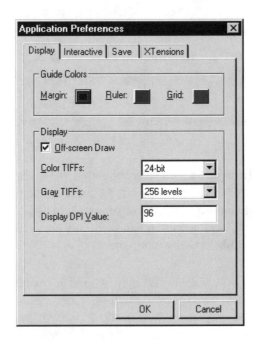

Reducing the color level display of pictures allows XPress to draw previews much faster than with increased color display levels. Setting the display of pictures does not affect how they print—just how they display. XPress enables you to set the display of color TIFF and gray TIFF picture files individually by choosing an option from their drop-down menus. Color TIFFs may be set to either 8-bit or 24-bit color on Windows platforms, or 8-bit, 16-bit, or 32-bit color on Macintosh platforms. Grayscale images may be set to either 16 levels or 256 levels of gray, as shown in the following illustration. The degree of display can make a significant difference in the amount of time it takes XPress to draw your document page, especially if the document contains a lot of pictures in high resolution.

Picture imported with grayscale
display options set to 16 levels

Same image imported with grayscale
display options set to 256 levels of gray

When using these display options for controlling the detail in your TIFF pictures, you may want to keep in mind that you will only notice results in imported images after the display options have been applied. This is because the preview of your picture is created by XPress when it is imported, instead of on-the-fly. So, if you import pictures into your document and subsequently change the preview display settings, you won't notice any difference in the screen appearance of your pictures unless you reimport the pictures using the Get Picture command.

TIP   *You can have XPress automatically create new previews for all the pictures in a document according to the current application preferences. To do this, close the document, and then choose File | Open. Press CTRL/CMD while clicking Open in the Open dialog box. (If pictures are missing, XPress will not create a new preview.)*

Using the Contrast Command

The capability to adjust the overall contrast of an image is one of the more powerful and complex features of picture control in XPress. It enables you to salvage poorly prepared pictures or use your design creativity to enhance the appeal of images by applying interesting visual manipulations. Applying contrast properties to your picture affects both the onscreen preview display and the printed output of pictures.

Picture contrast is set using the Picture Contrast Specifications dialog box shown in the following illustration. It is accessed by choosing Style | Contrast (CTRL/CMD +SHIFT+O/C) while your picture is selected. Working with grayscale images is perhaps the simplest operation, because only one color is available for the effect. While color images are selected, you may choose from various color models to adjust the contrast of your picture.

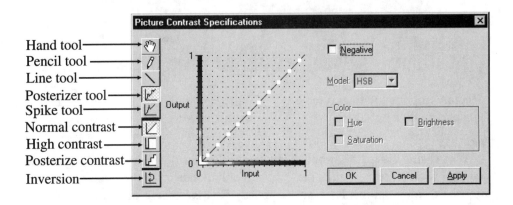

At first, the contrast tools you see in this dialog box may seem a bit overwhelming and intimidating. But in reality, you are seeing tool overkill. There are more tools here than are really necessary. First, in the center of the dialog box you see a graph representing the "curve" of the tones in your image. By default, this "curve" is always a straight line joining the bottom-left and top-right corners. The word *Output* identifies the Y axis of the graph, while *Input* identifies the X axis. To the left of the dialog box is a series of buttons that adds immensely to the confusion.

The diagonal curve line itself represents the "normal" state of your image when it was first imported into XPress. When certain tool buttons are selected (Spike and Posterizer), you may notice that the curve features 10 small white markers that correspond to the 10 divisions on each axis. Essentially these divisions represent 10 areas of tone of your image, ranging from highlight tones on the left side of the graph to shadow tones on the right. Highlight tones represent the whiter areas of your picture, midtones represent the middle gray tones, and the shadows represent the dark areas. The top of the graph represents what is, for all intents and purposes, 100 percent of a given color of ink, while the bottom represents zero percent. If you think of the graph in this way, it will be much easier to comprehend its use and anticipate the results of the changes made to the contrast curve. The following illustration may help in digesting the highlight-shadow contrast concept.

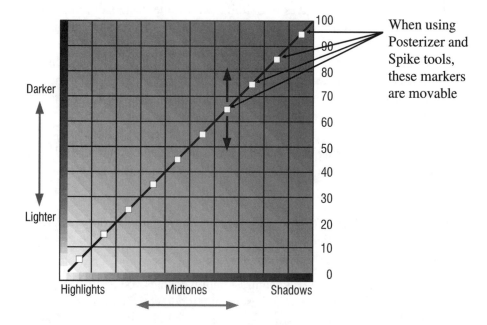

To the left of the graph is a series of buttons that has been subtly divided into two types of buttons: tool buttons and preset curve buttons. The tools enable you to shape the line of your contrast curve, and the preset curve buttons enable you to apply a preset effect. The following tools can be used for shaping your contrast curve.

- **Hand**   The Hand tool enables you to reposition the current shape of the curve anywhere on the graph simply by dragging anywhere on the curve with it.

- **Pencil**   The Pencil tool behaves like a freehand tool, enabling you to literally draw the shape of your curve directly on the graph.

- **Line**   The Line tool enables you to create straight lines on your curve. You may apply a straight line to the entire curve or only specific sections.

- **Posterizer**   The term *posterize* stems from the effect of applying inverse values to specific areas of a picture, which often results in dramatic effects. When selected, the Posterizer tool places markers at each 10-percent increment on your curve, enabling you to increase or decrease the intensity of your picture's tones as if they were flat levels.

■ **Spike** This tool behaves in a similar way to the Posterizer tool, enabling you to adjust your picture's contrast curve by 10-percent increments. Instead of flat levels, though, the Spike tool uses markers as if they were finite points on a line, enabling the curve to immediately change direction at each marker. Results achieved using the Spike tool instead of the Posterizer tool are often more dramatic, and picture contrast results appear more uncontrolled.

Although the preceding tools enable you to arrive at a custom-shaped contrast curve, the remaining buttons enact instant effects on the curve itself, each of which may be edited later.

■ **Normal contrast** Clicking the Normal button returns your curve to a diagonal straight line and the contrast in your picture to the state it was in when you first imported it onto your page.

■ **High contrast** The High contrast button enables you to change your picture's contrast curve to a preset condition to contain only white highlights and dark shadows—and very little tone between. By default, the highlights from 0 to 30 percent are converted to 0 percent of ink, and the 40- to 100-percent midtones and shadows are converted to 100 percent of ink shadows.

■ **Posterized** The Posterized button sets your curve to a preset condition where highlights, midtones, and shadow tones are somewhat more simplified and limited to specific values. Highlights are limited to 0 and 20 percent of ink, midtones are limited to 40 and 60 percent, and shadow areas are limited to 80 and 100 percent.

■ **Inversion** The Inversion button enables you to reverse the shape of a selected curve. The Inversion preset may be applied to either single or multiple-selected curves, setting its function apart from simply applying a negative effect on your picture. As a result, the Inversion preset button is most useful when working with color pictures.

TIP ────▶ *If the pictures you are using have been scanned or otherwise saved from original film negatives, the Negative option will be useful to you. You may apply a negative image effect on your picture image simply by clicking this option in the Picture Contrast Specifications dialog box.*

The results of applying and customizing these preset contrast buttons may be seen in the following illustration, where they were applied to a grayscale image.

Original image   High contrast preset   Posterized preset

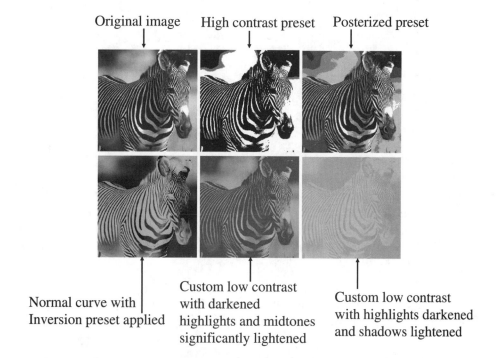

Normal curve with Inversion preset applied

Custom low contrast with darkened highlights and midtones significantly lightened

Custom low contrast with highlights darkened and shadows lightened

When working with color images, the tools become more complex. Color images may be adjusted in a number of ways, the operation of which is identical to the effects achieved while manipulating grayscale curves; the difference is you have either three or four colors to deal with. When a color picture is selected, the Model drop-down menu becomes available in the Picture Contrast Specifications dialog box. The Model menu includes a selection of color models on which you may *measure* the contrast changes to your color picture (it does *not* convert the color model on which the original picture file is based). It includes RGB, HSB, CMY, and CMYK color models. The first three models enable you to control three colors at a time; the latter model features the standard four-color process inks.

When a specific color model is selected, the dialog box reveals options for manipulating the curves of individual or multiple colors. For example, the following illustration shows how individual curves may be selected by checking or unchecking the option boxes beside the listed colors. While colors are selected, they may be manipulated using any of the available contrast tools in the dialog box.

8

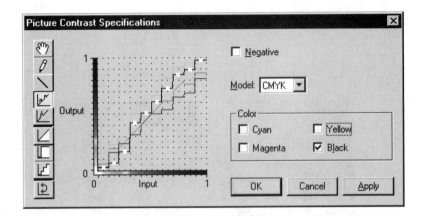

Clicking the Normal, High, Posterized, or Inversion preset contrast buttons affects only those colors that are selected. The same rule applies for resetting a color's contrast curve using the Normal button. Any selected color's curve may be returned to Normal independently of the other colors by clicking the Normal contrast button.

For some hands-on experience using the Picture Contrast Specifications tools, follow these steps (it will help to have a color TIFF bitmap prepared for this exercise):

1. Create a picture box and choose File | Get Picture (CTRL/CMD+E).

2. Choose a prepared color image, and to begin let's import it as a grayscale by holding the CTRL/CMD key while clicking the Open button in the Get Picture dialog box. Once Open is clicked, notice a grayscale preview of the image appears in the picture box. Size and position your picture as you wish.

3. With the picture selected by using either the Item or Content tool, choose Style | Contrast (CTRL/CMD+SHIFT+O/C) to open the Picture Contrast Specifications dialog box.

4. When first opened, the dialog box displays the picture's contrast curve as a diagonal straight line. And, because your current image is grayscale, notice that the Model drop-down menu is unavailable.

5. Click the Posterizer tool (fourth from the top of the row of buttons on the left). Notice your curve now features 10 markers.

6. Manipulate the markers by dragging the first two upwards to roughly one-third of the graph's height and clicking the Apply button. Notice the white areas of your picture become darker.

7. Drag the last three markers at the right of your contrast curve downwards to roughly one-third of the graph's height and click Apply again. Notice that the shadow areas of your picture become lighter, and the overall contrast of the image looks significantly flatter.

8. Click the High contrast button (third from the bottom in the row of buttons to the left of the graph) and click the Apply button. Notice that your picture now looks like a simple black-and-white image.

9. Drag the fourth marker (from the left) downwards to approximately two-thirds of the graph, drag the fifth marker downwards to approximately one-third of the graph, and click the Apply button. Notice that your picture now features two new shades of gray.

10. Take a moment to experiment with the Hand, Pencil, Line and Spike tools to familiarize yourself with their behavior. Click the Apply button any time you want to preview a new effect.

11. Click the Cancel button to close the dialog box without accepting the settings, and with your picture box still selected, choose File | Get Picture (CTRL/CMD+E) to open the Get Picture dialog box again. This time, import the same picture as a color image by simply clicking the Open button. Size and position your picture as you wish.

12. Choose Style | Contrast (CTRL/CMD+SHIFT+O/C) once again to open the Picture Contrast Specifications dialog box. Notice that with a color picture selected, the Model drop-down menu and Color options are now available.

13. Choose CMYK from the Model drop-down menu. Notice that the options for Cyan, Magenta, Yellow, and Black now appear in the dialog box.

14. Uncheck all the colors except Black, and choose the Spike tool from the series of buttons to the left. Notice 10 markers appear on your picture's contrast curve. Try manipulating the markers vertically to adjust their position. Notice that, as you do so, the other ink color curves are revealed underneath, but remain stationary as you move the Black ink contrast curve.

8

15. With your Black contrast curve altered from normal, click the Inversion button and observe the effect on the curve. Notice that the curve is now the reverse of what it was originally, with highlight, midtone, and shadow values reversed.

16. Select all the colors once again. Click the High contrast button and click Apply to see the effects. Notice that your picture's colors change dramatically.

17. Choose RGB from the Model drop-down menu and click the High contrast button again. Notice that the effect on your picture's color is different from that of CMYK. This is because the contrast is being measured and manipulated based on a different color model.

18. Take a moment to experiment with the effects of the different curve shapes created; use the various tools while manipulating one or more curves at a time. Click the Apply button each time to familiarize yourself with each tool's sensitivity.

To see the results of applying custom picture contrast specifications to color images, see the color insert in this book.

TIP *When working in most dialog boxes that include an Apply button, you may set Xpress to continually update the results of setting changes by pressing ALT/OPTION the first time you click the Apply button. In the case of the Picture Contrast Specifications dialog box settings, the pictures you modify will continually preview, although you may need to reposition this dialog box to see the results.*

Using the Halftone Command

The term *halftone* is borrowed from the traditional world of offset printing where halftones were created as film negatives exposed through a specialized halftone screen using a typical camera lens and light-sensitive orthographic film. The process was labor-intensive because film exposure involved controlled exposure times, lighting, and chemical processing procedures. The resulting halftone was manually assembled by literally taping film negatives into place for exposure to a paper or metal plate for offset printing. The process was (and to a certain degree still is) costly and quite environmentally destructive. Thankfully, much of this process can now be done digitally.

Halftones can now be produced using scanning hardware and image editors. Usually, the halftone produced from digital images features the default properties of the output device used to create the final film for offset printing, such as a high-end imagesetter. These properties are often set by the output device to match the resolution of the film and the output line frequency selected by the user, but default halftone properties can be overridden in XPress using the Halftone command (CTRL/CMD+SHIFT+H).

The Halftone command can have profound effects on the appearance of your document's pictures. It's also one of the trickier features to use because the properties you apply can't be previewed on screen. Instead, your choice for the style of your halftone must be based on previous knowledge of the effects applied. Halftone properties are a PostScript function, meaning they are applied at the film output stage of your document production process. In order to see the effects of applying halftone properties, you'll need to produce a reasonable-quality proof of your document before you decide which style and options work best for your picture. For the experienced halftone creator, the results of the halftone effect will be somewhat predictable. But for layout artists new to these effects, choosing halftone options will be (at least initially) by trial and error.

XPress' halftone arsenal includes Frequency, Angle, and Function options set using drop-down menus in the Picture Halftone dialog box, as shown in the following illustration. When left at default selections, these options enable your output device to take over the halftone screening functions.

8

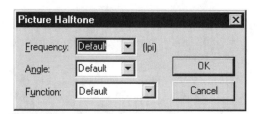

- **Frequency**   This drop-down menu contains preset choices for the number of dots or lines measured in a single inch in your final halftone. Options include Default, 60, 85, 100, 133, and 150 lines per inch; the industry standard is 150 when producing final output to a high-end film imagesetter. You may enter any value for your halftone within a range between 15 and 400 dots or lines per inch.

- **Angle**   When dots or lines are produced in your halftone, they are produced in rows; the size of rows varies according to the highlight, midtone, and shadow values in your original picture. These rows align at various angles, which are determined either by the default settings of your output device (usually 45 degrees for black plates), the settings entered in XPress' Print dialog box, or the angle you enter in this drop-down menu. Angles may be set to any measure based on a 360-degree rotation. Preset values in this drop-down menu include 0, 15, 45, 75, 90, and 105. Settings for 45, 75, 90, and 105 are standard screening angles for process color inks black, magenta, yellow, and cyan respectively, but certain imagesetters feature variations on these angles depending on the process screening technique in use.

NOTE   *Although the Frequency and Angle options enable you to enter custom values, certain PostScript devices may be incapable of exactly matching these values. In these cases, the closest value PostScript is able to reproduce is used instead.*

■ **Function**   The name of this option is slightly misleading in that the option actually describes the shape of the element used to describe the highlights, midtones, and shadows of your picture. The Function drop-down menu contains options for Default (usually dot), Dot, Line, Ellipse, Square, and Ordered Dither. When the Ordered Dither option is selected, both the Frequency and Angle options are unavailable.

The following illustration demonstrates the effects of various Picture Halftone settings applied to a grayscale image with an inherent resolution of 150 dpi.

Default Frequency, Angle, and Function options | Frequency = 60, Angle = 45, Function = Dot   Frequency = 25, Angle = 0, Function = Line

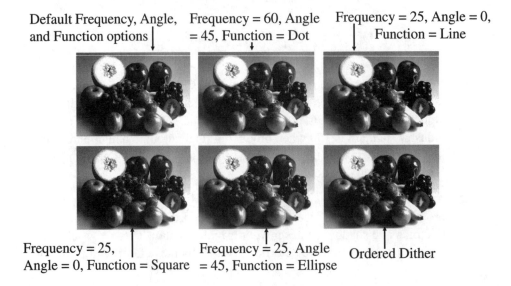

Frequency = 25, Angle = 0, Function = Square   Frequency = 25, Angle = 45, Function = Ellipse   Ordered Dither

Working with Picture Clipping Paths

If you're working with a picture that includes an entire scene or a collection of visual elements, and your design or layout calls for use of only one of those elements, you may need a clipping path. The term *clipping path* describes a manually or automatically created closed path that isolates specific areas of a picture, having the effect of acting as a window whose shape defines the view.

The ideal use for clipping paths is to isolate specific picture elements that are nonrectangular in shape. The most common use for clipping paths is for eliminating backgrounds that may be distracting or otherwise inappropriate for use in your document. XPress features several options for creating, editing, and applying clipping paths; the properties of these options may be set using the Modify | Clipping tab (CTRL/CMD+ALT/OPTION+T) dialog box shown in the following illustration.

File details
indicate
whether the
currently
selected
picture
contains
alpha or
embedded
paths

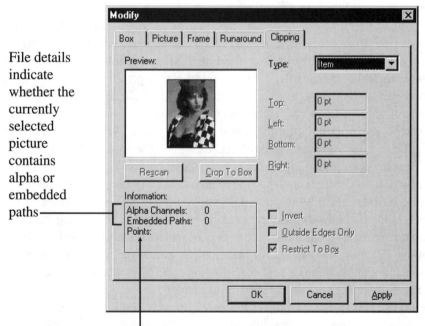

While a path is selected, the number of points on the
path is displayed

What's a Clipping Path?

A clipping path is usually an uneven shape that follows the contours of a picture element. The image is clipped along the path, leaving only the portion of the image that has been clipped visible, and the remainder clipped off. Where the image has been clipped, the background shows through as transparent by default. Clipping paths are often created in an image-editing program that supports multiple paths or channels, and are drawn using conventional Bezier tools. Paths may be saved in several modes, including actual named clipping paths or alpha channels, both of which are usable as clipping paths by XPress.

XPress Clipping Path Options

XPress enables you to create clipping paths in limited ways, and frankly, there are some picture conditions that simply won't allow you to create an accurate clipping path. And, as you might discover on your own, you cannot draw your own clipping path using the Bezier tools built into XPress. Bezier tools come into play only when editing embedded clipping paths or those that XPress enables you to create using available tools. In other words, if you intend to draw a path to use as a clipping path for your picture, be prepared to apply it manually as a shaded box rather than as a genuine clipping path embedded in your picture box.

Instead of creating clipping paths from scratch, XPress enables you to automatically apply clipping path effects using options in the Clipping tab dialog box. The way you create clipping paths using these features is based on the condition of the picture, its contents, and the type of elements it contains. The resulting setting will also be determined by which areas you would like to isolate. The best pictures to apply clipping paths to contain near-perfectly defined edges, are in clear focus, and feature uniformly-shaded areas that may be isolated easily into paths. Otherwise, the most efficient way to isolate the element you want to clip is by using an image-editing application or a manual clipping process in which you create a shape and place it over the area you want to eliminate.

With that little disclaimer out of the way, XPress' clipping path tools enable you to clip areas based on their shade and condition. The Type drop-down menu contains options for the following clipping path types.

- **Item**   By default, when your picture is selected, this option indicates that no clipping path is currently applied to your picture. It also indicates that, in fact, even the box your picture resides in is a crude clipping path of sorts.

Design: Steven Taylor

Description: Cover design, *Business Week*, December 30, 1996 issue

As with other examples from Business Week, this magazine cover design depicts the application of combined spot and process color using only carefully crafted text formatting for visual impact in a symmetrical and center-aligned layout.

■ **Embedded Path**   If your picture has already been worked on in an image-editing program, it may feature an embedded path. Image editors such as Adobe Photoshop or Corel PhotoPaint enable you to create and embed clipping paths from drawn paths, and then store them with the picture file in certain file formats. If your picture includes an embedded clipping path, the first path will be applied automatically when your picture is imported using the Get Picture command. Because of their accuracy, using embedded paths is one of the more favored options when working with clipping paths applied to picture files. When you apply embedded paths as clipping paths, the Path drop-down menu becomes available for selecting specific paths should your picture file feature more than one path. While embedded paths are in use, Noise and Smoothness options are available and affect the condition of the clipping path created; the Threshold option is unavailable. The following illustration demonstrates the effects of applying an embedded path as a clipping path.

Original picture

Embedded path created to isolate picture element

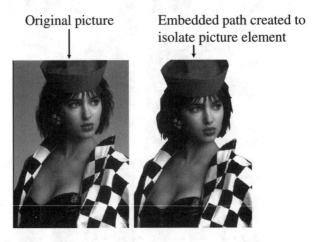

■ **Alpha Channel**   The Alpha Channel option also enables you to apply a clipping path that has been stored with your picture file as either a selection or a mask. The Alpha channel option is not automatically applied to imported picture files containing alpha channels, but may instead be applied by selecting this option from the Type drop-down menu. Alpha channels are often stored as selection channels with picture files and are created using image-editing applications. When the Alpha Channel option is selected, the Alpha Channels drop-down menu appears, enabling you to choose which channel you would like to use, should the file contain more than one choice. While an alpha channel is in use, all Tolerance options are available and affect the clipping path created. The following illustration shows an example of a clipping path based on an alpha channel.

Original picture

Picture's alpha channel used as a clipping path

- **Non-White Areas**   Using the Non-White Areas option works best on pictures in which the element you want to isolate is surrounded by a uniform shade or color. The Non-White Areas option can also be used when isolating areas with dark picture elements surrounded by light shades or vice versa. While using this option, you will rely heavily on the accuracy of the Threshold value, which we will discuss later in this section.

- **Picture Bounds**   The Picture Bounds option creates a clipping path based on the edges of your picture, regardless of their color or shade. For example, if your picture is surrounded by a white frame or border, the clipping path includes this area. While the Picture Bounds option is chosen, you may enter your own offset values for the top, left, right, and bottom margins of your picture's bounding box.

When the embedded path, alpha channel, and nonwhite areas of your picture are being used as clipping paths, several other options become available in the Clipping tab dialog box, including the Outset option, Tolerance settings for Noise, Smoothness, and Threshold; Invert, Outside Edges Only, and Restrict To Box options.

- **Outset**   The Outset value entered in this field controls how closely the clipping path contours created by XPress follow the edges of the detected areas. Outset may be set within a range between –4 and 4 inches. Entering positive values causes the clipping path to be created outside of the detected area, while negative values cause the path to creep into the area.

8

- **Noise**   The Noise value enables XPress to create a clipping path that ignores stray pixels, which may cause uneven contours and increase the number of points on the clipping path. The value entered corresponds to the size of the area encountered. For example, entering a value of 6 points causes areas 6 points and under to be ignored. Noise may be set within a range between 0 and 4 inches.

- **Smoothness**   The Smoothness value determines how closely the contours of your newly created clipping path will follow the shaded areas found in your picture. Smoothness may be set to any value within a range between 0 and 100 points. Lower values create smoother, but more complex, clipping paths, while higher values create less accurate, but less complex paths.

- **Threshold**   The Threshold value concept is critical to grasp if you intend to create clipping paths using the Non-White Areas option. Threshold is based on the percentage of shade or color, and enables you to set which areas of your picture are detected as hard "edges" of objects. Threshold operates on the basis of contrasting pixels, comparing dark pixels to light pixels. While using the Non-White Areas option for type of clipping path, pixels lighter than the Threshold percentage value are excluded from the clipping path, and darker pixels are included. The reverse of this concept applies when using alpha channels. The Threshold option is unavailable when you use the Embedded Paths option.

The following three options may be selected to work in combination with the previously discussed clipping path types and options. Availability of these options is determined by which type of clipping path is selected. Additional buttons in the dialog to Rescan and Crop to Box are defined below.

- **Invert**   This option has the effect of reversing the clipped area of the selected clipping path. Inverting a clipping path is usually required when alpha channels incorrectly isolate the background of a picture instead of the picture element. The following example depicts the effects of using the Invert option.

Original picture

Clipping path based on an alpha channel
reversed using the Invert option

■ **Outside Edges Only**   When used in combination with the Non-White
Areas clipping path option, this option enables areas of pixels that are
lighter than the Threshold value within the picture element to be excluded
from the clipping path. For example, imagine applying the Non-White
Area type clipping path to a picture of a chocolate-covered doughnut set
on a light-colored background. With this option active, only the area
outside the doughnut would be clipped out. With Outside Edges Only
inactive, both the outside and inside areas would be clipped. The
following example shows the effects of applying a clipping path with the
Outside Edges Only option selected and not selected. Notice that the
background areas *within* the picture element are clipped along with the
outside area.

Original picture   Outside Edges
Only active

Background
within the
picture
element is
also clipped

Outside Edges Only inactive

8

- **Restrict To Box**   When a clipping path is created using any of the supported types, the path created applies to the entire image, except the area created by the clipping path. With the Restrict To Box option active, the clipping path and picture box boundaries are combined to clip the image. With the Restrict To Box option inactive, the clipping path boundaries may extend beyond the edges of the picture box if more image exists.

- **Rescan**   Each time you choose a new clipping path type or change a clipping option such as Threshold, your picture is automatically rescanned and the new clipping path shape is applied. Your picture appears in the Preview window of the Clipping tab dialog box, and the clipping path appears in green (by default) within the preview. Areas that are clipped out of your image appear as white. You may force the path to be reapplied by clicking the Rescan button.

- **Crop To Box**   This button has the effect of eliminating portions of the clipping path that extend beyond the edges of the picture box. The goal is to simplify the clipping path and reduce the total number of points used to describe its shape.

TIP

Keeping your clipping path simple may be a priority when applying clipping paths that are described with excessive numbers of points. The more complex the clipping path, the longer your image will take to print. To simplify your clipping path, use the Crop To Box option in combination with adjustments to the Smoothness option.

Applying Clipping Paths

As with most complex features, the quickest way to learn their operation is through hands-on experience. The following exercise will provide you with a basic understanding of the powerful and complex capabilities that come from applying a clipping path to your picture.

1. If you use an image editing program, prepare a grayscale TIFF image with at least one alpha channel selection and one saved path, and import this image into your XPress document by creating an oval-shaped picture box and using the Get Picture (CTRL/CMD+E) command. Ideally, your picture will feature a well-defined visual element on a light-colored background.

TIP *If you need a picture to practice the effects discussed here, try the image named* Italy.tif *in Lesson 5 of the Xpress tutorials.*

2. Crop your picture by slightly reducing the width and height dimensions of your picture box.

3. With your picture selected, choose Item | Clipping (CTRL/CMD+ALT/OPTION+T) to open the Modify | Clipping tab dialog box. If your picture contains an embedded path, it may be automatically selected and applied as a clipping path to your picture and indicated as such in the Type drop-down menu. If not, the Type menu will display the Item option (meaning the clipping path is your picture box itself), and the options in the dialog box will be unavailable. Notice the representation of your picture is showing in the Preview window and is surrounded by a blue border. This blue border represents your picture box shape.

4. From the Type menu, choose Non-White Areas and be sure both the Restrict To Box and Outside Edges Only options are active. Notice the options in the dialog box change, and others become available. Notice a clipping path is immediately applied in the Preview window as a green border around the clipped area of your picture, as shown in the following illustration.

5. To increase the area of your picture's light-colored background, increase the Threshold option incrementally and click Rescan or Apply until the background completely disappears. Notice the image is cropped, and an empty green clipping path is left where your picture extends beyond your picture box.

8

Blue picture box border

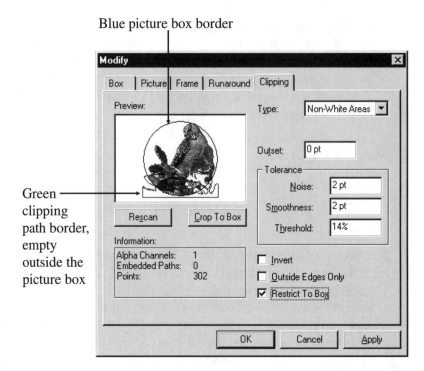

Green clipping path border, empty outside the picture box

6. Make a note of the current number of points used to describe the clipping path in the dialog box and increase the Smoothness option by 3 points. Click the Rescan button to have XPress recalculate the clipping path and check the results. After rescanning, check the number of points again and notice that a higher Smoothness setting reduces the number of points—but also reduces the accuracy of the clipping path.

TIP *If you find that the Rescan button does not recalculate and display the number of points on your clipping path, click the Apply button to force it to recalculate.*

7. Click the Crop To Box button in the dialog box. Notice the number of points is reduced even further and the Preview window indicates that the clipping path is now contained only within the confines of your picture box borders.

8. If your picture features areas *within* the outside edges of the item you want to isolate, click the Outside Edges Only option so that it is inactive and notice several things occur. Your picture is automatically rescanned to reveal the complete clipping path, the number of points that describe your clipping path increases, and the Preview window indicates that certain areas within your picture element are now clipped along with areas outside its previously clipped edges. The Preview window has also been updated to indicate the new shape of the clipping path in green. Notice the Crop To Box effect has been reset.

9. To reduce the number of points again, click the Crop To Box button a second time and notice that the number of points are again reduced.

10. Before accepting your clipping path, experiment with the Invert option and Noise settings to observe their effects on your picture. To apply your new clipping path, click OK.

TIP *Once a clipping path is created, it is applied to your picture regardless of the fact that you may change the size of your picture later on. Each time you resize your picture, the clipping path is also resized, avoiding the need to reapply it.*

Editing Clipping Paths

8

The capability to edit a clipping path enables you to customize—or correct—the results of XPress' automated clipping path creation features. Because clipping paths are essentially Bezier paths applied to your picture as masks, you may edit the clipping path shape the same way in which you would edit a Bezier path. While in the editing state, clipping paths appear as green lines over the top of your picture displayed in the same condition as it was in the Preview window of the Modify | Clipping tab dialog box. In this instance though, the difference is that the points are movable and editable.

You don't need to select any special tools in order to edit the path. By holding the Item or Content tool over a point, your cursor changes to a point-editing state, enabling you to reposition points, move their curve handles, or change one point type to another in order to tailor the path. As you edit the path, the clipping path results are updated immediately. Figure 8-1 shows a clipping path in the editing state.

TIP *While editing a clipping path, the Measurements palette displays the usual Bezier point and path properties, enabling you to quickly shape a path, as shown in Figure 8-1.*

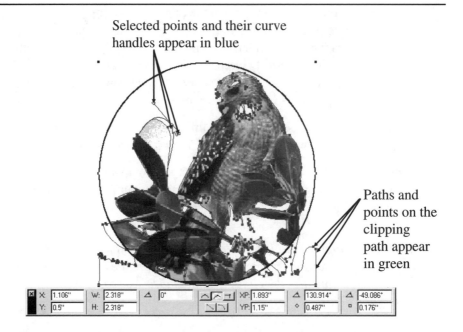

Selected points and their curve handles appear in blue

Paths and points on the clipping path appear in green

FIGURE 8-1   Editing a clipping path

To edit a clipping path applied to a picture, follow these steps:

1. Select the picture containing the clipping path you want to edit and choose Item | Edit | Clipping Path (CTRL/OPTION+SHIFT+F10/F4). Notice that the clipping path immediately appears along with the points and paths thatdescribe its shape.

2. Open the Measurements palette by choosing View | Show Measurements (F9).

3. Hold your pointer over the point or path you want to edit and click on it with your cursor. Notice the point's or path's marker and curve handles appear, and the Measurements palette displays the options available to you.

4. Reposition the path, point, or curve handles by dragging them.

5. Once you have finished editing the clipping path, and with your picture still selected, choose Item | Edit | Shape to return the display to normal and hide the clipping path details. Your clipping path editing is complete.

TIP *For more information on editing various types of Bezier paths, points, and curve handles, see* Drawing with Beziers *in* Chapter 5, Using Drawing Tools.

NOTE *When editing a path manually, you may find that the screen preview is not precisely accurate. However, when XPress creates a Non-White Areas path, it looks at the data in the high-resolution file. It's unlikely that you will be able to create a better path using the screen preview and drawing tools than what Xpress can create for you.*

Exporting Pictures from XPress

If at some point you want to use the picture properties you have applied in another application or XPress itself, you have the option of saving your pictures as encapsulated PostScript files. In fact, XPress enables you to export entire pages in your document—including the pictures they contain—with a single command; simply choose File | Save Page as EPS (CTRL/CMD+ALT/OPTION+SHIFT+S).

Saving entire pages in EPS format enables you to import the pages into other applications or back into your XPress document itself. The process of exporting and then reimporting pages is often used in order to place an entire page or spread onto a page and subsequently resize or reprint it in a different format.

The Save Page as EPS dialog box, shown in the following illustration, contains a number of options specifically geared toward handling the pictures on your page. You can control how the pictures are displayed, whether the pictures feature previews, and whether the EPS file representing your page includes the original picture data.

8

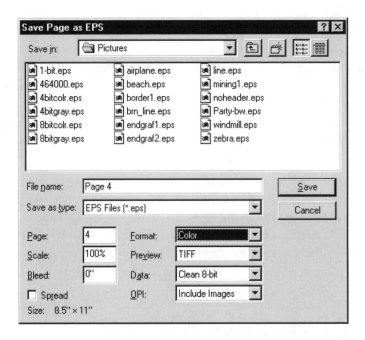

These options are set using the Format, Preview, Data, and OPI drop-down menus, which include a number of options.

■ **Format** The Color drop-down menu in the Format menu includes options for saving your page and pictures to Color, B&W (black and white), DCS, or DCS 2.0. The Color option saves your entire page and its pictures with all its applied colors; the B&W option saves the page in a single color of black, converting all type and pictures to black and grayscale. The DCS option enables you to use desktop color separation standards. DCS (essentially version 1.0) supports only process color, saving your page and all its contents to be reproduced in the standard four colors—cyan, magenta, yellow, and black (CMYK). The more up-to-date DCS 2.0 format supports both process and spot color. If your document contains spot colors applied to items on your page(s), the resulting EPS file will contain all colors specified.

■ **Preview** The preview applied to your page may be set to either TIFF or None (Macintosh platform versions also include PICT file formats) in the

Preview drop-down menu. Previews of entire pages often result in large file sizes, so setting a preview to None may help avoid overly-large files.

■ **Data**   The data representing your EPS may be set to ASCII, Binary, or Clean 8-bit; the latter is the most common format and default selection. Certain types of applications may require that ASCII or binary EPS files be supported. Before selecting either of these options, you may want to consult your output device documentation.

■ **OPI**   Open prepress interface (OPI) is a standard wherein the images you include on your page, and subsequently within your exported EPS file, may be contained within the EPS file or left as externally-linked files. The OPI option may be set to Include Images, Omit TIFF, or Omit TIFF & EPS.

TIP ⟶   *For more information on other options available in the Save Page as EPS dialog box, see* Chapter 16, Printing Your Pages.

Conclusion

As you might have concluded by working through the features and exercises described in this chapter, working with picture properties may be as simple or as complex as your design or layout requires. In this chapter, you've explored the capabilities available to you in applying color to your pictures, and you've seen how you can control your picture's appearance both on screen and in print. You've also learned the intricacies of one of the most complex tasks in XPress—applying picture clipping paths using both embedded paths and alpha channels, and creating clipping paths with XPress' own tool set.

But, pictures are rarely static elements that stand alone in a design or layout. They are often accompanied by text and other graphics in various formats. Complex designs and layouts often require that you tightly fit these elements together in order to communicate an idea or concept. So, although you may now have the impression that you know all there is to know about working with pictures, you have more to explore about creating layouts and documents in the next chapter, *Combining Text and Graphics.*

8

CHAPTER 9

Combining Text
and Pictures

Athena/ Acropolis/ Greece

305

Y ou may have thumbed to this chapter from one of several related areas. In fact, there are several points within this book that bring you here for the simple reason that this chapter is an absolute must read if you plan to use both text and pictures together on the same page.

Bringing text and graphics together in a single layout was previously a labor-intensive function usually left only to experienced electronic artists or designers. With the innovations in XPress, a multitude of capabilities have opened the doors for novices to explore and for experts to increase their productivity. In this chapter, you'll learn about all the ways XPress enables you to combine text and pictures on a single page, and how you may control these two types of objects in an effort to visually—and physically—integrate them. Along the way, you'll pick up tips and tricks for using these features effectively.

Setting Picture Runaround

Runaround is the term used to describe the effect of having text avoid an item on your page. If your publishing experience stems from the days when text runarounds required hours of cutting and pasting lines of text, you'll no doubt develop a profound appreciation of this feature. Although running text around your picture box might be considered slightly advanced by some users, it's one of the more commonly sought-after features for even the simplest layouts.

Creating a Simple Runaround

Runarounds may be applied not only to picture boxes, rules, and shapes, but to *any* type of item you can create in XPress. Runarounds are applied using the Modify | Runaround dialog box options and may be set in a number of ways. But, before you delve too far into all the variations of applying a runaround, let's explore how to apply one generically. To apply a runaround in XPress, follow these steps:

1. In an open document, create a simple text box using the Rectangle text box tool. Fill it with text by either typing, pasting, or importing the text. For now, leave the text alignment of your text at flush-left by selecting all the text with the Content tool (CTRL/CMD+A) and choosing Style | Alignment | Left (CTRL/CMD+SHIFT+L).

2. Create a second text box that is approximately the same depth as the first box by using the Oval text box tool, and then apply a color (such as solid black) to the box using the Modify (CTRL/CMD+M) | Box tab dialog box Color options.

3. Position the oval text box to straddle the right edge of the rectangular text box approximately half the width of the oval. Notice the oval text box automatically repels the characters in the rectangular text box, as shown in the following illustration, and the runaround is instantly reflowed as you position the oval. By default, XPress applies a runaround to all new objects.

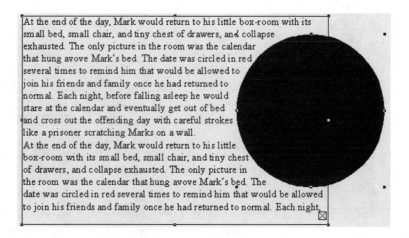

4. Select all the text in the rectangular text box and apply a justified alignment using the Content tool (CTRL/CMD+SHIFT+J). Notice the lines of text now match more closely the left contour of the oval text box.

5. Select the oval text box with the Item tool and open the Modify | Runaround tab (CTRL/CMD+T) dialog box. Notice the Type option in the dialog box currently displays Item, the Outset value is 1 point, and the Preview window reflects the effects of these options, as shown in the following illustration.

9

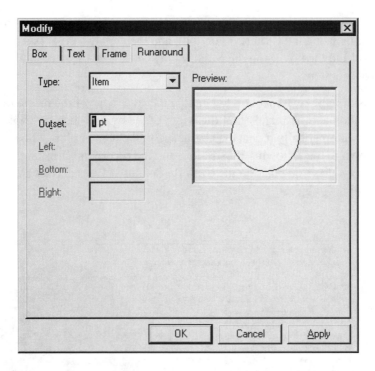

6. Change the Outset option to 6 points and click OK to accept the value. Notice that even before you click OK, the Preview window is updated to indicate the results of the new value.

7. Move the oval text box so that it is centered within space occupied by the rectangular text box by dragging it with the Item tool. Notice after it is in position, that the text is reflowed to the shape of the oval—but only on the right-hand side of the oval.

8. Select the rectangular text box and press CTRL/CMD+M to open the Modify dialog box, and then click Text to display the Text tab options.

9. Set the Run Text Around All Sides option to active and click OK to accept the new property. Notice the text now flows around all sides of the oval text box, as shown in the following illustration. You've just completed your first basic runaround.

At the end of the day, Mark would return to his little box-room with its small bed, small chair, and tiny chest of drawers, and collapse exhausted. The only picture in the room was the calendar that hung avove Mark's bed. The date was circled in red several times to remind him that would be allowed to join his friends and family once he had returned to normal. Each night, before falling asleep he would stare at the calendar and eventually get out of bed and cross out the offending day with careful strokes like a prisoner scratching Marks on a wall. At the end of the day, Mark would return to his little box-room with its small bed, small chair, and tiny chest of drawers, and collapse exhausted. The only picture in

The most significant concept to grasp from following the preceding steps is that text runaround is a function of *both* objects involved—not simply the object you want to run the text around. When you applied a runaround Outset value to your oval text box, you also needed to set the text running around it to accommodate the shape of all its sides.

TIP ➤ *To turn off the runaround effect, choose Item | Runaround (CTRL/CMD+T) to open the Modify | Runaround tab dialog box, and then choose None from the Type drop-down menu.*

The runaround options in the preceding example are limited because of the simplicity of the objects involved. The more complex the object, the trickier the runaround effect will be. In the following sections, you'll discover some of the more complex issues surrounding runaround effects applied to objects such as basic graphical pictures and pictures with applied clipping paths. You'll also find out that some new, powerful automated runaround features in XPress enable you to overcome much of the tedium involved in customizing runarounds to suit the visual elements in pictures.

9

Understanding Runaround Options

The type of runaround XPress enables you to apply to your item depends solely on the type of item you are working with. For example, in the preceding example you discovered that oval-shaped items may have only a single uniform runaround measure applied using the Outset option. The same limitation applies to all other available shapes in XPress except rectangular-shaped boxes. When rectangular-shaped items are selected, you may apply values individually to the top, left, right, and bottom sides of the box shape. Runaround values must fall within a range between 0 and 288 points (4 inches).

TIP *Although most runaround effects involve affecting your text to be "repelled" by the outside edges of a box shape, you may also apply runarounds to follow the contours of your shape within its borders by entering negative values. For example, an oval box with an outset value of –6 points repels text uniformly from 6 points* inside *its shape, as shown in the following illustration.*

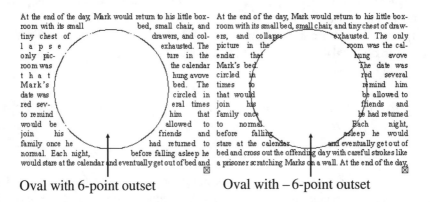

Oval with 6-point outset   Oval with –6-point outset

Before getting too far into XPress' runaround options, it may help to understand their capabilities and limitations. As you learn about these options, you may notice a striking similarity to the capabilities of applying clipping paths, discussed in the section called *Working with Picture Clipping Paths* in *Chapter 8, Advanced Picture Strategies*. In fact, clipping paths behave in combination with runaround options, as you'll see later on in this section.

■ **Item** When any item is selected in XPress, the Item option is selected automatically as the default for all shapes. As mentioned earlier, when the Item option is selected as the runaround type, other options become available in the Modify | Runaround tab dialog box. The Outset option becomes available for applying a uniform runaround to all shapes except rectangular shapes, for which you can set top, right, left, and bottom runaround values individually.

When text boxes and other types of boxes and lines are selected, your choice for runaround options is either Item or None. However, applying runarounds to pictures is more complex than for simple text boxes or other basic items. From this point, applying runaround options becomes a slightly more complex operation, enabling you to use XPress' more powerful runaround features. When pictures are selected, more options become available in the Modify Runaround tab dialog box, as shown in the following illustration.

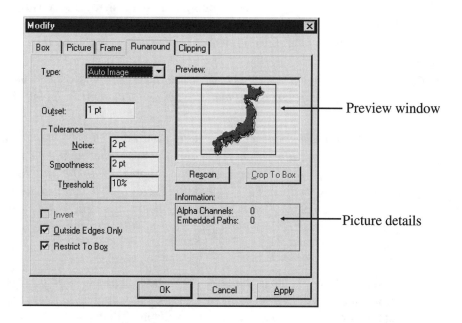

Preview window

Picture details

9

Although the Runaround tab dialog box contains much of the same options as the Clipping dialog box, the options are slightly reorganized to reduce confusion between the two. The Preview window indicates the effects of the selected options, various options appear depending on the runaround type chosen, and an Information area displays certain details about your selected picture.

Because the number of points used in describing your picture runaround shape is not as critical to output as the clipping path, this information is omitted from the Information area of the Runaround tab dialog box.

When working with pictures, the following runaround types may be available to you, depending on the format and condition of your picture, and how it has been prepared.

■ **Auto Image**   Selecting Auto Image enables you to quickly and automatically apply a runaround to the edges of your image. This could be considered perhaps the simplest of runarounds to apply to pictures. The Auto Image runaround type automatically detects the edges of your picture and sets the runaround shape accordingly. A uniform Outset value may also be applied to the resulting runaround shape; the sensitivity of this option is set using the Noise, Smoothness, and Threshold options shown in the preceding illustration and discussed later in this section.

While the Auto Image runaround is in use, the runaround created in the Runaround tab dialog box is automatically used as the applied clipping path.

Because Auto Image creates an automatic runaround shape, you may not choose the Invert option (discussed below) to reverse the runaround shape as with clipping paths. And, when a picture is applied with the Auto Image runaround type, runaround shape-editing controls become available whenever you select the picture on your document page. The behavior and resulting clipping and runaround paths are identical to those in XPress version 3.3.

■ **Embedded Paths**   If the picture you are working with has been prepared to include an embedded path using an image-editing application, you may select this option; otherwise it will be unavailable. Choosing the Embedded Paths option enables XPress to base the runaround's shape on that of the embedded path in the picture. The shape of embedded paths may also be adjusted using the Outset, Noise, and Smoothness options.

- **Alpha Channels**   If the picture you are working with has been prepared to include an alpha channel using an image-editing application, this option will be available. The runaround's shape will be based on that of the embedded path in the picture. The sensitivity of alpha channels may be set using the Noise and Smoothness options, but not the Threshold option.

- **Non-White Areas**   As with clipping paths, this option yields the best results when you use pictures that feature well-defined dark picture elements on light-colored backgrounds (or vice versa). Choosing Non-White Areas as your runaround type enables XPress to detect the edges of the picture element based on changes in pixel color and shade value, depending on the Threshold value entered.

NOTE   *Choosing an embedded path, alpha channel, or non-white area for the runaround has no effect on the clipping path, which controls the display of the picture.*

- **Same As Clipping**   If you have already gone to the efforts of creating or applying a clipping path to your picture, this option enables you to use the same shape. While Same As Clipping is selected, all options except Outset and Smoothness are unavailable. To check the values of these settings while Same As Clipping is selected, click the Clipping tab of the Modify dialog box. This option could be considered the reverse choice of using Auto Image.

- **Picture Bounds**   The Picture Bounds option creates a runaround based on the edges of your picture, regardless of their color or shade. For example, if your picture is surrounded by a white frame or border, the runaround is shaped to this area. While the Picture Bounds option is chosen, you may enter your own values for the top, left, right, and bottom offsets of your picture's runaround shape.

Depending on which type of runaround is chosen, the following options may become available.

- **Outset**   This option applies a uniform offset value to your runaround shape. Entering a positive value causes the runaround shape to be expanded from the edges of your item, while entering a negative

9

value causes the overall shape to be reduced into the edges of your item's shape. The Outset value entered in this field also controls how closely the runaround shape created by XPress' automated features follows the edge of the detected areas of pictures. Where this option applies, you may set it within a range between –288 and 288 points (–4 and 4 inches).

- **Noise**   The Noise value enables XPress to create a runaround that ignores stray pixels, which may cause uneven shapes and increase the complexity of the resulting runaround. The value entered corresponds to the size of the area encountered. For example, entering a value of 6 points causes areas 6 points and under to be ignored. Noise may be set within a range between 0 and 4 inches.

- **Smoothness**   The Smoothness value determines how closely the contours of your picture are followed when creating the runaround. Smoothness may be set to any value within a range between 0 and 100 points. Lower values create smoother, more complex runarounds; higher values create less accurate, less complex shapes.

- **Threshold**   As with clipping paths, the Threshold value is critical if you intend to apply runarounds using the Non-White Areas type. Threshold is based on percentage of shade or color and enables you to set which areas of your picture are detected as hard "edges" of objects. Threshold operates on the basis of contrasting pixels, comparing dark pixels to light pixels. When using the Non-White Areas type of runaround, pixels lighter than the threshold percentage value are excluded from the runaround shape, and darker pixels are included. The reverse is true when using alpha channels as runarounds. When using the Embedded Paths, or Same As Clipping runaround types, the Threshold option is unavailable.

The following options are available as check boxes when working with runarounds; they are available depending on the runaround type chosen.

- **Invert**   This option has the effect of reversing the runaround area of the selected clipping path. Inverting a runaround is usually required in cases where alpha channels incorrectly isolate the background of a picture instead of the picture element. Invert has a profound effect on the condition of your runaround, causing text to flow through the inside areas of your picture instead of running around the image.

- **Outside Edges Only** When used in combination with the Non-White Areas type of runaround, this option enables areas of pixels that are lighter than the Threshold value within the picture element to be excluded from the runaround. With this option active, only the area outside your picture shapes the runaround. With Outside Edges Only inactive, both the outside and inside areas form the shape of the runaround, enabling text to appear in open areas.

- **Restrict To Box** When a runaround is created, the subsequent runaround shape is formed from the shape of the entire picture, minus the area created by the runaround shape. With Restrict To Box active, the runaround shape and the picture box boundaries combine to form the runaround shape. With the Restrict To Box option inactive, the runaround boundaries may extend beyond the edges of the picture box if more of your picture exists.

- **Rescan** Each time you choose a new runaround type or change an option such as the Threshold value, your picture box is rescanned and a new runaround shape results. Your picture appears in the Preview window of the Runaround tab dialog box, and the runaround appears in magenta (according to your application preferences) within the Preview window. Areas that are not eligible for text flow appear empty. You may force the runaround to be recreated using the current settings by clicking the Rescan button.

- **Crop To Box** This button has the effect of eliminating those portions of the runaround shape that extend beyond the edges of the picture box.

Exploring Runaround Effects

With the preceding features and options in mind, let's explore some of the capabilities of automated runaround effects when integrating text with various types and conditions of pictures. Although there are many types of picture files, the two most common types you may need to run text around are bitmap pictures and graphical EPS images.

Bitmap Runaround Effects

Bitmap pictures inside of picture boxes that are rectangular in shape and don't include applied clipping paths need only have the Item type of runaround selected.

Entering runaround measures in the Top, Left, Right, and Bottom fields of the Modify | Runaround tab dialog box will enable you to control the distance between the picture edges and the text on individual sides. But, if the bitmap picture is uneven in shape, you may need to use one of XPress' automated runaround effects, such as Auto Image.

When creating any runaround effect, your aim is to choose the runaround type that requires as little manual editing to the shape of the resulting runaround as possible. Don't be too surprised if you encounter an image that simply cannot be set automatically for a perfect runaround within XPress. Although certain applied runaround types create perfect effects on some pictures, other picture runarounds often require editing. And, in certain cases, an image-editing application may be needed to create an alpha channel selection or embedded path.

The bitmap picture in Figure 9-1 shows various Threshold values applied at automated runarounds using the Auto Image runaround type. In this case, a well-defined visual element of a fisherman sitting on his beached boat is set on two different background types—a blue sky and a beach foreground. The ground is nearly uniform in color and isolates easily; the sky is a graduated blend of color ranging from dark to light, and it is difficult to isolate. Isolating the subject of this picture using automatic features is severely restricted (actually, impossible) because of the diverse conditions of these two background types.

In Figure 9-1, the image at the upper-left corner shows the original grayscale picture with no clipping or runaround effects applied; the image at the upper-right shows a Threshold value of 20 percent applied. At 20 percent, the sky background continues to appear in its darkest shades, while the highlight areas of the boat are already beginning to be clipped from the picture composition. The bottom-left example shows a Threshold value of 49 percent applied to eliminate the sky. Unfortunately, in the end, an alpha channel was used as the image clipping path, and Same As Clipping was used as the runaround type, as seen in the bottom-right example.

TIP ⟶ *When editing a runaround path, the same shaping and editing procedures apply as when working with Bezier tools and paths—with the exception of deleting points using keystrokes. To delete selected points, press ALT/OPTION+BACKSPACE/DELETE. After editing either your runaround or clipping path, both the runaround and clipping path types automatically change to User-Edited Path.*

In Figure 9-2, you'll notice that even this strategy doesn't always apply, and it seems some pictures are unavoidable candidates for manual editing of runarounds, independent of their clipping paths. In this grayscale bitmap example, there are two sunlit joggers on a darkening sky background. Their shapes are well-defined and in

Original

Threshold at
20 percent

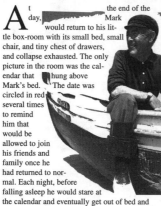

Threshold at
49 percent

Alpha channel
applied

FIGURE 9-1   Varying Threshold values applied using Auto Image
on a bitmap

focus, but the similarity of the shades of sky to shades in their clothing and hair coloring make isolating them using automatic features, clipping paths, or runaround effects quite tricky.

In Figure 9-2, the example at the top-left corner shows the original grayscale bitmap image with no clipping effect applied and a straightforward Item runaround of 6 points for the top, left, right, and bottom edges of the picture box. The example

at the top-right corner shows the same image with a Non-White Areas clipping path created with a Threshold value of 58 percent, and a Non-White Areas runaround type used with a Threshold value of 60 percent, and an Outset of 2 points. Even though the picture image is disappearing, the background insists on appearing in its darkest areas.

At the bottom-left of Figure 9-2, an alpha channel is created in an image-editing application and used as the clipping path, while the Same As Clipping runaround type is selected. But, because of the shape of the two main picture elements and the stray spaces left between them, the clipping path doesn't serve well as a runaround path. At the bottom-right corner, the runaround path has been manually edited to eliminate these spaces.

Graphical EPS Runaround Effects

While applying runarounds to bitmaps can be tricky at best, graphical EPS pictures are perhaps the other side of the coin. Graphical EPS images are often set on a pure white background, making them perfect candidates for XPress' automated runaround effects. When running text around unevenly-shaped graphics, you may effectively choose the Auto Image, Non-White Areas, or Same As Clipping types, each resulting in approximately the same level of efficiency. Figure 9-3 shows a black-and-white bitmap EPS applied with the Same As Clipping type runaround; the only alteration is an Outset value of 3 points. In fact, because this particular EPS graphic doesn't include any background shades, the same effects would result from using the Non-White Areas or Auto Image types.

The clipping path lets XPress know that the image is uneven in shape, and the runaround works to flow text around its contours. Figure 9-4 shows an example of a grayscale EPS image that includes no background shading, making it ideal for the Non-White Areas runaround. But, in order for the runaround to apply, the clipping path must also be applied using Non-White Areas first. Once you've thought it through, you'll deduce that the same results will occur if you choose Same As Clipping after applying the Non-White Areas type in the Clipping dialog box.

Even though it can often be straightforward to apply clipping paths and runaround effects to EPS graphics, you will eventually encounter an image shape

9

At the end of the day, Mark would return to his little box-room with its small bed, small chair, and tiny chest of drawers, and collapse exhausted. The only picture in the room was the calendar that hung above Mark's bed. The date was circled in red several times to remind him that would be allowed to join his friends and family once he had returned to normal. Each night, before falling asleep he would stare at the calendar and eventually get out of bed and cross out the offending day with careful strokes like a prisoner scratching marks on a wall. At the end of the day, Mark would return to his little box-room with its small bed, small chair, and tiny chest of drawers, and collapse exhausted. The only picture in the room was the calendar that hung above the end of the day, Mark would return to his little box-room with its small bed. The only picture in the room was the

calendar that hung above Mark's bed. The date was circled in red several times to remind him that would be allowed to join his friends and family once he had returned to normal. Each night, before falling asleep he would stare at the calendar and eventually get out of bed and cross out the offending day with careful strokes like a prisoner scratching marks on a wall.

At the end of the day, Mark would return to his little box-room with its small bed, small chair, and tiny chest

FIGURE 9-3   Applying a runaround to an EPS graphic using Same As Clipping

that does not lend itself well to automated runarounds, as seen in Figure 9-5. Integrating reference or design graphics such as maps into your text often results in highly-irregular shapes and difficult runaround spaces. In these cases, modifying an automatically-applied runaround is the quickest course of action. In this example, the Auto Image type of runaround was first applied to quickly create both a runaround and clipping path simultaneously, and then the runaround path was edited manually.

Editing a Runaround Shape

Editing a runaround shape is not unlike editing a clipping path. Your runaround path is edited manually using Bezier-like point-and-path editing operations. To enter the

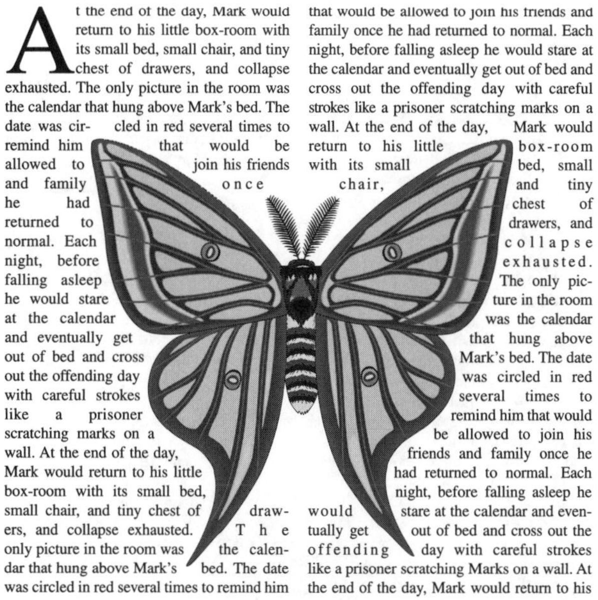

At the end of the day, Mark would return to his little box-room with its small bed, small chair, and tiny chest of drawers, and collapse exhausted. The only picture in the room was the calendar that hung above Mark's bed. The date was cir-   cled in red several times to remind him   that   would   be allowed to   join his friends and family   once he   had returned to normal. Each night, before falling asleep he would stare at the calendar and eventually get out of bed and cross out the offending day with careful strokes like   a   prisoner scratching marks on a wall. At the end of the day, Mark would return to his little box-room with its small bed, small chair, and tiny chest of   draw-ers, and collapse exhausted.   T h e only picture in the room was   the calen-dar that hung above Mark's   bed. The date was circled in red several times to remind him

that would be allowed to join his friends and family once he had returned to normal. Each night, before falling asleep he would stare at the calendar and eventually get out of bed and cross out the offending day with careful strokes like a prisoner scratching marks on a wall. At the end of the day,   Mark would return to his little   box-room with its small   bed, small chair,   and tiny   chest of   drawers, and   c o l l a p s e   e x h a u s t e d.   The only pic-   ture in the room   was the calendar   that hung above   Mark's bed. The date   was circled in red   several   times   to   remind him that would   be allowed to join his   friends and family once he   had returned to normal. Each   night, before falling asleep he   stare at the calendar and even-would   tually get   out of bed and cross out the offending   day with careful strokes like a prisoner scratching Marks on a wall. At the end of the day, Mark would return to his

---

■ **FIGURE 9-4**   When using EPS graphics and a Non-White Areas clipping path, setting your runaround to Same As Clipping is often the quickest way to create the runaround

9

runaround editing state, you must first choose the picture containing the runaround path you want to edit, and then choose Item | Edit | Runaround (CTRL/OPTION+F10/F4). Once the editing state is active, your runaround path is displayed on screen as shown in the next illustration, enabling you to change the shape of paths and the condition of points in the same manner as you would edit a Bezier path. Runaround points and paths appear on your screen in magenta by default (according to set application preferences) and are differentiated from the green display color used for clipping paths. Selected points, point curve handles, and paths appear in blue.

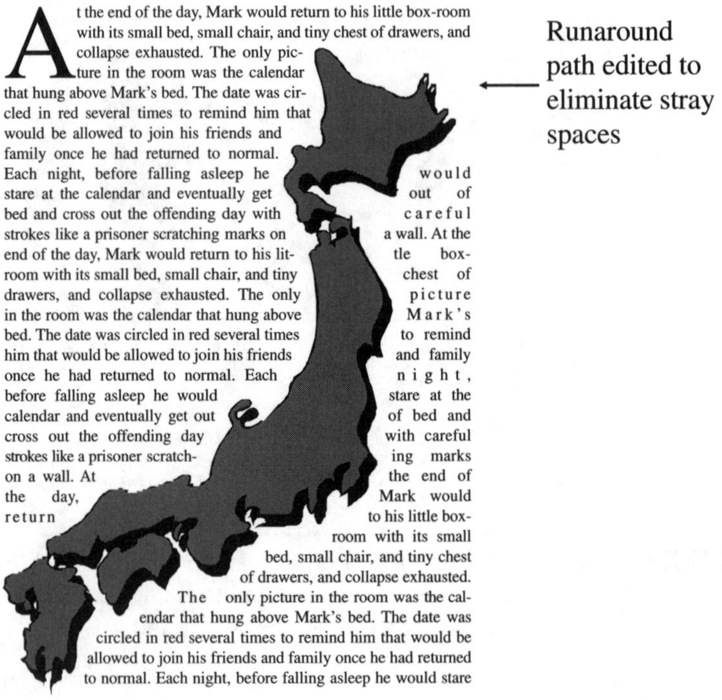

At the end of the day, Mark would return to his little box-room with its small bed, small chair, and tiny chest of drawers, and collapse exhausted. The only picture in the room was the calendar that hung above Mark's bed. The date was circled in red several times to remind him that would be allowed to join his friends and family once he had returned to normal. Each night, before falling asleep he stare at the calendar and eventually get bed and cross out the offending day with strokes like a prisoner scratching marks on end of the day, Mark would return to his lit-room with its small bed, small chair, and tiny drawers, and collapse exhausted. The only in the room was the calendar that hung above bed. The date was circled in red several times him that would be allowed to join his friends once he had returned to normal. Each before falling asleep he would calendar and eventually get out cross out the offending day strokes like a prisoner scratch-on a wall. At the day, return would out of careful a wall. At the tle box-chest of picture Mark's to remind and family night, stare at the of bed and with careful ing marks the end of Mark would to his little box-room with its small bed, small chair, and tiny chest of drawers, and collapse exhausted. The only picture in the room was the cal-endar that hung above Mark's bed. The date was circled in red several times to remind him that would be allowed to join his friends and family once he had returned to normal. Each night, before falling asleep he would stare

Runaround path edited to eliminate stray spaces

FIGURE 9-5   Certain EPS graphics will inevitably need to have their runaround shapes edited manually

TIP

When editing runaround paths, you do not need to choose any specialized tools—your cursor changes automatically to a hand-style cursor when it is held over a runaround point.

At the end of the day, Mark would return to his little box-room with its small bed, small chair, and tiny chest of drawers, and collapse exhausted. The only picture in the room was the calendar that hung above Mark's bed. The date was circled in red several times to remind him that would be allowed to join his friends and family once he had returned to normal. Each night, before falling asleep he would stare at the calendar and eventually get out of bed and cross out the offending day with careful strokes like a prisoner scratching marks on a wall. At the end of the day, Mark would return to his little box-room with its small bed, small chair, and tiny chest of drawers, and collapse exhausted. The only picture in the room was the calendar that hung above the end of the day, Mark would return to his little box-room with its small bed. The only picture in the room was the calendar that hung above Mark's bed. The date was circled in red several times to remind him that would be allowed to join his friends and family once he had returned to normal. Each night, before falling asleep he would stare at the calendar and eventually get out of bed and cross out the offending day with careful strokes like a prisoner scratching marks on a wall. At the end of the day, Mark would return to his little box-room with its small bed, small chair, and tiny chest

TIP

You may not edit certain types of applied runarounds—even when the clipping path remains editable. For example, choosing a Same As Clipping type runaround leaves the runaround editing state unavailable. Editing the clipping path automatically causes changes to the shape of the runaround path to occur.

To exit the editing state and return the display of your picture to normal, choose Item | Edit | Runaround (CTRL/OPTION+F10/F4) again. After making changes to your runaround path, the Modify | Runaround tab dialog box will display your runaround type as User-Edited Path.

9

Strategies for Shaping Boxes

If the layout you are creating calls for unusually-shaped text boxes, XPress features some powerful capabilities in this regard. Creating an unusually-shaped text box can be a tedious but rewarding exercise. Because of the Bezier capabilities of XPress, you may shape a text box to be virtually anything you want and have the text in your document flow freely within the shape.

Creating a shape for your text involves several steps. In essence, you'll be creating basic shapes and combining and reshaping them to suit your needs. Although the shapes you create on your own can be nearly unlimited, the two following exercises involve creating two basic shapes: a key-shaped box (created using text boxes, Merge commands, and text modifications), and a box shape based on an existing character (created using XPress' Text to Box command). Although these two exercises demonstrate creating specific shapes, you are limited only by your imagination.

Creating a Key-shaped Box

The capability to shape boxes using Beziers opens the doors of creative opportunity for picture or text box applications. As a practical exercise in creating an unevenly-shaped box in the shape of a key, follow these steps:

1. In an open document, choose the Oval text box tool from the Tool palette and while holding the SHIFT key to constrain the shape to a circle, create a text box.

2. With the text box selected, press CTRL/CMD+D to create a duplicate.

3. Resize the new text box to roughly one-third the size of the first. Holding the SHIFT key while resizing the oval shape will constrain it to a circle.

4. Using the Item tool, position the two circles so that the smaller circle is perfectly centered within the larger circle.

5. Choose the Rectangle text box tool from the Tool palette while holding the ALT/OPTION key to keep the tool perpetually selected, and then create a tall text box extending from the bottom of the large circle, as shown in the following illustration.

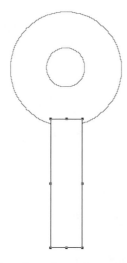

6. Position this rectangular-shaped text box so that it is centered vertically with the two circles.

7. Create two more rectangle text boxes, roughly similar in size, to serve as the shapes for the serrated edge of the eventual key shape. Position them to overlap the lower right side of the first rectangle.

8. Now we will combine the shapes. Choose the Item tool from the Tool palette and while holding the SHIFT key, click each circle box to select it.

9. With the two circles selected, choose Item | Merge | Combine. The two circles are merged into a single circular shape with a cutout hole in the center to represent the handle of the key.

10. To combine the rectangle boxes, hold the SHIFT key and click each of the three rectangle boxes with the Item tool.

11. Choose Item | Merge | Union to combine the three rectangles into a single shape.

12. With the newly-created shape still selected, hold the SHIFT key again, click the circular shape created earlier, and choose Item | Merge | Union to unite the shapes into one. Your key-shaped text box is complete. To verify that it is indeed a text box, choose Item | Content and ensure the box state displays as Text.

TIP → *Although you created the initial shapes using text boxes, and the results created a text box, you may also use picture boxes and simply convert their content state to text after the final shape is complete.*

13. Choose the Content tool from the Tool palette and import text into the shape by pressing CTRL/CMD+E to open the Get Text dialog box and load a text document, as shown in the following illustration.

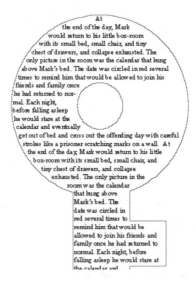

With text now inside your key-shaped box, you'll notice that by default the text does not completely fill the shape. To set the text to follow all sides of the text box shape, choose Item | Modify | Text tab. Click Run Text Around All Sides, and then click OK to accept the modification. Your text now follows throughout the shape. Apply your text properties in the usual way. When working with text inside unevenly-shaped text boxes, set smaller character sizes with tight tracking and justified alignment, as shown in Figure 9-6.

Creating a Character-shaped Box

XPress' Text to Box command enables you to create box shapes based on text characters, fonts, and styles. The resulting shape may be filled with color, text, or

BusinessWeek

FEBRUARY 3, 1997   A PUBLICATION OF THE McGRAW-HILL COMPANIES $3.50

Our Annual Ratings

THE BEST MUTUAL FUNDS

Building A Winning Fund Portfolio

Up-and-Coming Funds to Watch

NEW Improved Performance Guide

Design-Francesca Messina

Designer-Elaine Chu
Illustrators-Stuart Bradford, Richard Downs, LeVan/Barbee Studio

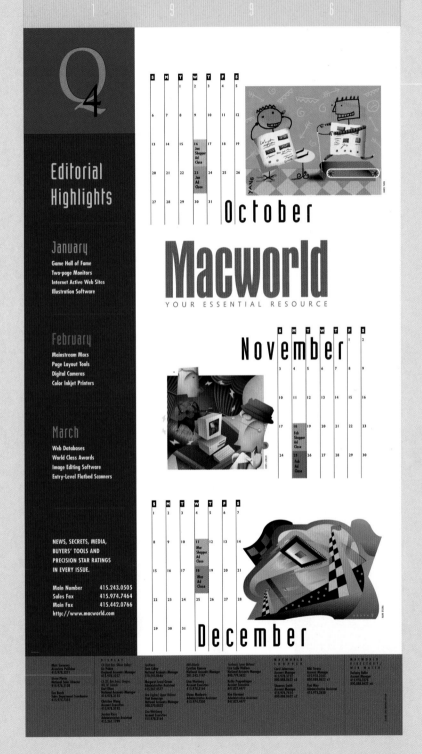

Designer-Elaine Chu
Illustrators-James Yang, Chris Lensch, Hank Osuna

Canada is the Competitive Alternative...

Published by Prospectus Inc.

Exhibit I-4
Comparison of Total Annual Costs
All Industries, by Country (US $'000)

	Index
Canada	94.6
Sweden	96.3
United Kingdom	98.3
United States	100.0
Italy	102.6
France	103.6
Germany	107.2

©KPMG Canada and Prospectus Inc. 5,000 10,000 15,000 20,000
■ Location-insensitive costs ■ Location-sensitive costs

... to France, Germany, Italy, Sweden, the UK and the US. Conventional wisdom has it that investors targeting North American markets usually do best by operating from low-cost US production sites. The reality, according to a new report, is that in 1997 most of these investors may have been better off locating in Canada.

A NEW STUDY RECENTLY RELEASED by KPMG Canada called *The Competitive Alternative: A Comparison of Business Costs in Canada, Europe and the United States*, reveals that Canada now boasts the lowest business costs among seven leading North American and European countries — including a 5.4 percent advantage over the United States.

MANY AMERICAN ENTREPRE-neurs have already recognized that Canada has become a useful base from which to penetrate North American markets — most notably, markets in their own country. US direct investment in Canada, currently estimated at $122.7 billion, has risen by 62 percent since 1988, the year before the FTA and subsequently NAFTA came into effect.

But, as any Canadian business executive who travels abroad is well aware, the nuances of what makes Canada a good place to do business are a bit of a North American secret. Surveys reveal that many European investors often have little or no awareness of Canada and harbour significant misconceptions about Canada as a potential investment location. Most of their North American target markets, of course, are located in the US. So Canada is often ignored when these people are making decisions about where to lay down production facilities on this side of the Atlantic.

The advantage was both sectoral and geographic: the top 14 low-cost cities on the list are Canadian. In fact, all 17 of the Canadian cities in the survey finished in

That cost advantage, coupled with easy Canadian access to US markets under the 1994 North American Free Trade Agreement, will undoubtedly enhance Canada's reputation as a springboard to the North American marketplace.

This independent study should give the Europeans pause. KPMG Canada is a member of KPMG International, the highly respected professional services firm. The current study is an update and extension of KPMG surveys conducted annually since 1994. This year's international edition is sponsored by Royal Bank of Canada, Ontario Hydro, the Atlantic Canada Opportunities Agency, and Canada's Department of Foreign Affairs and International Trade, and published by Prospectus Inc.

KPMG FOUND THAT THE CANADIAN cost advantage prevails to varying degrees across a range of eight production sectors, from labour-intensive to techno-logy-intensive. In fact, Canada finished first in every one of the sectors scrutinized: electronics, food processing, medical device, metal fabrication, pharmaceuticals, plastics, software production, and telecommunication equipment.

the top 20 of the 42 cities surveyed.

The most cost-competitive European cities were both located in Sweden — Karlskoga (15th), and Goteborg (16th). Two UK cities, Telford (21st), and Cardiff (22nd), ranked ahead of all US cities. The highest-ranking US cities were Norfolk, VA (23rd), Austin, TX (24th), and Raleigh, NC (25th).

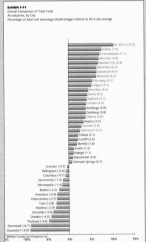

Exhibit I-11
Overall Comparison of Total Costs
All industries, by City
Percentage of total cost advantage (disadvantage) relative to US 4-city average

City	
St. John's (10.3)	
Halifax (7.9)	
Charlottetown (7.7)	
Moncton (7.1)	
Quebec City (6.8)	
Edmonton (6.4)	
Saskatoon (6.4)	
Montreal (6.2)	
Winnipeg (5.4)	
Calgary (5.2)	
Hamilton (4.4)	
Sarnia (4.3)	
Sudbury (4.1)	
London (4.0)	
Karlskoga (3.9)	
Goteborg (3.8)	
Ottawa (3.8)	
Malmo (3.4)	
Toronto (2.8)	
Vancouver (2.5)	
Telford (2.1)	
Cardiff (2.0)	
Norfolk (1.8)	
Austin (1.2)	
Raleigh (1.1)	
Manchester (0.9)	
Colorado Springs (0.7)	
Scranton (-0.3)	
Bellingham (-0.6)	
Columbus (-0.7)	
Sacramento (-1.3)	
Minneapolis (-1.4)	
Boston (-2.2)	
Avezzano (-2.6)	
Valenciennes (-2.7)	
Turin (-2.8)	
Modena (-2.9)	
Grenoble (-3.6)	
Toulouse (-4.6)	
Darmstadt (-4.7)	
Dusseldorf (-4.9)	

©KPMG Canada and Prospectus Inc. -10% -5% 0% 5% 10% 15%

THE STUDY FOCUSED ON 42 LOCATIONS: 27 in North America and 15 in Europe. The investment model used was based on the establishment and operation of a new plant, employing a minimum of 90 workers over 10 years, in each of eight industry sectors. For the purposes of international comparison, three to four comparable cities in each country were averaged, with results shown for a number of categories, such as labour costs, property costs, construction costs, transportation costs, utility costs, taxes, and so on.

According to Stuart MacKay and Glenn Mair, co-authors of the report, labour costs typically represent more than half of location-sensitive costs. Among the countries studied, the UK recorded the lowest combination of base wages, benefit costs and wage-based taxes. Canada finished second, followed by Sweden and Italy. Marginal productivity advantages in Germany, the US and France were not enough to offset the relatively high labour rates in those countries.

North America has a significant advantage over Europe on land and building costs — for example, industrial land is about 12 times more expensive in Germany than in the United States. Canada finished second to the US in the land costs category, and first in terms of construction.

KPMG found that the Canadian cost advantage prevails to varying degrees across a range of eight production sectors.

Electricity costs were lowest in Sweden, followed by Canada. Germany and the UK led the field in transportation and delivery costs. The Europeans couldn't compete with North American telecommunication costs, where Canada placed first, followed closely by the US.

Canada's low interest rates placed it first in financing costs. Loan money is relatively plentiful in Canada, partially because of the federal and provincial government cutbacks in recent years.

Canada finished second only to Sweden in minimizing the corporate tax burden. Canada, France, Sweden and the UK offer effective combined corporate tax rates of less than 35 percent, providing a significant advantage over other countries. Relatively high property-based taxes in France and the UK partially offset their income tax advantage, leaving Sweden and Canada with the lowest overall corporate tax burden. Canada's R&D tax incentives are the most generous in the countries studied.

The 5.4 percent Canadian cost advantage over the US may surprise some Europeans, but the cost hierarchy in Europe will be well-known. The Canadian advantage was 1.7 percent over second-place Sweden and 3.7 percent over third-place UK, and was a much more formidable 8.6 percent over Italy, 9.0 percent over France, and 13.8 percent over Germany.

THE STUDY FINDINGS ARE SENSITIVE to exchange rates. The Canadian advantage over the US would disappear, for instance, if the value of the Canadian dollar were to rise above US $0.83.

That, however, would require a surge of more than 14 percent in the value of the loonie relative to the US dollar — possible, of course, but certainly not probable anytime soon. The Canadian dollar hasn't travelled in that rarefied atmosphere for many years and the rate hasn't climbed above US $0.75 in more recent years.

NOTWITHSTANDING THE EXCHANGE RATE caveat, the case for locating in Canada has never been better documented than it is in this report. The Canadian cost advantage over three of the five European countries surveyed (Germany, France, and Italy) is formidable. More importantly, the cost advantage over the United States helps dispel the myth that setting up shop in US locations, such as the heavily-promoted Sun Belt, is necessarily the most cost effective way to go.

The study focused almost entirely on business costs, but its authors also point out that many other factors need to be considered in the selection of a business location. These include a variety of considerations with regard to economic and corporate environments and quality of life issues.

These are areas in which Canada has a reputation for having an edge. On the economic side of the coin, the fact that federal and provincial governments have made such significant progress in deficit reduction in recent years has lowered inflation and heightened business and con-sumer confidence to the highest levels in 15 to 20 years.

The fact that Canada has ranked first on the United Nations' Human Development Index four years in a row is more than a peripheral consideration for investors who are considering locating here.

THIS STUDY SHOULD OPEN A FEW eyes or investors aiming at EU markets only, it may well be that locating in Sweden or the UK will still be more logical than locating in Canada. But for investors aiming at North America, it is now hard to argue that Canada shouldn't be examined as an option.

The Competitive Alternative offers up this new evidence in a relatively low key way. It doesn't constitute proof positive that there are better profit opportunities in Canada than there are in the United States. But it will point out that the facts suggest investors would be foolish not to take a look at Canada before making a North American investment decision.

Indeed, To order copies of *The Competitive Alternative*, please contact the publisher, Prospectus Inc. at: **1-800-575-1146**, (toll-free in North America) or **(613) 231-2727; www.prospectus.com**.

To contact KPMG, please call Stuart MacKay (tel: 604-691-3410) or Glenn Mair (tel: 604-691-3340) in Vancouver.

"We have to work harder and smarter to spread the word about Canada's economic renaissance. The KPMG study is evidence that Canada can compete and win with the best in the world."

*John E. Cleghorn
Chairman and CEO
Royal Bank of Canada*

Design-Cotie Communications

Art Director-Andree Kahlmorgan/ **Illustrations-**Dave Jonason

Art Director-Francesca Messina/ **Photographs-**Elizabeth Hathon

MIDYEAR OUTLOOK

BusinessWeek

JUNE 16, 1997   A PUBLICATION OF THE McGRAW-HILL COMPANIES $3.50

SPECIAL INVESTMENT GUIDE

HOW TO PLAY THIS MARKET

SMART PLAYS IN **TECHNOLOGY**

 MUTUAL FUNDS | **MERGERS**

GLOBAL MARKETS **BONDS**

REAL ESTATE AND MORE

Internet: www.businessweek.com America Online: Keyword: BW

Design-Molly Leach/ **Illustrator**-Gary Hallgren

A t
the end of the day, Mark
would return to his little box-room
with its small bed, small chair, and tiny chest
of drawers, and collapse exhausted. The only picture in the room was the calendar that hung above
Mark's bed. The date was circled in red several times to
remind him that would be allowed to join his friends and
family once he had   returned to normal. Each
night, before falling   asleep he would stare at
the calendar and even-   tually get out of bed
and cross out the   offending day with
careful strokes like a   prisoner   scratching
marks on a wall. At the   end of the day, Mark
would return to his little box-room with its small bed, small
chair, and tiny chest of drawers, and collapse exhausted.
The only picture in the room was the calendar that
hung above Mark's bed. The date was circled in
red several times to remind him that would
be allowed to join his friends and
family once he had
returned to normal.
Each night, before
falling asleep he
would stare at the
calendar and eventually get out of
bed and cross out the offending
day with careful strokes like a
prisoner scratching marks on a
wall. At the end of the day, Mark
would return to his
little box-room with
its small bed, small chair, and tiny
chest of drawers, and collapse
exhausted. The only picture in the
room was the calendar that hung
above Mark's bed. The date was
circled in red sever-
al times to remind
him that would be
allowed to join his
friends and family

FIGURE 9-6   The completed key-shaped text box

9

pictures as your layout requires. As a practical exercise in creating a box shape based on a character, follow these steps:

1. In an open document, create a text box using any of the text box tools found in the Tool palette, and then enter the character for a question mark (?) using the Content tool.

2. Apply a font that features wide, bold characteristics, such as Helvetica Black or Bold Extended, and increase the size to the maximum preset

available (192 points). To do this quickly, highlight the character (CTRL/CMD+A) and increase the size repeatedly using the keyboard command CTRL/CMD+SHIFT+> until the character size stops increasing.

3. With the character still selected with the Content tool, choose the Style | Text to Box command. A duplicate of your character is created automatically in Bezier form. If you want, delete the original text box by selecting it with the Item tool and pressing CTRL/CMD+K.

4. Increase the size of the new shape by a factor of three using the Measurements palette and entering ***3** after the width and height measures in the palette and pressing RETURN/ENTER after each entry. The item is now three times the size of the original character.

5. By default, the new shape is in picture box state. If you want, you may stop following these steps and use the resulting shape as a picture box by importing a picture into it. To do this, select the Item tool and choose File | Get Picture to open the Get Picture dialog box and open a picture. From there use the picture box commands to manipulate the picture as you want.

6. To convert the picture box to a text box, choose Item | Content | Text. The picture box changes to a text box.

7. With the shape still selected with the Content tool, choose File | Get Text to open the Get Text dialog box and import a text document. Your shape is now loaded with text, but the text doesn't completely fill the text box shape yet.

8. With the text box shape still selected, open the Modify | Text tab dialog box and choose the Run Text Around All Sides option, and then click OK to accept the change. Notice that even though your text is flowing through what appears to be two separate boxes, no link exists. Only the fact that this box is shaped using a compound path enables the text to flow from one shape to the other.

9. Apply your text characteristics as you would normally. As you do, you'll discover again that when working with text inside unevenly-shaped text boxes, smaller character sizes set with tight tracking and justified alignment reflect the shape of the box most efficiently, as shown in Figure 9-7.

A t
the end of the day, Mark would return
to his little box-room with its small bed, small chair,
and tiny chest of drawers, and collapse exhausted. The only picture
in the room was the calendar that hung above Mark's bed. The date was circled in red several times to remind him that would be allowed to join his friends
and family once he had returned to normal. Each night, before falling asleep he would
stare at the calendar and eventually get out of bed and cross out the offending day with
careful strokes like a prisoner scratching marks on a wall. At the end of the day, Mark would

return to his little box-room with its	small bed, small chair, and tiny chest of
drawers, and collapse exhausted. The	only picture in the room was the calen-
dar that hung above Mark's bed. The	date was circled in red several times to
remind him that would be allowed	to join his friends and family once he
had returned to normal. Each night,	before falling asleep he would stare at
	the calendar and eventually get out of
	bed and cross out the offending day with
	careful strokes like a prisoner scratching
	marks on a wall. At the end of the day, Mark
	would return to his little box-room with its small
	bed, small chair, and tiny chest of drawers, and
	collapse exhausted. The only picture in the
	room was the calendar that hung above
	Mark's bed. The date was circled in red
	several times to remind him that
	would be allowed to join his
	friends and family once he had
	returned to normal. Each night,

before falling asleep he would stare at
the calendar and eventually get out of
bed and cross out the offending day
with careful strokes like a prisoner
scratching marks on a wall.
At the end of the day, Mark would
return to his little box-room with its
small bed, small chair, and tiny chest

FIGURE 9-7   Creating a box in the shape of a character may be done using the Text to Box command

Applying Text to a Path

Although many applications try to perfect the effect of running text along a path, few do it as well and efficiently as XPress' text-path tools. Text that follows a path is often used for special effects where short strings of characters or words themselves become graphic elements that create visual interest as well as communicate a message. The path that your text follows may originally be virtually any type of shape you may create in XPress, including rounded, concave, beveled, oval, or rectangular shapes. You may convert any of these shapes to accept path text by using the Edit | Shape submenu andchoosing any of three line types, as shown in the following illustration.

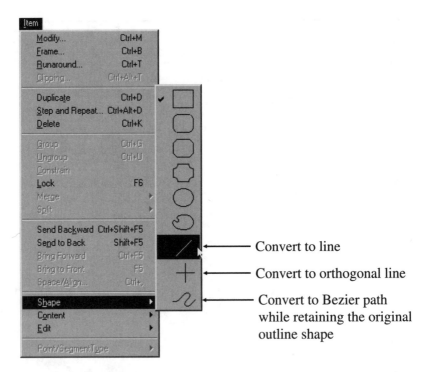

Convert to line

Convert to orthogonal line

Convert to Bezier path while retaining the original outline shape

The first of these shape selections has the effect of converting your selected box to a line; the second restricts the shape to an orthogonal line oriented either vertically or horizontally, depending on how the shape was originally created. The last shape condition on the list is perhaps the most useful. It enables you to convert any box shape to a text path, without distorting or destroying its inherent shape as do the first two selections. When a box shape is converted to a text path, defaults enable text to follow the outside shape of the box in a clockwise direction beginning at the lower-left area of the shape. The following illustration shows rectangle, oval, rounded-rectangle, and Bezier shapes converted to this state and used as text paths.

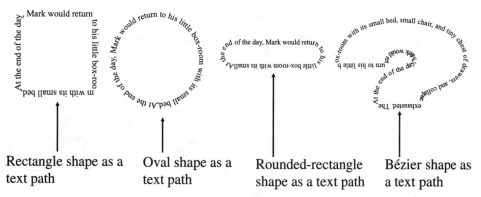

Rectangle shape as a
text path

Oval shape as a
text path

Rounded-rectangle
shape as a text path

Bézier shape as
a text path

The text path may also be created manually using any of XPress' text path tools. These line tools are nearly identical to similarly-named line tools found in the Tool palette—the only difference is that creating a line with any of these tools automatically sets it to accept text characters along its path. The four text-path line tools are the Orthogonal text path, Line text path, Bezier text path, and Freehand text path, which are grouped together in the Tool palette, third from the bottom. The following illustration shows various effects achieved by creating path shapes and applying text using text path tools.

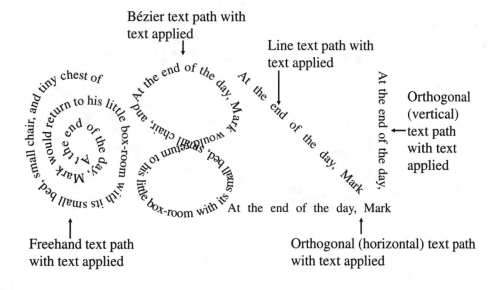

Bézier text path with
text applied

Line text path with
text applied

Orthogonal
(vertical)
text path
with text
applied

Freehand text path
with text applied

Orthogonal (horizontal) text path
with text applied

9

QuarkXPress 4 IN ACTION

BULL MOOSE MUSIC
Frequent Buyer Club

Fine-Print Section

one additional club benefit:

Besides your purchase points, Bull Moose also keeps track of any store credit you may have accumulated through gift certificates, the sale of used CDs, or exchanges.

caveats and disclaimers:

1. please present your card or mention club membership at the time of your purchase. once you leave the register, we cannot add points for that particular purchase
2. if you don't use your card for more than a year, we will need to delete your account.
3. we will gladly replace any lost cards for 50¢.

for more information about our promotions, in-store concerts, or any other exciting Bull Moose news, visit our web site at http://www.bullmoose.com

Happiness, a sense of belonging, consumer goods:

We all want what the Plastic People want. But how do we get it?

Join the *Bull Moose Frequent Buyer Club*, that's how! You can have it all!

with every purchase you make at Bull Moose, you'll earn points toward discounts on future purchases. you can also use your purchase points to get free Bull Moose merchandise. in addition, club members are eligible to win other good stuff that we scam from big, greedy record companies. wearing and owning these items will greatly enhance your sense of identity!

as an added bonus, you can use our exciting club recruitment pyramid scheme to get extra points by signing up your friends and family!

Everyone will share in the joy!

Design: Thomas Puckett
Firm: Intelligent Design Enforcement Agency (I.D.E.A.)
Client: Bull Moose Music
Description: Frequent Buyer Club brochure design

QuarkXPress 4 IN ACTION

Here's how the program works:

- ☑ sign up at any bull moose store and receive your club membership card.
- ☑ present your card each time you make a purchase.
- ☑ bull moose keeps track of your points for you. your receipt shows you how many points you have accumulated after each purchase.
- ☑ the point system works this way.

1. five points give you 50% off any item that is worth $5 or less.
2. ten points give you 50% off any item that is worth $10 or less.
3. twenty points give you 50% off any item that is worth $20 or less.
4. etc., etc., etc. (you get the point, no pun intended.)
5. your points earn discounts on all merchandise at bull moose.
6. there is no limit to the number of points you can earn.

Our club recruitment pyramid scheme:

- ☑ sign up your friends.
- ☑ as your friends accumulate points, you also accumulate points worth 10% of their purchase points.
- ☑ there's more! if you have signed up someone who then recruits someone else, you get points worth 1% of the second person's purchase points.
- ☑ you also get points worth 1% of all additional second-tier people's purchases. unfortunately, the pyramid scheme must stop here. we would need a giant univac supercomputer to calculate beyond that.

if all of this sounds complicated, that's because it is. just remember that bull moose does all the work! if you have questions, or want to know how many points you have, ask any of our salespeople.

for even more obscure details about the program, read our fine-print section, which is conveniently located on the back of this brochure.

Join the Plastic People!
Recruit your friends! Get more stuff!

name:

street address:

zip:

phone:

e-mail:

birthday:

who referred you to our club?

what is his/her card number?

if you do not want to be on our mailing list, check here. ☐

This brochure is part of a music store's campaign to have customers sign up for a frequent buyer club. The client requested a design that was eye-catching and fun. The tiny plastic figures were photographed with a macro lens and the brochures were designed using QuarkXPress and Live Picture.

Using the text path tools to create shapes is identical to using the usual line tools in XPress, and applying, editing, and modifying text on text paths is identical to working with the usual text tools in text boxes. However, even more flexibility exists when working with text paths through the Path dialog box, which is accessed by selecting text on a path and opening the Modify | Text Path tab dialog box, as shown in the following illustration.

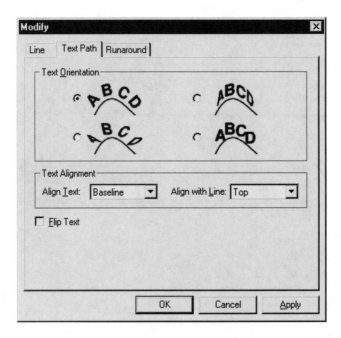

Options in this dialog box enable you to control how the text on your shape or path behaves in relation to the path itself. You may control how the text is oriented, aligned, or flipped using the following options.

■ **Text Orientation**   Four orientation styles are available. The first style (the default) enables the text path characters to follow the path or shape without any distortions; characters simply align with the path as if it were the baseline of the text. As the path changes angle, each character is rotated. The second option (top-right) applies a distortion to the characters based on the curve of the path they are following. The characters themselves are oriented vertically; however each character is skewed to mimic the curve of the path. The third option (bottom-left) preserves the baseline orientation, but the vertical character orientation is adjusted to mimic the curve of the path or shape. The fourth option (bottom-right) preserves each character shape without applying rotation or skew, allowing each character to be attached to the path at its center point. Figure 9-8 shows the effects of each of these options when working with text on an oval-shaped path.

TIP ──────▷ *When selecting text path items, you may use either the Content or Item tools. But clicking the characters themselves will not select the items. Instead, you must click the path that the text follows.*

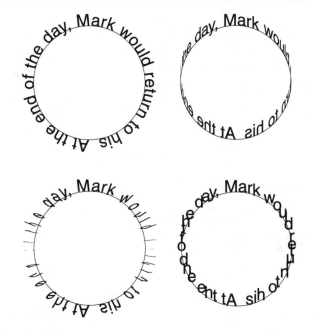

9

FIGURE 9-8 Using Text Orientation options with text applied to a circular path

- **Align Text** This drop-down menu features options for aligning the text path characters to the Baseline (the default), Center, Ascent, or Descent; these effects are shown in the following illustration.

AaBbCcDdEeFfGg ⟵ Baseline text alignment
AaBbCcDdEeFfGg ⟵ Ascent text alignment
AaBbCcDdEeFfGg ⟵ Center text alignment
AaBbCcDdEeFfGg ⟵ Descent text alignment

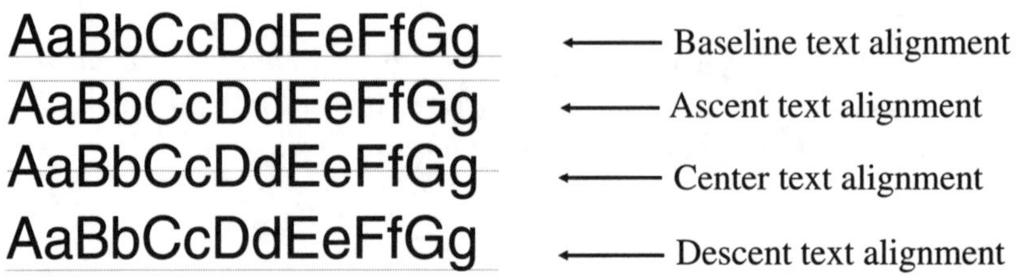

- **Align with Line** This drop-down menu enables you to choose the specific point at which your characters align with the edge of your line. When applying text to lines that have small width measures (or none at all), this option has little visual effect. However, if your line is thicker, you may want to specify to which edge of the path the characters align by choosing the Top, Center, or Bottom option; these effects are shown in the following illustration.

AaBbCcDdEeFfGg ⟵ Top alignment
AaBbCcDdEeFfGg ⟵ Center alignment
AaBbCcDdEeFfGg ⟵ Bottom alignment

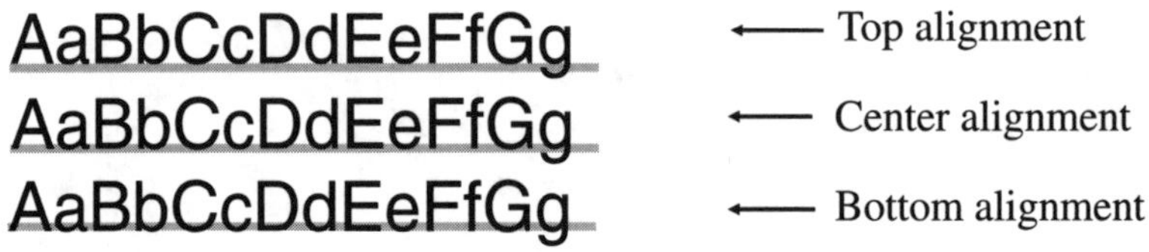

- **Flip Text** This option enables you to apply the text to the opposite side of the text path, as shown in the following example. The Flip Text option is also available while using the Content tool and working with text paths by choosing Style | Flip Text or clickingthe Flip Text button in the center of the Measurements palette (F9).

AaBbCcDdEeFfGg   ⟵ Flip Text option not applied

AaBbCcDdEeFfGg   ⟵ Flip Text option applied

Conclusion

In this chapter, you have learned the workings of a few of XPress' most powerful tools. You've seen how automated runaround and clipping features enable you to apply sophisticated properties to digital photographs and graphics, and you've strategized how to use their associated options. You've also discovered that you may turn your text boxes into unevenly-shaped objects and attach text to nearly any type of path.

You've also approached a milestone in this book by reaching the end of *Part 2: Creating Layouts and Documents*. This part of the book has taken you on a journey where you experienced working with text, applying picture properties, and using strategies for handling more advanced picture issues. You ended by learning to integrate text and pictures. Now that you know exactly how to use the powerful tools covered in this part, you may move on to *Part 3: Putting It All Together.*

9

PART III

Putting It All Together

CHAPTER 10

Laying Out Documents

Over the course of Parts 1 and 2 of this book, you've progressed from installing XPress to learning how to use core XPress features such as boxes, text formatting, drawing tools, and picture manipulation. Having a comprehensive understanding of these functions will help you to solve layout puzzles on an individual basis as you use XPress in the production of your documents. Now it's time to round out your knowledge of specific layout support tools in XPress. In the next three chapters, you'll discover strategies for maximizing production time while laying out documents, learn to use time-saving long-document features, and find out how to tailor your XPress tools and application behavior to suit the way you work.

In this chapter, you'll explore XPress' document support tools for working more efficiently with content. You'll discover how to use the Append command to capitalize on some of the properties you've applied to items in other documents. You'll learn how to move content quickly within your document or to other documents, and you'll find out how to anchor and lock items in your text and on your pages. And, you'll learn how to format, and build and work with lists, tables of contents, and indexes in your documents.

Resources from Other Documents

As you produce documents using XPress, it may occur to you from time to time that you're performing a task you swear you've done all too often in the past. In fact, if layout is your primary task, the likelihood is quite high that you've created documents that are identical or similar in many respects. Many users often forge ahead in their production processes without thinking twice about whether or not they're repeating a task they did yesterday, last week, or last year. A wise old layout artist once told me, "There's no such thing as an original layout." And with all the rules and guidelines we apply to layout, this is probably true.

Because you're using XPress, some of the repetitive tasks you perform everyday may be unnecessary. These include tasks such as formatting text, specifying styles and colors, setting up hyphenation and justification (H&J), and making textual lists, custom dashes and stripes, and so on. In order to benefit from the efforts you put into other documents, XPress enables you to use the Append dialog box options shown in the following illustration to quickly transfer properties of various types of items between documents

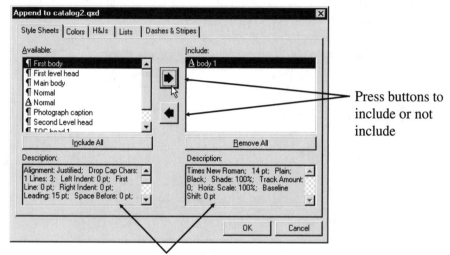

Press buttons to include or not include

Selected attribute details display here

The Append command enables you to transfer all types of attributes from other documents. Once attributes are appended, they are essentially copied and stored with your current document. In other words, no association or link exists between your current document and the one from which you are appending attributes. For example, if you append a color from another document and subsequently edit the color in the source document, it will not change in the target document. The procedures used in appending attributes are the same no matter which attribute you are appending. In fact, except for the tab name and the specific contents of each list, the tabs are identical.

NOTE

As you work with each type of attribute in XPress, you may notice each feature (Style Sheets, Colors, H&Js, Lists, and Dashes & Stripes) includes its own Append command, the options of which are used in exactly the same manner as the Append command discussed in this chapter. The only difference is that when the Append command is accessed from the File menu, you may have access to all *types of attributes in a single dialog box.*

10

To access the Append dialog box, choose File | Append (CTRL/CMD+ALT/OPTION+A). The first dialog box to appear is not the Append dialog box, but instead is a dialog box enabling you to locate the file or document from which you want to append attributes, as shown in the following illustration. Using the Windows version of XPress 4, you may also limit the display of file types by making a choice from the Files of Type drop-down menu.

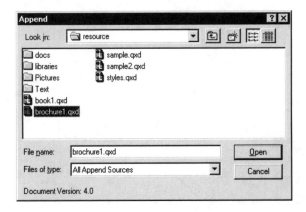

While All Append Sources is selected, all eligible files type are displayed, including the following:

QuarkXPress documents (QXD)
QuarkXPress templates (QXT)
QuarkXPress libraries (QXL)
QuarkXPress automatic save files (ASV)
XPress tags (XTG)
WordPerfect 3.x (WP, WPD, WPT, DOC)
WordPerfect 6.x (WP, WPD, WPT, DOC)

Once a file is selected, and OK is clicked, the Append dialog box opens to display the available attributes in the file. The Append dialog box is divided into two halves: Available and Include. When a specific tab is selected, the attributes are automatically displayed in the Available list. When an attribute is selected in the list, a detailed description of the selected attribute appears in the Description field below, and the right-pointing arrow button becomes available. Clicking this button moves the selected attribute from the Available list to the Include list. You choose all listed attributes by clicking the Include All button.

TIP ──────────▷ *You do not need to have a document open in order to append attributes from it.*

Any attributes you move to the Include side of the dialog box will be appended to your current document when you click OK. When an attribute is selected in the Include list, the Description area directly below displays details about the attribute, and the left-pointing button becomes available. Clicking this button returns the selected attribute to the Available list, while clicking the Remove All button returns *all* the attributes listed on the Include side to the Available side. Once the OK button is clicked, all your selections are copied to your current document. After clicking OK, a warning appears to notify you of the types of attributes being copied, as shown in the following illustration. If you're confident that the choices you make are always correct, you may choose the Don't Show This Warning Again option.

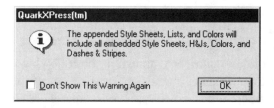

TIP ──────────▷ *Once you have selected specific attributes to copy to your document, select another attributes tab by clicking it before clicking the OK button. The OK is a common button to all attributes; clicking it will copy the selected attributes but immediately and automatically close the dialog box. You may also select more than one attribute at a time by holding SHIFT to select sequentially-listed attributes or by holding CTRL/CMD to select attributes that are listed nonsequentially.*

When a document is accessed through the Append command, any number of attributes tabs may appear, including Style Sheets, Colors, H&Js, Lists, and Dashes & Stripes. If the document from which you are appending does not contain certain attributes, the tab representing those attributes simply doesn't appear. For example,

10

if you open an XPress document that doesn't contain custom dashes and stripes, the Dashes & Stripes tab will not appear.

TIP

Create a master document that contains only established layout and design attributes for styles, colors, H&Js, and dashes and stripes. Keeping a master document such as this will enable you to establish and easily maintain design standards while working in a publishing environment. If you work in a networked environment, make the document available across network drives.

Ironing Out Append Conflicts

With the capability to copy certain attributes from other documents using the Append command comes the hazard of overwriting attributes with the same name. Without a method of resolving these types of conflicts, you might be faced with a situation where you could lose valuable attribute information. Fortunately, XPress implements a conflict feature to help avoid this.

The Append Conflict dialog box, shown in the following illustration, appears only when an attribute features the same name as an attribute in your current document but has different properties applied. In other words, if you are using the Append command to copy a style sheet from another document, and the style sheet has the same name but different character or paragraph attributes as a style sheet that already exists in your current document, the Append Conflict dialog box appears. You cannot access the Append Conflict dialog box through menu options or keyboard shortcuts.

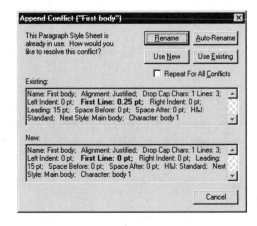

When resolving conflicts, the Append Conflict dialog box offers four choices in the form of command buttons and displays detailed descriptions of the conflicting attributes. The Existing area details the attributes of the item about to be copied over, and the New area details the item you want to append to your current document. The command buttons leave the choice for conflict resolution up to you, as follows:

- **Rename**   Clicking this button opens a dialog box enabling you to assign a new name to the attribute being copied to your existing document, as shown in the following illustration. Enter a new name for your attribute in the New Name field and select OK to rename the attribute.

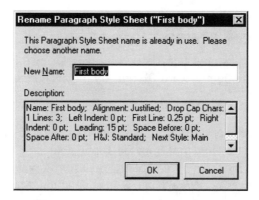

- **Auto-Rename**   Clicking the Auto-Rename button enables XPress to assign a different name to your attribute. The new name is automatically applied with an asterisk preceding its current name.

- **Use Existing**   Clicking the Use Existing button cancels the Append selection, enabling XPress to leave the attributes in your current document as they are.

- **Use New**   Clicking this button enables XPress to overwrite the existing attribute with the new one.

- **Repeat For All Conflicts**   Selecting this option enables you to choose the current conflict resolution method for all subsequent conflicts. For example, if you choose the option and then click the Auto-Rename button, all conflicts will be resolved by adding an asterisk to conflicting attribute names.

10

NOTE *Operation of the Append Conflict command is the same, regardless of whether you are resolving conflicts for style sheets, colors, H&Js, lists, or dashes and stripes attributes.*

Moving Contents

Shifting picture or text boxes or entire layouts you have created from one location to another could be considered a basic operation. Whether you choose to move content to another page or a completely different document, the operation is quite similar and virtually seamless. The following operations are described in steps.

Moving Items Between Pages

There are several ways to move items between pages. Using the clipboard is perhaps the easiest and most straightforward. To quickly move contents with the clipboard, follow these steps:

1. With your document opened to the page containing the items you want to move, choose the Item tool from the Tool palette, and then select the items by clicking them once. Holding the SHIFT key while clicking items enables you to select more than one item at a time. Marquee-selecting the objects enables you to select objects within a given area.

2. With your objects selected, choose Edit | Cut (CTRL/CMD+X) to delete the items from their current position and copy them to the clipboard.

TIP *If you want to copy your selected items from one page to another without removing the original, choose Edit | Copy (CTRL/CMD+C) instead of Edit | Cut.*

3. Change your view to the destination page by selecting it from the Page View pop-out menu at the bottom of your document window.

4. Choose Edit | Paste (CTRL/CMD+V) to paste the items on your clipboard into the current page. By default, pasted items appear in the center of the page, so you may need to reposition them using the Item tool once they have been pasted onto the new page.

NOTE *If the items you are moving are on pages in close proximity to each other (for example, from page one to page two), you may select and drag them, although dragging is considerably more time-consuming than using the clipboard features described above.*

Moving Pages Within a Document

There are two methods to choose from when moving pages from one location to another within your document. You may use the Page | Move command or the Document Layout palette. To use the Move command to move one or several pages, follow these steps:

1. With your document open, access the Move Pages dialog box by choosing Page | Move. The dialog box opens, as shown in the following illustration.

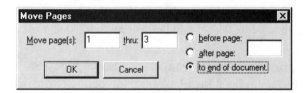

2. Enter the number of the page you want to move in the Move Pages field. If you want to move a sequence of pages, enter the first page number of the sequence in this field and the last page number in the Thru field.

NOTE *If the pages you want to move have been designated with prefixes and page number styles using the Section command, the prefixes must be entered in order for XPress to correctly locate the pages. However, you may also designate an "absolute" page number by entering a plus symbol (+) before the number. An absolute page number identifies the page's current position according to your document layout. For example, the first page in a document can always be identified as +1 regardless of its assigned page number.*

3. Choose a destination for your pages by clicking either the Before Page or After Page option, each of which requires you to enter a page number in the adjacent field. Or, choose the To End of Document option to move your selected pages to the end of your current document.

4. Click OK to move the pages. Your pages and all items they contain are moved to their new positions.

One of the limitations you'll discover when using the Move Pages command is that you cannot move noncontinuous pages. And when moving pages, page numbering is always an issue. If you have chosen to apply automatic page numbering, the numbering of the pages you move is updated automatically according to the layout of your document.

TIP ⟶ *You do not need to have a particular page in view when using the Move Pages dialog box to move pages.*

Moving pages with the Move Pages command is perhaps less interactive than moving them with the Document Layout palette, so it may be wise to adapt your work habits to use of the palette because its capabilities are so expansive. To move pages using the Document Layout palette, follow these steps:

1. With your document open to any page, choose View | Show Document Layout (F4/F10) to open the Document Layout palette shown in the following illustration.

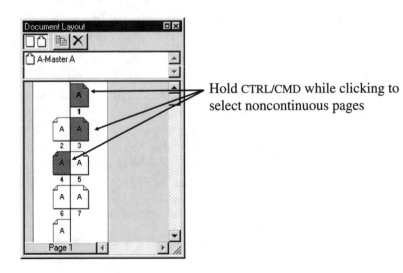

Hold CTRL/CMD while clicking to select noncontinuous pages

2. Select the pages you want to move by clicking them once. To select continuous pages, hold the SHIFT key while clicking the first and last pages in the sequence. To select noncontinuous pages, hold CTRL/CMD while clicking the pages.

3. To move the pages to a different location in your document layout, drag them within the Document Layout palette to the new location. This location may be between two existing pages, after an existing page, or at the end of the document. Once you release your mouse button, the pages are moved.

CAUTION *Beware of the following hazard when moving page contents from one document location to another. XPress will not change the linking relationship between moved pages and their text boxes. For example, if the text on page 1 is linked to page two, and page 1 is subsequently moved to the end of your document, the text will continue to flow from what was once page 1 to what was once page 2, regardless of their new position in your document layout. Another hazard to watch for when moving pages involves moving an uneven number of pages in a facing-page layout. This move results in all pages being reshuffled and left-facing pages being changed to right-facing pages, which is often undesirable when creating a layout based on facing pages.*

Copying Items Between Documents

Copying content between two different documents is similar to copying between pages. Whether you are copying picture, text, or shaped boxes between documents, the operation is seamless; no dialog boxes appear, and you have no special decisions to make (other than deciding which content you want to copy and to where you want to copy it). To copy content from one document to another, follow these quick steps:

10

1. Open both documents in XPress and size their document windows and page views so that both the source page and destination page are visible to you, as shown in Figure 10-1. If you are using the Windows version of XPress 4, you may choose Window | Tile Vertically or Window | Tile Horizontally to quickly arrange and size your document windows. If you are using a Macintosh version, choose View | Windows | Tile Documents.

2. Select the items you want to copy from the source document.

3. Drag the items from the source document directly onto the page of the destination document and release the mouse. Even if your documents are set to different view magnifications, as shown in Figure 10-1, the operation is seamless.

CAUTION➤ *If you attempt to copy text boxes that are linked to other text boxes in the source document, the copy operation will fail and none of the selected items will be copied to the new document. XPress warns of failed link duplication with the alert shown in the following illustration. If you really need a copy of the box in another document, you can duplicate it and move the duplicated copy. The new box will contain all the text in the current box plus all the text following it (indicated by the overflow symbol).*

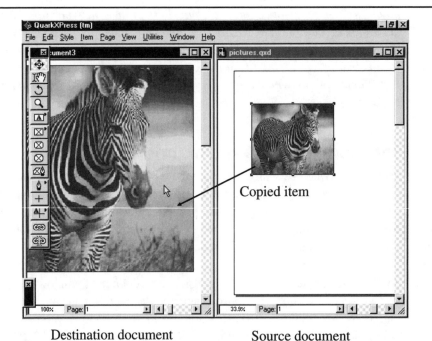

Destination document   Source document

■ **FIGURE 10-1**   Copying items from one document to another

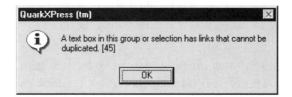

Locking and Anchoring Items

The capability to freely move items on your page and throughout your document is extremely convenient for creating all types of layouts, but there may come a time when you would like to restrict the movement of items or control how they flow within your page layout. XPress enables you to lock items on your pages and anchor items within text. You might assume these two operations behave similarly, but they are applied differently and result in different conditions.

Locking an item is a command function of XPress. Once an item is locked, it can no longer be moved or manipulated with your mouse; you can still modify it with the Measurements palette or Modify dialog box. *Anchoring* is a term used to describe pasting items into text boxes at specific points, so that the items can flow freely as your text flows but remain in a fixed position in relation to the text content. Anchoring items allows automatic flowing of content—regardless of the type of item, while locking items ensures they don't move once they are positioned.

How to Anchor an Item

To anchor an item in a text box and have it flow with your text, follow these steps:

1. In an open document, create or select the item you want to anchor in a text box, choose the Item tool from the Tool palette, and copy (CTRL/CMD+C) or cut (CTRL/CMD+X) the item to the clipboard.

NOTE *You cannot anchor a group or a text box that already contains anchored items.*

2. Choose the Content tool from the Tool palette, select the text box into which you want to anchor the item, and click with the I-beam cursor to select an insertion point.

10

3. Paste the item into your text by choosing Edit | Paste (CTRL/CMD+V). The item is now anchored and will flow with your text.

TIP *To unanchor an item anchored in text, select the item and choose Item | Duplicate. This creates an unanchored copy, which enables you to delete the anchored oiginal.*

When pasting an item into a line of text, the item aligns (by default) to the baseline of the line of text it is pasted into. Once the item is anchored, your text's leading properties take over. With Auto Leading applied to the text, the item causes the space to expand to accommodate its height according to Modify | Runaround default settings. If the item already includes an applied runaround, these values will still apply after it has been anchored. Once an item is anchored in a text box, you may alter the way in which it aligns with the baseline using options in the Modify dialog box, which is shown in the following illustration.

TIP *To anchor items so that they reside on their own paragraph space, position your cursor immediately after the item and press RETURN to insert a full return. To delete an anchored item from your text, choose the Content tool, highlight the item, and press BACKSPACE/DELETE.*

Alignment options for box items ——→

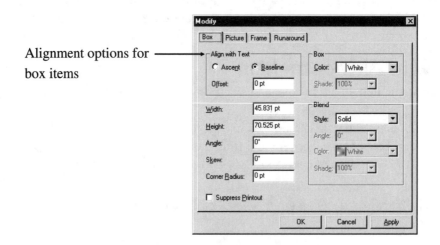

> TIP *Anchored items may be picture boxes, text boxes, shapes, or lines, depending on your needs. You may modify the properties of an anchored item by choosing the Item tool, selecting the object, and either double-clicking the item or pressing CTRL/CMD+M. When a specific item is selected, the Modify dialog box displays tabs associated with the item's properties. You may also set runaround properties of anchored items, enabling you to apply outset values to them.*

When an item is anchored in text, Modify dialog box options enable you to set its alignment to the ascent or baseline of the item, or apply a custom offset within a range between -36 and 828 points.

> TIP *You may also change the alignment quickly with alignment buttons on the Measurements palette.*

Locking and Unlocking Items

Operation of XPress' Lock command is much more straightforward than anchoring an item. To lock an item so that its properties may not be changed with the mouse, choose Item | Lock (F6). When an item is locked, a "padlock" symbol appears whenever you attempt to apply changes to the item using tools. However, you may still select a locked item by clicking it, and then change its properties through use of dialog boxes or keyboard shortcuts. To unlock an item, simply select the item and choose Item | Unlock (F6).

10

Spacing and Aligning Objects

You may organize the items on your page based on their shape, dimensions, and distance from each other using XPress' Space/Align Items feature, which is accessed by choosing Item | Space/Align (CTRL/CMD+,). The Space/Align Items options enable you align objects horizontally and vertically using the various dialog box options shown in the following illustration.

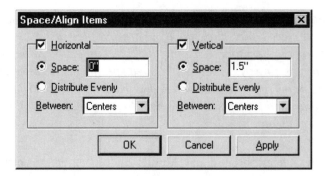

The Horizontal and Vertical options may be selected individually or at the same time by clicking their respective check boxes. Deciphering the functionality of these options without some explanation is confusing at best. Spacing and aligning controls are split into two separate functions: Space (evenly) and Distribute Evenly. When either Space/Align Items option is selected, the type of space used is determined by options set in the Between drop-down menu.

- **Space**   The Space option enables you to add a specific amount of equal physical space between your items either vertically or horizontally. Entering a value in the Space field tells XPress how much to space out your selected items. The space XPress adds between your items is determined by the option chosen in the Between drop-down menu. Space may be added based on your items' width or depth measure (Item), the center of items, the left edges of items, or the right edges of items. The value entered in the Space field may be based on an absolute distance measure, a percentage of the current space between items, or a specific distance. The measure entered in the Space field must fall within a range between 0 and 10 inches.

- **Distribute Evenly**   Selecting this button enables you to spread your selected items evenly either vertically or horizontally. When items are distributed, the point at which they are measured may be the width or depth measure, the center, or the left or right edges of the items. The overall space within which your items are distributed is determined by the space between the two items that are the farthest apart.

Working with Style Lists

If you've had the opportunity to work with style sheets, you already know how critical they are to streamlining the application of text formatting. If you create and apply styles as part of your everyday work habits, the Lists feature will be of interest. The Lists feature enables you to quickly and automatically compile large documents comprising tables of contents text based on the styles you have applied to text—specifically headings. Once these documents have been created, you may update them, build new lists, apply styles to them, and navigate your document with them.

The capability to create lists isn't a new invention by any stretch. But it is a powerful feature that enables you to capitalize on work you have already done in your XPress document. This section explains how to build lists from your existing text documents and details their function. The Lists feature is tricky to use, so you may want to review the available options and follow the upcoming exercise.

Using the Lists Command

The Lists command is completely based on paragraph styles that have already been *created and applied*. In order for lists to be compiled, styles must have been already created and applied in your current document (or in another document from which you may append the lists).

The quickest way to grasp operation of the Lists feature is to understand the principles on which it operates. When you create styles and apply them to headings, you are essentially creating tags by which these headings may be identified. When the Lists feature examines your document, it searches for these tags in the order they appear and makes a copy of the text to which they are applied. The copies are then reassembled in the same order when the list is built. Options in the Lists feature enable you to determine which headings are first-, second-, or third-level in your newly-created list, based on the style of the headings and the order they appear in your document.

Because lists are based on styles, they can only be built if styles are applied to headings. So, the first order of business before you attempt to build a list is to apply styles to (at least) all headings. You may also want to plan how your list is going to appear in your document in terms of font, styles, layout, and so on. And, it will also help if you create a new set of styles on which to base the listed headings in your new list document. Before building your list, decide which numbering scheme you would like to apply to your list. Numbering may be based on the page number where the headings in your document fall.

10

The next step in working with lists is to create a new list based on applied styles in your document. Lists are compiled, managed, and edited using command buttons in the Lists dialog box shown in the following illustration. If you've had experience creating styles, colors, Dashes & Stripes, or H&Js, you may already realize what these commands accomplish.

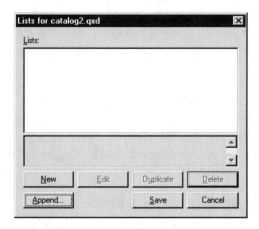

Creating a New List

Clicking the New button in the Lists dialog box opens the Edit List dialog box shown in the following illustration. Here, you can provide a unique name for your list and begin assembling your styles. From here, the mechanics of list creation take on a methodical approach. Let's assume for a moment that you have an XPress document opened in front of you that includes two levels of headings applied with styles. And, you have already formulated what you would like your list to look like by setting out styles for these two levels of heading in the list you are about to create. Let's also assume this list is a simple table of contents for your existing document.

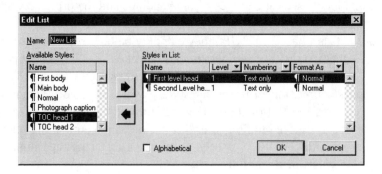

To create a new list, follow these steps:

1. If you haven't already done so, apply the styles you want to use in your list to the headings in your document.

2. Choose Edit | Lists to open the Lists dialog box.

3. Click the New button to open the Edit List dialog box, and then enter a name for your new list. Because we are creating a table of contents, enter **Table of Contents** in the Name field.

4. Select the style to which the first level of heading in your document has been applied, and then click the right-pointing arrow to add the style to the Styles in List side of the dialog box. Notice that the Level, Numbering, and Format As columns include properties associated with the style you just added. Notice also that each column heading is accompanied by a drop-down menu.

5. Select the style to which the second level of heading has been applied, and then click the right-pointing arrow button again to add this second style to the list. Because our table of contents will only feature two levels of heading, this is the end of adding styles. If you want, you may add up to eight levels of headings to a list.

TIP ─────────► *You may assign up to 32 styles in a single list, but the text for each list entry is limited to 256 characters.*

6. In the Styles in List side of the dialog box, select the first style in the list by clicking it. From the Level drop-down menu choose 1 if it isn't already selected. This sets your heading to be automatically formatted as the first level of heading.

7. From the Numbering drop-down menu choose Text...Page# to set the numbering scheme to include the page number after the heading. You may also set this in reverse order or leave the listing as text only.

8. From the Format As drop-down menu choose the paragraph or character style you (ideally) set up previously to apply to the first level of heading in your list.

10

9. Select the second style in your list and set Level to 2, Numbering to Text...Page#, and Format As to the style you have created for your list's second level of heading.

10. Click OK to create your list criteria and return to the Lists dialog box.

TIP *To make changes to the list you just created, select the list in the Lists dialog box listing and click the Edit button to reopen the Edit List dialog box. Editing functions are identical to those covered in the preceding steps. Once you have completed your changes, click OK to return to the Lists dialog box, and then click Save to save your list criteria and exit the dialog box.*

Building and Updating Lists

So far, you haven't actually built a list, but instead have told XPress what your list will look like by defining style parameters. Once you have defined styles and formatting for your new list in the Lists dialog box, the next step is to create the list. To do this, use commands in the Lists palette shown in the following illustration. To open the Lists palette, choose View | Show Lists (CTRL/OPTION+F12/F11). As soon as the Lists palette opens, you'll notice any lists currently available in your document are shown in the List Name drop-down menu.

The Lists palette includes the following options:

■ **Show List For**   This drop-down menu enables you to select which lists are displayed in the List Name drop-down menu. If you have only a single QuarkXPress document open, the selection remains at Current Document. If you have other documents opened, such as a book document, these will also be available from this menu.

■ **List Name**   The List Name drop-down menu enables you to select a list from the document shown in the Show Lists For drop-down menu. As soon as a list is selected, it will display in the lower portion of the Lists palette.

■ **Find**   This field accepts text entries for finding items in your currently-displayed list. As you enter text to find, the palette automatically highlights the first match it finds in the list.

■ **Update**   This command button enables you to automatically update the listed text displayed in the palette. Updating is often required when the text applied with the styles specified in your list has changed in the document. For example, if you change the text in headings compiled in the list while the Lists palette is open, clicking Update will cause XPress to search your document and update the display to match your text changes.

■ **Build**   This command button enables you to compile a text document on your page, based on all the parameters set in your selected list. When the new list document is built, all text found during the search of your document is assembled and applied with the styles you have specified in the originally-compiled list, as set in the Lists dialog box. Once a list has been built, you may edit it as you would a normal text document.

NOTE *A list is simply an association of the styles and text in your document. Appending a list from another document to your current document, transfers only the list and its associated styles—not the list itself. In order for your current document to build a new list document based on list styles in other documents, you must import a text document and apply the same styles to it. Once the styles used in the appended list have been applied to text in your current document, a new list may be built based on the applied styles.*

10

The whole purpose of the Lists palette is to enable you to quickly and automatically create a text document based on styles applied to your text. So, to build a list using the Lists palette, follow these steps:

1. With your document open and the styles used in your list already applied to the text in your document, choose Show Lists (CTRL/OPTION+F12/F11). The Lists palette opens.

2. If it isn't already selected, choose Current Document from the Show List For drop-down menu.

3. From the List Name drop-down menu, select the list name you have created, based on steps followed in the preceding exercise. If the styles in the list type you have selected have already been applied in your document, the Lists palette will immediately display results.

4. With the list displayed in your palette, double-click one of the entries in the palette list. Notice your view changes to display the exact location of the text you clicked in the list. This is one of the key capabilities of XPress' Lists feature.

Although the list appears in the Lists palette, it still has not been created in your document. To generate the list as an actual document, follow the next two steps.

5. Choose the Content tool and change your page view to the area of your document into which you would like your new list document to flow. If you haven't already done so, create a text box to insert the built list into. Or, select an existing text box and click an insertion point. The list you build will be created at the insertion point you select.

6. Click the Build button in the palette. The list document is created. If the styles you specified in your list are complete, you will not need to perform any extra formatting in order for your list to appear exactly as you want it to.

TIP

To avoid the need to constantly update your list, generating a list document should be one of the last steps you perform in the construction of your document. Be sure your list doesn't add extra pages to the beginning of your document, which results in reshuffled pages and inaccurate page numbers in the list.

7. To edit the text on which your list is built, double-click the text in the list to display the original text on your page, and then perform any required text editing. To have the list in the palette reflect the changes to your original text, click the Update button.

8. After the contents of a list has changed, you must rebuild it in your document in order for it to match your original text. To do this, click the Build button after the final edits have been made to your original text. The message shown in the following illustration appears on your screen offering two choices: Replace the current list, or insert another list based on your current document text. If you would simply like to update the list, click Replace to proceed. If you would like to create an additional list, click Insert.

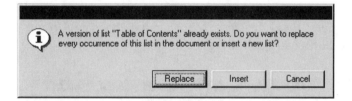

TIP   *When a list is unusually long or complex, it may be wiser to delete the original list before attempting to build a new one.*

Working with Indexes

10

Creating index entries for your document is perhaps one of the most critical functions in creating a user-friendly publication. Indexes are often used as maps to the inner contents of long documents. A well-structured and complete index enables readers searching for information in the document to find what they are looking for quickly and easily. In the world of publishing, index creation is often done by professionals who have honed their skills to a fine art.

XPress' Index feature enables you to automatically create an index based on the text in your document and your inserted index entries. Indexes are created by tagging words in your document. These tags may apply to single words, several paragraphs, or an entire selection of text. After your tags have been applied, you may build the index based on the applied entries and the index formatting you decide on.

The Index feature enables you to control which entries appears in the index, the number of levels in the index, and the format of the entries it lists. Creating an automated index using this feature saves an immense amount of time and effort that is traditionally expended combing through text manually. And, because indexes are always one of the final portions of a document to be created, any type of automation is usually worth the effort—especially if your document production process follows a tight deadline.

Installing Index Tools

If you've recently installed QuarkXPress and you are about to create an index, you may be puzzled to learn that your version lacks the necessary tools. The Index features operate by way of an Index XTension, which must be installed in order for the tools to be available. XTensions in XPress are controlled through use of the XTensions Manager. To check whether the Index feature is enabled in your XPress application, open the XTensions Manager by choosing Utilities | XTensions Manager, as shown in the following illustration.

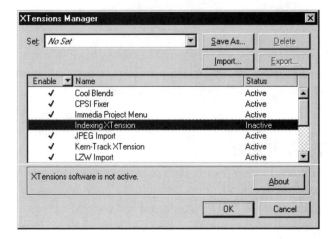

TIP *You do not need to have a document opened in order to access the XTensions Manager.*

If the Indexing XTension is installed, it will appear in the XTensions Manager list. If it is currently inactive (as shown in the preceding illustration), you may

Art Director & Design: Malcolm Frouman

Description: Cover design, *Business Week*, March 30, 1998 issue

This cover design on the best performing Standard & Poor 500 companies integrates text as a graphic on the right side of the layout together with finely-tuned text formatting to fit a justified column.

10

activate it by selecting it and choosing Yes from the Enable drop-down menu. You will need to exit (CTRL/CMD+Q) and relaunch QuarkXPress in order to reset your XTensions.

Once the Indexing XTension has been activated, and XPress is relaunched, the Index feature will be available. Functionality of XPress' Index feature is controlled through tools in the Index palette, which is opened by choosing View | Show Index.

Using the Index Palette

The primary function of the Index palette is to create entries—not to create the index document itself. Once the Index palette is opened, you'll notice it includes a number of fields, buttons, and drop-down menus, as shown in the following illustration. If the function of these controls doesn't seem obvious to you at first, don't be too concerned—they are highly specific and perform a complex function. The following definitions detail their use and operation.

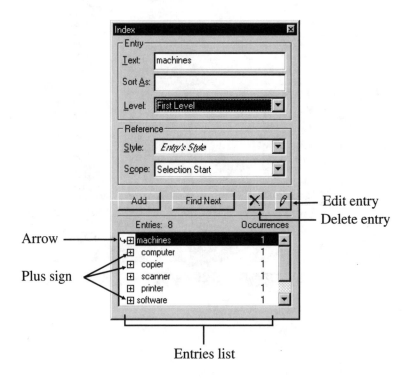

Entries list

Entry Options

The Entry area is composed of three fields: Text, Sort As, and Level. These fields enable you to designate which text in your document is destined for your index and how that text is to be tagged. To define an index entry, browse the text boxes in your XPress document and use the Content tool to highlight the text you would like to appear in your index. Once the text is highlighted in your document, it will automatically appear in the Text field. To define your selected text as an index entry, you must also specify at least the level before proceeding.

TIP —————▶ *Pressing CTRL/CMD+ALT/OPTION+SHIFT+I enables you to quickly add highlighted text in your document to the Index palette Entries list, according to current settings in the palette.*

The Level drop-down menu enables you to define whether your text should appear as a first-, second-, third-, or fourth-Level entry in your index. Varying the levels of entries in an index provides it with a structure. First-level entries appear more prominently than second level entries, which appear more prominently than third levels, and so on. Levels also enable you to organize entries so that second-level entries fall under first-level entries when their topics are related.

The Sort As field enables you to sort the index entry in a way other than the alphabetical method XPress uses normally. Entering a character (or series of characters) in this field causes the entry to be sorted under a different alphabetical listing. This feature is perhaps most useful when creating entries for text that begin with numerals rather than characters.

Reference Options

Reference options enable you to control how your index entries are formatted and numbered, and the range of text an entry covers. These options take the form of two drop-down menus: Style and Scope. The Style drop-down enables you to set the character or paragraph style sheet for your entry as you would have it appear in your index. By default, the style is automatically applied with Entry's Style; this means the same style that is applied to the index entry will apply to it when the index is created. The remaining options in this drop-down menu include styles that you have created in your document.

The Scope drop-down menu is a little more complex. The term *scope* refers to the range of your entry. Your entry can be a single word or several pages of text. The Scope option works with the index numbering scheme and enables you to set

10

whether the index entry location is numbered by its beginning or end, or the complete range of the entry. The Scope drop-down menu includes the following options:

- **Selection Start**   This choice enables XPress to identify the page number where the index entry starts. Selection Start is useful for indexing a short word or phrase that is unlikely to break across pages.

- **Selection Text**   This selection is perhaps the second most-commonly chosen option in the drop-down menu. Choosing Selection Text enables XPress to list a range of pages, beginning with the page number where the entry begins and ending with the number where it ends. The Selection Text option is used for indexing a short range of text, such as a paragraph that might break across two pages.

- **To Style**   Choosing the To Style option enables XPress to number the entry in a range format, beginning with the page number where the entry begins and ending with the page number on which a specified paragraph style appears next. The specified style may be set using the additional drop-down menu that appears when To Style is chosen. Choose To Style for quickly indexing from the start of one section to the start of another section (that is, between subheads).

- **Specified # of Paragraphs**   Choosing Specified # of Paragraphs enables XPress to number the entry in a range format, beginning with the page number where the entry begins and ending after the number of paragraphs you specify in the additional field that appears when this option is selected. Select Specified # of Paragraphs when an entry spans text such as a bulleted list.

- **To End Of**   Choosing the To End Of option enables XPress to number the entry in a range format, beginning with the page number where the entry begins and ending either at the end of the story or the document, depending on the selection made from the additional drop-down menu that appears with this choice. This choice is useful for providing the full range of pages a chapter covers, provided chapters are contained in single XPress stories.

- **Suppress Page #**   If the page number on which the entry you are defining is irrelevant, choosing this option enables XPress to omit listing the page number of the entry.

- **X-Ref**   X-Ref is an abbreviation for *cross reference*. You may need to define an entry as a cross reference if your entry relates to other defined entries. Cross references may be set to simply point to another index entry or to text you enter in the field. Choosing X-Ref displays an additional drop-down menu and field. From the menu you may choose the See, See Also, or See Herein option to refer to other entries specified by entering the related entry text in the field.

Command Buttons

Commands in the palette include buttons to add, find next (or find first), delete, or edit entries.

- **Add**   Once an entry has been highlighted in the Text field, and the other parameters in the palette have been selected, clicking the Add button enables you to add the entry to the index. Once an index entry has been added to your list, tags are applied in your text. When tags are applied to text, nonprinting brackets appear at the beginning and end points of the entry.

NOTE ———▶ *Tags display only when the Index Xtension is running and the Index palette is open.*

- **Find Next**   Choosing this option finds the next instance of an index tag in a document.

- **Delete**   This button deletes an entry from the index list and the tags associated with it in your document. To delete an entry in the index, select it in the Entries list of the Index palette and click Delete. If you delete an entry with subentries, an alert will warn you that all subentries will be deleted as well.

- **Edit**   The Edit button enables you to change properties associated with an entry after the entry has been applied. When an entry is selected, you may change the Text, Sort As, and Level properties. When page numbers or cross references are selected, you may set the Style and Scope options. To edit an entry, select it in the Index palette's Entries list, click the Edit button, and apply your changes. Selecting a different entry ends the editing mode automatically.

10

TIP *Double-clicking an entry or a cross reference in the Entries list of the Index palette enables you to quickly enter editing mode.*

As a practical exercise in creating a list of entries, follow these steps:

1. In an open document containing the text to which you want to apply index entries, open the Index palette by choosing View | Show Index.

2. Viewing the text in your document, highlight your first index entry using the Content tool. Notice the same text appears in the Text field of the palette.

3. Click the Add button in the palette. Notice the entry is added in the Lists area of the palette and automatically includes several identifying features. First, an arrow appears beside the entry (along with a plus symbol in the Windows version or a triangle symbol in the Macintosh version). Above the Entries list you'll see Entries: 1 and an Occurrences heading showing an occurrence of 1 beside your entry.

4. Click the plus symbol to reveal details about your entry. The numeral that appears indicates the page number on which the index entry occurs in your document.

5. Add several more entries to your list using the same steps. Notice each time you add an entry it is added alphabetically. And, by using the default settings in the palette, each new entry is added as a first-level heading.

6. Click a point to the left of one of the entries you have created and notice a small arrow appears beside it. This arrow indicates where the subentry will go.

Select another instance of text in your XPress document, choose Second Level from the Level drop-down menu, and then click the Add button. Notice the new entry is inserted below the arrow indicator and appears slightly indented.

7. Select another instance of text in your XPress document, but this time choose First Level from the Level drop-down menu and Suppress Page # from the Scope drop-down menu, and then click Add.

8. Click the plus symbol beside the entry you just created and notice it displays a minus (-) symbol, indicating the page number is suppressed. Numbering properties are displayed in this area.

9. Select another instance of text in your XPress document, choose X-Ref from the Scope drop-down menu and See from the additional drop-down menu that appears. Then, click your cursor in the field to the right and click a related subject in the Entries list. Notice the entry you clicked appears in the field. Click Add to add the new entry, and then click the plus symbol beside it. Notice the related subject text appears below the entry. You have just created a simple cross reference.

TIP *The Preferences command enables you to set marker color and separation character preferences for your Index XTension. To set these, choose Edit | Preferences | Index to open the Index Preferences dialog box shown in the following illustration. This dialog box enables you to specify marker colors and character types when your index document is created.*

Index Entry Strategies

Although creating an index document is an automatic feature of XPress, as you may have already guessed, creating the index entries to support it is anything but automatic. Structuring an index may be a long, laborious task, depending on the length and complexity of your document. One simple strategy is to identify the index strategies in your text using features in the word-processing application used to create your documents—if that is where your text documents were originally prepared.

If you are using XPress to apply the index entries, you'll want to use as many shortcuts as possible. If you approach the creation of an index methodically, you may be able to reduce your index creation time. The first shortcut to keep in mind is CTRL/CMD+ALT/OPTION+SHIFT+I, which automatically adds text to the Index palette's Entries list. Adding the text to this list is the most laborious part of the procedure, and this shortcut will help a great deal. Enter the entries regardless of their level or the properties you want to associate with them such as numbering, styles, and so on.

Once all the entries have been added to the Entries list, you may return to the palette and edit them. For example, changing the Sort As and Level properties may be the first property you want to change, following which you may want to create and apply specific styles for your index. Regardless of the approach you take, the next step will be a delight, enabling you to reap the rewards of all your hard work.

Building an Index

Once you have defined your index markers, the next step is to generate the index document and be sure you have created a master page with an automatic text box and all the style sheets needed for the index. To do this, choose Utilities | Build Index to open the Build Index dialog box shown in the following illustration.

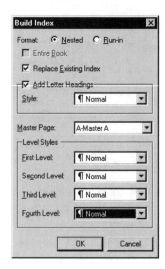

The Build Index dialog box enables you to specify the complete appearance of the index you are about to create, including the general format, letter heading styles, master page format, and level styles.

TIP   *In order for the Build Index command to be available, you must have index entries applied to text in your document and have the Index palette open.*

- **Format**   The Format option enables you to select either Nested or Run-in styles of text for your new index. Choosing Nested enables you to preserve the structure you created in the Index palette based on various levels of headings. Choosing Run-in causes the index to be created with hard returns between first-level entries, but none between second, third, or fourth levels.

- **Entire Book**   Selecting this option enables XPress to build the index based on entry information in all files associated with a book. If the document you are building the index in does not feature associated book files, this option will be unavailable.

- **Replace Existing Index**   Selecting this option enables XPress to overwrite the current index page(s) with the newly-created index. Deselecting this option when building a new index creates an index at the end of your document, regardless of whether one exists already.

- **Add Letter Headings**   Selecting this option enables the creation of alphabetical letters that organize your alphabetic index subsections. With this option selected, you may also choose a paragraph style for the letters to be created. By default, letters appear as individual paragraphs.

- **Master Page**   Choosing a master page from this drop-down menu enables you to control which master page is used when your index is created. Only master pages featuring an automatic text box are listed.

- **Level Styles**   This area enables you to choose a paragraph style for each of the first, second, third, and fourth levels of your index. These styles are automatically applied when your index is created.

Clicking the OK button in the Build Index dialog box instantly creates your new index according to the options you have selected in this box.

10

NOTE ━━━━▶ *By default, the Build Index command appends the index to the* end *of your current document, adding exactly enough pages to accommodate its length. The pages it adds are based on the master page selection you choose in the dialog box.*

NOTE ━━━━▶ *You must rebuild the index if you edit text; there is no dynamic link between the text in the document and the text in the index.*

Conclusion

In this chapter, you've discovered a *pot pourri* of features that all relate to making your layout tasks a little more efficient. You've seen how to avoid the wasted effort of reapplying properties used in other documents, how to move small and large amounts of content within your document and across documents, and how to anchor and lock items in your text and on your pages. You've also learned how to work with powerful style lists, and you've unearthed the mysteries associated with XPress' powerful index feature.

In being exposed to these features, you've learned quite a bit about how well XPress is geared toward working with large, complicated documents. But, there's even more you need to know. In the next chapter, you'll discover how to work with books, chapters, and sections, and see the features that make it easier to work with highly-complex layouts.

CHAPTER 11

Working with Long Documents

It's no secret that QuarkXPress provides you with precision tools for creating and controlling the layout of highly complex documents. In earlier versions of XPress (and other layout applications on the desktop), creation of long documents was often a coordination nightmare. Long documents—such as those ranging to several hundred pages or more in length—were often chopped into shorter documents to maximize their manageability. Since long documents often evolve by passing through several publishing processes, managing editorial and production traffic was often a challenge.

But, with this latest release of XPress come a special tool geared toward working with lengthy documents: Books. Through use of the Books feature, you may automatically compile individual documents as Book components—or chapters—and broadly manage certain properties associated them. Whether your main function involves creating only very large books or you are presently faced with a one-time project, the Books feature is definitely something you should look into using. This chapter takes a very close look at how XPress' new Books feature can help you work more efficiently and points out the pitfalls to watch for along the way.

Strategies for Long Documents

It seems only yesterday that production artists would spend hours—or even days—planning the appearance of a long publication. This process often involved mock-up layouts of various book parts, such as covers, sections, and chapter introductions. Following the layout and design, the type and font treatment for nearly all text in the document would be mapped out by hand on hard copies of the text. If all went as planned, a typesetter would correctly follow the naming scheme and instructions. The result would be long printed galleys of the text, ready for paste-up and assembly into pages. This process was often closely monitored by one or more copyeditors who would review all layout during production. As this checking process evolved, the final pages would move between editing and production (often several times) until all was complete.

Much of the labor involved in laying out documents has been reduced with the advent of electronic publishing. But other tasks such as editing remain woven into the fabric of the publishing process. And since layout and production are often performed by two different individuals or teams, document files now become a shared commodity. It's during the sharing process that publishing procedures can often become confused by such issues as multiple document versions and difficult file-naming schemes. These problems are further compounded by the fact that content can change drastically from the beginning to the end of the publishing process of any long document—causing pages, chapters, and sections to vary in both length and design, right to the final printing.

With the release of XPress 4 come quite a few new features for dealing with long documents. The following features have been either added or beefed up to improve efficiency:

- The maximum number of style sheets, colors, H&J sets, tabs, and paragraphs *per story* has been expanded to support thousands

- When editing existing style sheets, you may now apply changes at more than one million locations in a document

- You may now create more than one million paragraphs per QuarkXPress document

- QuarkXPress document length has been expanded to support a maximum of 2,000 pages, or 2 gigabytes

- You may insert index entries and create four-level nested as well as two-level run-in indexes

- You may add index entries and create cross-references with an Index palette, including choices for six options that determine an entry's scope (such as length of the entry, number of paragraphs, or the next style sheet change)

- You may specify the format, punctuation, master page, and style sheets for creating indexes

- You may automatically create formatted tables of contents and other paragraph-style-sheet-based lists, and regenerate lists and indexes after your text has been edited

Now that you're using QuarkXPress 4 to create your documents, you have quite a few electronic conveniences to use. Still, you'll want to consider a number of things *outside* XPress. The following may serve as a checklist when you're planning production of a large document using XPress:

■ **Define styles**   Defining your text appearance at as many levels as possible is the first and perhaps most critical of all steps in planning a long document. Most important is those for paragraph formats that can include multiple heading levels and all variations of body text. Style definition may also precede the layout stage in QuarkXPress. By naming and defining styles in the word processing application you use to write or edit the published text, you enable editors to roughly plan for length and appearance. For information on creating paragraph styles, see *Using Styles and Style Sheets* in *Chapter 6: Working with Text.*

■ **Create master pages**   Before you import the text into XPress, create the master pages that your publication design calls for. Master pages may be set to include properties such as single or facing page formats, page size, margins, text boxes, logo type, auto page numbering, automatically linked text boxes and so on. When adding large numbers of pages to your long document, you'll be able to specify the exact master page format. For more information on creating and applying master pages, see *About Master Pages and Sections* in *Chapter 3: Tackling a Layout.*

■ **Define Colors, H&Js, and Dash & Stripe**   Setting these properties before you lay out your text isn't as critical as defining your styles and master pages. But you will appreciate having already defined these in XPress before proceeding too far in the construction of your document. Colors, H&Js, and Dash & Stripe properties can affect your layout the same way font selection does. If you plan to create a TOC across a book, defining lists will also be a critically important feature to use.

■ **Use templates**   Once you have applied styles and master pages, it may be convenient to save your resulting specifications in template format; this stores all the settings. The template you create may then be used to begin each new chapter in your publication. To save a document as a template, choose Template from the Files of Type drop-down menu in the Save As dialog box. For more information on using templates, see *Opening Templates* in *Chapter 1: XPress Train Quickstart.*

■ **Use automation**   Use the CTRL/CMD+3 command to create automatic page numbers, instead of creating them manually. The use of automation will enable you to take full advantage of the auto-numbering capabilities of XPress' new Book feature. Also use the Lists feature, which enables you to instantly create or update content listings such as table of contents, indexes, figure and illustration tables, and so on. For more information on using XPress' index feature, see *Working with Indexes* in *Chapter 10: Laying Out Documents*.

■ **Use Books and libraries**   As you'll discover shortly, XPress' new Books feature enables you to assemble and manage multiple files together as a unit—aptly named a "book." Once your document is part of a book, you may control its ordering, numbering, and printing, and monitor certain aspects of its status—all with a simple click or drag of your mouse. In addition, you may use XPress' library feature to store, manage, and retrieve frequently used items. Libraries may store a range of QuarkXPress-specific items ranging from entire layouts to individual items such as text paths, picture and text boxes, lines, and groups of items. For more information on using the Book and Library palettes, see the following two sections.

Working with Books

As mentioned earlier, the Books feature in XPress enables you to assemble and manage the individual chapters that compose large publications. The Books feature is controlled by way of a Book palette through which you may take advantage of the following strengths:

■ Create and assemble book components consisting of multiple QuarkXPress files. You may add up to 1,000 chapters to a book, and XPress enables you to open up to 25 chapters at a time

■ Manage books and their components across multiple users or network drives for efficient, network-based construction of long documents

■ Automatically and instantly synchronize page numbering, style sheets, colors, H&Js, lists, and dash and stripe styles in all book components

■ Reorganize, add, or delete book chapters instantly, in turn updating the content of the entire document to accommodate the new content

■ Control printing by choosing all or selected-only chapters in a book

For electronic layout artists creating large documents, the Book feature provides long-awaited solutions to the risks involved in manually setting page numbers for publications that span multiple QuarkXPress documents. The convenience of

11

automatic numbering across collections of documents *alone* makes the Book feature worthwhile.

Books are controlled through use of the Book palette (shown following this paragraph). As with other palettes, the Book palette may be minimized or maximized by double-clicking its title bar, but it may also be resized vertically or horizontally, depending on how much of the content you need to view. The Book palette is slightly different from other palettes in XPress in that it can't be opened from the View menu or through keyboard shortcuts. Instead, a book must first be created and named in order to open, as well as for the palette itself to display. Items available in the palette are as follows:

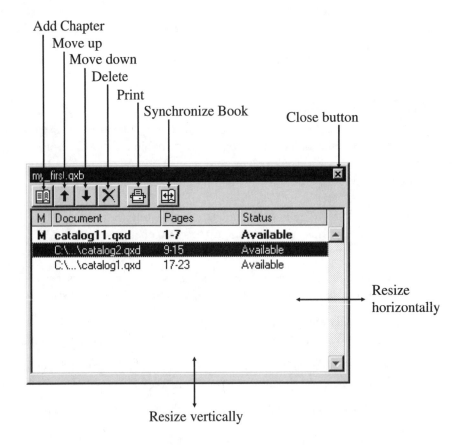

- ■ **M** The bold M in this column identifies a chapter as the Master Chapter. By default, whichever chapter is added to the book first is the Master Chapter. Master chapters define which colors, styles, H&Js, lists, and dashes and stripes properties are used throughout the book and also when synchronizing chapters.

- **Document**   This column lists the document name, including the chapter's location path. The path is set when you first add a chapter to the list.

- **Pages**   This column lists the range of pages in the document. When a chapter is added to a book, the rest of the page numbers in the book are automatically updated. The actual page numbers of the book are determined by where the chapter is added. If you've defined Section starts in your documents, the page numbers will have asterisks next to them.

- **Status**   This column lists the current condition of each chapter. Status may be displayed as *Available, Open, [*username*], Modified,* or *Missing.* When a chapter's status is *Available*, this indicates that the file path has been verified, and the chapter may be successfully opened at any time. The *Open* condition indicates that you currently have the chapter open in XPress. When a user name is displayed, it indicates that someone else on the network you're currently using already has the chapter open and is working in it (only one user at a time may work in a file). User names are determined by your network administrator, who sets file-sharing options for the network's system software. When a chapter is listed as *Modified*, this indicates that the chapter modification date has changed since it was lasted examined by the Book feature. The *Missing* status simply indicates that the chapter is no longer at the end of the path first used to add it to the Book. To locate a missing chapter, simply double-click the chapter name and locate it using the dialog box controls.

NOTE   *To close a Book palette, click the Close button in its title bar. Closing the Book palette causes all chapters associated with the book to close as well. If unsaved changes have been made to the chapter documents, you'll be prompted to save them each time a document is about to close.*

11

To create a new Book file, open the Book palette and add chapters to it, following these steps:

1. Choose File | New | Book. The New Book dialog box opens.

2. Enter a name and set a location for your new book.

3. Click OK. The new book file is created and the Book palette containing it opens. Notice the palette features the name of the new book in its title bar.

4. To open an existing book file, choose File | Open to open the Open dialog box, click the Book file (indicated by QXB in Windows), and click OK. Each time you open a new or existing Book file, another Book palette opens.

TIP *You don't need to have a document open in order to create a new book file or open the Book palette. In addition, you may open more than one book file at a time.*

5. To add chapters to your new Book palette, click the *Add Chapter* button—the first button at the top of the palette. The Add New Chapter dialog box opens.

6. Locate the chapter you wish to add and click OK. The chapter is added to the palette.

To add more chapters, repeat these steps. As you do, you may notice that the position where the chapter is added becomes a key factor in the ordering of automatic page numbers. You may also want to keep in mind that a chapter may only belong to one book at a time. If you wish to add the chapter to other books, you must make a separate copy for each book. To reorganize chapters in your book, use the Add Chapter, Move Chapter Up, Move Chapter Down, and Delete buttons in the palette. Besides Add and Delete, command buttons in the palette are defined as follows:

■ **Move Chapter Up/Down**   While a chapter is selected in the palette, pressing the *Move Chapter Up* or *Move Chapter Down* buttons moves the selected chapter up or down one level each time they're clicked.

■ **Print**   The Print button opens the main Print dialog box, enabling you to print selected chapters in a book. This button enables you to print chapter pages without having to open any of the chapters; QuarkXPress, however, *does* need to open the chapters "behind the scenes," requiring that the chapters you want to print have a status of *Available*. For more information on printing, see *Chapter 16: Printing Your Pages*.

■ **Synchronize**   Clicking the Synchronize button has the effect of ensuring that all the chapters in your book are using the same style sheets, colors, H&Js, lists, and dashes and stripes as those found in the master chapter. The Synchronize command doesn't delete information, but instead does the opposite: It compiles a comprehensive list of all ingredients and copies them to all chapter documents. When conflicts occur (such as with two different styles using the same name), the styles specified in the master document are used. Synchronize may also be used for making global changes to the style sheets, colors, H&Js, lists, and dashes and stripes in documents; you do this by editing properties in the master chapter itself and clicking the Synchronize button.

TIP   *Before using the Synchronize command on your book chapters, delete as many unused style sheets, colors, H&Js, lists, and dashes and stripes as possible from your document. To do this using style sheets as an example, choose Edit | Style Sheets (SHIFT+F11) to open the Style Sheets dialog box, choose* Style Sheets Not Used *from the* Show *drop-down menu, select the unused styles, and click first* Delete *and then* Save. *Reducing the number of style sheets, colors, H&Js, lists, and dashes and stripes stored in your documents will help reduce their file size.*

Books and Networks

Although the Book feature in XPress is geared toward book management for teams of users who may be working across local or wide area network drives, there are a few considerations:

When you first create a new book file and subsequently add chapters to it, the path that leads to the chapter is stored in memory. Each time you reopen a book file, these paths are checked and the status of the book at the end of that path is displayed. If an individual chapter is listed as missing in your Book palette, then either the original file is no longer located at the end of the path or the filename has been changed. In order for a chapter to be available, it must be located by the Book palette with its original path and filename.

TIP   *When working in the Books palette, any user who has the book open may add, reorder, or delete chapters, or may change section starts in chapters.*

11

When working across a network as well as with book components stored on network drives, this operational rule becomes even more important. Since the full path of the document must be validated in order for the document to be available, it makes sense that you be connected to the network before attempting to open the book file. Otherwise, your book components may not be available to you.

Taken a little further, if you're working in a team publishing environment where other team members require access to shared files, it also makes sense that all book components be stored on the network instead of on your computer's local hard drive. That way, even after you've finished working and turned your computer off, the shared files will still be available to other team members.

Although it has little to do with the operation of XPress, network mapping is also a consideration when working with book files. Because a book's files and its components may be shared, the path names must be constant. This means that the network drives for all users must be named identically. If you suspect yours isn't, it may be necessary contact your network administrator to rename the drives.

In networked environments, including both Macintosh and Windows systems, you can't mix platform version files. For example, if you open a book chapter using QuarkXPress for Macintosh operating systems, a user in QuarkXPress for Windows with the book open wouldn't know the chapter is open. In other words, if you're using a Macintosh version of XPress 4, and you wish to include a Windows version XPress file, it must first be converted and subsequently stored on a Macintosh-compatible network drive. Avoid sharing files across platforms when using the Book feature.

Setting a Book Chapter Start

If you've used automatic page numbering to number the pages in your QuarkXPress documents, you'll be able to quickly customize your section starts or enable the Books feature to number pages automatically. By default, when a chapter is added to a book, the chapter immediately becomes a Book chapter start and any automatic page numbers are updated accordingly. There's nothing more you need to do.

When your document becomes a chapter of a book, an asterisk (*) appears beside the first page of the document in the Page Indicator field, indicating a manual chapter section start. If the book has been set up with overriding section starts, the chapter that follows will automatically begin with the next sequential number. If you wish, you may change, override, or customize page numbering in your chapters by using the Section command dialog box options shown in the following illustration.

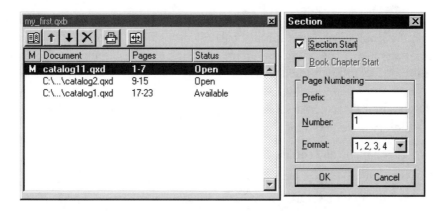

With no options selected in the dialog box, you may notice that the grayed-out Book Chapter Start option is selected already and the numeral in the Number field matches the chapter sequence. You can't actually select this option yourself—it's selected on your behalf when you add your document to a book. If you wish, you may override the automated book numbering by choosing the Section option. Once the Section option in the dialog box is selected, the Prefix, Number, and Format options become available and the automatic chapter numbering is overridden, as shown in the previous illustration.

For information on setting Prefix, Number, and Format options, see *Working in Sections* in *Chapter 3: Tackling a Layout.*

TIP

When working with multiple open documents and using the Book palette, you may bring a document to the fore quickly by double-clicking its name in the palette chapter list.

Working with Libraries

Although the Library feature is not as comprehensive as the Books feature, its usefulness when working with large documents is just as significant. Actually, the Libraries feature may be used for any length of document—long or short. Libraries may be used to store frequently-used items such as layouts, logos, forms, table formats, and so on. Library items may be text or picture boxes, or shapes or lines, or grouped items, and so on. Items stored in a Library file may be quickly identified, selected, and copied to your document page or traded between library files.

Library items are stored in files that are managed through the Library palette. As with the Book palette, the Library palette can't simply be opened and viewed. Instead, you must create or open a library file using the File commands. To create a new Library file, follow these steps:

1. Choose File | New | Library (CTRL/CMD+ALT/OPTION+N). The New Library dialog box opens.

2. Enter a name and set a location for your new library.

3. Click OK. The new library file is created and the Library palette containing it opens as shown in the illustration on the next page. Notice that the palette features the name of the new Library in its title bar.

4. You may create or open as many libraries as you wish. To open an existing library file, choose File | Open to open the Open dialog box, click the Library file (indicated by QXL on Windows), and click OK. Each time you open a new or existing library file, another Library palette opens.

NOTE *To close a Library palette, click the Close button in its title bar.*

TIP *Library save functions are controlled through your Application Preferences. If you select Auto Library Save in the Save tab, you won't need to save library files by closing them. With this option selected as your preference, each time you make a change to a library collection, the changes will automatically be saved.*

The Library palette behaves as do any other palettes. You may maximize or minimize a palette by double-clicking its title bar, resize it vertically or horizontally, or close it by clicking the Close button in the title bar. When a library file is first created, what you see is an empty shell with no existing content. In this state, the library is ready for adding content. To add items to your new library file, follow these steps:

1. Open a document from which you wish to copy an item to your new library (CTRL/CMD+O).

2. Choose the Item tool from the Tool palette.

3. Click the item you wish to add by clicking on it in your document window. You may select more than one item to add, but keep in mind that if multiple items are selected and added simultaneously, they'll be considered a single item in the library.

4. Drag the item(s) from your document into the Library palette, but before you release the mouse button notice that an eyeglass-style cursor appears in the palette as you drag your item into it. Notice also that two small triangles appear. These triangles indicate where the item will be placed in your library and also that the original document still holds a copy of the items you dragged into the library.

5. Open a second QuarkXPress document by choosing File I Open (CTRL/CMD+O), selecting a document, and clicking OK.

6. Add your library item to the document by dragging it from the palette onto one of the pages of the second document. Notice that the item has merely been copied and the library item remains in the palette.

7. Drag at least three more items into your Library palette as in the example below. As you do, notice the small triangles that appear each time, indicating the resulting position of the library item you're adding. Items are positioned to the right of or below the triangle's indicated position.

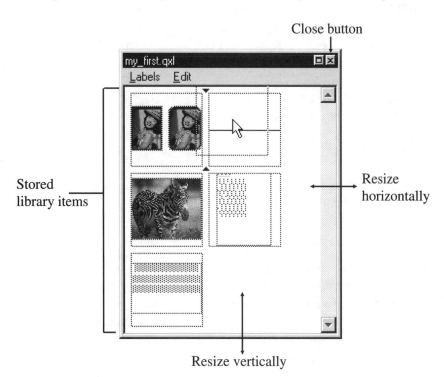

Close button

Stored library items

Resize horizontally

Resize vertically

11

8. Select one of the items in the Library palette, drag it to a different position in the palette, and release the mouse. Notice that as you dragged the item, the triangles reappeared to indicate the new position.

TIP *To delete a library item using a Windows version of XPress 4, choose Delete from the Edit menu at the top of the Library palette. XPress will prompt you before an item is deleted. To delete an item while using the Macintosh version of XPress, select it and choose Edit | Clear or press the DELETE key.*

Working with Library Content

The Library palette is equipped with either one or two menus for managing the items in the library, depending on your platform version. On Windows versions, an Edit menu enables you to perform typical clipboard functions, including Cut (CTRL/CMD+X), Copy (CTRL/CMD+C), Paste (CTRL/CMD+V), and Delete. These commands apply specifically to library items, and not to the items in your document. On both Windows and Macintosh versions, a Labels menu enables you to control how you view items in your library. With no labels applied to items, the menu simply includes *All* and *Unlabeled* selections, the default of which is *All*. To apply a label to a library item, continue from the above exercise by following these steps:

1. Double-click one of the items in your newly created palette. The Library Entry dialog box appears.

2. Enter a label for the library item in the Label field.

TIP *When applying labels to items in your library, choose labels that will enable you to clearly identify the items.*

3. Click OK to apply the label.

4. Select another item and apply a different label to it in the same manner. Do the same for the remaining two items. (You may also label items by selecting an existing label from the drop-down list in the Label Entry dialog box.) Notice that each time you add a label to a library item, the label becomes available from the Label drop-down menu.

5. Click the Labels menu in the palette and notice that the new labels you applied to your library items now appear in this menu along with *All* and *Unlabeled*.

6. Choose *Unlabeled* from the Labels menu in the palette. If you labeled all the items in your palette, the palette will appear empty.

7. Choose one of the label entries you applied to a library item from the Labels menu. Notice that the specific item now appears by itself in the palette.

8. Repeat this for other labels you entered and notice that, each time, the labeled item appears. Notice also that the selections in the menu remain selected and the items they apply to remain visible until you deselect them or choose *All* or *Unlabeled*.

Because the Library palette may only display items either greeked or in thumbnail form, when working with large collections of library items, these view commands will be invaluable for identifying and locating the items you need to copy to other documents. But the feature is only as efficient as the person creating the labels—so labeling items correctly and accurately becomes all-important to making effective use of this feature.

NOTE *If you wish, you may also apply the same label to multiple items—for example, you might put the same label on all the logos for a given publication, project, or client.*

For the most part, items stored in library files are available independent of the documents from which you originally copied the items. Libraries may be exchanged between locations and users, although there are more than a few hazards to be aware of; the most significant of these are font issues. These limitations also include naming schemes for such things as style sheets, colors, H&Js, lists, and dashes and stripes. It's a good-news/bad-news scenario.

First the *bad news*. The problem of font compatibility may come up when exchanging libraries between users. For example, copying an item to a library and subsequently copying the library file to a different computer may result in missing fonts if the second computer isn't furnished with the same fonts as the library item

11

uses. In cases where fonts are missing, you'll likely need to substitute other fonts, or take steps to install the missing fonts on the new system.

A similar hazard may result when copying pictures to—and subsequently from—a library file after the file has been moved to a different computer. Although previews of pictures may be copied, the original data representing the picture will be listed as missing until the correct path is restored.

When copying items with identical style, color, H&J, list, or dashes and stripes names, you may also experience conflicts—often without warning! In cases where the names of these ingredients match those used in the destination document, the document's specifications are used. This could result in items that are copied from libraries changing color, or in text formatting changing, or in text reflowing or looking quite different from the document the library item was originally copied from. This is definitely a concern if you plan on making widespread use of the Library feature. The same hazard applies when copying items to a library file that already contains an item with a style, color, H&J, list, or dashes and stripes that features an identical name. In these cases, the item will change as soon as it's copied to the library.

The *good news* is that, when copying items with compatible fonts, all style sheets, colors, H&J, and dashes and stripes contained in the library item are automatically copied to the destination document. Unfortunately, when using libraries, the bad news is more significant than the good news.

NOTE *Library files don't port successfully across platforms (that is, move from Macintosh to Windows or vice versa).*

Working with Baseline Grids in XPress

As mentioned at the beginning of this chapter, when preparing to tackle a long or complex document it's always a good idea to begin by planning the appearance and layout of certain things carefully before you proceed too far with production. One of these things is baseline alignment across columns of text, which opens a basic guideline of good layout—establishing a baseline grid.

Establishing such a grid for your publication enables the baseline of text in adjacent columns to align with each other regardless of the occurrence of headings, which usually are set in a larger font. Baseline grids also enable you to align picture and text boxes with baselines or X-height of text. The result of a well-planned baseline grid is a neat and orderly layout appearance. It's not absolutely necessary

Art Director: Steven Taylor
Firm: *Business Week* Magazine
Description: Cover Design, *Business Week*, March 9, 1997 issue

This cover design depicts inside coverage of the best and worst performing boards governing corporations. It integrates text as a graphic together with center formatted text columns in a staggered layout to guide the reader's eye.

that you establish a baseline grid, but it *will* help improve the overall appearance of the publication you are creating. Some might even say it's a design function rather than a layout function. In reality, few desktop layout artists pay much attention to this issue. But for high-end, quality layout and professional-looking results, following a baseline grid is an integral part of the layout function.

Baseline grid options are set in your Document Preferences dialog box, opened by choosing Edit | Preferences | Document (CTRL/CMD+Y) and selecting the Paragraph tab shown next. The dialog box options consist of fields for Start and Increment.

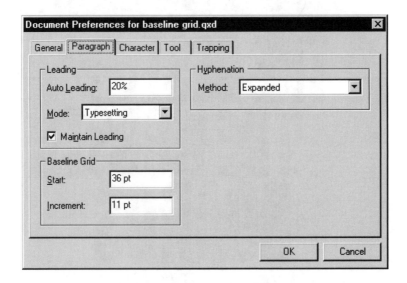

Baseline grids often follow the leading measure of the body text of a document. For example, if the text leading is set to 13 points, then the increment of the baseline grid is set to match. When headings or subheadings occur in text, they may not align with the baseline of the body text, but the body text to follow definitely will. To plan this out, you need to first establish the size of your body text and any headings or subheadings that will occur. Once these sizes are established, you'll need to set spacing above and below the headings to enable all body text, and variations of it, to align with the grid as shown in Figure 11-1.

TIP   *When establishing styles to fit a baseline grid, be sure to use exact leading measures rather than the Auto Leading feature. Auto Leading applies vertical spacing as a percentage of the size of text, not of an absolute measure.*

Photograph aligned manually with baseline of text ——

Each night, before falling asleep he would stare at the calendar and eventually get out of bed and cross out the offending day with careful strokes like a prisoner scratching marks on a wall.

Letter to shareholders

At the end of the day, Mark would return to his little box-room with its small bed, small chair, and tiny chest of drawers, and collapse exhausted. The only picture in the room was the calendar that hung above Mark's bed. The date was circled in red several times to remind him that would be allowed to join his friends and family once he had returned to normal. Each night, before falling asleep he would stare at the calendar and eventually get out of bed and cross out the offending day with careful strokes like a prisoner scratching marks on a wall.

Caption for photograph, caption for photograph, caption for photograph

Body text automatically aligns across three columns

Tackling foreign markets

At the end of the day, Mark would return to his little box-room with its small bed, small chair, and tiny chest of drawers, and collapse exhausted. The only picture in the room was the calendar that hung above Mark's bed. The date was circled in red several times to remind him that would be allowed to join his friends and family once he had returned to normal. Each night, before falling asleep he would stare at the calendar and eventually get out of bed and

cross out the offending day with careful strokes like a prisoner scratching marks on a wall.

Gold Standards

At the end of the day, Mark would return to his little box-room with its small bed, small chair, and tiny chest of drawers, and collapse exhausted. The only picture in the room was the calendar that hung above Mark's bed. The date was circled in red several times to remind him that would be

allowed to join his friends and family once he had returned to normal. Each night, before falling asleep he would stare at the calendar and eventually get out of bed and cross out the offending day with careful strokes like a prisoner scratching marks on a wall.

International money market funds

At the end of the day, Mark would return to his little box-room with its small bed, small chair, and tiny chest of drawers, and collapse exhausted. The only picture in the room was the calendar that hung above Mark's bed. The date was circled in red several times to remind him that would be allowed to join his friends and family once he had returned to normal. Each night, before falling asleep he would stare at the calendar and eventually get out of bed and cross out the offending day with careful strokes like a prisoner scratching marks on a wall.

—— Photograph aligned manually with X-height of text

Photograph captions automatically align with body text across columns ——

Returns on investment

At the end of the day, Mark would return to his little box-room with its small bed, small chair, and tiny chest of drawers, and collapse exhausted. The only picture in the room was the calendar that hung above Mark's bed. The date was circled in red several times to remind him that would be allowed to join his friends and family once he had returned to normal. Each night, before falling asleep he would stare at the calendar and eventually get out of bed and cross out the offending day with careful strokes like a prisoner scratching marks on a wall.

Caption for photograph, caption for photograph, caption for photograph

FIGURE 11-1   Planning a baseline grid

The other function of baseline grids comes into play when specifying your body text style. Choosing the *Lock to Baseline Grid* option in the Formats tab of the Paragraph Attributes dialog box (CTRL/CMD+SHIFT+F) (shown in the following illustration) enables your body text to adhere to the underlying grid at all times. When specifying options for such styles as body text or photograph captions, choosing this option locks styles to align with the baseline grid, and in turn with each other, no matter where they appear on the page.

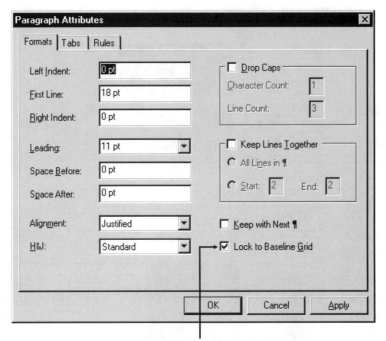

Use this option to align body styles to the
baseline grid increment

While the document in Figure 11-1 is set with a baseline grid increment of 11 points, the text is set with four styles: body text, two heading levels, and a style for the photograph captions. The type specifications consist of the following:

- **Body Text**   Normal + Alignment: Justified; First Line: 18 pt; Leading: 11 pt; Lock to Baseline Grid; Next Style: body text

- **Heading level 1**   Alignment: Left; Left Indent: 0 pt; First Line: 0 pt; Right Indent: 0 pt; Leading: 15 pt; Space Before: 9 pt; Space After: 2 pt; H&J: Standard; Keep With Next ¶; Next Style: Heading level 1; Character: (Times New Roman; 14 pt; +Bold; Black; Shade: 100%; Track Amount: 0; Horiz. Scale: 100%; Baseline Shift: 0 pt)

- **Heading level 2**   Alignment: Left; Left Indent: 0 pt; First Line: 0 pt; Right Indent: 0 pt; Leading: 12 pt; Space Before: 9 pt; Space After: 2 pt; H&J: Standard; Keep All Lines in ¶ Together; Keep With Next ¶; Next Style: Heading level 2; Character: (Times New Roman; 11 pt; +Bold +Italic; Black; Shade: 100%; Track Amount: 0; Horiz. Scale: 100%; Baseline Shift: 0 pt)

- **Photograph caption**   Alignment: Justified; Left Indent: 0 pt; First Line: 0 pt; Right Indent: 0 pt; Leading: 11 pt; Space Before: 0 pt; Space After: 0 pt; H&J: Standard; Lock to Baseline Grid; Next Style: photo caption 1; Character: (Times New Roman; 10 pt; +Bold +Italic; Black; Shade: 100%; Track Amount: 0; Horiz. Scale: 100%; Baseline Shift: 0 pt)

Although each layout and individual design case may differ slightly, the principles of the baseline grid remain constant. Notice, in the above style specifications, that the baseline grid is set to locked only for the photograph captions and the body text. The paragraph spacing has been added above and below the two heading levels in order to accommodate the grid. Space above and below the headings is equal to the total leading value of a single line. In these two cases, space above of 9 points added to space below of 2 points equals the leading of both the body text and the photograph caption: 11 points.

Conclusion

This chapter has focused on some of the more specific tools QuarkXPress 4 includes for working with long documents. You've explored a number of the issues surrounding planning a large document, and you've seen how the Books feature enables you to simplify assembly of potentially enormous publications. You've also found out about the workings of the Libraries features and a few not-so-simple issues surrounding their use. For the complete low-down on all that's customizable in XPress, and to find out how to squeeze out that last drop of productivity, see the next chapter, on fine-tuning XPress.

11

CHAPTER 12

Fine-tuning XPress

I recall taking a course in woodworking years ago. Our class instructor was an elderly gentleman with an extremely pronounced German accent whose most frequent words were: "You vill use zee right tool for zee right jop!" He never revealed the logic behind it—we just feared him and followed his commands to the letter.

This chapter is one of the most valuable you'll visit. If you're using XPress only for on/off projects or for quick, specific tasks, then taking time to customize the application isn't really going to help much. But, if you intend to use XPress for creating a wide variety of documents or multiple documents of a specific type, then customization is something you'll want to pay close attention to; the time you spend will pay off in ease of use and consistency of output. This chapter uncovers all the various ways you may customize XPress—no small feat, considering the program's vast capabilities. To a certain degree *everything* in XPress is customizable. This chapter, however, concentrates on only those customization steps that will save you time, effort, or both.

When Does Customization Make Sense?

Each time you launch XPress, open a new document, use a tool, or enter text, you're very likely to spend time changing options or entering similar or even identical settings. You'll be pleased to know there's probably a way to streamline XPress to minimize these potentially wasted efforts.

Customizing makes sense particularly if you work in an environment where specific standards must be followed. For example, say you work in an environment where the corporate standard typeface used in all documents is limited to Helvetica, but each time you create a new text box and enter text, it's automatically set to Times Roman. And, each time you find yourself changing the font, creating a style, applying a standard style, or all three. The same applies to standardized colors, dashes and stripes, and so on. Customizing your application settings will change this.

Or let's say your job is to create long or highly-complex documents that result in large file sizes and lengthy Save operations. As you work, you're constantly interrupted by XPress' Auto Save feature. Don't worry—you can customize this too.

Or, each time you reach for the Line tool, you find you've chosen the Orthogonal tool in error—a tool you never even use. Or each time you need an oval text box you choose the Bevel-corner text box instead. Or each time you create a box or shape, the line is too thick or thin. You can change these too—by customizing. The more you customize, the less you'll need to set options—and the faster and more productive your work will be.

Default Settings and Beyond

XPress assigns application default properties to any new item you create in your document. As mentioned earlier, changing these default settings saves you time spent resetting properties later on to match your particular document's design. All default properties may be changed through use of Edit commands. If XPress has been launched, and no documents are yet open, you'll notice (among other things) that commands for accessing XPress' default Style Sheets, Colors, H&Js, Lists, and Dashes & Stripes are available from the Edit menu.

Setting Defaults for All New Documents

Although the procedure for changing actual application defaults settings is specific to the command dialog boxes you choose, the results are the same. To change application default settings generically, follow these steps:

1. Launch XPress, or close all currently-open documents so that only the program window (Windows) or command menus (Macintosh) are showing. If you attempt to change defaults while a document is opened, the changes will apply only to that document.

2. Choose the Style Sheets (SHIFT+F11), Colors (SHIFT+F12), H&Js (CTRL/OPTION+SHIFT+F11), Lists, or Dash & Stripes commands from the Edit menu to change:

   - **Default Styles Sheet settings** Choose either the *Normal* paragraph or *Normal* character style and modify these with your new default paragraph or character settings. Although you may modify both the *Normal* styles, they can't be deleted or renamed. If your work environment includes use of standardized character or paragraph style sheets, adding them will ensure that they're automatically available to all new documents. For more information on creating and saving styles, see *Using Styles and Style Sheets* in *Chapter 6, Working with Text*.

12

■ **Default Color settings**   The default colors first installed with XPress are a mix between RGB (red, green, and blue) colors and CMYK (cyan, magenta, yellow, and black) colors, with no spot colors specified. If you work in an environment where specific spot ink colors are frequently used, you might consider adding them to this list. This way, each new document you create will feature colors specific to your needs. For more information on adding, creating, and saving Colors, see *Creating New Colors* in *Chapter 13, Working with Color*.

■ **Default Dashes & Stripes settings**   Adding any custom dashes & stripes will ensure that they're available to items in all new documents. By default, the *Solid* dash is the default for all items and can't be changed, edited, or deleted. However, if your default collection contains selections you're certain you'll never use, you may delete them. If you change your mind later on, you may use the Append command to copy them from any document created earlier or from documents stored on the XPress 4 program disc. For more information on creating and saving dashes and stripes, see *Creating Dash & Stripe Styles* in the next section of this chapter.

■ **Default Lists**   Normally, no default lists are included in XPress. Properties associated with Lists are so specific that they may differ for each document they're associated with. And because lists rely so heavily on Style Sheets, creating default lists useful for all users is nearly an impossibility. Instead, XPress has left the default list creation up to you. You may use the Edit | Lists command to create default lists based on your default styles you've set and then apply any list properties available. To make this easier, be sure you've already created both document default styles and list default styles to choose from.

■ **Default H&J settings**   Modify the *Standard* H&J (hyphenation and justification) settings for default automatic hyphenation, character spacing, and capitalization. Although the *Standard* H&J may be edited, it can't be deleted or renamed.

3. Once you've finished making changes to any of the above, choose File | New (CTRL/CMD+N) to verify that the default settings have been changed. To do this quickly, open the Measurements palette by choosing View | Measurements (F9).

4. Create a new text box and enter some text to check your new default font, size, and style settings displayed in the Measurements palette.

5. Select the text by highlighting it and choose Style | Colors to view your new color collection.

6. Choose Style | Paragraph Style Sheet and Style | Character Style Sheet to view any default styles you've added.

7. Choose Style | Formats (CTRL/CMD+SHIFT+F) to verify any H&J settings you may have added.

8. Choose Item | Frame (CTRL/CMD+B) to check for your new Dash & Stripe styles.

9. Close your document without saving the changes by clicking the Close button and answering *No* to the prompt screen that appears.

■ **Default Auxiliary Dictionary** Although no documents are open, you may also set the default dictionaries used by XPress for all new documents. If you've spent the effort required in building a personal, professional, or project-specific dictionary, making a dictionary available to all new documents will save you (or someone else) hours of time verifying spelling instances that have already been saved. Auxiliary dictionaries enable you to avoid misspelling commonly-used names and terms, as well as to verify spellings of words specific to the industry or subject matter discussed in your documents. To set the default auxiliary dictionary, choose Utilities | Auxiliary dictionary to open the Auxiliary Dictionary dialog box, locate and select the dictionary file you want to use from now on, and click Open to complete the operation and close the dialog box.

TIP *When sending your document to others, include the Auxiliary Dictionary file with any other files related to your document such as image, font, tag, or preference files. Without your Auxiliary dictionary file, any specialized spelling you may have added yourself won't be found.*

12

Creating Dash & Stripe Styles

XPress enables you to apply dashes & stripes to virtually any drawn item, including text and picture box frames, lines, and freehand and Bézier boxes. You may choose from a brief collection of existing default styles, with certain items selected from the Style menu, the Frame dialog box, or the Measurements palette. Custom dashes & stripes may be created and saved by choosing Edit | Dashes & Stripes to open the Dashes & Stripes dialog box. Individual dialog box controls allow you to create new dashes or new stripes to suit your fancy and add flair to your publications.

Creating New Dash Patterns

Dashes are simply repeating "horizontal" line patterns that may be applied to any line or box frame in XPress. You may set any existing or new dash pattern to any line width, color, or shade. You may even control the gap color and shade *between* the dashes. To create a new custom dash, open the Edit Dash dialog box shown next by clicking the New button from the Dashes & Stripes for [*document filename*] dialog box and select Dash.

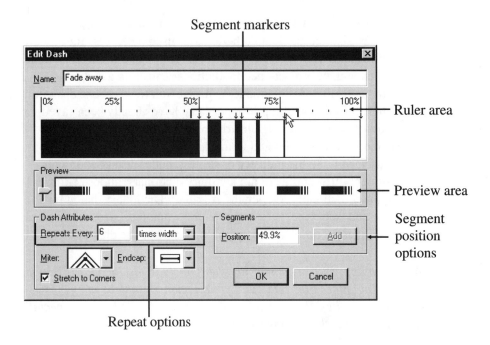

The Edit Dash dialog box includes an assortment of options to apply to your new pattern. New dash options in the dialog box involve the following features and parameters:

■ **Ruler area**   The area at the top of the dialog box enables you to interactively create your new dash pattern. This features operates in a similar way to setting tab markers. Click-dragging in the top of this area enables you to set the start and end points of the segments in your new pattern. Dragging the endpoint markers sets the length and position of each. You may also enter the positions in the Segment field and click the Add button to apply them. Once the start and end points of a dash segment have been created, you may drag the entire segment using a hand-style tool. You may create a maximum of only five individual segments per pattern.

■ **Preview area**   The Preview area features a slider control that enables you to vary the width of the new dash pattern and immediately preview the results. As you move the slider up or down, the line width increases or decreases and a pop-up flag from the slider control indicates the current width of the line in points.

TIP *To delete a dash segment from the Ruler preview area, simply drag the segment to any point outside the Preview window.*

■ **Repeats every**   You may use this option to establish whether the pattern of the dash is fixed within a given distance, or whether it changes frequency with the width of the line or frame it's applied to. Choosing the Times Width option from the drop-down menu and entering a repeat value sets your new dash to repeat based on a percentage of the width of the line or box frame. Choosing points and entering a repeat value sets the pattern as absolute within a given measure regardless of the width of the line or box frame. With times width selected, the Ruler area displays pattern segments based on position settings from 0 to 100 percent; with points selected, the Ruler displays increments between 0 points and the

12

repeat value you enter. The illustration below demonstrates the results of dash patterns applied with both repeat styles.

Repeats every 5 times width

12-point line

24-point line

Repeats every 25 points

12-point line

24-point line

- ■ **Miter**   The Miter styles affect the shape of the corners. The drop-down menu offers sharp corner (the default) shapes, round corner shapes, and beveled corner shapes. Their effects are shown below on identical text boxes given a custom solid-dash pattern.

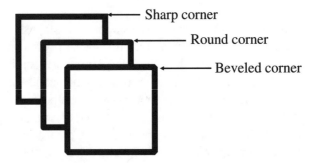

Sharp corner

Round corner

Beveled corner

- ■ **Endcap**   The Endcaps option control the appearance of the ends of dashes. The drop-down menu is composed of butt caps (the default), round caps, and projecting square caps. The butt cap style terminates the shape of the end of each dash segment ("butting" up against it), causing it to appear flat, while round cap applies a rounded end to the segment based on the width of the frame or line. The projecting square cap is perhaps the most distorted of the three styles, and causes each dash segment to be applied with a complete square shape centered on the end of the segment and changing size with the width of your frame or line. The effects of the three cap styles are shown in the following illustration, applied to the same dotted dash pattern. Vertical ruler lines have been added to show the subtle difference between butt and projected square cap styles.

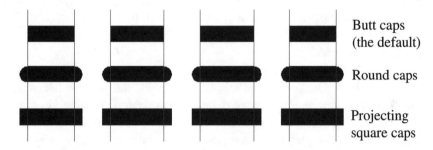

Butt caps (the default)

Round caps

Projecting square caps

- **Stretch to corners**   This option enables you to set the dash pattern to be positioned evenly and symmetrically at corners when applied to box frames and lines. This option is best left selected (the default) when creating dash patterns so that the segment patterns are able to define the corners of shapes. If you want, you may deselect it for the results shown next. In both examples shown, the same basic dash pattern is used.

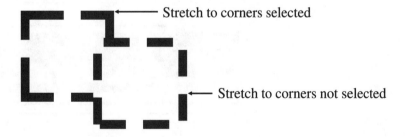

Stretch to corners selected

Stretch to corners not selected

12

- **Segment position**   Although it may be faster and simpler to position markers using your mouse pointer, you may enter marker segments in the Segments field of the Edit Dash dialog box and click the Add button to create them.

*When using the new dash pattern options for the first time, try editing a copy of an existing pattern rather than creating a new one from scratch. To do this, click the dash pattern in the Edit Dash dialog box and click Duplicate. A duplicate named Copy of [*dash pattern*] immediately opens into the Dash Edit dialog box.*

Creating New Stripe Patterns

The procedure for creating new stripe patterns is very similar to that of making new dashes. Whereas dashes enable you to create patterns that repeat "horizontally" along the length of a pattern applied to a frame or a line, stripe patterns set the "vertical" stripes along its *width*.

As with dash patterns, you may set any existing or new stripe pattern to any line width, color, or shade. You may also set the gap color and shade *between* the stripes. Stripe patterns may be much more detailed than dash patterns, and options in the Edit Stripe dialog box enable you to create as many new stripe segments as you've got patience for. You may be limited, though, by the detail rendered by your output device. For example, a highly-detailed stripe pattern may not appear as you created it when your document is printed to a bubble jet printer.

To create a new custom stripe, open the Edit Stripe dialog box shown next by clicking the New button from the Dashes & Stripes for [*document filename*] dialog box and select Stripe.

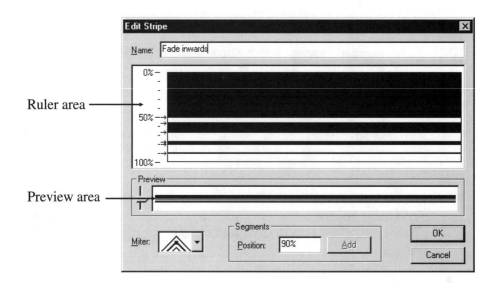

The Edit Stripe dialog box includes a simpler set of options than for that of new dashes. Options in the dialog box consist of the following:

- **Ruler area**   The area at the top of the dialog box enables you to interactively create stripes of varying widths by dragging markers at the left side of the Preview area. Dragging the markers vertically sets the width and position of each. You may also enter the positions in the Segments field and click the Add button to apply them. Once the start and end points of a stripe segment have been created, you may drag the entire segment using a hand-style tool.

- **Preview area**   Using the Preview area features a slider control that enables you to vary the width of the new stripe pattern at various box frame or line widths. As you move the slider up or down, the preview width increases or decreases indicated by a pop-up flag from the slider control indicates the current width of the line in points.

TIP   *To delete a stripe segment from the Ruler Preview area, simply drag the segment to any point outside the preview window.*

- **Miter**   The Miter styles for stripes affect corners of shapes. These are applied identically as with creating new dash patterns described above, and result in the same line effects. Styles are selected from the Miter drop-down menu and are composed of sharp corner (the default) shape, round corner shape, and beveled corner shape.

Creating Custom H&Js

The appearance of hyphenation in your document has always been one of the more subtle issues surrounding document design. If you create documents that are short on text, but long on pictures, you may not be too concerned with hyphenation. You may merely need to either turn it on or turn it off.

But for many text-heavy or high-end publications, the ability to control hyphenation is extremely critical to controlling the look of text. Hyphenation affects all text, but mostly text set in very large sizes or to very narrow column widths (or both). Hyphenation factors also come into play when creating runaround effects between text boxes and pictures or uneven shapes. The best rule of thumb to follow is: *Less Is Better*. In fact, ideally, no hyphenation is the best scenario. But, turning hyphenation off in many instances causes text length to end far short of the margin

12

(particularly in academic or technical publications that tend to use long words) or distracting spaces between words—especially if your text is justified.

XPress comes with only one H&J recipe—*Standard*—which serves as the default when applying any paragraph text formatting or when simply entering text into a text box. Options for hyphenation and justification are set in the Edit Hyphenation dialog box shown next, which is accessed by clicking the Edit button in the H&J dialog box. To open the H&J dialog box, choose Edit | H&Js (CTRL/OPTION+SHIFT+F11).

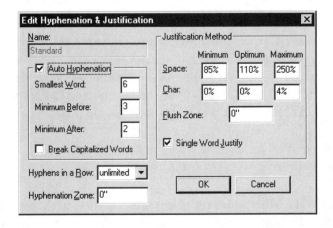

The thrust of this feature is to create an H&J recipe that minimizes the number of hyphens that appear at the right margin of your text, so that the reader won't be distracted by repetitious hyphens. The Standard H&J is set to these properties:

■ **Standard H&J**   Auto Hyphenation Enabled; Smallest Word: 6; Minimum Before: 3; Minimum After: 2; Don't Break Cap Words enabled; Hyphens in a Row: unlimited; Hyphenation Zone: 0"; Space Minimum: 85%; Optimal: 110%; Maximum: 250%; Character Minimum: 0%; Optimal: 0%; Maximum: 4%; Flush Zone: 0"; Single Word Justify

If you're not familiar with the terms used, this H&J might seem like secret code. In an effort to understand hyphenation options, the following terms are defined.

■ **Auto Hyphenation**   With this option selected, XPress' currently-selected hyphenation settings are enabled. When it's not selected, hyphenation is essentially turned off (but the justification controls on the right side of the dialog box *still* take effect). The way Auto Hyphenation breaks words is determined by the built-in hyphenation dictionary (not the spelling dictionary) as well as by XPress' automatic hyphenation algorithm. When Auto Hyphenation is enabled, the next three options are available.

■ **Smallest Word**   Enter the minimum number of characters a word must be to become eligible for auto hyphenation.

■ **Minimum before**   When a word is divided by an automatic hyphen, portions are left on two different text lines. Enter the smallest number of characters that may precede the hyphen. The higher the value the easier the text will be to read, and the higher the risk that poor word spacing may result in your text.

■ **Minimum after**   As with *Minimum before*, enter the smallest number of characters that may follow a hyphen.

■ **Hyphens in a row**   By default in the *Standard* H&J, this option is set to *unlimited*, meaning that potentially every line could end with a hyphen. Realistically, you probably won't want this to happen. Setting this to 2 or 3 hyphens in a row is probably the most you would ever want to see in your text. However, the fewer hyphens in a row you specify, the greater the risk of poor spacing in justified text.

■ **Hyphenation Zone**   The hyphenation zone is the area between the right margin of your text column and the space value you enter in this field. Any word in the hyphenation zone is fair game for a hyphen when length makes it spill over the right margin. Wide hyphenation zones increase the likelihood of hyphens, while shorter distances decrease this. The Standard H&J has a hyphenation zone of 0 inches.

Justification of your text is determined by the settings chosen in this area of the H&J dialog box. Justification is divided into two main treatments: character spacing and word spacing. These two properties may be adjusted in order for text to justify to meet both margins. To justify text, choose *Justified* or *Forced* from the *Alignment* drop-down menu in the Paragraph Attributes tab dialog box; these controls can be used to fine-tune the spacing in already-justified text. The amount of adjustment to word spacing and character spacing is determined by the settings you enter in the space fields.

- **Space Minimum, Optimum Maximum**   Every font has its own degree of word spacing as an integral characteristic. The spacing options in these three fields enable you to set limits for the least and most amount of space XPress may add to or subtract from the original spacing, based on percentage. The *Optimum* space is used for lines that don't require adjustments to justify, such as left, right, and center alignments.

- **Char. Minimum, Optimum, Maximum**   As with word spacing, every font has its own degree of built-in character spacing. The spacing options here enable you to limit the percentage of space applied between characters. *Optimum* value is also used for left, right, and center alignments.

- **Flush Zone**   The flush zone may sound like an uncomfortable place to eat your lunch, but actually enables you to control whether or not to justify the last line in a justified paragraph even if the line doesn't completely fill your column width. The flush zone is measured from the right margin of your column and by default is set to 0 in the Standard H&J, meaning the last line isn't justified until it reaches all the way to the right margin. This option applies only to the last line in a justified paragraph.

- **Single Word Justify**   Selecting this option (the default) enables XPress to justify words alone on a single line, or essentially turns off justification where no word spaces exist. When this option is not selected, lines that contain a single word are left unjustified—even if they reside in the middle of a paragraph.

Customizing the Tool Palette

If having the right tool for the right job makes sense to you, then you may agree that having the right assortment of tools will most certainly help. The Tool palette in XPress may be customized to varying degrees, making it unique among palettes. On Windows, you may orient the palette horizontally or vertically (the default). (Macintosh versions of XPress 4 don't enable you to change the Tool palette orientation.) You may also reorganize the tools, or hide the ones you don't use—a welcome feature since many of the tools in the Tool palette are so closely related.

To orient the Tool palette horizontally as shown next, hold CTRL while double-clicking the title bar of the Tool palette. Only the palette changes orientation—not the tool buttons. To return the palette to vertical orientation, double-click its title bar again.

Reorganizing buttons in the Tool palette is slightly trickier. You may pull a tool button out of any *pop-out* and have it display independently in the palette. Pop-outs are buttons in the Tool palette that expand to enable access to related tools and are indicated as pop-outs by a small black arrow. You may also "hide" a tool button from view and install it back into its pop-out. The following two illustrations demonstrate the Tool palette fully expanded to display all tools, and then condensed to show only the minimum number.

Pulling a tool button from a pop-out to display in the main Tool palette is a tricky maneuver. You must first press and hold down the CTRL key, and then click and hold on the pop-out button in the palette until the row of buttons appears. Then, while still holding the CTRL key, release your mouse button over your tool button choice. Your chosen tool will be installed in the Tool palette below the pop-out button.

To install a button back into its pop-out row, hold the CTRL key *first* while clicking on the tool button. The button you clicked will seem to disappear, but double-checking the pop-out will reveal it. Don't try to click-and-drag it or press CTRL a second time. At least *one* tool button from each tool group must appear in the palette at all times.

NOTE ➤ *Each time you quit XPress, your current tool settings are saved in XPress' Preferences file. When XPress is relaunched, all tool positions will be restored.*

Use the following keyboard commands with the Tool palette and tools:

Tool Choice	Command/Action
Show/Hide Tool palette	F8
Show/Hide individual tool	CTRL+CLICK to select
Select tool below current tool	CTRL/CMD+ALT+TAB
Select tool above current tool	CTRL/CMD+ALT+SHIFT+TAB
Invoke Page Grabber Hand	Press and hold ALT/OPTION

Tool Choice	Command/Action
Invoke Zoom In tool	CTRL (+SPACEBAR under Windows versions)
Invoke Zoom Out tool	CTRL+ALT (+SPACEBAR under Windows versions)

Changing Tool Behavior

Each time you select a tool and create a box, line, or shape in XPress, the resulting item features certain default properties. In cases where you find yourself constantly changing item properties to suit the type of documents you regularly produce, over time this added step can accumulate to more than a little lost productivity. Luckily, you can change the defaults of properties associated with new items for each and every tool in XPress through the use of tool customization.

Tool preferences are changed via the Tool Preferences dialog box shown next. This dialog box is opened by choosing Edit | Preferences | Document (CTRL/CMD+Y) to open the Default Document Preferences dialog box and then selecting the Tool tab. As mentioned earlier, you may change these defaults for all new documents or simply for the document you're currently working in, depending on when you choose to change them. If you'd like to change tool properties for all new documents, apply the changes while no documents are open. To change them for only a certain document, change them while the document is open.

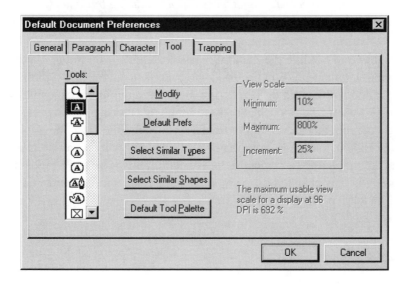

This dialog box features a list of all the tools available in XPress' Tool palette, plus five command buttons for accessing tool options or applying preference states. The command buttons are defined as follows:

- **Modify**   With one or more tools selected, clicking this button opens the Modify dialog box. The tabs that appear indicate the options you may change, specific to the type of item the tool creates. In cases where more than one tool is selected when this button is pressed, you may also see a Group tab that features common options for the selected tools.

- **Use Default Prefs**   Clicking the Default Prefs button with one or more tools selected returns the tools to their original defaults when XPress was first installed.

- **Select Similar Types**   Because XPress includes many tools that perform related functions such as the various text, picture, and line tools, you may automatically select all related tools by clicking this button.

- **Select Similar Shapes**   Because several tools create similar type shapes in text, picture, or shape conditions, selecting one of these tools and clicking this button selects all the tools that create the same type of shape.

- **Default Tool Palette**   Clicking this button returns the Tool palette to its original default state.

TIP ▸ *To open the Document Preferences | Tool tab dialog box quickly, double-click the Zoom tool, or double-click any Text, Picture, or Line tool.*

- **Zoom tool**   While the Zoom tool is selected, the Minimum, Maximum, and Increment fields in the Tools tab become available. By default, the Zoom tool is set to XPress' maximum and minimum capabilities. If you want, you may change these limits by entering new settings in the Minimum and Maximum fields. And, each time the Zoom tool is clicked on your page, your magnification changes by a preset value according to the Increment field. By default this is set to 25 percent, but you may change this to any increment value within a range between 1 and 400 percent.

NOTE *In Windows, the Maximum magnification factor of the Zoom tool is limited by the display settings set in your Application Preferences | Display tab (CTRL+ALT+SHIFT+Y).*

■ **Text box tools**   When any text box tool is selected, you may modify Box, Text, Frame, and/or Runaround properties associated with the selected tool(s).

■ **Picture box tools**   When any picture box tool is selected, you may modify Box, Picture, Frame, and/or Runaround properties associated with the selected tool(s).

■ **Line tools**   With any line tool selected, you may modify Line and/or Runaround properties.

■ **Text-Path tools**   With any text-path tool selected as Line, you may modify the tool's Line, Text-Path, and/or Runaround properties.

TIP *To reset your currently-selected tools to their default preferences, click the Default Prefs button. To change all the tools in the palette to defaults, select them all by holding SHIFT while clicking the first tool (Zoom) and then the last tool (Freehand Text-Path) in the list. To reset only the Tool palette to its default state, click the Default Tool Palette button.*

Setting Application Preferences

Application preferences enable you to control the overall program performance when working in any document. Exploring these settings will give you a chance to hone your copy of XPress to perform to match exactly how you prefer to work. While Display, Interactive, and XTensions behavior could be considered fine-tuning, the most critical features to pay attention to in terms of application preferences are the all-important Save preferences.

These preferences are set using the Application Preferences dialog box opened by choosing Edit | Preferences | Application (CTRL/CMD+ALT/OPTION+SHIFT+Y). The options are divided into four tabbed areas as follows.

12

Setting Display Preferences

While working in the Windows version of XPress 4, the Display tab dialog box shown next enables you to set the colors of onscreen display guides, including Margin, Ruler, and Grid colors. By clicking these color buttons you may select from one of 48 basic colors or create your own color by clicking the *Define Custom Colors* button. Display options also enable you to choose between high- and low-quality display of Color TIFFs (choose from 8-bit or 24-bit) and Gray TIFFs (choose from 16 or 256 levels of gray), or to set the onscreen Display DPI [dots per inch] Value (choose a value between 36 and 300 dpi). While working in Macintosh versions of XPress, the margin, ruler, and grid color buttons display the Apple color wheel; the Color TIFFs menu also has 16-bit, and there is no Display DPI Value. Macintosh versions also include *Tile to Multiple Monitors* and *Full-Screen Documents* options.

If you work with extremely-high-resolution color images, you may want to disable the Off-Screen Draw option (selected by default), which enables XPress to draw the complete representation of an image or item even though it may reside off your current screen view. Screen draw time can be excessive when working with high-resolution color images or documents containing highly-complex shapes.

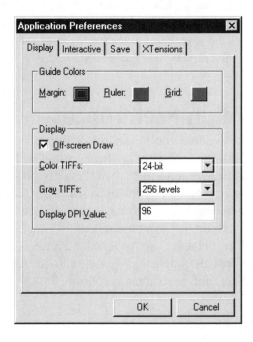

TIP → *Setting the Ruler color also changes the onscreen color of clipping paths while in editing mode. And, setting the Grid color also changes the onscreen editing color of runarounds.*

Setting Interactive Preferences

The Interactive tab shown next enables you to control screen-draw speed performance, quote character, and dragging preferences. By default, the options are set to enable XPress to behave at ideal performance levels, although you may want to change certain settings depending on your system capabilities and the type of work you do. You'll also find when exploring these settings that increasing the performance requirements of one setting causes others to perform poorly.

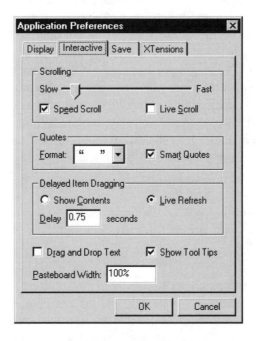

For example, settings such as fast screen scrolling and forcing XPress to show details of items as they're dragged may consume incredible amounts of system resources. By default, XPress' scroll speed is set very low, meaning that each time you click an elevator button the screen contents change only slightly. If you increase the scrolling speed, screen contents change more dramatically, but with your display settings set to their highest—such as Color TIFFs set to 24-bit and Off-Screen Draw to Active—you may notice that scrolling actually takes longer.

The Speed Scroll option enables XPress to greek both pictures and blended colors in boxes, which can often be time-consuming to repeatedly draw when scrolling. Selecting Live Scroll (off by default) forces XPress to update your screen contents as you drag a scroll box (thumb box) but may drain your system resources.

TIP

You may turn Live Scroll on or off (depending on whether it's selected in the Application Preferences dialog box) by holding ALT/OPTION while dragging the scroll box (thumbbox).

Select the quote character you want to use, when quotes are converted during text import operations, choosing from a selection of six styles in the Quotes drop-down list. Choose the Smart Quotes (on by default) to enable XPress to automatically substitute the selected open and close quotes as you type in text boxes.

As you drag items on your screen, you may notice that subtle time delays have been built in to control item-drawing behavior. For example, hesitating slightly between the time you click an object and the time you actually drag it is controlled by the *Delay* value entered. After your hesitation, XPress may either draw the selected text or picture in detail as you drag it (choose Show Contents), or may draw the item as you drag it *and* periodically refresh your complete screen, including item layering and text flow.

TIP

To enter straight quotes to abbreviate feet (') or inches (") when Smart Quotes is enabled, press CTRL/CMD+' for feet (') or CTRL/CMD+ALT/SHIFT+' for inches (").

The remaining options compose a potpourri of options. You may enable drag and drop text functions that automate clipboard cut and paste functions and enable you to drop text from other applications directly into text boxes. Choose Show Tool Tips to enable XPress to display flags while working with tools and screen features in your program or document window—this is ideal if you're new to XPress or a recent upgrader to version 4. Or set the width of your Pasteboard (the working area found around your document page borders). The Pasteboard may be set within a range between 0 and 100 percent of your document page width—the length of the document is ignored. Pasteboard width won't be less than 0.5 inches or more than 48 inches.

Setting Save Preferences

If you value your work (and your sanity), you'll want to pay very close attention to how XPress saves your document, whether and where backups are stored, and how often backups are updated. By default, the way XPress saves documents is quite basic—it's completely manual. Should your application or system crash for one reason or another, all the work you did up to your last save will be lost. The save options selected on by default are those for *Auto Library Save* and *Save Document Position*. The Library option enables library files to be saved the moment changes are made to it, while the document position option enables XPress to record the last size, position, and shape of your document window.

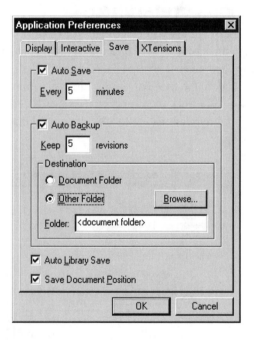

Other Save options in the dialog box aren't selected, but it may be wise to consider using at least one of them. Choosing *Auto Save* forces XPress to perform a minisave periodically, according to the time interval entered in the Every [*value*] minutes field. Be as daring as you like here, and keep in mind that each time your file is auto saved, you'll lose a few moments of productivity—especially if you work on a network where save times are even slower than to a local drive.

Choose *Auto Backup* to force XPress to make complete copies of your document. The number entered in the Keep Revisions field determines how many copies are

12

made. Each time a Save command is manually performed, a numbered copy of your document is stored in either the document folder or a folder of your choosing. After the maximum number of revision copies have been created (the default is 5), the files are renumbered automatically. Again, be as daring as you like here, but keep in mind that saving multiple copies of each document you work on may consume incredible amounts of memory and disk space as well. Also, consider changing the default location of the auto backups. By default, they're stored in the same folder as the document—leaving you with multiple copies of the same document with very similar names, on the same possibly vulnerable drive. There's a lot of potential for you to open the wrong file—or to delete the right one.

Setting XTensions Preferences

The XTensions Manager enables you to govern your use of XTensions in XPress. By choosing options in the Application Preferences dialog box shown next, you may set how the XTensions Manager is loaded each time XPress is launched. The more XTensions you have loaded, the more of your system's resources must be dedicated to running XPress, so if you rely heavily on the use of XTensions for performing specific tasks, then you may want to see the XTensions Manager at each launch by choosing the Always option.

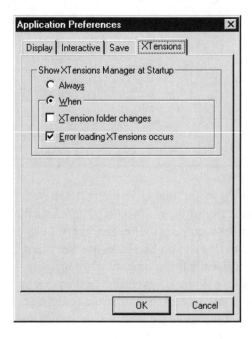

The remaining options in the dialog box become available by choosing the *When* option, which sets XPress to automatically open the XTensions Manager at startup only when loading errors occur or when XTensions are added to or removed from the XTensions folder. By default, two XTensions folders exist in your XPress program folder—one named *XTension* and one *XTension Disabled*. Any changes made to the XTension folder are detected when XPress is launched.

TIP ▸ *Using Windows platforms, you may identify XTensions by their three-letter XNT extension.*

Setting Document Preferences

When it comes to enabling you to assert control over both the display and behavior of XPress documents, all the stops have been pulled out. Other programs often provide far too many customization options to make life easy. But XPress' options are logically organized, neatly presented, and relatively straightforward to select. Options have been organized into five main tabbed areas composed of General, Paragraph, Character, Tools, and Trapping. This section covers setting General, Paragraph, and Character preferences, while Tools preferences are discussed earlier in this chapter. For information on XPress 4's trapping features, see *Chapter 14, The Basics of Trapping*.

TIP ▸ *By setting Document Preferences with no documents opened, you're actually setting the defaults for all newly-created XPress documents. If this isn't your intention, first open only the document you want to apply the preferences to, before opening the Document Preferences dialog box.*

General

General preferences include a mixed bag of options that mainly affect the measurement and display of items and also interface elements in your document as shown below. The default settings of these options are selected by XPress based on user feedback. But the choice to keep them or not is yours.

12

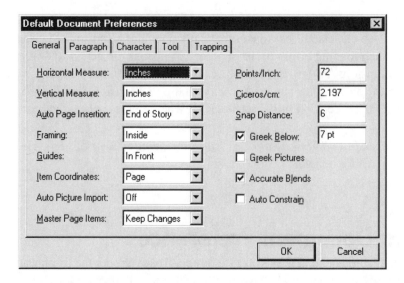

■ **Horizontal and Vertical Measure**   Choose from Inches (Standard or Decimal), Picas, Points, Millimeters, Centimeters, Ciceros, or Agates for display of each ruler measure. The choice you make here also affects the default measurement display of interface elements such as drop-down menus and numeric fields in dialog boxes and palettes. However, you may enter any measurement you want, on-the-fly, as you work, by adding the measure abbreviation after the value. For information on these abbreviations, see *Appendix B, Keyboard Shortcuts.*

■ **Auto Page Insertion**   When text documents are imported into your XPress document, the text may not always fit in your selected text box and overflow will often occur. Select this option *Off* or *on* under three conditions: *End of Story, End of Section*, or *End of Document* from the drop-down menu to tell XPress whether and where to add pages containing automatic text boxes to hold the overflow text. The additional pages will be based on the last master page in use.

■ **Framing**   Choose whether the frames (such as dash patterns or stripes) of your text or picture boxes are displayed and printed *Inside* (the default) or *Outside* your text or picture boxes. Choosing Outside framing from the drop-down menu has the effect of enabling solid, dash, or stripe patterns to be applied around the outside of your boxes, which has the effect of making boxes larger and is more difficult to work with than the *Inside* option. The difference between these two states is shown next.

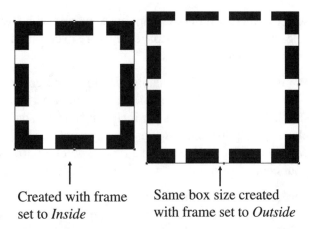

Created with frame
set to *Inside*

Same box size created
with frame set to *Outside*

- **Guides**   Set your guides to display In Front (the default) or Behind the items that you see on your screen. Guides include margin, ruler, and grid marks on your screen as well as shapes for clipping paths and runarounds.

- **Item Coordinates**   This option enables you to set how item positions are measured and displayed by choosing Page (the default) or Spread. With Page selected, item positions are measured from the ruler zero point of each page. With Spread selected and facing pages in use, item positions are measured continuously across page spreads, starting at the ruler zero mark.

- **Auto Picture Import**   This option is simply set to *Off* (the default), *On,* or *On (verify)*. Set to *On*, it has the effect of forcing XPress to looks for all pictures and verifies their location. Using this option, Modified pictures are updated automatically; if a picture is missing, a dialog box will appear. And, set to On (verify), has the effect of reimporting all pictures and then displaying a warning dialog box if pictures are missing; it also provides options for updating any missing or modified pictures.

NOTE ⟶ *On (verify) lists all missing or modified pictures and lets you update them—it does* not *reimport all pictures.*

12

- **Master Page Items**   This option may be set to *Keep Changes* (the default) or *Delete Changes*. If you choose at some point to reapply a new master page to a page that already contains items, XPress looks here for guidance on whether to keep any previous master page items, depending on whether the master page item has been modified. With *Keep Changes* selected, modified master items are kept, and with *Delete Changes* selected, modified master page items are overwritten with the newly applied master page items.

■ **Points/Inch**   This field enables you to enter a conversion setting for your document. Unless you have a specific need for changing this, it should be left at 72 points per inch, which is the standard used in electronic publishing. Some users may want to adhere to older standards where an inch can be equal to either 72.27 or 72.307 points, depending on your country of origin.

■ **Ciceros/cm**   As with the Points/Inch measure, this field enables you to enter a more exact value for ciceros per centimeter. The standard in electronic publishing has been rounded to 2.197 (the default) and it's probably wise to leave this as is. If you have a specific need, you may change this to the more exact traditional value measure of 2.1967.

■ **Snap Distance**   The snap distance determines the distance between which items are magnetically drawn to guides on your page, such as margin, ruler, and grid lines. Snap distance is 6 points by default, but may be changed to any value within a range of 1 to 216 points.

■ **Greek Below**   This option controls when text on your page is greeked. Greeking significantly speeds screen draw time,. The higher this setting, the faster your pages will screen draw, but the less you'll be able to read on screen (unless you zoom in). By default, this is set to 7 points. The Greek Below feature works in direct relation to the view scale magnification you're currently using.

TIP ⟶ **TIP:**   *Increasing your Greek Below size to 12 or 14 points will significantly improve your screen draw speed, without significantly reducing the readability of large or headline-sized text.*

■ **Greek Pictures**   Allowing pictures to be greeked has the same effect as for text, enabling XPress to fill picture boxes with a gray screen until selected. This is an extremely powerful feature to use if your documents contain more than a few pictures. By default, it's not selected, but it may be a wise choice to activate it.

- **Accurate Blends**   XPress' blends feature enables you to create exciting color blends of various styles for your box backgrounds. For faster display of blended colors onscreen, select Accurate Blends off. If your monitor is limited *only* to 256 colors (8-bit color), leave Accurate Blends selected to eliminate color banding.

- **Auto Constrain**   This option is for users who are accustomed to the way XPress behaved in earlier versions. In those days, boundaries for all items on a document page were defined by other boxes. If this is your favorite way to work in layout, you may select Auto Constrain to return XPress behavior to these quirky days. Otherwise, you're advised to leave it unselected.

Paragraph

Setting Paragraph preferences enables you to make decisions about how Auto Leading is applied, how baseline grids are set up, and which paragraph text hyphenation method to use, by selecting options in the Paragraph Preferences dialog shown next. Options specific to paragraph preferences are as follows:

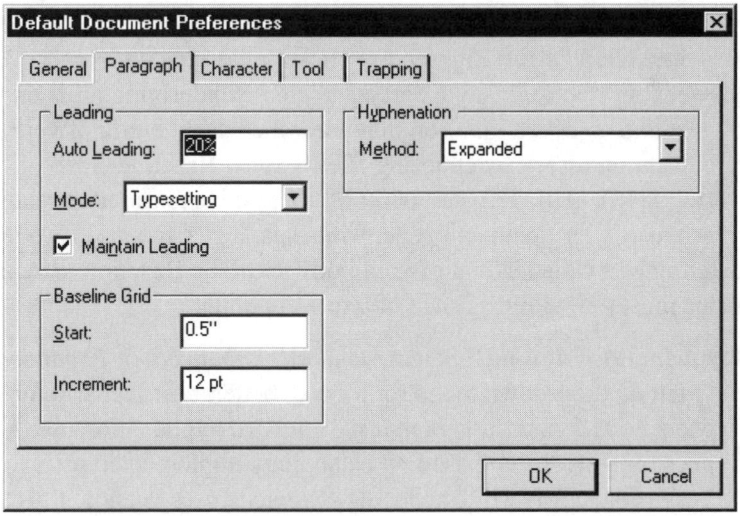

12

■ **Leading** When leading in your document is set to Auto, the spacing between lines of text is applied based on a percentage of the font size. Auto leading is a powerful feature to use, because of its flexibility in applying spacing between lines based on the line's content and font size. By default, this value is set to 20 percent leading, meaning for example that 10-point type will be applied with a leading of 12 points (that is, with 2 extra points added to the leading value). You may set the auto leading percentage to any percentage value between 1 and 100 percent, depending on your design aesthetics.

You may also set the mode used by XPress for leading to *Typesetting* or *Word-Processing*. Choosing *Typesetting* (the default) enables XPress to measure leading upward from baseline to baseline, while choosing *Word-Processing* measures leading downward from ascender to ascender.

TIP ➤ *You may also enter incremental values in the Auto Leading field option. For example, entering +1 in the field sets Auto Leading at 1 point more than the largest font size in your line of text. You may also specify Auto Leading in other measurements by appending the value with measure abbreviations such as mm for millimeters and so on. The value will be converted to points next time you open the dialog box.*

■ **Baseline Grid** Most high-end publication designs use such grids, for they enable electronic layout artists to create underlying grids on which all text and objects align. You may view the baseline grid of your document on screen by choosing View | Show Baseline Grid (CTRL/OPTION+F7). The start point of the grid is measured in relation to the edge of your document page, while spacing of the grid is usually determined by the leading of your body text. The Baseline Increment value must fall within a range of 0 to 144 points.

■ **Hyphenation Method** Select *Standard, Enhanced*, or *Expanded* from the Method drop-down menu for a good, better, best scenario for hyphenation of your paragraph text. *Standard* hyphenation uses a hyphenation algorithm based on technology implemented prior to XPress version 3.1, while choosing *Enhanced* uses version 4's internal hyphenation dictionary. Choosing *Expanded* uses the *Enhanced* algorithm in combination with any Hyphenation Exceptions saved with the document.

NOTE *If you open a previous version document, the Expanded method of hyphenation is used as the default.*

Character

The Character Preferences dialog box options shown next will be of significant interest to designers or professional typesetters who need to customize document characters to a specified or established character design.

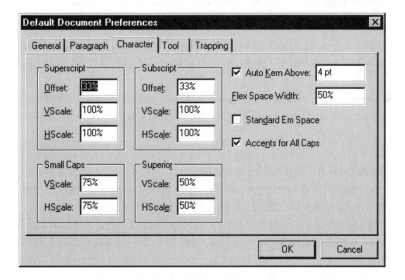

Character preferences include the following options:

- **Superscript and Subscript**   Superscript characters are usually smaller and are positioned above the baseline of text, while subscript characters are usually smaller but appear below the baseline of text. You may control superscript and subscript characteristics using the offset and scale options here. Offset controls the amount of the baseline shift, while the vertical (VScale) and horizontal (HScale) values set the change in size relative to the font size. By default both baseline offsets are set to 33 percent, while the scaling is left at 100 percent of the font size.

- **Small caps and Superior**   Small caps and superior caps are hybrids of a font's uppercase character formatting. In essence, applying this style converts upper- and lowercase text to all uppercase characters, leaving

12

uppercase (small caps) characters larger than lowercase (superior) to simulate the shape of upper and lowercase text. The degree to which the characters are reduced may be set by entering vertical (VScale) and horizontal (HScale) values based on percentage changes from the original font size. By default, small caps are 75 percent of the original font size while superior caps are 50 percent.

- **Auto Kern Above**   Choosing this option and entering a value enables you to set at the font size at which the automatic kerning tables kick in. The default is the option selected: a font size of 4 points.

- **Flex Space Width**   Flex spaces are spaces that you enter in text manually in an effort to fine-tune spacing of justified text—or for whatever reason you choose. Flexible spaces are fixed-width spaces.

> **TIP** *To enter a breaking Flexible Space in text, press CTRL/CMD+SHIFT+5/SPACEBAR; to enter a nonbreaking Flexible Space press CTRL/CMD+ALT/OPTION+SHIFT+5/SPACEBAR.*

- **Standard Em Space**   To use Standard em space measures in your text, select this option. A standard em space is as wide as the font is tall, meaning that a standard 12-point em space is 12 points wide. By default, this option is not selected, enabling XPress to use its own measure for creating em spaces based on the width of two zeros of the font in use. XPress' method enables em spaces to change in width if vertical or horizontal scaling is applied to your text.

> **TIP** *To enter an en space (one-half the width of an em space) in your text, under Windows press CTRL+SHIFT+6, while on Macintosh versions press OPTION+SPACEBAR to enter an em space, type two en spaces.*

- **Accents for All Caps**   Selecting this option (the default) enables XPress to apply accents to capital letters in your text. Sometimes, accents can adversely affect the appearance of text set with little or no extra leading, causing the accents to jut up into the descenders on the line of text above. Also, some publications' editorial styles prohibit accent marks on headlines in all caps.

- **Ligatures**   Macintosh versions of XPress 4 also feature an option for Ligatures in the Character tab.

Design: Elaine Chu

Firm: Elaine Chu Graphic Design, 748 Oakland Ave., #302, Oakland, CA 94611
(Phone) 510-547-7705, (Fax) 510-597-1087, e-mail egchu@aol.com

Client: Ziff-Davis Publishing Company

Description: *MacWEEK* Magazine product demo directory

The client needs a high-impact directory cover for trade show purposes. This piece was
printed in process colors. I used the same screen build colors as those of the MVB logo to
create a Quark color palatte. The bars and square shapes were created directly in Quark
and filled with these custom colors. The overlapping letterforms image was created in
Photoshop to achieve the transparent effect, then saved as an EPS and imported into
Quark where it was easily sized and cropped.

12

NOTE ────────▶ *For information on setting Trapping preferences for your document, see* Setting XPress Trapping Preferences *in* Chapter 14, The Basics of Trapping.

Custom Kerning and Tracking

XPress users often pride themselves on their software's sophisticated ability to edit or customize kerning and tracking tables, while in reality few users know how to do this properly. And, if you don't have the need to or the experience in editing kerning or tracking tables, it may be best to leave these as they are. Existing kerning and tracking tables in XPress serve well for many average applications. Both kerning and tracking are controlled through use of the Kern-Track Editor XTension. Kerning and tracking are specified by the font designer, so if you select a quality font where attention has been paid to kerning and tracking, customization shouldn't be necessary.

Customizing Kerning

The controls for editing kerning tables are accessed by choosing Utilities | Kerning Tables Edit. After choosing the command, you're presented with a dialog box that enables you to select the font for which you want to create a custom kerning table. Once the font is selected, clicking Edit opens the Kerning Tables for [*font name*] dialog box shown next.

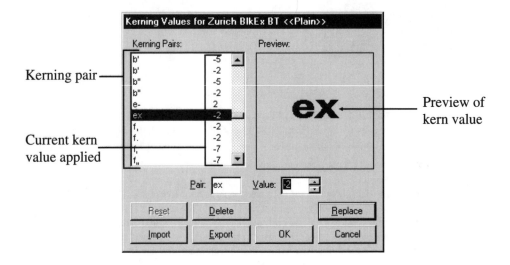

On one side of the dialog box are the available kern pairs to edit, while on the other side is a preview window that reflects the effects of applied values; below both, command buttons are available for applying your editing changes. To adjust a kern pair, follow these steps:

1. Select the pair in the Kern Pair window or enter the pair in the Pair window. The pair appears in the preview window.

2. With the pair selected, edit the kern spacing by clicking the Value spinners or entering a value. Each time you click a spinner, the value changes kerning by 1/200 ems within a range between –100/200 to 100/200 ems. Negative values reduce the kern space while positive values increase it.

3. To apply the changes, click the *Add* button.

4. To restore the font to its original built-in kerning value, click the *Reset* button.

5. To delete a kerning pair, highlight the pair and click *Delete*.

6. Once you've finished editing the kerning table for your font, click OK to return to the first dialog box and then click *Save* to save your editing changes to the table and close that dialog box.

While the above steps make kerning table editing seem simple, it is anything but. Kerning a font to appear uniformly kerned across all characters can take hours. But if you have knowledge and expertise in this area the results can be rewarding. To ease some of the labor involved in creating and applying kerning pair edits, you may use the Import and Export buttons to save your kerning edits and apply them to other fonts. By clicking the *Export* button, you may save the information in your kerning table as an ASCII text file and reimport it for use with other fonts by clicking the *Import* button. Because of the different character shapes and weights designed for different fonts, the imported kerning values will likely need to be customized for the new font.

Customizing Tracking

The controls for editing the tracking table for a font are accessed by choosing Utilities | Tracking Edit. After choosing the command, you're presented with a dialog that enables you to select the font whose tracking table you want to edit. Once the font is selected, clicking Edit opens the following Tracking Values for [*font name*] dialog box.

Add up to four handles per curve

Tracking value in 1/100 ems

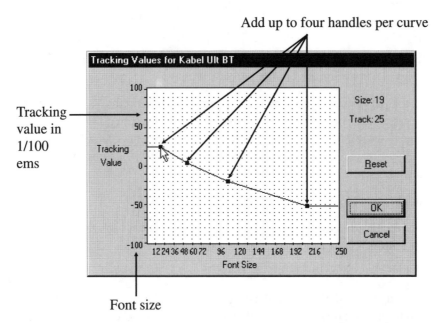

Font size

As the graph illustrates, tracking values from –100/200 ems to 100/200 ems may be applied to measure at the left axis; these values may be applied to fonts ranging in sizes from 2 to 250 points, measured along the bottom axis. A zero value indicates that no tracking is applied to a font at a given size. The tracking curve may be manipulated by adding curve handles to it; simply click your cursor directly on the tracking curve. A curve may include up to four handles. Clicking the Reset button flattens the tracking curve to zero for all font sizes.

To save edits to the tracking curve, click the OK button to return to the previous dialog box and then click Save to exit the Tracking Edit feature. Tracking applies whenever a font is used in XPress, regardless of whether you edited the tracking with a document open or closed.

TIP *To remove a curve handle from a tracking curve, hold CTRL/CMD while clicking on the handle.*

Unfortunately, to really see the results of your tracking you'll need to view text—a great deal of it, and the kind of material you typically use—with the tracking in use. There's no preview feature in the dialog box. And, if you edit the tracking for a particular font, be sure to edit the same tracking curve to each of the font's related styles. For example, if you edited Univers Plain, be sure to edit tracking for the Bold, Bold Italic, and Italic styles, as well as any other variations you have in use.

Kerning and tracking changes are saved to XPress' Preference settings file. If you edit kerning or tracking and subsequently open a previously-created document, XPress will warn you of changes to the Kern/Track values with the following dialog box:

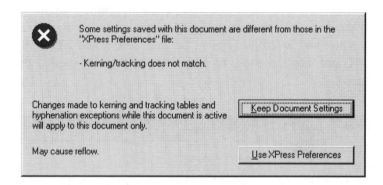

If you exchange files with another XPress user working on a different computer and XPress program, this message will also appear. In order to keep the same kerning and tracking settings as were created originally for the document, the correct response to this dialog box is *Keep Document Settings*. For example, if you send your document to a service bureau for printing, this will always be the correct response. However, each time the document is opened, this warning will reappear, which may become tiresome over time. But, there's no real solution to keeping both the *document* preferences and the *program* preferences valid. If *Use XPress Preferences* is selected in this dialog box while the text kerning and/or tracking (and/or hyphenation exceptions) for the document being opened have been edited in another copy of XPress, it's likely that text reflow will occur.

Creating Custom Print Styles

Printing your XPress document is often an operation you perform when nearing or having reached the final stages of layout. For highly-complex documents you may repeatedly print the same document over and over again in an effort to proof it or view how you've fine-tuned it. You may also print different documents in the same way to the same printer using identical print settings each time you do so. In cases such as these, it's worth spending the time naming and saving your print settings using your own Print styles.

Printing styles contain all the parameters set in XPress' main Print dialog box. Creating a print style is more a customization feature than it is a printing function, although it *does* help to know about the specifics of your printer and the required output of your document. Print styles are created by choosing Edit | Print Styles to open the Print Styles dialog box shown next. Clicking the New button opens the Edit Print Style dialog box that enables you to select all the printing parameters for your document. By making selections in the Document, Setup, Output, and Options tabs of the dialog box and entering a name for your new print style, you may save accumulated hours of option-choosing each time you print a document that matches your parameters.

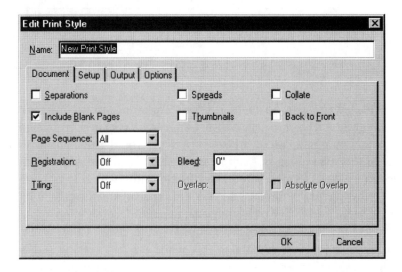

After creating a print style, simply select it from the *Print Style* drop-down menu in the main Print dialog box and proceed without reselecting your print options. When a print style is created, it's made available to all documents. For more information on printing your XPress documents and choosing print options, see *Chapter 16, Printing Your Pages.*

Checking Out Your XPress Version

If you're a new user to XPress and you happen to need information about your copy of XPress for one reason or another (such as when calling technical support), it may help to know where the version and revision number are recorded. The quick way to check your version number is to hold ALT/OPTION while choosing Help | About QuarkXPress. Choosing this displays a dialog containing all the information about your XPress version, including all applicable XTensions, their individual serial numbers, your hardware and operating system, and any relevant drivers, as shown below.

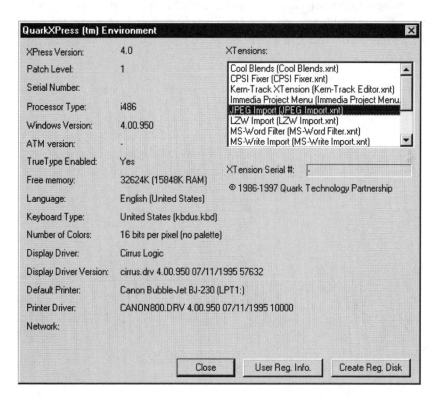

The User Reg. Info and Create Reg. Disk buttons in this dialog box also enable you to record this information on paper, should you ever be incapable of launching XPress. These methods are similar to keeping your home insurance documents in a bank's safety deposit box in case your house burns down. Clicking Create Reg. Disk creates a new XPress document complete with a text document containing the information listed in this dialog box. Clicking the User Reg. Disk creates an encoded Quark registration date file to save to disk as a backup to that created when you first installed the program. Both are wise backups to have in the event that something unfortunate happens.

12

Conclusion

Although bits and pieces of XPress customization features are spread throughout other chapters in *Fundamental QuarkXPress 4,* they're listed here in their entirety for your convenient one-stop shopping. Regardless of your user level, this is likely one of the most important chapters you have read. This chapter has explored all the customization available to you in XPress. This chapter also concludes *Part 3, Putting It All Together.* But, you still have one more section to explore in the next part: *Beyond XPress Basics.*

PART IV

Beyond XPress Basics

Athena, Acropolis, Greece

CHAPTER 13

Working with Color

At this point, the close study of XPress 4 moves into areas that affect how your documents are viewed by the outside world. Whether your documents are simple or complex, you may eventually be publishing them in one form or another, either by offset printing or online publishing. This first chapter in this final part on *Beyond XPress Basics* explores the higher functions of both XPress and publishing. In it, you'll delve into the world of XPress color: how to measure it, apply it, customize it, and feel comfortable working with it.

How XPress Sees Color

In the software world there's no shortage of ways in which you can measure and apply color. Color can be as simple or as complex as you need it to be, but before you venture too far into how XPress sees color, it may help to know a few of the limitations involved with working in color.

Although your eyes are able to detect a huge range of colors, your monitor and printer are only capable of reproducing a very small fraction of that range. And, in cases where you use devices that record color, the limitations are similar. In an effort to re-create the color seen by input devices and those that you see on your computer and in print, various color standards have been established. If there were only a single application for color, the solutions would be simple. But with the variations that exist in today's publishing industry, each niche area has adopted its own specific type of color.

For example, each color monitor has its own characteristics and capabilities, directly affecting how you view the colors on your screen—which may be where the complications begin. In the software world there are system colors, browser palettes, and platform issues to consider. And, in the real world, there are various ink colors and reproduction methods to consider. The easy solution is to become completely familiar with the specific color measurement system you deal with regularly, and then stick with it.

XPress, like other software applications, uses color measurement systems called *models*. Color models are mathematical definitions of color properties, and they vary in theory from model to model. Ultimately, you'll be viewing all the items on your document page—at least initially—by way of your monitor, which renders only in RGB (red, green, blue) color. And so, any of the color models you choose to work in will become RGB *interpretations* of those colors.

If your document is destined for offset reproduction, you'll likely be applying either spot or process color to your items. While the CMYK (cyan, magenta, yellow, black) color model enables you to measure, view, and formulate colors to apply to your items, it's merely a color model and not an organized system of color. Although the CMYK color model enables you to create nearly any combination of process ink colors, the device you're printing your document to may not be capable of reproducing the complete range of ink percentages. For example, a low-end printing press using paper plates may not be capable of reproducing a 3 percent black screen without the screen dots fading away, nor might it be capable of producing a 97 percent black screen without the holes in the screen plugging up. The correct strategy to follow is either through use of an organized system of color such as the matching color systems included with XPress, or through consultation with your printing vendor.

About Color Models

As mentioned earlier, color models enable you and your software to measure, display, and apply consistent and reproducible color. The most significant point to remember when working with color models is that they merely provide a way to measure color and are not color collections themselves (except for Multi-Ink). To create and apply a color in XPress, you must first create the color as a named color style using the controls accessed by first selecting Edit | Colors (SHIFT+F12) and clicking either the Edit button to alter an existing color or New to open the Edit Color dialog box shown next with the RGB color model selected.

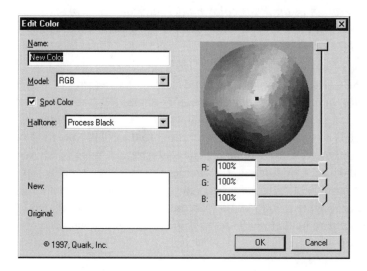

Later on in this chapter, you'll learn to create new colors according to the needs of your document and reproduction methods, but for now the priority is to grasp the principles of how color in XPress is measured. There are four basic color models included in XPress 4, each accessed from the Model drop-down menu. XPress also features the Multi-Ink model, which has its own specialized use. Their functions are defined as follows:

- **RGB** When it comes to your monitor and what you see on your screen, the RGB color model is the master model of all color. Your monitor renders color using the RGB model on a full-time basis—regardless of which color model your items have been formatted with. Nearly all monitors use an RGB color gun to project color to your screen, while essentially interpreting the particular color model you have selected to use. The RGB color model is based on "transmitted" or additive color, divided into units of red, green, and blue light in values ranging from 0 to 100 percent.

  Combined RGB values of red=100 percent, green=100 percent, and blue=100 percent will produce pure white. All RGB values set to zero percent will render pure black. Color values may be changed interactively using the three color sliders and the Brightness slider in the Edit Color dialog box. Raising or lowering the Brightness slider has the effect of increasing or decreasing the percentage values of all three RGB values simultaneously.

TIP *Operation of the RGB color model interface controls is similar to that of HSB, LAB, and CMYK color models, with slight variations for the specific colors involved.*

- **HSB** The HSB color model measures color in terms of the transmitted color values of hue (the actual color), saturation (the amount of color), and brightness (the intensity—that is, the amount of white—in the color). Hue is measured in degrees according to the color's position on the color wheel, shown in the previous illustration, which is divided into its 360 degrees, beginning at a value of 0 at the three o'clock position and increasing counterclockwise. Saturation and brightness are measured in color ranging from 0 to 100 percent. In this color model, the Brightness slider is redundant with the brightness percentage value.

■ **LAB**   The LAB color model is defined by luminance (L), plus chromatic components A and B, or color ranges from red to green (A) and blue to yellow (B). LAB color is a standard that first originated with the Commission Internationale d'Eclairage (CIE) in 1931, and is a model designed to render accurate color independent of the device outputting the image (monitor, printer, or scanner). This color model is perhaps the most widely-used model for color translation between software applications, and is sometimes referred to as CIELAB. Colors in this model are described numerically; such descriptions serve as critical notations of the way in which color mode conversions are calculated during display and printing. Luminance is divided into values ranging from 0 percent (darkest) to 100 percent (lightest), while the A and B components may range in color unit values ranging from -120 to 120. The Brightness slider on the color wheel has the effect of increasing or decreasing the luminance value, while making only slight changes to the A and B color component values.

TIP
Reproduction and translation to RGB screen color and CMYK color conversion in XPress 4 is achieved through LAB color space-conversion.

■ **CMYK**   If you work in offset printing, you may already be aware of the importance of the CMYK color model. The abbreviation CMYK represents color based on the four-color ink printing method used by many color printers, and ultimately included by the traditional four-color process used in offset printing. The four basic colors measured in this color model are cyan, magenta, yellow, and black. Each color is divided into percentages ranging from 0 to 100. As with other models, cyan, magenta, and yellow values may be selected by manipulating their respective slider controls or by picking a color in the color wheel. In this color model, the Brightness slider has the effect not only of changing the black color component, but also of increasing or decreasing the values of C, M, and Y ink colors.

TIP
To obtain an equivalent color across color models or the matching systems discussed below, first select the original color from a color model or matching system, and then immediately select the color or matching system you want the equivalent color for. XPress' Edit Color dialog box will automatically display the closest or equivalent color.

13

- **Multi-Ink**   Choosing Multi-Ink enables you to combine colors created and based on other colors and then to combine them with still other process colors or spot colors, to create a color that you may apply, in various percentages, to items in your document. To learn more about the tricky procedure for creating a multi-ink color, see *Multi-Ink Colors* later in this chapter.

Using Matching System Colors

You might assume that the remaining selections under the Model drop-down menu measure color, although in fact there's a subtle difference not indicated as such in the dialog box. True, the first four selections of RGB, LAB, HSB, and CMYK measure color, but the remaining selections are actually called *matching systems*. A matching system is a collection of colors that display in RGB on your monitor, but may be set to print as specified ink colors. The term *matching system* actually stems from the fact that each of these systems is supported by printed hard-copy sample books called *color swatches* to refer to the actual printed inks. Each of these color "systems" has its own specialized method for identifying specific colors. Using a matching system is far more reliable than judging ink colors from how they appear on your monitor.

XPress 4 includes ten different choices, including Multi-Ink and matching systems for Pantone, TOYO, DIC, Trumatch, Focoltone, Pantone Process, Pantone Coated, Pantone Solid to Process, Pantone Uncoated, and Hexachrome Coated. The matching system you choose depends on how your document will eventually be reproduced. And, since these swatches are developed and distributed by different, competing companies, their properties vary widely.

Pantone

The largest and most comprehensive color matching system of them all is offered by Pantone, one of the first internationally recognized color standardization systems to dominate the printing industry. Pantone was on the scene long before digital color fell into the hands of the general public. The Pantone electronic palettes found in programs such as XPress 4 are supported by a hard-copy collection of high-quality color swatches available in both uncoated and coated paper stock versions. The Pantone electronic process color collection contains more than 3,000 different colors, all of which the manufacturer claims will fall in the printable screen range. Colors are composed of screen percentages ranging from 0 to 100 in 3 and 5 percent increments. The Pantone electronic spot color collection shown next contains over 220 different colors. Pantone spot colors also display the process color equivalent in the CMYK fields.

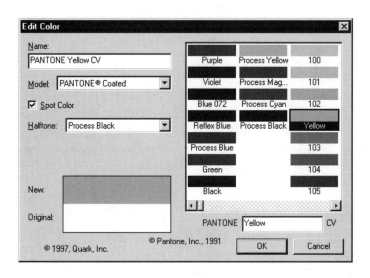

TIP *The Pantone Process color palette contains more than 3,000 different printable colors, while the Pantone Spot color palette contains more than 220.*

Pantone uses its own numbering system for process colors. Its coding is geared more toward locating the colors on its hard-copy printed swatches. For example, an ink color such as S 97-1 may be recognized first by S, which indicates that SWOP inks (explained later) were used for print reproduction. The letter is followed by the number 97, indicating the page number of the color swatch. The last number, 1, indicates the position on that page, counted down from the top. All colors are arranged in chromatic order according to the natural-light spectrum, and each page contains nine tints.

TIP *Pantone's Solid to Process color matching system enables you to select the closest possible process colors based on your choice of spot colors, without the need for purchasing a spot-to-process conversion swatch.*

The inclusion of Pantone's electronic spot and process colors in XPress is just the tip of the iceberg when it comes to the full extent of the company's entire matching system. The complete Pantone matching system includes a line of

13

slickly-packaged products including color formula guides, color selectors, color-specifying chips, color tint selectors, color foil selectors, color papers, markers and inks, transfer systems, and digital color imaging software—to name just a few.

TIP

*If you'd like to contact Pantone for more information about its products, see its Web site at **www.pantone.com** or contact one of its three world-wide offices as follows:*

Pantone, Inc.: America, 590 Commerce Blvd., Carlstadt, N.J., 07072-3098, Tel: (201) 935-5500, Fax: (201) 896-0242

Pantone UK, Inc.: 115 Sandgate Rd., Folkstone, Kent, CT20 2BL, England, Tel: 44-0303-259959, Fax: 0303-259830

Pantone, Asia: Room 904, New World Tower, 16-18 Queen's Rd. Central, Hong Kong, Tel: (852) 845-8388, Fax: (852) 845-7841.

About TOYO and DIC

The TOYO and DIC color matching systems are widely used in Asia and other Pacific Rim countries—especially Japan. Each contains its own numbering system and collection of different process colors. The TOYO collection of colors shown below has been developed using manufacturer TOYO's own special process ink colors, which vary in density and color from other standard process color inks.

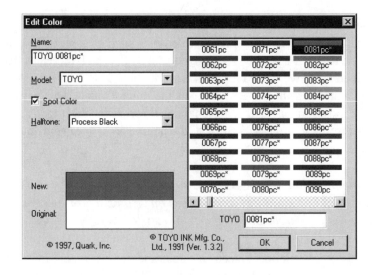

The DIC color system has been developed using the DIC (Dainippon Ink and Chemicals, Inc.) brand of process color inks and is divided into three categories of color, including DIC, DIC Traditional, and DIC Part II. When the DIC color samples are viewed in the Edit Colors dialog box, as shown next, the DIC category is identified by asterisks accompanying the associated color number. Standard DIC colors are identified with no associated asterisk, while DIC Traditional colors are identified by one asterisk (*) and DIC Part II colors by two asterisks (**).

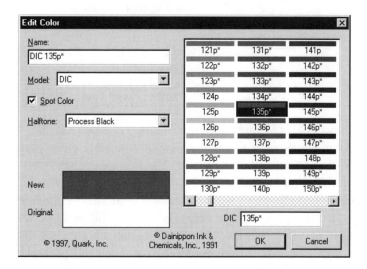

Trumatch

The Trumatch color matching system is composed of over 2,000 easily printable colors. Trumatch has specifically customized its color matching system to suit the digital color industry, using the Computer Electronic Prepress System (CEPS). The collection of colors comprises 40 tints and shades of each hue, shown next. Black is varied in six increments of percentages.

13

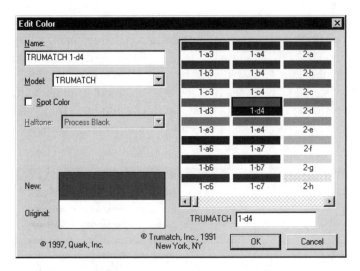

As with other color matching system vendors, Trumatch has also developed its own numbering system. For example, a green color that's numbered Trumatch 23-C2 can easily be tracked by its number. The first number indicates a particular hue value. Hues are numbered sequentially around the color wheel of the visible color spectrum. The following letter indicates the tint of the hue graduated from "A" or 100 percent to "H" or 5 percent screens. The number following the letter indicates the percentage of black present. Black is divided up into six increments of percentages, from a zero value (indicated by no number) to 42 percent (indicated by the number 7).

The Trumatch numbering system may take some time to get used to. Trumatch has designed and printed process color swatches composed of coated and uncoated versions, printed using a standard set of SWOP (Standard Web Offset Printing) inks using a common screen frequency of 150-line. The printed Trumatch colors are broken down into YMCK—ordered differently to match the order in which the process inks are printed. Most other color matching systems are broken down into CMYK, which indicates a different printing order.

Although Trumatch is a relative newcomer to the digital color world and is new as far as color matching systems go, its system is quite solid and well-conceived. Trumatch palettes can be seen in other software products such as CorelDraw, Photoshop, Illustrator, Freehand, PageMaker, PhotoStyler, and Micrografx Designer. The Trumatch technology has also been adopted by imagesetter manufacturers such as Scitex, Linotype-Hell, and Du Pont.

TIP

Trumatch can be reached at 25 West 43rd St., Suite 802, New York, N.Y., 10036-7402, Tel: (212) 302-9100, Fax: (212) 302-0890.

Focoltone

The Focoltone color matching system has existed for years. Focoltone, a European-based company, designed this 750-color palette to reduce much of the need for tedious color trapping. The Focoltone color collection shown next works by standardizing CMYK screen percentages to 5 percent increments. The thrust of this standardization is to increase the likelihood of common, color screen percentages by reducing the variety of screens used. The Focoltone matching system has been arranged in such a way that a full spectrum of colors is displayed on the palette at any given point.

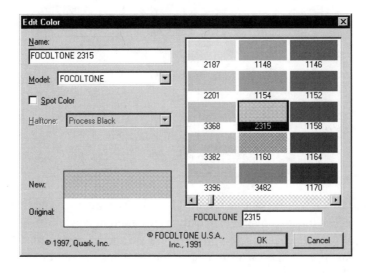

TIP

*Focoltone's head offices are located in the United Kingdom. Visit its Web site at **www.focoltone.com** or contact its sales offices by phone at 44-0785-712677, or by fax at: 44-0785-714587. Its main office number is 44-0222-810940, or fax: 44-0222-810962.*

13

Hexachrome

The Hexachrome system has been developed by the Pantone company and is relatively new in comparison to the others. Hexachrome is based on technology that allows for high-fidelity, or *HiFi*, color matching systems that consist of colors printed with six process colors instead of the standard four—hence the name. Orange and green are added to the CMYK plates to create more impact and increase the range of reproducible colors. Hexachrome printing is far more costly than printing ordinary process color, while for many designers, printing to process color is often a luxury in itself. The selection scheme for Hexachrome colors is shown next.

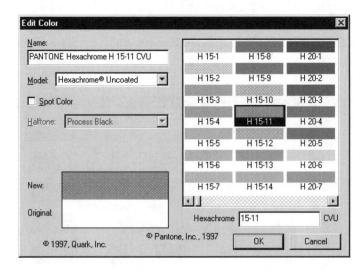

Because Hexachrome printing requires that six inks precisely overlap each other at various angles, the ink coverage, density, and screening angles are quite different from those of usual process-color printing. Be sure to consult with your printing vendor before applying Hexachrome ink colors to items in your document.

Applying Colors

Colors are easily applied in XPress. But, unfortunately, you can't simply choose any item on a page and formulate a color for it the way you can in certain illustration programs. Colors must first be created and named in order to be available in dialog boxes and menus. Once a color exists, though, you may apply it to nearly any item you want.

Because colors may be applied in many ways—to text, boxes, frames, lines, dashes, and stripes—there is no one all-encompassing procedure to follow. Most commonly, colors are applied to text, to boxes, or to their frames. Options for doing this are all contained in various tabs of the Item I Modify dialog box. As a practical example in reviewing the procedure for applying color to text in a box, follow these steps:

1. In an open document, create a text box and add text to it.

2. Open the Measurements palette (F9) and format your text. Notice that the Measurements palette contains no color option.

3. Using the Item tool, double-click the box to open the Modify dialog box, select the Frame tab, and apply a 6-point frame.

4. Click the Text tab and apply a text inset of 6 points. Click OK to accept the changes and close the dialog box.

5. Open the Colors palette by choosing View I Show Colors (F12). The palette opens onto your screen.

6. Click the Frame mode button to display Frame colors and click a color or shade, or both. Changes are immediate.

7. Click the Background mode button and click a background color or shade, or both, for your box. For now, leave the color blend at Solid.

8. To apply color to the characters themselves, you must choose a different tool. Choose the Content tool and highlight the text in the box to which you want to apply a new color.

9. Click the Text mode button and click the color or shade, or both, to apply it to your text. Using color tools in XPress, you have now colored as many of the elements of the text box as you can.

TIP
You may also apply color or shades to text, through selections in the Style menu, the Modify dialog box (CTRL/CMD+M), or the Colors palette while text is selected.

13

Creating New Colors

If you've just followed through the above exercise, you likely have a colored text box with colored text on your page, using colors you probably hadn't intended to use. What happens when you don't see on the list the color you want to use? The answer is to create or add the color manually. There's no other way to apply a color than to first make it available.

As a practical example of creating colors to apply, continue from the exercise in the previous section and follow these steps:

1. With your colored text box containing colored text selected, return to the Colors palette.

2. To create a new color and add it to your available colors list, open the Edit Colors dialog box. To do this quickly, hold the CTRL/CMD key and click on any color listed in the Colors palette. The Colors for [*document name*] dialog box opens.

3. To create a new color, click the New button. The Edit Color dialog box opens to reveal RGB color controls by default. To create a screen-only color, choose RGB, LAB, or HSB from the Models drop-down menu and click a color in the color wheel. For a specific ink color, choose from Pantone, Focoltone, Trumatch, TOYO, or DIC, and then select an ink color from the electronic catalog that appears, by clicking on it once. For the sake of this example, though, you'll create your own process color by choosing CMYK from the *Model* drop-down menu. The color wheel appears.

4. Pick a purple color from the color picker by clicking near the lower-right corner of the wheel, or by entering a value of **20** percent in the *C:* field and **60** percent in the *M:* field. These two fields represent cyan and magenta ink colors.

5. Experiment with the effects of the Brightness slider by moving it up and down. Notice that as you move the slider up the color brightens and the values you entered change, as do the slider positions adjacent to the color fields. If necessary, reenter your C: and M: values after experimenting.

6. Enter the name Medium Purple for your new color and uncheck the Spot Color option to allow this color to separate to different plates when printed. Leaving the Spot Color option selected forces the color to print on its own individual printing plate when your document colors are separated during printing.

7. Click OK to accept the properties for your new color and click Save in the Colors for [*document name*] dialog box to save your color and close the dialog box.

8. If the Colors palette is hidden, press F12 to view it. Notice that your new color now appears in the list of available colors. You may now apply this color to items in your document.

TIP

If you want to use colors created in other documents in your current document without re-creating them from scratch, use the Append command in the Colors for [document name] dialog box to select and append colors. If you want the colors you've created both to be available for all *documents and to appear in your default available colors list, close all documents and repeat the append process.*

NOTE

In the past, and still today in some other software applications, the naming scheme you use for your colors has been critical to identifying their color type and make-up. Thankfully, XPress alleviates this need with the ability to sort and display colors and their details in the Colors for [document name] dialog box. To sort and identify colors using this feature, choose Edit | Colors (SHIFT+F12) and use the Show drop-down menu to select All Colors, Spot Colors, Process Colors, Multi-Ink Colors, Colors in Use, or Colors Not Used. To view details of a color, select it in the available colors list and read the description given in the lower section of the dialog box. Colors will be listed as Spot or Separated, and the color model or associated values will be listed.

Types of Color

With all these terms identifying spot, process, registration, and multi-ink colors mentioned, it may help to have a primer on exactly what these color types are, what they represent, and how they will affect the items to which they're applied. Plus, there are other options you've seen in the dialog boxes that up to now have remained a mystery. This section explores specific properties you may apply to new or existing colors.

13

Spot Color Option

When creating or editing a color using the Edit Colors dialog box, you may set the color to print as a spot color regardless of whether you've specified it as a separated process color using one of the process color models such as CMYK, Pantone Process, Trumatch, Focoltone, or Hexachrome. Because of this fact, this option should be carefully chosen. For example, if your document is to be eventually reproduced in process colors only, selecting any of your process colors as spot will cause extra color plates to be created when your final CMYK separations are printed. Since the costs associated with printing separations to certain types of printers can be high, this can be a costly mistake if chosen in error.

TIP ————————▶ *You may quickly locate a specific color in any collection by entering its color number in the field below the color collection list.*

By default, the Spot Color option is automatically checked when selecting any of the spot colors from Pantone Coated or Uncoated, TOYO, or DIC color collections. So in this same regard, unchecking the Spot Color option for any of these colors will cause them to print as separated colors in a matching formula of process color percentages. This too may be a costly error if your actual intent is to use these ink colors as spot colors. For example, if your document is destined to be reproduced in two or three spot colors of ink, but one or more of your spot colors has been specified as process by unchecking the Spot Color option, you'll end up with four additional process color separation plates when the document is printed to separations—costly indeed.

Halftone Color Option

While the Spot Color option is selected, the Halftone drop-down menu becomes available and contains choices for Process Cyan, Process Magenta, Process Yellow, and Process Black. But the naming of this option may be slightly misleading or confusing. The real purpose of this option is to specify the *screen angle* of colors when the items in your document have been specified to print as a shade of the selected color. The screen angle is the angle at which dot percentages that compose the shades of ink colors are angled. Screen angles are measured in degrees.

When you select a specific color from the Halftone drop-down menu you're actually setting screen angles to match process color screen angles, which (by default) print at the following settings:

Process Cyan: 105 degrees

Process Magenta: 75 degrees

Process Yellow: 90 degrees

Process Black: 45 degrees

NOTE ───▶ *Screen angles for process or spot colors may be overridden at the printing stage either by settings in the printing device in use, or through use of options in the Print dialog box. For more information on setting spot and process screen angles, see* Output Options *in* Chapter 16: Printing Your Pages.

Multi-Ink Colors

If you've been working with desktop software equipped with color printing capabilities for more than a few years, you may be pleased to have access to this next feature. The Multi-Ink feature enables you to create a single color composed of two or more different ink colors and apply them to a single item on your document page. When items are applied with a Multi-Ink color, the colors they're composed of may be set to separate as individual colors when printed.

The procedure for creating a multi-ink color is slightly different from that of a single spot or process color. Multi-ink colors are selected by choosing them from the available colors list. So, to use a specific color, you must first create it and add it to the list. Once it's available, it may be used in a multi-ink color composition.

As a practical exercise in creating a multi-ink color based on two different spot colors not yet available in your current list of colors, follow these steps:

1. Open the Colors for [*document name*] dialog box by choosing Edit | Colors (SHIFT+F12). The dialog box opens.

2. For this exercise, you'll create a single multi-ink color based on yellow and blue spot colors, which will in essence enable you to create a shade of green to apply to items in your document. Click the New button to create the first color. The Edit Color dialog box opens.

3. Choose Pantone Coated from the *Model* drop-down menu and select Pantone 106 CV (a yellow color) from the color collection that appears. Notice that the name automatically appears in the Name field and the Spot Color option is automatically selected.

13

4. Click OK to add the color, close this dialog box, and list the color in your currently-available colors list.

5. Click New a second time, select Pantone Coated again, choose Pantone 292 CV (a blue color) from the color collection, and click OK to close the dialog box and add this second color to your list.

6. Click New a third time—this time to create your final multi-ink color. Choose Multi-Ink from the *Model* drop-down list and notice that the colors you just created are both present in the list that appears on the right of the dialog box. By default, all colors are currently applied with *no* shade, meaning your current multi-ink color contains no ink colors. Notice that the Spot Color option in the dialog is also unavailable while Multi-Ink is selected. This indicates that the multi-ink color you're specifying may not be printed to a single plate when your document is printed, meaning the colors will separate to their own individual plates and the Halftone screen angle will be controlled by the options set for the individual multi-ink colors.

7. Observe that above the colors are two-column labels—one for the color name and one for Shade.

8. Select Pantone 106 CV in the list and click the Shade button as shown below. Set the shade to 100 percent by selecting 100 from the drop-down menu that appears, as shown next. Notice that the New area to the lower left changes to reflect the change in color, indicating yellow.

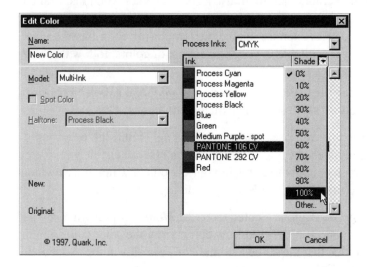

9. Select Pantone 292 CV in the list, click the Shade button, and set the shade to 100 percent. Notice that the New area to the lower left changes to reflect the change in color, now indicating green.

10. Enter a name for your new color in the Name field, such as Multi-ink green.

11. Click OK to add the color, exit the dialog box, and add the color name to your colors list.

12. Before clicking Save to save your new colors, click on the multi-ink color you just created and observe its details at the bottom of the dialog box. Notice that it describes the color as "Multi-Ink color; Components: 100% PANTONE 106 CV; and 100% PANTONE 292 CV."

TIP ───────▶ *When combining spot colors from different color models for a multi-ink to create a single color, avoid mixing spot colors from different matching systems such as Pantone, TOYO, and DIC. Because of their different color and ink coverage properties, rarely do print vendors use inks from different swatch books in a printed job.*

With a multi-ink color created, you may now apply it to various kinds of items in your document such as backgrounds of boxes, frames, lines, dash and stripe patterns, and so on. Because you're combining two colors of ink, you will now be capable of creating a third color for items in your document without the expense of printing a third ink color! You may even apply the multi-ink color in percentages by specifying shade values.

Applying "Registration" Color

You may have already noticed in your list of available colors a listing named "Registration." The availability of this "color" is both a blessing and a curse if you aren't aware of its effects. Applying an item with Registration has the effect of forcing the item to appear on all printed plates when your document colors are separated during printing. By default, Registration appears as black on your screen, set to RGB colors 0%, 0%, and 0% respectively.

The purpose of setting items to appear on all plates enables you to use any item as a registration element while still positioned on or close to your page. This definitely has its advantages when printing your document pages to a printing device that can't include the usual registration marks (which appear by default outside your page dimensions). Creating registration marks outside your printed page is a method often used when printing to sheet-fed offset printing presses where the final printed product will be physically trimmed to a given size.

High-volume, lower-quality flyers or newspapers use Registration color to enable registration, since this type of printing is fed by web-type printing presses where the final printed product isn't trimmed to size.

The curse of using Registration arises if you apply it to an item in error. When an item in your document prints on all separation plates instead of only the one you intended, it often causes a printing puzzle that's difficult to solve, and the mistakes can be costly if your document needs to be reprinted to correct the error.

NOTE *The Registration color in XPress can't be deleted from the list of available colors in your document or from the default list. However, you can edit the on-screen appearance of registration. For example, if you don't want to confuse it with black accidentally, you may edit the RGB color to appear differently.*

Exploring XPress Color Blends

The ability to apply color blends to items in your document page certainly opens the door to more than a little design and creative ingenuity. Blends may be applied to any closed-path item, such as various shapes of text and picture boxes, Bezier shapes, text converted to boxes, and all sorts of variations in between.

NOTE *Blends can't be applied to text in boxes, box frames, or lines.*

Applying a "blend" to an item in XPress causes a smooth gradation between two colors. The colors you blend may be any of those you've created in your available colors list. Blends may be applied using either the Modify | Box tab dialog box shown next or the Background mode of the Colors palette (F12). In certain instances, the blend feature may enable you to blend from a spot color to a process color, between two process or spot colors, or from one multi-ink color to another. Blends may also be set with certain angles or rotation, depending on the type of blend selected.

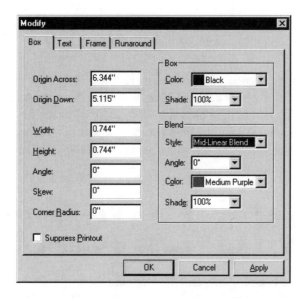

In order for the entire list of blends discussed here to be available to you, you must have the Cool Blends XTension listed as *Active* in the XPress XTensions Manager. If the XTension isn't listed in the XTensions Manager, install it from the XPress program disc using the Import command. If you're using a Macintosh version of QuarkXPress, you may simply drag the Cool Blends Xtension over from the program disc on your desktop. After importing, you'll need to Quit and relaunch XPress in order for Cool Blends to be available.

With Cool Blends active in the XTensions Manager, XPress 4 enables you to create and apply six basic styles of blends as follows:

■ **Linear Blends**   The Linear blend style enables you to blend in an even gradation between two colors at any angle. The gradation of color occurs at a steady rate starting at color #1 on one side of your object and continuing to color #2 on the other side as shown next. The distance between the two sides determines how much space it takes for one color to gradate to the other. The less space the colors have to blend with each other, the less smooth the blend will appear. Entering a degree value between –360 and 360 enables you to set an angle for the blend.

TIP *When using the Modify | Box tab dialog box to apply blends, the box color serves as color #1, while the blend color serves as color #2.*

- **Mid-Linear Blends** The Mid-Linear blend style enables you to create a blend of color where color #1 blends to color #2 at the mid-distance of the box shape, and then blends back to color #1 at the far side of the box, as shown next. Again, the blend smoothness is determined by the size of the box. Entering a degree value between −360 and 360 enables you to set an angle for the blend.

MID-LINEAR

- **Rectangle Blend** This and the Diamond blend, described next, are perhaps the more stylized of the blend styles. The Rectangle blend style begins with color #2 at the center of the box shape and blends it outward in a square or rectangular shape to color #1, until reaching the edges of your box shape, as shown next. The resulting shape of the blend is determined by the overall proportions of your box shape. Entering a degree value between −360 and 360 enables you to rotate the blend effect within the box shape.

RECTANGLE

- **Diamond Blends** The Diamond style creates a blend in a similar way to the Rectangle style, beginning at color #2 in the center and blending to color #1 outward until reaching the outside edges of the box shape, as shown next. The shape of the Diamond blend is determined by the overall proportions of the box shape. Entering a degree value between −360 and 360 enables you to rotate the blend effect within the box shape.

DIAMOND

- **Circular Blends**   The Circular blend style creates a circular-shaped blend beginning at color #2 in the center and blending outward to the edges of your box in color #1, as shown next. Entering a degree value between –360 and 360 enables you to control how quickly the blend effect occurs. Positive values cause the blend to occur more slowly, while negative values cause it to occur more quickly.

- **Full-Circular Blends**   The Full Circular blend style behaves nearly identically to the Circular blend style. It creates a circular-shaped blend beginning at color #2 in the center and blending outward to the edges of your box in color #1, as shown next. But in this case the blend occurs more naturally and more smoothly (as shown in the examples) than for that of the Circular style. Entering a degree value between –360 and 360 enables you to control how quickly the blend effect occurs. Positive values cause the blend to occur more slowly, while negative values cause it to occur more quickly.

FULL-CIRCULAR

As a practical exercise in creating a blend using the Colors palette, follow these steps:

1. In an open document, create any box shape using either a text or picture box tool.

2. If you haven't already done so, open the Colors palette by choosing View | Show Colors (F12).

3. Select the box you just created by clicking on it, and click the Background mode button in the Colors palette. By default, the drop-down menu that appears reads Solid.

13

4. Choose Linear Blend from the drop-down menu. Notice that two color option buttons appear below the drop-down menu.

5. Click the #1 option, click a color in the list, and choose a shade for the starting color of the blend.

6. Click the #2 option, click a color in the list, and choose a shade for the ending color of the blend. Your box blend appears immediately.

7. By default, your blend angle is set to 0 degrees, meaning it's vertically-oriented. Enter a new angle for your blend by entering 180 in the degree field. Your box is now blended in the opposite direction.

8. Set the blend on an angle by entering 45 in the degree field. Your blend is now angled.

9. Apply a new blend style by selecting Mid-Linear from the drop-down menu. The effect is immediate and your box now features more realistic-looking depth.

10. Choose Diamond from the drop-down menu and observe the effects. Enter a different rotational value by returning the blend to **0** degrees (enter **0** in the degree field).

11. Next, choose Circular from the drop-down menu and observe the results.

12. Adjust the blend by entering 200 in the degree field and notice that the blend now occurs more slowly than before.

TIP ══════════▷ *To remove a blend applied to a box, choose Solid from the drop-down menu in the Colors palette.*

Conclusion

Color can add dramatic impact to your documents, and if you have the luxury of using it, you'll want to squeeze as much creative freedom as possible from the ability to use it. This chapter has explored both the technical side of color and the creative possibilities of color in XPress. And, because XPress 4 has superior power when it comes to preparing documents destined for offset printing, you've seen that many of the issues surrounding color are directly tied to printing your documents.

TIP   *For information on working with color in pictures and applying color to certain picture types, see* Setting Picture Color in XPress *in* Chapter 8: Advanced Picture Strategies.

It's nearly impossible to think about color without considering the complex issues of printing your final document. Before printing a color document, there's something that a few creative types like to get too caught up in: color trapping. Don't worry, the next chapter, *The Basics of Trapping*, will help you overcome some of your trepidation.

13

CHAPTER 14

The Basics of Trapping

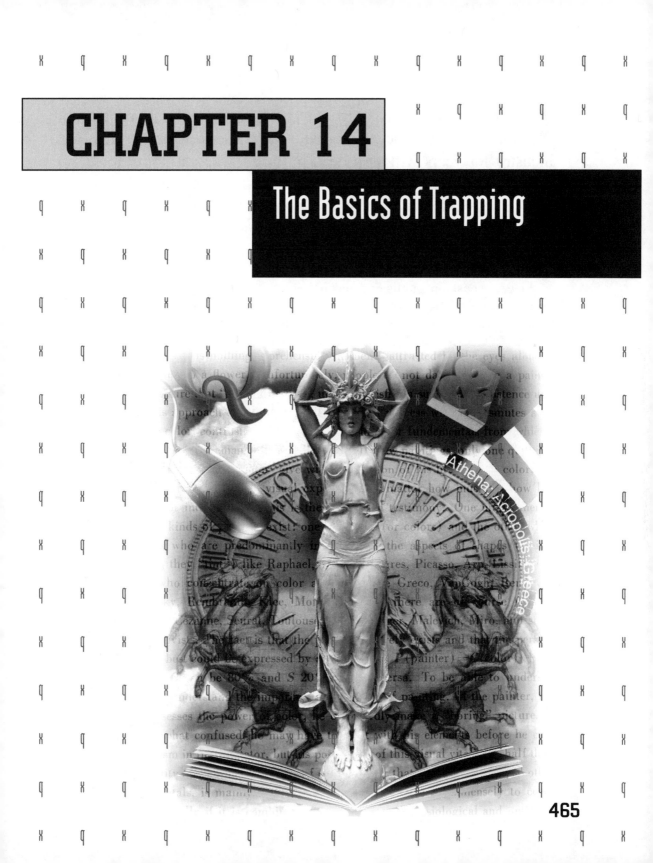

Athena, Acropolis, Greece

Understanding the concept of trapping is certainly not for the meek. Even tradespeople who have been in the prepress industry for years will stop dead in their tracks and think for a moment when faced with questions regarding color trapping. If you're new to the subject, you'll need a clear head and a quiet spot where you can absorb some of the logistical theory behind trapping and learn to use the tools in XPress to control it.

In early desktop publishing technology, color trapping desktop-created documents was a disaster, to put it mildly. Developers neatly avoided the entire issue, opting instead to leave trapping to the user through content workarounds and plenty of grief. In time, the problem was partly overcome through use of highly specific, automated "prepress" software capable of interpreting color desktop files and applying trapping values to color items. What many designers and electronic artists discovered was that trapping was not entirely an automatic process, and rarely could they depend on these applications' correctly interpreting and applying all instances of trapping.

In this chapter, you'll learn what trapping is and whether it's even something you need to be concerned about. If it is a concern, you'll learn about all the automated features and manually applied options in QuarkXPress 4 that enable you to apply trapping to color items in your document. You'll learn the three levels on which trapping may be controlled, and you'll explore some strategies to use when approaching the trapping stage of preparing your document for print.

What Is Color Trapping?

When the terms and phrases involved in describing trapping were first coined, the creators must have been having a bad day. The term "trapping" itself conjures some unappealing images, and the trend continues with other terms such as "knockouts" and "choking," to name just a few.

If you've ever had the opportunity to see poor-quality printing, you may have experienced firsthand the results of poor press registration and poorly trapped color. The old comic books you probably read as a child may come to mind. Imagine the black outline of a comic book character whose clothing color is slightly out of alignment with the shape of his clothes. When inks print out of register, gaps or color shifts appear between objects. Trapping compensates for this misregistration by slightly expanding one adjacent color into another, as shown in the following example.

Improperly
registered color

Properly
registered color

In fact, poor color registration and color trapping are interconnected issues. Color registration is the process of correctly aligning multiple colors of ink on the printed page, while color trapping is the process of creating slight overlaps where colors in your document meet. Consider for a moment the forces at work to make color inks align correctly. As the printing press is running at high speeds, it vibrates, causing rollers and guides to misalign and paper to shift position. Temperature and humidity changes in the press room also affect the paper material your document is being printed onto. The more sophisticated the printing press, the less readily this happens, but these issues are always factors to consider when preparing a multicolor document for print.

NOTE   *Color misregistration can occur any time a multicolor document is reproduced. This is an issue not only when reproducing documents on a conventional offset printing press, but also when documents are being silk-screened, stamped, or lithographed.*

In addition, the larger the size of the printed document and the color shapes being printed, the less noticeable misregistration is. And, the larger the color shapes in your document are, the more opportunity you'll have to build in color *traps* in order to reduce misregistration. Color shapes may be any item on your document page such as text and picture boxes, lines and shapes, and the various colored parts they're composed of. For example, the trapping values associated with a document such as a postage stamp will be much smaller and more difficult to print than those of a transit bus sign.

14

Once the color trapping has been applied in your document, the next step in preparing it for printing is generating color separations. You may even need to prepare a color proof of the separations to check color accuracy, registration, and trapping. Color proofing often involves creating color acetate overlays of the actual separated film output, in an effort to create a "match print" or color key. Match prints are often preferred over color keys because of the fact that they reflect accurate color. Matchprint and Color-Key (both spelled like this) are trademarks of 3M Corporation; the generic terms are "single sheet color proof" and "overlay color proofing system."

Do You *Really* Need to Trap?

Whether you even need to think about trapping your document depends on answers to a number of questions you need to ask yourself:

- Is the document destined to print in more than one color?

- Do different colors meet at any point on your pages?

- Is there a possibility the press will poorly register these colors?

If your answer to all these questions is *no*, proceed to the next chapter. If you answer *yes* just once, you'll need to consider applying color traps either throughout your entire document or to individually selected items. How you proceed depends on how extensive the color printing, how many colors are involved, and the capabilities of the offset press that will print your document.

There will of course be instances when you don't need to—or can't—color trap your document. For example, if there's a single process color photograph in the document that doesn't feature any type of frame, isn't positioned on top of a color background, and doesn't meet with any other color items on the page, then it won't be possible to trap the process colors—even though the person operating the press would love to have a black frame around the photograph to hide any improper ink registration.

Understanding Traps and Terms

To understand trapping and the terms used to describe certain types of trap situations, you'll need to take a close look at a few simple trap examples using color shapes (or in this case shaded ones). Try to imagine them in color here, or refer to the trapping examples in the previous chapter of this book.

- **Trap**   The term *trap* describes adding a small portion or area to a shape to reduce the hazards of poor color registration. Shapes of different color are trapped in a direction from the lighter color to the darker color in such a way that the two colors overlap.

- **Spread**   When two colors meet in a situation where the lighter-colored shape is positioned in front of the darker-colored shape, portions are added to the edges of the lighter-colored shaped in order to *spread* into the darker color. Figure 14-1 is an example of a simple spread.

- **Choke**   When two shapes meet in a situation where the darker-colored shape is positioned in the foreground and the lighter-colored shape is in the background, the lighter background is *choked* where the two colors meet, meaning the lighter background's edges overlap into the darker shape's edges where the two shapes meet, as shown in Figure 14-2.

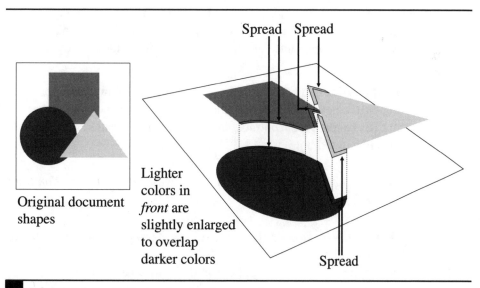

Spread   Spread

Original document shapes

Lighter colors in *front* are slightly enlarged to overlap darker colors

Spread

FIGURE 14-1   Effects of a simple spread

14

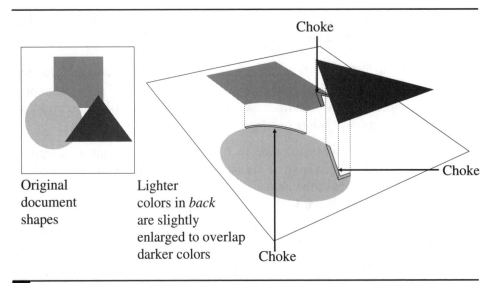

Choke

Choke

Choke

Original document shapes

Lighter colors in *back* are slightly enlarged to overlap darker colors

FIGURE 14-2   Effects of a simple choke

- **Overprint**   As the name implies, when one colored item overlaps and *overprints* another item of a different color, the ink coverage in the areas where the two shapes overlap is combined, as shown in Figure 14-3. In other words, one ink color prints on top of another. Overprinting can cause the two colors to combine to create the illusion of a third ink color, which can either cause unexpected results or be manipulated to an advantage.

- **Knockout**   When one colored item overlaps another item of a different color, the usual method of handling this is to remove the portion of the item that lies beneath the frontmost item. This action is called *knocking out* and is illustrated in Figure 14-3.

TIP   *Keep in mind the golden rule of trapping: Always trap in a direction from light to dark.*

In QuarkXPress 4, you have essentially three levels of trapping control available:

- Default trapping controlled by options in the **Trap Preferences**
- Color trapping controlled by options in the **Color | Edit Trap** dialog box
- Item trapping, controlled by settings in the **Trap Information** palette

Original document
shapes   Knockout   Overprint

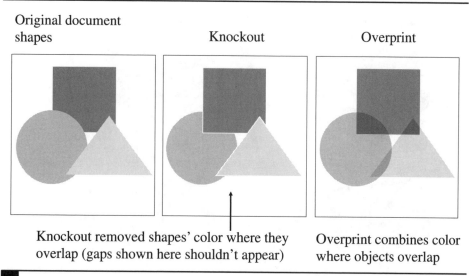

Knockout removed shapes' color where they   Overprint combines color
overlap (gaps shown here shouldn't appear)   where objects overlap

FIGURE 14-3   Effects of overprinting and knocking out color

Even before XPress prints your document, it examines each item for trapping conditions and looks to these three control areas for information and guidance on how to proceed. Each subsequent level of control supersedes the previous. Trap preferences are followed in a very general sense for all objects not applied with any further trap options. The Color trap options override all preference settings, so if your item contains a color that has specific trapping options applied to it in the Edit Color dialog box, these options are used. If trap options have been applied to an item using the Trap Information palette, these settings override all others.

When it comes to trapping text, the same trapping rules apply, only the resulting trap effect is much more complex—especially when you're dealing in process color. Figure 14-4 demonstrates the effects of applying trapping to text characters.

Note that for text up to 24 points and small items (dimensions up to 10 points), QuarkXPress attempts to preserve the item's shape during process trapping by not allowing automatic spreads or chokes when the item's shape would be compromised. QuarkXPress does this by comparing the darkness of each process component of an item to the darkness of its entire background. A spread is applied only when the process components of an item are less than or equal to half the darkness of its background. A choke is applied only when the process components of a background are less than or equal to half the darkness of the item in front of it.

14

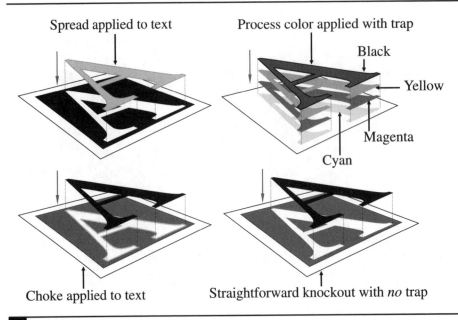

Spread applied to text

Process color applied with trap

Black

Yellow

Magenta

Cyan

Choke applied to text

Straightforward knockout with *no* trap

FIGURE 14-4   Applying various trapping effects to text characters

When trapping text or other small items, the chances are good that your text or item's shape may become distorted or disfigured. Fortunately, XPress has a built-in feature that examines any text characters below 24 points and other items less than 10 points in one dimension to determine whether trapping will distort the item's shape when printed. To do this, XPress compares the difference in luminance value between the text or item and its background or foreground color. Spreads and chokes are then applied only when the difference in color is less than half the color (luminance) of the background or foreground.

Setting XPress Trapping Preferences

Since many instances of trapping can be guided by a certain set of rules or principles, much of the labor involved in applying traps may be automated. As you select options in your document preferences, you're actually defining which rules XPress follows when it applies automatic color traps. Automatic trapping is performed according to the basic principles of trapping, meaning lighter colors are spread or choked according to their layering position and color. Colors may also be automatically knocked out or overprinted according to various user options set.

TIP *Keep in mind that color trapping is only applied when a document is printed. Simply applying a trap value to items in your document won't enable you to actually view the traps. For that, you'll need to examine the resulting printed page.*

Commands in XPress' document preferences control the top level of color trapping, and as you'll soon discover, XPress has a unique collection of terms all its own for describing and setting these options. The Default Document Preferences (CTRL/CMD+Y) | Trapping tab dialog box shown next features what could be considered the master set of controls for determining the trapping of colored items in your document.

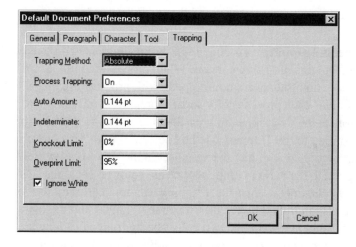

For the most part, trapping options enable you to apply overall trapping in the most common instances. The choices you make in the Trapping dialog box will answer questions such as *when* to trap, how much to trap *by*, as well as limits on when to knockout and overprint. In an effort to understand these options and how they'll affect your document's color, the following definitions identify their capabilities:

■ **Trapping Method** This drop-down menu contains three choices for controlling trapping and is perhaps the most important of all the options you'll select in this dialog box. Select *Knockout All* to turn trapping off and deactivate the remaining options in the Trapping dialog box. Select

14

Absolute to enable XPress to apply trapping according to the values set in the *Auto Amount* field discussed below. Select *Proportional* to enable XPress to use the most complex option of the three, whereby trap values are based on the *Auto Amount* value and then multiplied by the difference in lightness and darkness (luminance) between the two colors being trapped. Using *Proportional* is perhaps the most-automated and forgiving choice, allowing the amount of trapping to be larger as the difference in colors increases. For example, if your item colors differ only marginally, then the chance of a misregistration gap being noticeable is lessened. If the colors differ greatly, then misregistration gaps will be more noticeable, so the resulting trap value applied is larger.

TIP ▸ *To have your trapping preferences apply to all future documents as default settings, set them while no documents are open. To have them apply to a specific document, set them while the document is open.*

- **Process Trapping**   Process trapping may be selected by using *On* or *Off* from this drop-down menu. When process trapping is *Off*, process-color items are not trapped. With process trapping *On*, XPress examines each process color separation individually in relation to other colors being overlapped in your document. The resulting trap is set according to the Trapping Method selected. With *Absolute* chosen, the trap is applied with half the value set in the *Auto Amount* field and applied to the darker component of the color on each plate. With *Proportional* chosen as the Trapping Method, half the *Auto Amount* value is multiplied by the difference in lightness and darkness (luminance) between the two colors being trapped. Below are examples of the results of process trapping applied using *Absolute* and *Proportional* trapping methods.

Color	Front item	Back item	Absolute trap	Proportional trap
Cyan (C)	40	10	Spread at ½ Auto Amount	Auto Amount (40–10)÷2
Magenta (M)	50	70	Choke at ½ Auto Amount	Auto Amount (50–70)÷2

Color	Front item	Back item	Absolute trap	Proportional trap
Yellow (Y)	60	70	Choke at $\frac{1}{2}$ Auto Amount	Auto Amount $(60-70) \div 2$
Black (K)	40	35	Spread at $\frac{1}{2}$ Auto Amount	Auto Amount $(40-35) \div 2$

NOTE *All values above are percentage values.*

- **Auto Amount** The value entered in the Auto Amount field controls the width of the spread or choke amount XPress applies to items in your document when trapping. By default, Auto Amount is set to 0.144 points, but you may enter any value within a range between 0 and 36 points. *Auto Amount* is the value used in automatic trapping in general as well as while *Auto Amount* is set for specific colors in the Trap Specifications dialog box discussed later in this chapter. You may also choose Overprint as the Auto Amount, which results in the item overprinting other colors instead of an automatic trap being applied.

- **Indeterminate** This may be one of the strangest terms you'll encounter in XPress' new trapping dictionary. Essentially it means a value "cannot be determined." Indeterminate is a fancy way of describing items whose color can't be identified because of its value (such as colors with equal luminance values) or color composition (such as imported color pictures). In these cases, the Indeterminate trapping value is automatically applied. For example, when XPress encounters an item that's in front of an *Indeterminate* background, the Indeterminate value is used. Like Auto Amount, the Indeterminate default is 0.144 points, but you may enter any value within a range between 0 and 36 points. You may also choose Overprint as the Indeterminate value, which results in the item overprinting Indeterminate colors instead of an automatic trap being applied.

- **Knockout Limit** The Knockout Limit value enables you to control whether a color is knocked out or not and is expressed as the percentage difference between a foreground and background item color; this enables you to control the point at which an object color knocks out a background color. If a color isn't knocked out, settings in the Auto Amount field apply. The default is 0.

14

- **Overprint Limit**   All items colored solid black (100 percent) overprint by default. If the item is less than 100 percent black, XPress checks your preference for how much black should be present before overprinting. By default, overprint is set to 95 percent, meaning all items between 95 and 100 percent will overprint and all items below 95 percent will be trapped according to both the remaining trap options and the amount set in the Auto Amount field.

- **Ignore White**   This item is checked by default, enabling XPress to knock out the shape of items colored with white. When left unchecked, all items overprint the white item, and the results may be undesirable. For example, if a white item is between two differently-colored items, the item on top will be trapped to the item on the bottom, meaning traps could be visible in the white area when the final document is printed. Unchecking *Ignore White* should only be used when trapping under special printing circumstances.

Setting Ink Color Trap Specifications

The next level of trapping is set according to options applied to ink colors in the Trap Specifications for [*color name*] dialog box shown next. These options override those set in the Trapping preferences dialog box and are essentially a function of ink color. To open the Trap Specifications dialog box, choose Edit | Colors (SHIFT+F12), choose an ink color, and click the Edit Trap button. The dialog box opens to display your current list of available colors.

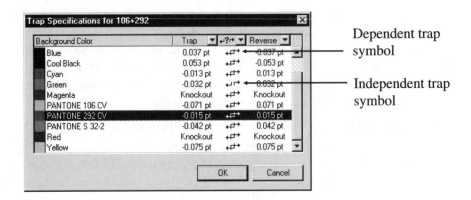

Dependent trap symbol

Independent trap symbol

TIP *To have your trapping specifications apply to all future documents as default settings, set them while no documents are open. To have them apply to a specific document, set them while the document is open.*

The Trap Specifications dialog box includes a number of options for controlling how your selected color traps when it comes in contact with other colors in your document—regardless of which type of item the color has been applied to. The dialog box displays three columns of settings according to the colors in your document list. When a color is selected, the following options are available in the form of drop-down menus in the headings of the columns:

- **Trap** This column displays the current trap amount that XPress will automatically create when your selected color overlaps another color—in this case listed as background colors. Choose *Default* to leave the trap amounts to be created at the options selected in the Trapping preferences dialog box, or choose *Overprint, Knockout, Auto Amount (–)* for chokes, *Auto Amount (+)* for spreads, or *Custom* to override the preference settings for all instances. When *Knockout* and *Overprint* options are selected in this list, the *Knockout* and *Overprint Limits* in the Trapping Preferences dialog box determine how the color will print.

TIP *For quick reference, XPress indicates values other than defaults in the Trap Specifications list with an asterisk (*).*

- **Reverse** The concept of Reverse trap can be a little confusing. The options in this dialog box are geared toward cases where your selected color is applied to an item *in front* of an item applied with one of the colors in this list. In this case, the other colors serve as backgrounds. Reverse enables you to apply a trap value in the opposite situation, when your *selected* color serves as the background and the listed colors are applied to the object in front of it. By default, Reverse traps are simply negative values of the Trap value. If you want, you may override the defaults by choosing *Overprint, Knockout, Auto Amount (–)* for chokes, *Auto Amount (+)* for spreads, or *Custom* to override the preference settings for all instances. As with the Trap options, *Knockout* and *Overprint* options are determined by the *Knockout* and *Overprint Limits* in the Trapping Preferences dialog box.

- **Dependent/Independent**   As discussed above, *Trap* values and *Reverse* values are, by default, essentially the opposite of each other. For example, if the *Trap* value for a color is 0.144 points (a positive value), then the *Reverse* value will be –0.144 points (negative value). The *Dependent/Independent* option enables you to break this relationship if you choose to, so that the *Trap* and *Reverse* values may be set independently of each other. The unconnected arrow symbol represents a Dependent condition, while the overlapping arrow symbol represents an Independent condition. To toggle between conditions for any given color, click once on the currently-displayed symbol.

NOTE ➤ *The Indeterminate color listing enables you to specify a trap value or printing condition when your selected color comes in contact with an Indeterminate color, such as an imported color picture or a color of equal luminosity.*

Once you've completed editing the traps for your color, click the OK button to close the Trap Specifications for [*color name*] dialog box, and click Save in the Edit Color dialog box to save your trap editing and close the dialog box.

Using the Trap Information Palette

The final level of trapping options is set directly in your document and applied to selected items. This is perhaps the most labor-intensive operation when trapping a document, but it's also the most significant of all three levels. Options set at this point override both your document preference options and the options chosen in the Trap Specifications list. Applying traps directly to items in your document using the Trap Information palette (shown next) is referred to by XPress as *item-specific* trapping. To open this palette, choose View | Show Trap Information (CTRL/OPTION+F12).

Trap Information			
Background:	Default ▼		
Frame Inside:	Default ▼	-0.136 pt	?
Frame Middle:	Default ▼	-0.067 pt	?
Frame Outside:	Default ▼	0.144 pt	?
Gap Inside:	Default ▼	-0.069 pt	?
Gap Outside:	Default ▼	0.144 pt	?
Text:	Default ▼		

When applying item-specific trapping you have a number of things to consider. First of all, the items you're applying trap properties to may feature more than one element. For example, a text box could conceivably be composed of text, a background, and a frame dash and stripe—including both the frame and the gap. And each of these elements could be assigned a different color or shade.

The Trap Information palette is context sensitive, meaning the available options change depending on the type of item selected. When setting the item-specific trap for various elements of the items in your document, you'll notice that the Trap Information palette features the same set of trapping options for each element, composed of selections for *Default, Knockout, Overprint, Auto Amount (–)* for applying chokes, *Auto Amount (+)* for applying spreads, and *Custom* for entering your own trap value. The effect of selecting these trapping options is identical to those applied in the Document Preferences | Trapping tab and the Trap Specifications dialog box.

■ **Background**   When a text or picture box item with no frame property applied is selected, the background option becomes available. Although the background of a text or picture box is usually the largest area, it's the simplest part to identify. The background is the interior portion of any text or picture box.

14

- **Frame Inside, Frame Outside** A frame is perhaps one of the most complex elements to trap—especially if a dash or stripe pattern is applied to it. When a box or line with any frame value is applied, the two frame elements *Frame Inside* and *Frame Outside* become available. *Frame Inside* controls the trap properties where the innermost edge of the frame overlaps the background color (or an item beneath this edge while the box background color is set to None). *Frame Outside* refers to the trap properties where the outermost edge of the frame overlaps a background item's color.

- **Frame Middle** Frame Middle trap options control the edges of colored portions of a frame style. This option becomes available when you apply boxes with complex frame styles containing interior elements such as the default frame styles Double or Dash Dot or the bitmap style.

- **Gap Inside, Gap Outside** When a box or line is selected with a patterned frame style applied and the gap set to a color, the *Gap Inside* and *Gap Outside* trap property options become available, in addition to the three frame trap options discussed above. *Gap Inside* controls the edges where the gap color overlaps the interior elements of the box such as the background (or an item beneath this edge while the box background color is set to None). *Gap Outside* controls trapping for the edge of the gap that overlaps background items beneath it.

- **Text/Picture** When text in a box is selected, the text color may be set with trap properties using the *Text* options. When a picture box containing a picture is selected, the *Picture* trap options are available. In the case of pictures, you may only set trap options to Default, Knockout, or Overprint—otherwise the process color trapping set in the Document Preferences dialog box is used.

- **Line, Line Middle, Gap** When lines are selected, the *Line* trap option becomes available, enabling you to control the edges of the line where it overlaps other background items. If the line is applied with a pattern, the *Line Middle* trap option becomes available to control trap for the edges where the frame dash or stripe color overlap into background items beneath. If a gap color has been applied to the line or frame, the *Gap* option enables you to apply trap properties where the gap color edges contact the line (or frame) dash color, any background colors, and any color items beneath.

The Trap Information palette has one last function: the capability of actually providing information about the intended trap, as shown next. When an item is selected and certain elements of the item are available for trap options, XPress displays information about the trap properties applied whenever you click and hold on the question mark symbol adjacent to the trapping option.

The information box that appears lists information about the element's color, the color of elements underneath, the source of trap values in use (Edit Trap or Trap Preferences), plus any trap preferences currently in use by the element such as Proportional, Process Trapping, Rich Black, Overprint Limit, Knockout Limit, or Smallest Trap Value.

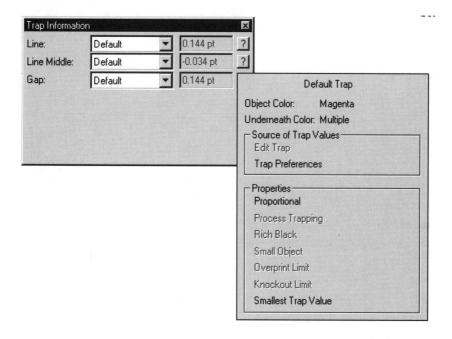

Conclusion

As promised, the topic of trapping color in documents is a heady topic not for the faint of heart, and it helps to know a little about the issues before delving too far into it. Without at least some knowledge of printing production processes, discussing trapping can be like explaining the details of brain surgery to medical students on their first day of classes.

14

This chapter has explored XPress' three levels of trapping in detail. You discovered what trapping is about, how it affects the colors of items on your document, and how to set both automated and manual trap options in an effort avoid ugly misregistration during offset printing. Next you'll pursue further complexities of color use, in *Chapter 15: Using Color in Documents.*

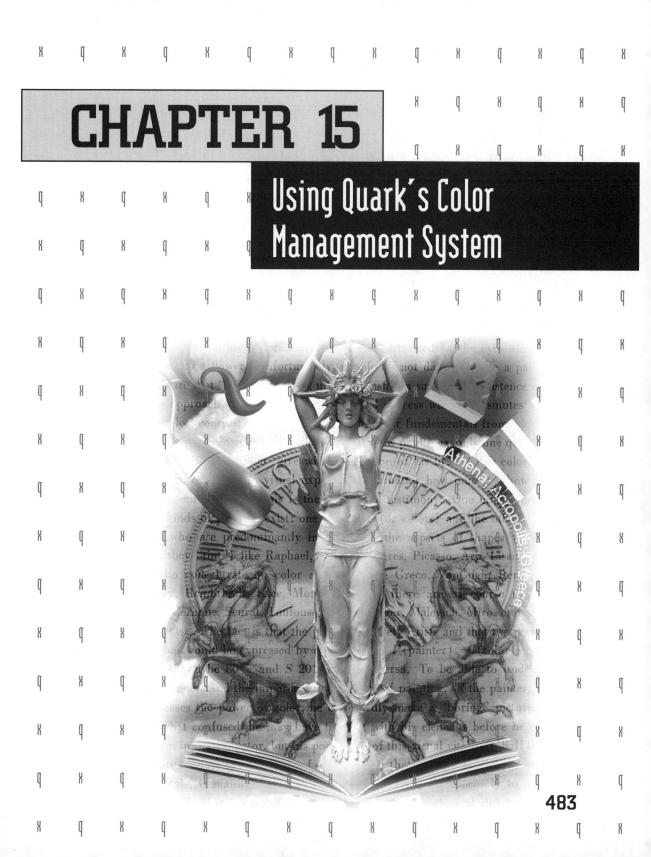

CHAPTER 15

Using Quark's Color Management System

Athena, Acropolis, Greece

483

In the world of digital color production there are, needless to say, almost as many hardware and software variables in production processes as there are reproducible colors. The key to achieving proper color through controlling these variables is to know your digital tools, but with color technology changing so quickly, this is no small feat. Yet through use of some sophisticated tools aimed at achieving color correctness, this latest version of XPress *does* have advantages over lower-end applications.

This chapter fleshes out the capabilities of Quark's Color Management System and provides you with directions on how to use it. You'll discover how to install and activate it, set profiles for your color devices, and apply color profiles to pictures. The journey begins with a primer to help you prepare to work in color and to rely realistically on what you see on your screen.

Setting Up an Accurate Color System

Color designs of even the best designers and illustrators can get poor reviews simply because they use an uncalibrated desktop system. Calibration is the process of adjusting and verifying displayed color to scanned color and through to printed color. Reasons for inaccurate color may stem from a poorly calibrated monitor or color proofing device, to poor print reproduction—or to any of the many processes between. The trick to avoiding color errors is to first understand all the processes involved, loosely represented in Figure 15-1.

Watch That Monitor

Essentially, the process begins with your eyes and what they and your brain interpret from what you see on the screen of your color monitor. But it continues on down the line to include your color page layout software, color scanner, desktop color proofing device, and finally the imagesetter and printing press or equivalent reproduction method.

Begin your calibration process with your monitor. Following these steps will ensure a controlled environment for viewing colors:

■ Begin by obtaining a printed hard-copy color reference such as a color swatch. Be sure your swatch is recent; over time swatch colors can fade. If you purchase a new swatch, be sure to mark it with the date you purchased it.

■ When viewing colors, be sure your monitor is sufficiently warmed up. Waiting roughly half an hour will ensure that the color has stabilized.

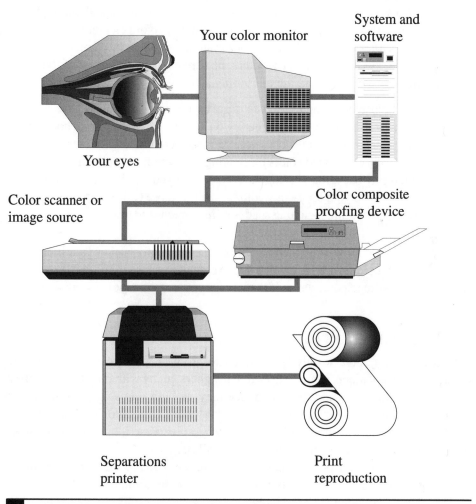

FIGURE 15-1   Desktop color process for printed documents

- Set your work area lighting to your usual working light level. Controlled lighting is ideal; avoid having natural light coming into the room, because levels of natural light change during the day. Bright light reduces the spectrum of light our eyes let in; vice versa for low light. This in turn affects how the colors on your monitor appear.

- Take steps to shield your system from power surges. Power levels can fluctuate during various times of the day, and consequently affect the color generation of your monitor.

- If your monitor is a recent model, it may feature brightness and contrast controls. Be sure to set these to comfortable levels and tape them in place or use built-in hardware software to lock them. Avoid changing these settings after you've calibrated your system. If you share a common working system with other workers, be sure everyone is aware of the importance of not changing the settings.

- When adjusting brightness and contrast, try matching as closely as possible your swatch colors to those appearing on your screen. In XPress, choose the color swatch book that matches your reference color swatch. Compare screen colors to printed colors by creating a selection of colored items on a neutral-gray background using the color model you've chosen, and compare these colors to your hard-copy color swatch. Choose colors that range across the color spectrum, including shades of red, green, and blue.

Following these steps will at least stabilize the color information your monitor is providing. If the colors on your monitor look reasonably close to those in your color swatch book, you're in good shape. If they don't, you may have some work ahead.

Look Good in Print

You may be using a black-only laser printer to proof all your color documents. If you are, you're not alone. Many artists and designers get by with only the color they see from their monitors and the experience they've built on using the same color schemes over and over again. If you have the luxury of a color proofing device capable of producing accurate color, you may be able to use it to obtain at least an "impression" of what your final output color will be.

A multitude of color printer manufacturers in the industry use various printing technologies, such as laserjet, bubblejet, laser, color sublimation, or thermal wax transfer. These technologies vary widely in the way they interpret and reproduce color; some reproduce colors based on cyan, magenta, yellow, and black ink models, while others use their own special recipes.

As far as your software is concerned, only two different breeds of printers may be considered for use with QuarkXPress: PostScript and non-PostScript. PostScript is a page-description language developed by Adobe, and it has become the virtual standard for the desktop industry. PostScript-based color printers build color based on information in your PostScript driver. The accuracy of these printers depends on how their drivers read the color information from the print engine of your software (that is, QuarkXPress). Non-PostScript printers interpret the color from your software's print engine, but usually have drivers that interpret PostScript color information.

Another determining factor in color proofing is the resolution of your printer. The higher the resolution, the more accurate your color proof will be. Although technology is advancing quickly, most color proofing devices still commonly print to either 300 or 600 bits per inch (bpi) of resolution. Compare that to the final imagesetter film resolution that often lies within a range of from 2,400 to 3,600 dots per inch (dpi).

Scan for Color

Desktop scanning technology has revolutionized the ability for most layout artists and print designers to use color pictures in desktop color. What used to be a costly prepress step in obtaining color separations is now electronic wizardry. But, with this wizardry comes a heaping helping of "visual illiteracy" on the part of users. Many often find, after scanning an image, that it lacks the satisfactory color they wanted to capture from the original. And the problem is compounded by placing these unrefined images into page layouts. Keep in mind that the scanner is simply a recording device. Just as with a stereo amplifier, you may have to adjust the bass and treble a bit to hear all the sounds in the correct balance (or, in this case, see all the colors). As with monitors, not all scanners are created equal—especially if you work in the Windows platform.

Scanners operate with various kinds of optic technology, whereby a light bar or a laser records the colors of an original image, and then subsequently converts into data the information it records. This data is then converted into RGB (red, green, blue)—the only color model used by your monitor to render images. If you're reproducing your image in black-and-white, you need only to convert it to grayscale for it to print properly to film. But, if you're producing a spot or four-color process document and want to reproduce your image in the available colors, you'll need the aid of an image editor capable of converting your color picture to your desired colors.

TIP *For process color, convert to CMYK and save the file as a TIF to have it be compatible with XPress. For duotones using spot colors, convert the picture to grayscale, then duotone adding your chosen spot color, and finally save the file as an EPS. Once in XPress, the file will separate correctly at the printing stage.*

When you scan an image, you'll need to make a number of decisions concerning resolution, compression (if any), and file format. Resolution is determined by the final print resolution of your document, while compression and format are determined by the image editor or utility you're using to acquire the color image. The TIF file format is widely accepted and usually importable into most desktop applications such as QuarkXPress 4.

For more information on film imaging and other output issues, see *Chapter 16, Printing Your Pages.*

Using Quark CMS

When it comes to color management, QuarkXPress 4 puts its own twist on how to accurately translate and display color across devices. This twist comes in the form of Quark's own CMS (Color Management System), which enables you to specify the properties of your monitor, composite printer, and separations printer in the form of device profiles. A device profile is a file containing the color capabilities of a color device. Standard profiles conform to established color standards. Quark's CMS is managed through use of a CMS XTension. Once installed and activated, CMS enables you to use Quark's Color Management Module (CMM)—a built-in color engine capable of interpreting and translating colors based on the properties of the device in use. Properties of compatible devices are interpreted by data contained in ICC (International Color Consortium) device profiles, which conform to standards followed by color-capable publishing software developers—such as Quark.

The purpose of any color management system is to display accurate color across devices. The issues surrounding color management can often be complex and confusing, but suffice it to say that the whole thrust is to be able to view on your color monitor what you'll eventually hold in printed color form in your hands. Quark's CMS works as the intermediary between all your devices, in an effort to regulate color and provide your eyes with color information accurately portraying what will end up in your hands when printed. Figure 15-2 loosely shows a graphic representation of this process. When you specify device profiles, you're essentially

15

telling the color engine what your device limitations and capabilities are so that it can reflect the color back to you.

In an effort to understand how the color manager operates, follow this highly simplistic scenario. Let's say your color printer can only print blue and its device profile contains data describing this crippling limitation. Let's also assume your monitor is capable of reproducing just about any color under the sun, as is your color scanner. After correctly defining their profiles to Quark's color management system, you launch XPress and view your document; everything looks normal. However, when you import a recently-scanned full-color picture specifying color correction for your printer, all you see are various blue shades in what was supposed to be a

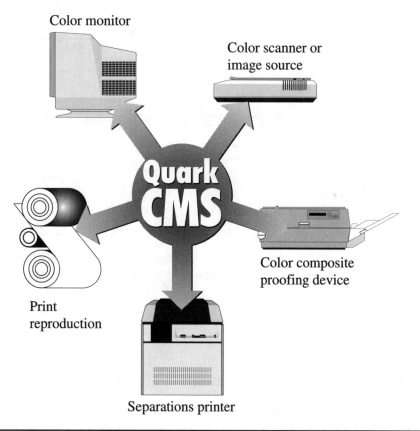

Color monitor

Color scanner or
image source

Color composite
proofing device

Print
reproduction

Separations printer

FIGURE 15-2   Quark's CMS manages, interprets, and reflects back color
to your hardware devices based on the data contained in
device profiles

full-color picture. Believe it or not, your CMS setup is working just fine. Confused? Read on.

Installing the Quark CMS XTension

The first step in benefiting from color management in XPress is to install it. The CMS XTension is installed through use of the XTensions Manager. To check if yours is installed and active, open the XTensions Manager by choosing Utilities | XTensions Manager to open the dialog box shown next.

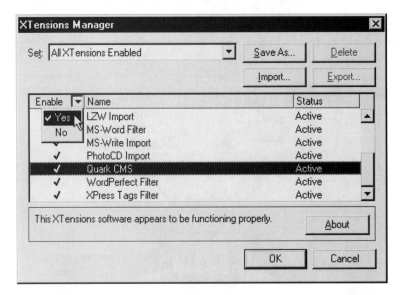

To enable the Quark CMS XTension, highlight it and select *Yes* from the Enable drop-down menu or click in the column to the left of the XTension, to display a check mark. After changing the XTension from Inactive to Active, you'll need to exit and relaunch your XPress program for it to become active. Once XPress is relaunched, you'll notice the CMS XTension has added specific color-related menu items to you application, as follows:

- Color Management is added to the Edit | Preferences submenu.

- The Profile Manager is added under the Utilities menu.

- The Show Profile Information command is added under the View menu.

- An additional tab named Profiles is added to the Utilities | Usage dialog box.

15

■ Color Correction and Profile options are added to the Get Picture dialog box.

■ A Profiles tab is added to the Print dialog box.

Setting Color Management Preferences

Once your CMS XTension is successfully activated, choose Edit | Color Management to open the Color Management Preferences dialog box (shown next) and specify the profiles for the color devices you're using to create, display, and print your document. As you do this, you're essentially feeding in the data that describes the capabilities and limitations of all the hardware devices you're currently working with. The device profiles you specify contain data that describe the color properties of your system hardware, including color monitors, color scanners, color composite printers, and color separation devices. Quark's CMS will then be able to reflect back to your monitor a reasonable interpretation of the colors you'd expect in print, based on these properties.

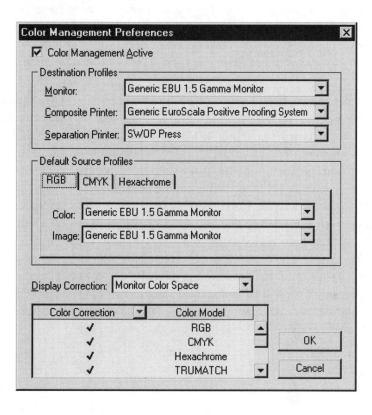

To activate CMS, click the *Color Management Active* option at the top of the dialog box and enable the remaining dialog box options. Once CMS is activated, a number of significant color profile-related features spring to life behind the scenes. These include the appearance of additional tabs in the Usage and Print dialog boxes, and a Color Correction option in the Get Picture dialog box. If CMS isn't selected as active, these items will simply not appear. With CMS inactive, the Profile information palette will open but will remain dormant and the command for viewing the Profile Manager will be unavailable in the Utilities menu.

First, choose the devices you're using to view and print your document from the *Monitor*, *Composite Printer*, and *Separations Printer* drop-down menus in the Destination Profiles area. The purpose of selecting options in the Destination Profiles area is to enable QuarkXPress to display and print your document's color pictures accurately to the selected devices.

NOTE ➤ *For the CMS features to accurately reflect the color properties of your device, you must select a corresponding profile, but Quark doesn't supply device profiles, nor does XPress enable you to create your own device profiles as do other applications. If you discover that the device you're using isn't listed in the drop-down menus, obtain the device profile from your hardware manufacturer or select the profile for a device with similar color properties.*

Next, choose the options for device profiles associated with your picture input devices from the Default Source Profiles area. This area includes choices for the Color and Image profiles for conditions where your color picture is in RGB, CMYK, or Hexachrome color. For example, choose your monitor profile from the Color drop-down menu, and then from the Image drop-down menu choose the profile that represents your scanner (or other image source device).

Finally, select the Display Correction mode in which you want your color items to be rendered to your screen. The Display Correction drop-down menu includes options for choosing corrected color for your *Monitor Color Space*, *Composite Printer Color Space*, and *Separations Printer Color Space*. You may also choose *None*, which has the effect of deactivating the color correction feature entirely. For example, choosing *Composite Printer Color Space* enables Quark's CMS to attempt to render color items to your monitor based on the color space represented by your composite printing device.

Color space is the model on which the display of your picture is based. And a composite printer is the color printer you'd normally use to print your document prior to final separation output to check the color accuracy in your documents. The term composite *refers to a printer that prints all colors at one time on a single sheet.*

The remaining options in the Color Management Preference dialog box enable you to activate color correction for items in your document set to specific color models or swatch book colors. The available choices include *RGB, CMYK, Hexachrome, Trumatch, Focoltone, Pantone Process, Pantone Solid to Process, Hexachrome Coated,* and *Hexachrome Uncoated.* To activate color correction for any of these, highlight the model or swatch book in the list and choose *Yes* or *No* from the *Color Correction* drop-down menu or click once in the area adjacent to the color model/swatch book to toggle it on or off. Once a color model is specified for color correction, Quark's CMS will attempt to display accurate color based on your Color Correction choice (that is, your monitor or printer).

As with other preference features, you may apply color management to a single document or to all subsequently-created documents. To set these preferences for a specific document, make your selections with the document open. Doing so applies your choices only to the document. To have your profile preferences apply to all subsequently-created documents, close all documents before opening the Color Management Preferences dialog box and selecting your profiles.

Applying Color Correction to Pictures

When you first create a new document and import your first color picture, you'll see an option for color correction in the Get Picture dialog box (shown next). Beyond setting overall application and document Color Management Preferences, this is the first step in actively applying color correction while working with imported items on your page. While your color picture is selected to be imported into a picture box and the CMS feature is active, the *Color Correction* option becomes available, as does the *Profile* drop-down menu. Choosing Color Correction enables you to set the device profile for which the color in your imported picture will display.

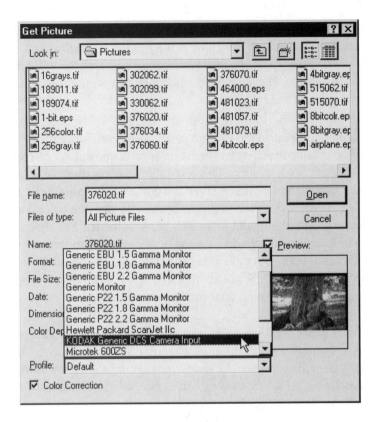

To apply color correction to your imported picture, click Color Correction and choose your device profile from the Profile drop-down menu. Once the picture is imported, XPress will attempt to reproduce accurate color, depending on the printer selected in your Color Management Preferences dialog box.

TIP ➤ *If Quark's CMS feature isn't selected as active in the Color Management Preferences dialog box, the Color Correction option and Profile drop-down menu won't appear in the Get Picture dialog box. To activate CMS, Choose Edit | Preferences | Color Management and click the Color Management Active option at the top of the dialog box.*

Using the Profile Information Palette

Although your Color Management Preferences dialog box enables you to set the overall color profile settings for your document, you may still need to edit or override these settings in some cases. This is the role of the Profile Information palette. Once a picture has been imported, you may change its color correction color space (or deactivate it) at any time using the Profile Information palette (shown next). To open the Profile Information palette, choose View I Show Profile Information.

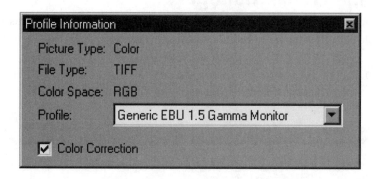

NOTE   *The Color Correction and Profile options in the Profile Information palette only become active while color pictures are selected.*

TIP   *If Quark's CMS feature isn't active, the Profile Information palette won't operate. To activate CMS, Choose Edit I Preferences I Color Management and click the Color Management Active option at the top of the dialog box.*

The Profile Information palette displays specific information about selected pictures, including the Picture Type, the File Type, and the Color Space for your imported picture. The palette also includes an option to activate or deactivate *Color Correction* and a *Profile* drop-down menu that enables you to choose the color profile to apply to the picture, just as you're able to do in the Get Picture dialog box.

NOTE   *XPress supports color correction only for certain types of picture file formats. If your selected picture can't be color corrected, the Profile Information palette will display the Picture Type and Color Space as* Unknown *while still indicating the File Type information. Unsupported file types include EPSF (EPS), and DCS (desktop color separations) file formats, both of which feature predetermined color and can't have their color space information altered for printing. For information on using various file format types, see* Working with Picture Formats *in Chapter 7,* Adding and Controlling Pictures.

TIP *Choices made in the Profile Information palette override those made previously in the Color Management Preferences dialog box.*

Using the Profile Manager

The Profile Manager is your master control when working with various types of device color profiles in XPress. It lists all the device profiles that are currently available to you, and it enables you to activate or deactivate them at any time using options in the Profile Manager dialog box (shown next). To open the Profile Manager, choose Utilities | Profile Manager.

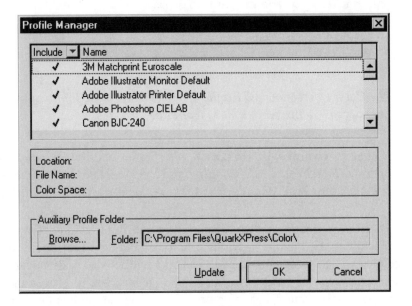

The Profile Manager displays a list of all the profiles available on your system and subsequently to Quark CMS. You may activate or deactivate any of the device profiles listed by clicking to highlight one and choosing Yes or No from the Include drop-down menu or by clicking on the check mark to the left of the listing to toggle the active state on or off. You may also define and update an Auxiliary Profile Folder by clicking the *Browse* button to locate alternate profile locations and clicking *Update*.

If Quark's CMS feature isn't selected as active in the Color Management Preferences dialog box, the Profile Manager won't be accessible from the Utilities menu. To activate CMS, Choose Edit | Preferences | Color Management and click the Color Management Active option at the top of the dialog box.

Checking Profile Usage

As with other types of usage features, such as fonts and pictures, the Profile Usage command enables you to obtain a quick snapshot of what's going on in your document file in terms of profiles and color correction. To open the dialog box shown next, choose Utilities | Usage and select the Profiles tab.

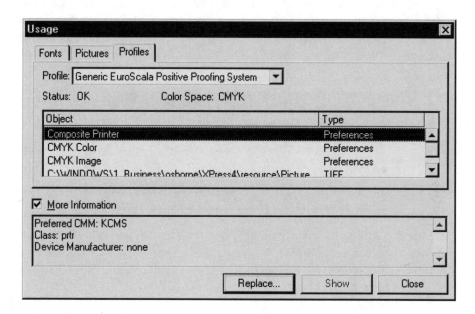

To obtain only the profile used for a given picture file, select the picture before opening the Usage dialog box. To obtain information about all the profiles used for pictures in your document, open the dialog box while no pictures are selected.

Options in the dialog box enable you to select a profile being used from the *Profiles* drop-down menu and also to obtain an instant summary of the pictures associated with it in the list. The list itself is composed of two columns, representing the type of item using the profile and the type of profile assigned to correct the item's color.

If Quark's CMS feature isn't selected as active in the Color Management Preferences dialog box, the Profile tab won't appear in the Usage dialog box. To activate CMS, Choose Edit | Preferences | Color Management and click the Color Management Active option at the top of the dialog box.

You may use the Profiles tab of the Usage dialog box to replace the device profile in use for a given item by highlighting the item in the list and clicking the Replace button to open the Replace Profile dialog box (shown next). Select the new profile to replace the current one by choosing it from the *Replace With* drop-down menu, clicking OK to close the dialog box, and clicking the Close button to close and exit the Usage dialog box.

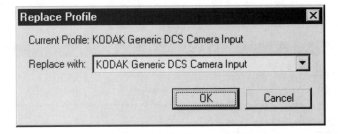

The lower portion of the Usage dialog box features an option to display more information about a selected profile. When selected, the dialog box expands to reveal profile information such as the CMM (Color Management Module), the Class of the device, and its manufacturer.

Choosing Profiles at Print Time

The final step in applying device profiles comes into play when you choose to print your document. Quark's CMS feature installs a Profiles tab (shown next) in the Print command (CTRL/CMD+P) dialog box, which enables the color engine to interpret the device profiles of both your composite and separations printers and to send the appropriate color data to your selected printer.

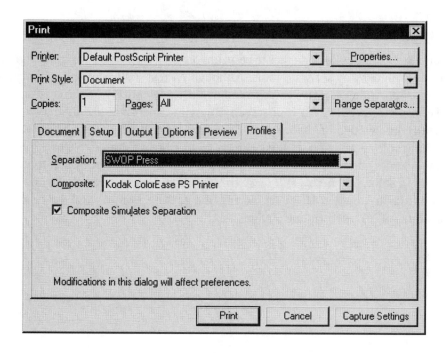

If your selected printer is incapable of producing color, the Profiles tab options will be unavailable.

By default, when you first open the Profiles tab, it displays the device profiles you originally specified in the Color Management Preferences dialog box. Be aware that this is your last chance to change them prior to printing. Choose device profiles for your separations printer or composite printer, or both, from the *Separation* or *Composite* drop-down menus. If you're actually proofing the color separations that you intend to eventually print to your separations printer, you may check the Composite Simulates Separation option in the dialog box.

If Quark's CMS feature isn't selected as active in the Color Management Preferences dialog box, the Profiles tab won't appear in the Print dialog box. To activate CMS, Choose Edit | Preferences | Color Management and click the Color Management Active option at the top of the dialog box.

Conclusion

Obtaining accurate color continues to be an ongoing concern for artists and designers working with desktop software tools. Although XPress' color correction tools are capable of providing accurate color, you shouldn't rely entirely on the accuracy of the color images you see on your screen. But with experience and diligence, plus a healthy knowledge of the printing processes, you'll be well on your way to achieving color perfection. In this chapter, you've been exposed to Quark's color management system in an effort to provide you with the necessary tools for printing in color, but there's still more to learn regarding printing. Continue your exploration in Chapter 16 by exploring the precise control and far-reaching capabilities of XPress' printing features.

CHAPTER 16

Printing Your Pages

If there's any point at which producing your document actually becomes exciting, printing is *it*. This is the time when all your hard work laboring over your computer bears fruit. And, for many desktop designers and layout artists, printing can be a rewarding experience when their creative efforts become tactile, informative, and functional products—and often portfolio samples or prizewinners as well. But, depending on how you've prepared your document, printing can be a time of joy… or a nightmare come to life.

If your QuarkXPress 4 document is destined for offset reproduction—as most are—it still has several stages to travel through. As it does, you'll be faced with options to choose that you may not be entirely familiar with. You may also be faced with the prospect of handing your document to a service bureau for remote output. In either case, you'll have to follow a certain order of things. This chapter walks you through the steps and options involved in printing your document to your desktop printer, and it covers what you'll need to know when taking your file to a service bureau for remote output.

Printing with 4.0 versus the *4.02 Updater*

Shortly after the release of QuarkXPress 4, Quark released a 4.02 Updater for both Macintosh and Windows version, which introduced several performance improvements and corrected printing problems associated with the original release. If you've purchased a recent copy of XPress, you have likely the updated version. But, if you purchased the original 4.0 version and are experiencing problems related to printing, installing the 4.02 updater should be tops on your list. The updater may be obtained by contacting Quark directly, or by downloading it from the company's World Wide Web site at **http://www.quark.com**.

The updater corrects the following printing-related problems:

- Program crash that occurs if you click Print in the Print dialog box while the Pages field is empty

- Incorrect printing of hairlines

- A problem occurring when choosing landscape orientation in the New Document dialog box, which doesn't properly set the page orientation to landscape in the Setup tab of the Print dialog box

- A PostScript error problem while printing a document with a LaserWriter version 7.x selected as the printer and a PostScript Printer Description (PPD) that uses a page size of *Custom*

- Frame-trapping problems

- Problems associated with drag-and-drop printing *(Windows 95/NT only)*

- Problems when separating Canvas 3.5.1 Desktop Color Separation (DCS) *(Macintosh versions only)*

- Printing problems that occur when the *Paper Height* drop-down menu (File | Print | Setup tab) is set to *Automatic (Macintosh versions only)*

- A printing problem that clips documents to 11.0 inches while the Generic Imagesetter printer type is selected *(Macintosh versions only)*

NOTE ———————▶ *Even if you aren't having problems while printing, it may be wise to obtain the 4.02 Updater, since certain other features have been changed or improved since the program was first released. For more information on improvements covered in the Updater, see the* Introduction *at the beginning of this book.*

Using a Service Bureau

Before the advent of desktop publishing, there were (and still are) businesses dedicated solely to word processing, design, typesetting, and prepress, employing experts in these particular areas. Preparing text, artwork, or photographs for any of these traditional processes was usually a practical or mechanical task rather than an electronic one. But things have changed quickly in the last dozen years or so, and procedures aren't exactly what they used to be. Now, much of the expertise involved is falling on the shoulders of the electronic artists who use a personal computer and a layout program. Using QuarkXPress 4, virtually anyone can have the tools necessary to create professional layouts and designs. With version 4, the tools have been developed to a point where even the most demanding professional can achieve sophisticated results. But in certain cases, layout artists who may not be familiar with remote output from a service bureau can find themselves wandering in unfamiliar territory.

When using XPress 4 to create documents destined for offset printing, you may be faced with the prospect of using a service bureau for film output, scanning, or color-matched proofing—operations that ordinarily are their core business. High-resolution film, used to produce offset press printing plates, is a common requirement. Film output can range from simple single-color output, to complicated process color separations employing both process and spot color. With process color, four separate pieces of film are needed to print the cyan, magenta, yellow, and black plates. With each additional spot color, an additional piece of film is required—and additional skill is required.

Most professional service bureaus are intimately familiar with XPress, since it has nearly become a standard for professionals in the publishing industry. And you'll find that many workers at such bureaus pride themselves on their expertise in handling, troubleshooting, and outputting client files. If you're a first-time client, you may find yourself being carefully eyed by the operators as they try to determine if you really know what you're doing. And you may also be eyeing them from the other side of the counter as you try to determine if *they* know what they're doing. Both of you are justified in doing so, since service bureau output can often be a complex exercise in "information coordination."

It has often been said that giving three different people the same document to create will result in three completely different documents—even if they appear to be identical on screen. The first may create a document that that looks and prints just fine. The second will look fine, but take forever to print. And the third simply won't print at all.

With inexperienced layout artists, problems can often be encountered. Files may be created in strange ways, causing grief and unnecessary expense for all involved. This is the type of thing everyone tries to avoid. If you're fully-prepared for the experience of buying output, you can substantially reduce your chance of having output problems. Whether you're a first-time purchaser of output, or a seasoned professional, you'll find that printing your files at a service bureau *can* be a pleasant experience—as long as you've slowly and carefully reviewed the information in the chapters in this part of the book.

Understanding Imagesetters

This section provides some background on what an imagesetter is and the acrobatics it performs to image your file. Whether you ask for a single page of output or high-resolution film for a hundred-page book, your data will likely go through the same channels.

All imaged files must first be downloaded through a raster image processor (RIP) according to the specific directions you've provided. In the case of print files, the files may be downloaded directly to the imagesetter on the premises. Or, if you provided a source file, the file may be imaged directly out of XPress 4. In most cases, the service bureau uses a spooler to hold the data until the imagesetter is ready for it. A healthy service bureau business likely has its imagesetters running 24 hours a day and uses dedicated print spoolers to handle the flow of traffic between the operators' computers and the actual imagesetters.

Next, after your data starts feeding to the imagesetter, the image is burned onto a layer of photographically-sensitive film. From there, the film is fed into a chemical processor that develops, fixes, washes, and dries the film, much like the way your local one-hour film processor handles your photos. After processing, the finished output is cut into separate film pages and packaged.

Two principal models of imagesetters are currently used. First, a *capstan* imagesetter uses a 200-foot roll of film that's loaded into the imagesetter much like the film in an ordinary camera. The film enters the imagesetter and is fed by rollers to a laser device that exposes the film. From there it's fed into a light-tight cassette that can be easily removed from the imagesetter without exposing the contents. The service bureau operator removes the cassette for processing, just as from a regular camera.

The second type of imagesetter is the *drum model* imagesetter. Drum model imagesetters image film that has been cut into large sheets and vacuum-mounted to the inside of a light-tight, half-barrel-shaped housing. An imaging laser moves back and forth inside the drum to expose the film. The exposed film is then track-fed into a take-up cassette (again, light-tight), and a new sheet of film is fed into place.

Imaging Output Material

You likely will order two types of film output from the service bureau: paper or film, sometimes both depending on your needs. These materials can be easily confused with each other since both are photographically-sensitive and considered *film* even though one is paper-based. Once the film has been imaged by the imagesetter, film processors are used to automatically process, fix, wash, and dry both types of output. A properly maintained processing system is fed by a filtered, constant water supply that's temperature-controlled. Like imagesetters, processors require regular maintenance to provide consistent results. The professional service bureau continually monitors both imagesetters and processors for such things as dust, dirt, static, and film density.

If you've prepared your files properly and provided the service bureau with everything it needs, you won't have any surprises when your film comes back. If a problem occurs and your output isn't satisfactory, the first thing to do is check your output order form to ensure that your order is correct.

If your files are complex, the service bureau may charge you for additional processing time in the form of surcharges. Most service bureaus follow a rule of thumb that allows 15 minutes for each letter-sized page to be imaged and processed. Beyond that, you may be charged up to a dollar per minute for the additional time needed to image the page. This practice isn't uncommon, but keep in mind that good customers are rarely charged extra.

Setting Print Options

Because of the multitude of situations involved with printing documents, an enormous number of variables may be set in XPress' Print command dialog box (CTRL/CMD+P). The options you choose will depend on your own particular needs and the device you're using to print your document. The main Print dialog box (shown next) has been subdivided into five basic areas, in the form of tabs. These areas include *Document, Setup, Output, Options*, and *Preview* tabs, the details of which follow. If you're using Quark's Color Management System (CMS) and it's active, a sixth tab for setting your color, *Profiles*, will also appear. The following section will serve as a guide in choosing these options.

Choose a Printer

Choosing a printer in the Print dialog box is the very first step in beginning your print procedure. Once selected, the capabilities of your printer are reflected through options available in XPress' various tabbed Print dialog boxes. The most significant factor in the capabilities of your printer is whether it's a PostScript or non-PostScript type. Since QuarkXPress is fully PostScript-compatible and heavily geared toward describing items in your document in this format, PostScript printers feature many more capabilities for printing documents than do non-PostScript printers.

For example, while a PostScript printer is selected, you'll be able to print color separations for any or all colors, specify page size options, and use Quark's PostScript Error Handler to troubleshoot any printing problems that occur. While a non-PostScript printer is selected, these options are unavailable. To select a printer using a Macintosh, use the Chooser under the Apple menu. Choosing a printer using Windows versions is slightly simpler; make your selection from the Printer drop-down menu.

NOTE   *If your printer doesn't appear in the Printer drop-down menu, this may indicate it's unavailable, not operating properly, or not installed on your system. On Macintosh platforms, if your printer is already installed and operating properly you may only need to select it by opening the Chooser from the Apple drop-down menu. Using Windows versions, this often indicates that the printer isn't installed. In either case, consult your system documentation and follow the procedures to install or select the printer.*

Once your printer is selected, its associated printer driver will enable or disable the available options in the remaining tabs of the Print dialog box. The printer driver contains data associated with the printer you've chosen and essentially tells XPress about its capabilities. If you're using the Windows version, a button to review the Properties associated with your chosen printer is available, enabling you to verify the printer's capabilities if you choose to do so. The illustration below shows the properties associated with a Linotronic 630 imagesetter. The majority of options contained in this dialog box are duplicated by options set in the various tabs of the Print dialog box. On the Macintosh, most of the options in the Properties dialog box are available through dialog boxes that display when you click the Page Setup and Printer buttons at the bottom of the Print dialog box.

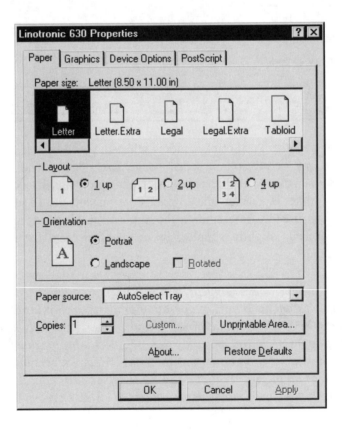

Common Print Dialog Box Buttons

In the Print dialog box, a number of options are available regardless of which type of printer you've chosen or which dialog box tab is selected. These include options for choosing a Print Style, the number of Copies you want to print, a Pages field, a Range Separators button, and a Capture Settings button, the operation of which is detailed as follows:

- **Print Style**   Choosing a print style enables you to instantly define all the printing options in all dialog boxes. If you've created Print Styles as described below, you may select this from the drop-down menu.

- **Copies**   Use this field to enter the number of copies of the selected page(s) you want to print. This field accepts a value of up to 999 copies for each printed page.

- **Pages**   Enter the page numbers you want to print in this field. You may print All the pages in your document (the default) or specify continuous or noncontinuous page numbers by using range separators between the page entries as described below.

- **Range Separators**   This button opens the Edit Range Separators dialog box, shown next, which enables you to customize how you enter continuous or noncontinuous page numbers to print in the Pages field. By default, a dash (-) separates continuous pages while a comma (,) separates noncontinuous pages. For example, to print pages 1, 4, 5, 6, 7, 8, 21, 22, 23, 24, 25, and 40 of a 40-page document, you would enter "1, 4-8, 21-25, 40" in the Pages field. Range separators may be any single character you want. Any spacebar characters entered in the *Pages* field are ignored.

NOTE *The only reason to change the Range Separators is if your section page numbers conflict with the defaults (e.g., your pages are numbered A-1 or 3-1).*

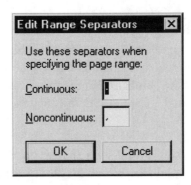

- **Capture Settings** This button enables you to save your currently-chosen printing options to be set automatically the very next time you open the Print dialog box. In essence, after clicking the Capture Settings button, your chosen options become your printing default settings. Use the Capture Settings button as the alternative to the Cancel button to close the dialog box, and to make your current settings available the next time you open the Print dialog box.

Using Print Styles

Print styles are more of a productivity tool than anything else. They enable you to immediately select printing options that have been previously saved using the Print Styles command. When a print style is created and saved using this feature, it becomes available to all subsequently printed documents, as opposed to being saved to a specific document. If no print styles exist in your Print Style drop-down menu, it indicates that none are available, and it may be wise to create some—at least for the most common documents.

To create a print style, choose Edit | Print Styles to open the Print Styles dialog box shown next.

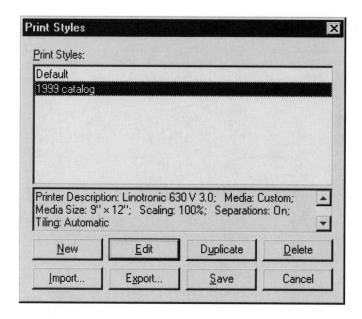

Command buttons in the Print Styles dialog box are identical to those seen in the Style Sheets, Colors, H&Js, Lists, and Dashes & Stripes commands found under the Edit menu, with a slight variation: When a print style is selected in the Print Styles dialog box list, a brief description of it appears in the lower area of the dialog box, just as with other property style creations. There's no *Append* command button since print styles are available to all documents. Instead, the Append command is replaced by the addition of *Import* and *Export* command buttons, discussed below. The remaining buttons include commands for New, Edit, Duplicate, Delete, Save, and Cancel. To create a new print style, click the New button to open the Edit Print Style dialog box shown next.

The Edit Print Style dialog box is subdivided into four tabbed areas, *Document,*
Setup, Output, and *Options;* these contain selections identical to those found in the
Print dialog box. To create a new style, you merely enter a name for your new style
in the Name field, choose the options you want to apply to your print style, click
OK to exit the dialog box, and click Save to close the Print Styles dialog box and
save your print style. The new style will be available the very next time you open
the Print dialog box while a PostScript printing device is selected. See the sections
to follow for information on setting print style options.

NOTE *Print styles may be used only while a PostScript-compatible printer is*
selected from the Printers drop-down menu.

■ **Import** Click the Import button in the Print Styles dialog box to import
a style created by another user. Imported styles are data files that store all
the options selected by another user. On Windows versions of XPress, a
print style may be identified by its three-letter QPJ extension.

■ **Export** If you want, you may make print styles you have created
available to other users through use of the Export button. When a print
style is exported, it takes the form of a data file. Windows version files
also feature the extension QPJ.

Setting Document Options

While the *Document* tab (shown next) in the Print dialog box is selected, the options defined below may be available, depending on the type of printer you've selected.

```
┌─────────────────────────────────────────────────────────────────┐
│ Print                                                         ✕   │
│                                                                   │
│ Printer:    │Linotronic 630                      ▼│  │Properties...││
│                                                                   │
│ Print Style:│Document                                          ▼││
│                                                                   │
│ Copies:  │1│   Pages: │All                    ▼│ │Range Separators...││
│                                                                   │
│ ┌Document│ Setup │ Output │ Options │ Preview │ Profiles │        │
│                                                                   │
│  ☑ Separations          ☐ Spreads          ☐ Collate             │
│                                                                   │
│  ☑ Include Blank Pages  ☐ Thumbnails       ☐ Back to Front       │
│                                                                   │
│  Page Sequence: │All      ▼│   Bleed:  │0"      │                 │
│                                                                   │
│  Registration:  │Centered ▼│   Offset: │6 pt    │                 │
│                                                                   │
│  Tiling:        │Automatic▼│   Overlap:│3"      │  ☑ Absolute Overlap│
│                                                                   │
│                      │  Print  │  │ Cancel │  │Capture Settings│  │
└─────────────────────────────────────────────────────────────────┘
```

■ **Separations**   If your document contains more than one color, choosing the Separations option will enable you to separate the colors to a compatible printer type. Separation options may be selected later on in the Output tab. For each selected plate of color, a separate sheet of output material will be generated for each of your selected pages.

TIP

> *For more information on printing and working with desktop color separation (DCS) files, see* Chapter 17, Printing Color Separations.

■ **Spreads**   If your document features left and right pages or pages arranged in a horizontal row in the Layout palette in the form of spreads, you may want to choose this option. The Spreads option has the effect of enabling you to print pages across defined page boundaries, provided your chosen printer supports a page size large enough to do so. In cases where it doesn't, you may need to use the Tiling option discussed later in this section.

- **Collate**   If you've chosen to print more than one copy of selected pages, the Collate option becomes available. Choosing this option essentially has the effect of duplicating the print data sent to your printer once for each copy you select to print. As a result, choosing the Collate option increases the time it will take to print your pages relative to the number of copies you select.

- **Include Blank Pages**   This option is off by default, because few users require blank pages to print in their documents, especially when printing to an imagesetter or any printing device whose output material is costly. Choosing Include Blank Pages causes XPress to print pages that don't include user-created items.

- **Thumbnails**   Choosing to print thumbnails has the effect of printing your pages at the smallest possible size (less than 10 percent of the original)—even less than the 25 percent minimum that may be set in the Reduce or Enlarge field (discussed later in this section) found in the *Options* tab. While Thumbnails are selected to print, other options such as the Separations option are unavailable.

- **Back to Front**   Choosing this option simply enables you to print a document consisting of more than one page in reverse order, the last page being printed first.

- **Page Sequence**   This drop-down menu features three choices for printing All (the default) pages or the *Odd-* or *Even-*numbered pages of your document. This is helpful if you're going to print a double-sided document. In that case, first you print all the odd pages, and then you flip the paper over, put it back in the printer, and print all the even pages.

- **Registration**   This option includes three options for printing registration marks with your document. Registration marks consist of trim (corner) marks that define the page edges of your document, plus registration symbols—sometimes referred to as "target dots"—that enable film separations to be aligned during the stripping stage of offset printing. Choosing *Off* (the default) omits registration marks from your printed pages. Choosing Centered has the effect of printing four registration symbols centered at each of the four sides of your document pages. Choosing Off Center also prints four registration symbols at the sides of your document, only they're not printed to align with the center marks of your pages.

- **Tiling**   Choose an option from the Tiling drop-down list if you need to print your document to a page size that is smaller than your document page without reducing its size. Tiling has the effect of printing your document page(s) in sections, with the eventual aim of assembling them manually after printing. Choosing *Off* (the default) turns the tiling feature off, while choosing either *Manual* or *Automatic* activates the feature. While Manual is selected, the origin of your tiles is dependent on your Ruler origin (zero) position, beginning each tile at the upper-left corner. Choosing *Automatic* enables XPress to set the portion of your document page that appears on each tile and centers the tiles on each page. The number of tiles required to print your entire document is indicated in the Print | Preview tab. Choosing *Automatic* also enables you to set the two options described below.

- **Bleed**   This is another of those violent terms you'll encounter when working in the offset printing industry. Bleed refers to the amount of space between the printed edges of your document and the imaginary border around your page in which items overlapping the edge may appear. In desktop publishing *bleed* is used to describe situations where ink is allowed to overlap into the area of a page that will eventually be trimmed from your final printed document. Color backgrounds and photographs are a popular item type to have bleed off your page. The Bleed value may be set within a range of between 0 and 6 inches, with a default of 0.

- **Offset**   With Registration marks set to print with your document, the Offset option becomes available and enables you to set the distance between your registration marks and the outer edges of your page. Offset may be set within a range of between 0 and 30 points, with a default of 6 points. (This field is new to XPress version 4.02.)

TIP   *When XPress prints Automatic tiles, tick marks and page information are included with the tiled pages to ease the task of reassembling the printed pages.*

- **Overlap** With *Automatic* tiling selected, you may set the *Overlap* value of each printed tile. Setting an overlap value makes it much easier to assemble individual tiles for transparent output material, such as film. *Overlap* may set in inches within a range of between 0 and 6 inches, with a default of 3 inches.

- **Absolute Overlap** With *Automatic* tiling selected, the Absolute Overlap value also becomes available. When selected, *Absolute Overlap* enables XPress to print each tile without centering it on the output material.

TIP   *For more information on Tiling, see the section* Special-Needs Printing *later in this chapter.*

Setup Options

Print setup options enable you to control options both for your printer and for the output material you'll use to print your document onto. While the *Setup* tab (shown next) in the Print dialog box is selected, the following options may be available, depending on the type of printer you've selected:

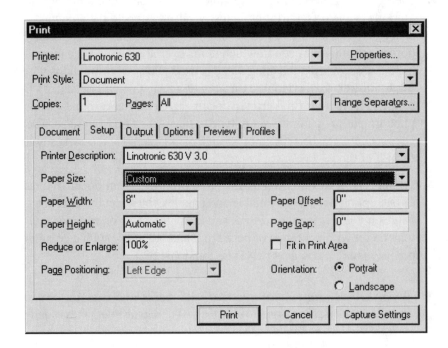

- **Printer Description** The Printer Description drop-down menu contains the list of all available printer types according to the printers enabled in the PPD Manager. For more information on enabling or disabling the printers that display in this list, see *Using the PPD Manager* later in this chapter.

- **Paper size** For new users, this option may be slightly misleading—it refers to "paper" when in fact the material you're printing your document onto may not be paper at all. Paper size also refers to the size of your *output material* rather than the page size of your document. Output material is measured in page formats such as *Letter*, *Legal*, *Tabloid*, and so on, influenced by your choice of Printer Description. While a specifically defined paper size is selected, the following two options are unavailable.

TIP ➤ *If you've selected Registration marks to print, be sure to select an output page size larger than your document page size, to accommodate these marks. Add at least 0.5 inches of space to each of the four sides of your printed page. For example, if your document page is 10 inches by 15 inches, choose an output material size of 11 inches by 16 inches. For standard sizes such as Letter, Legal, and Tabloid, preset sizes appended with the term ".Extra" are often available with your PPD, such as* Letter.Extra *(which sets an output material size of 9.5 inches by 12 inches).*

- **Paper Width/Height** To enter your own paper width and height values, choose a paper size of *Custom* from the Paper Size drop-down menu. Custom is often the last option listed in the Paper Size menu. Once selected, you may enter the *Width* and *Height* for your output material. Both the *Custom* Paper Width and Height values must fall within a range of between 1 and 240 inches. Paper Height may be set to Automatic (the default).

- **Reduce or Enlarge** If you require your document to change size when printed, enter a reduction or enlargement value in this field, based on a percentage of the original size. Values entered below 100 percent reduce the size, while values entered above 100 percent enlarge it. Reduction or enlargement values must fall within a range of between 25 and 400 percent.

■ **Page Positioning**   For the Page Positioning options to be available, you may need to choose *Custom, MaxPage,* or *MaxMeasure* as your output material size from the *Paper Size* drop-down menu. Choosing *Custom* enables you to enter your own page sizes in the *Paper Width* and *Paper Height* fields. Choosing *MaxPage* has the effect of imaging your document to the largest size of which your selected printer is capable. While a paper size of *MaxPage* is selected, *Page Positioning* may be set to *Left Edge, Center, Center Horizontal,* or *Center Vertical* from the available drop-down menu.

■ **Paper Offset/Page Gap**   While a *Custom* paper size is selected, the *Paper Offset* and *Page Gap* fields become available. *Paper Offset* enables you to control where the left edge of the document page begins from the left edge of the output material and must be set within a range of between 0 and 48 inches. The *Page Gap* value enables you to control the amount of space between individually printed pages and is useful when printing multiple pages to roll-fed printing devices where the pages are printed one after another. The shorter the distance, the less output material is wasted. *Page Gap* may be set within a range of between 0 and 5 inches. The default value for both options is 0.

■ **Fit in Print Area**   The *Fit in Print Area* option becomes available when QuarkXPress detects that the page size you're printing to is smaller than your document page size. Choosing this option has the effect of enabling XPress to automatically calculate a page reduction size for you. For example, if your document pages are *Tabloid* size (11 by 17 inches) but your chosen paper size is *Letter,* choosing *Fit in Print Area* enables XPress to calculate an automatic page reduction size of 70.7 percent. Unchecking the options returns the Reduce or Enlarge option to 100 percent.

■ **Orientation**   The term *orientation* describes the manner in which your page is "fed" into your printer. Orientation of your document often matches the orientation of your output material. Orientation is directly related to the width and height measures of your chosen paper size, such as Letter, Legal, Tabloid, and so on. The term has always been surrounded by confusion, since users often mistake orientation of the document with the orientation of their output material. Thankfully, XPress' print feature includes a Preview tab, discussed later in this chapter, that enables you to view both your document orientation and your output material selection at once. If you feel any uncertainty about which option is correct for your print setup, check out the Preview tab.

Output Options

The Output tab options enable you to set virtually all the color, resolution, and line frequency settings for your printed output. While the *Output* tab (shown next) in the Print dialog box is selected, the options defined below may be available, depending on the type of printer you've selected.

16

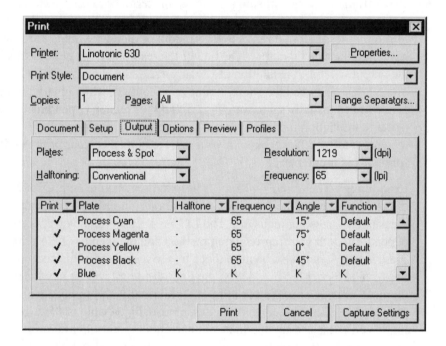

- **Plates**   While the Separations option in the *Document* tab is checked, the Plates drop-down menu is displayed. This option includes two choices for displaying all the *Process and Spot* colors in your document, or changing all colors in your document to four-color process using the *Convert to Process* option. While Convert to Process is selected, only cyan, magenta, yellow, and black plates appear in the Options tab colors list.

- **Print Colors**   While the Separations option in the Document tab is *unchecked*, the Print Colors drop-down menu (instead of the Plates drop-down menu) is available in the Output tab. Choose from *Black and White, Grayscale,* or *Composite Color* printing.

- **Halftoning**   This term is used to describe the screening method used to reproduce shades of color and digital photographs. Two methods of halftoning may be selected from this drop-down menu: *Conventional* or *Printer*. The Conventional option enables XPress to include halftoning information with the print data sent to the printer. Choosing Printer lets the selected printer use its default halftoning method instead.

- **Resolution**   Much confusion surrounds this term, because resolution may refer to scanning resolution, screen resolution, and so on. In the case of printing resolution, it refers to the amount of detail the imagesetter will build into the printed output. The higher the resolution, the more detailed the output will be. A resolution of roughly 1,270 dpi (dots per inch) is often the default used for photographic paper output, while photographic film output is usually set to roughly 2,540 dpi or higher, depending on the offset reproduction method in use. If you're unsure about which resolution to specify, check with your service bureau or your print vendor for their requirements.

- **Frequency**   The term *Frequency* is used to describe the number of rows of dots measured in the dot screen halftone of your printed output and is measured in lines per inch (lpi). The LPI Frequency value you choose depends on both your reproduction method and the quality of the printing press in use. It may also be influenced by the resolution value chosen above. The higher the Frequency, the finer the detail will be in your final output. Common sheet-fed printing presses usually accommodate up to 150 lpi, while high-speed web presses are usually capable of 85 to 100 lpi. If you're unsure about which value to choose, consult your print vendor. Setting the Frequency value sets the default value for the Frequency associated with each ink color listed in the lower area of this dialog box.

The lower area of the Options dialog box is fashioned into a list of colors, together with their associated printing properties. For this color list to display more than simply Black, you must be printing to a PostScript printer selected in the Printer drop-down menu, and the Separations option in the Document tab must be selected as active. Each color in the list represents a separate printing plate, and each may be controlled individually by selecting it and choosing the available options from drop-down menus at the top of the Print, Halftone, Frequency, Angle, and Function columns. Options are defined as follows:

- **Print**   The Print drop-down menu enables you to turn printing for a particular plate *on* or *off* as indicated by a check mark. To turn printing on or off, choose Yes or No from the drop-down menu or click in this column to the left of the Plate name to toggle the appearance of the check mark.

- **Plates**   The plates column simply identifies the available colors in your document.

- **Halftone**   Another repeated option name here. But, in this case, the *Halftone* option refers to setting the screen angle for nonprocess colors for shades, pictures, and digital photographs to match that of a process color ink. Choose C (cyan), M (magenta), Y (yellow), or K (black, the default) from the drop-down menu to have the angles of shades, pictures, and digital photographs match a process color angle. By default, cyan=105 degrees, magenta=75 degrees, yellow=90 degrees, and black=45 degrees.

- **Frequency**   Using the Frequency option, you may set lines per inch (LPI) frequency for a specific color differently from others, if you want. Choose Default (the default) to have the Frequency match the value selected in the Frequency option in the upper area of the dialog box, or choose Other to enter your own value and override the default.

- **Angle**   Using the Angle option, you may set the angle at which the rows of dots describe shades of color, pictures, and digital halftones for a specific color individually. By default, process colors will already be entered, but spot colors will each be set to match Black (45 degrees). Choose *Other* to enter your own value and override the default.

- **Function**   The Function for each printed color may be selected individually from this drop-down menu. Function is the shape of the dot that describes shades of colors, pictures, and digital photographs, and this option may be set to *Dot, Line, Ellipse, Square,* or *Tri-dot*.

Printing Options

The Options tab contains a potpourri of options for setting picture output options, page flipping and negative printing options, and EPS overprinting. While the *Options* tab (shown next) in the Print dialog box is selected, the options defined below may be available, depending on the type of printer you've selected.

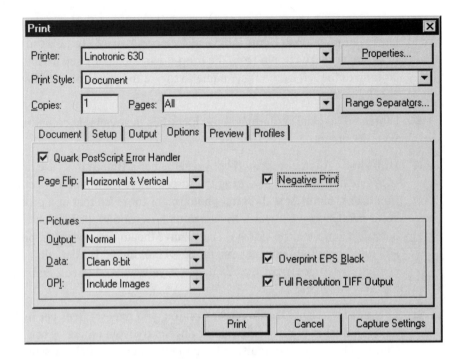

■ **Quark PostScript Error Handler**   Quark has gone one better when it
comes to identifying PostScript errors, with an improvement to the
usual—and often cryptic—error messages associated with complex page
items that may halt printing. Besides the usual error messages that print
when a particular page refuses to print, Quark's improvements involve
printing a bounding box around the offending item encountered in your
document, identifying it with a box featuring a black border and a 50
percent black background. Plus, a message at the upper-left corner of the
unsuccessfully printed page indicates the cause of the problem. To locate
(and usually replace or delete) the offending item, match the position of
the bounding box that appears with an object on your page. To activate
Quark's Error handler, simply click the check box.

■ **Page Flip**   The Page Flip drop-down menu enables you to print your
page backward or upside down, or both, by choosing Horizontal (to print
backward), Vertical (to print upside down), or Horizontal and Vertical
(both backward and upside down). Although these options might seem
ridiculous when printing to a laser printer, for high-resolution film output
they're invaluable and enable you to control the side on which the film

16

emulsion faces. Emulsion is the photo-sensitive layer adhered to film that enables it to appear either black or clear, to reflect the items on your page. Flipping your printed page causes the emulsion side to appear on the back side of the film, for the emulsion side to contact the photosensitive side of the printing plates during plate production. Setting the Page Flip option to *None* (the default) enables the pages to print normally.

- **Negative Print**   This option is another function of generating film output and enables you to print your pages as negative images. Where items are usually white on your page, they'll appear black on the film.

- **Picture Output**   The purpose of the *Output* drop-down menu is to give you choices for printing pictures in Normal, Low Resolution, or very Rough conditions. This option is useful when proofing the text of documents that are image-intensive, causing them to take additional time to print. Choosing *Normal* (the default) leaves pictures to print in the usual way. But choosing *Low Resolution* enables XPress to forego the high-resolution data that describes pictures, and instead replace them with the 72 dpi screen resolution previews. Setting Output to *Rough* completely suppresses the printing of pictures in your document, leaving only the picture's frame and background properties to print.

- **Picture Data**   The ability to choose the Data type that describes the pictures in your document gives you flexibility when printing your document through a print spooler and to a wider range of printer types. *Clean 8-bit* (the default) is similar to *Binary*, but omits additional data strings that *Binary* adds to communicate with parallel port printers. The *ASCII* format is a more versatile format, compatible with a wide range of printers and print spooling software.

- **Picture OPI**   This option enables you to fine-tune the printing of pictures for OPI (open prepress interface) systems. OPI systems have the capability of substituting high-resolution data files that describe picture files in place of the images you've imported onto your pages. High-end OPI systems are used for ultra-high-resolution color pictures where importing the enormous picture files associated with such resolution just wouldn't be practical. Before printing, the high-resolution images are substituted for lower-resolution placeholders. Choose *Include Images* (the default) if you aren't using an OPI system to print your document. To add the OPI comments to your low-resolution TIFF picture placeholders at print time, choose *Omit TIFF*; while using OPI for both TIFF and EPS picture files choose *Omit TIFF & EPS*.

TIP ━━━━━▶ *For information on working with systems that use digital separations, see* Working with DCS *in* Chapter 17, Printing Color Separations.

■ **Overprint EPS Black**   Although other items on your document page can be controlled through automatic or manual trapping properties, EPS pictures can't. For these, you'll need to rely on the diligence of the creator of these files to have added the proper trapping. Choosing the *Overprint EPS Black* option has the effect of forcing all black elements in an EPS picture to overprint, regardless of their applied internal trapping properties.

■ **Full Resolution TIFF Output**   Choose this option if you'd like your TIFF pictures to print at the highest line frequency supported by the printer you're using at your selected printer resolution (see Output tab options). With this option selected, TIFF pictures will automatically be set to print at the highest line frequency (lines per inch, or lpi) possible. For example, with a resolution of roughly 2,540 dpi selected to print on an imagesetter printer, the line frequency choices range from 100 to 150 lpi for all shades of color, pictures, and digital photographs. With *Full Resolution TIFF Output* selected, all TIFF images will print at 150 lpi, independent of the lpi setting chosen for the rest of the printed document. Leaving *Full Resolution TIFF Output* unchecked leaves the Frequency value set in the Options tab as the lpi setting used for TIFFs.

Previewing Your Print Selections

A good habit to adopt is to check the Preview tab just prior to pressing the Print button, regardless of how large or small your printing job happens to be. The Preview tab enables you to view certain printing-related options you've set in the Document and Setup tabs, such as page size, output material size, registration mark printing, thumbnail printing, tiled printing seams, bleeds, and so on. The display consists of a statistical display in text form, plus a viewing window indicating your document (as shown next.) The main purpose of the Preview feature is to ensure that your document fits correctly on the output material when Document and Setup options have been set.

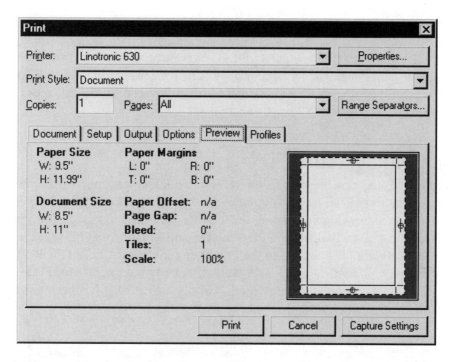

Unfortunately, the display of your document in the Preview tab has limited abilities. It doesn't display any details of the content of your pages, bleeds, or any options that may be selected in the Output or Options tab, including resolution display, number of pages to print, flipping, negative print, picture handling, or other conveniences found in some applications.

NOTE ▶ *If you're using Quark's Color Management System (CMS) feature, the Profiles tab will also appear in the Print dialog box. For information on using CMS and choosing related options at print time, see* Chapter 15, Using Quark's Color Management System.

Using the PPD Manager

The purpose of Quark's PPD (PostScript Printer Description) Manager is to enable you to manage the display and your access to printer description files. PostScript Printer Description files are needed to describe the properties of your printer; they appear in the Printer Description drop-down menu of the Setup tab of XPress' main Print dialog box. They're often supplied by manufacturers with the purchase of a new printing device. A single PPD file can contain entire lines of printer models for a single manufacturer brand, making PPD lists long and time-consuming to navigate. For example, the PPD files included with AGFA printers include more than 30 entries that are displayed numerically and alphabetically in the list of PPDs. If the PPD that you need to select each time you print comes at the end of the list, repeatedly searching for and selecting it can be annoying.

Fine-tuning Your PPD List

The PPD Manager enables you to control which printer types appear in the Printer Description drop-down menu (of the Setup tab in the Print dialog box) by either checking or unchecking the mark to the left of each listed printer, as shown in the PPD Manager, next. To open the PPD Manager, choose Utilities | PPD Manager. To change whether a PPD appears in the Printer Description list, select the PPD and choose Yes or No from the *Include* drop-down menu, or click next to the PPD in the list to toggle display of the check mark. Once your PPD list has been changed, clicking the *OK* button saves your changes.

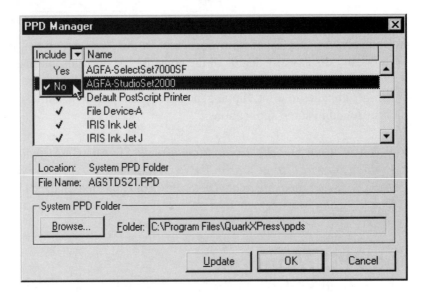

While a PPD is selected, the location and associated file name appear below the PPD list. By default, PPDs are located in your system folder for your operating system. But if you want, you may set the folder location for your PPDs using the *Browse* button in the dialog box. In fact, it may be wise to keep all your PPDs in a single folder separate and secluded from system files, to easily keep track of them. To do this, create a folder named PPDs in your QuarkXPress program folder and store your PPDs there. After changing the folder location, the PPD list is automatically updated, or you may click the *Update* button to manually update the list.

TIP

When choosing which PPDs display in the list, you may select multiple continuous and noncontinuous PPDs using the SHIFT and CTRL/CMD keys, respectively, while making your selection. Once a selection of PPDs is highlighted, you may select Yes or No from the Include drop-down menu to change the display conditions of all of them at once.

Getting a PPD

Usually, PPD files are distributed on disk with new printing hardware. But you may be in a situation where you simply can't, for unknown reasons, locate the PPD file for your printer. Bottom line: If you don't have the correct (or compatible) PPD, you simply can't print. Obtaining these files is easier than it has been in the past, but still it takes some hunting. Quark doesn't supply PPD files on the XPress 4 program disc, so if you misplaced the disk that came with your printer, you have some work to do.

The absolute best source for getting a PPD file is through the World Wide Web. If you don't have access, contact your manufacturer by phone, call the vendor who originally sold you the printer, or locate another user who owns the same printer model as you. If you have access to the Web, try visiting Quark's Web site at **http://www.quark.com**. At the time of this writing, Quark's collection of downloadable PPDs was limited.

The best source for PPD files in the world may be Adobe, inventors of the PostScript page description language. There, you'll find PPDs for nearly every printer manufacturer in the world, including INF files that are often needed for color management systems. The following sections (with most-recent drivers listed first, then in alphabetical order) identify Adobe's Web site URLs where PPDs for both Macintosh and Windows may be found.

PostScript Printer Drivers for Windows

http://www.adobe.com/supportservice/custsupport/LIBRARY/pdrvwin.htm

Release date	Manufacturer	Language	File size
03/05/98	AdobePS 4.1.1I	Italian	1111K
01/13/98	AdobePS 4.2.3	Brazilian Portuguese	1053K
01/13/98	AdobePS 4.2.3	Chinese Simplified	1052K
01/13/98	AdobePS 4.2.3	Chinese Traditional	1047K
01/13/98	AdobePS 4.2.3	French	1059K
01/13/98	AdobePS 4.2.3	German	1057K
01/13/98	AdobePS 4.2.3	Italian	1055K
01/13/98	AdobePS 4.2.3	Japanese	1057K
01/13/98	AdobePS 4.2.3	Korean	1062K
01/13/98	AdobePS 4.2.3	Spanish	1053K
12/23/97	AdobePS 4.2.3	U.S. English	1049K
08/07/97	AdobePS 4.1.1BP	Brazilian Portuguese	858K
08/07/97	AdobePS 4.1.1D	German	1113K
08/07/97	AdobePS 4.1.1E	Spanish	1095K
08/07/97	AdobePS 4.1.1F	French	1130K
07/12/96	AdobePS 4.1	U.S. English	1017K
03/17/98	AdobePS 3.1.2 (Win 3.1)	Brazilian Portuguese	1024K
12/23/97	AdobePS 3.1.2 (Win 3.1)	U.S. English (all versions)	998K

Manufacturer PPD files for Windows

http://www.adobe.com/supportservice/custsupport/LIBRARY/pdrvwin.htm

Release date	Manufacturer	File size
09/08/97	Xerox	196K
08/22/97	AGFA	122K
07/21/97	3M	48K
05/30/97	Hewlett-Packard	135K
05/30/97	Eastman Kodak	75K
03/06/97	Adobe	26K
03/06/97	Apple	135K
03/06/97	Birmy Graphics	32K
03/06/97	CalComp	39K
03/06/97	Canon	142K
03/06/97	Digital	128K
03/06/97	EFI	114K
03/06/97	Seiko Epson	68K
03/06/97	Fuji Xerox	104K
03/06/97	IBM	51K
03/06/97	Linotype-Hell	179K
03/06/97	Mutoh	31K
03/06/97	Okidata	139K
03/06/97	PrePRESS Solutions	172K
03/06/97	QMS	95K
03/06/97	Samsung	196K
03/06/97	Seiko Instruments	83K
03/06/97	Shinko	22K
03/06/97	SofHa GmbH	46K
03/06/97	Sony	114K

16

Release date	Manufacturer	File size
03/06/97	Tektronix	305K
03/06/97	XANTE Corporation	189K
12/02/96	AST	22K
12/02/96	Autologic	174K
12/02/96	Bull Italia	23K
12/02/96	COLORBUS Software	57K
12/02/96	Colossal	41K
12/02/96	Compaq PageMarq	43K
12/02/96	Crosfield Electronics	50K
12/02/96	Dataproducts	82K
12/02/96	Dainippon	150K
12/02/96	Dainippon Printing Co. Ltd.	24K
12/02/96	DuPont	24K
12/02/96	Fargo Electronics	34K
12/02/96	Fuji Film (LuxSetter)	26K
12/02/96	Fujitsu	22K
12/02/96	GDT Softworks	31K
12/02/96	Hitachi	46K
12/02/96	IDT	21K
12/02/96	Indigo	36K
12/02/96	Laser Graphics	30K
12/02/96	Laser Press	31K
12/02/96	Management Graphics	29K
12/02/96	Mannesmann Scangraphic	33K
12/02/96	Mitsubishi Electric	50K
12/02/96	Monotype	52K

Release date	Manufacturer	File size
12/02/96	NEC	81K
12/02/96	NeXT	21K
12/02/96	Oce Graphics	22K
12/02/96	Panasonic	37K
12/02/96	Pix ColorLink	23K
12/02/96	Qume	22K
12/02/96	Radius	36K
12/02/96	Ricoh	43K
12/02/96	Schlumberger	22K
12/02/96	Scitex	72K
12/02/96	Sun	24K
12/02/96	Texas Instruments	130K
12/02/96	Unisys	31K
12/02/96	Varityper	214K
12/02/96	VerTec Solutions	24K

INF Hardware Device Profiles for Printers

http://www.adobe.com/supportservice/custsupport/LIBRARY/pdrvwin.htm

Release date	Manufacturer	File size
06/05/96	3M, AGFA, and Apple	219K
06/05/96	Autologic to CalComp	194K
06/05/96	Canon to Crosfield	193K
06/05/96	Dainippon and Fuji	219K
06/05/96	DataProducts to EFI	219K
06/05/96	Epson to Indigo	219K
06/05/96	Laser Graphics to Oce Graphics	219K
06/05/96	Oki, Panasonic, and Pix	219K

Release date	Manufacturer	File size
06/05/96	PrePRESS Solutions	219K
06/05/96	QMS to Sun Microsystems	219K
06/05/96	Tektronix, Texas Instruments, and Unisys	293K
06/05/96	Varityper	208K
06/05/96	VerTec Solutions, XANTE, and Xerox	189K
02/07/96	Acrobat PDF Writer 2.1 (Win95)	7K

PostScript Printer Drivers for Macintosh System Version 8.x

http://www.adobe.com/supportservice/custsupport/LIBRARY/pdrvmac.htm

Release date	Manufacturer	Language	File size
03/09/98	AdobePS 8.5.2	Japanese	1680K
01/28/98	Virtual Printer Plug-in 8.5.1	U.S. English	157K
01/28/98	Watermark Plug-in 8.5	U.S. English	293K
01/12/98	AdobePS 8.5.1	Brazilian Portuguese	1674K
01/12/98	AdobePS 8.5.1	Chinese Simplified	1664K
01/12/98	AdobePS 8.5.1	Chinese Traditional	1664K
01/12/98	AdobePS 8.5.1	French	1676K
01/12/98	AdobePS 8.5.1	German	1677K
01/12/98	AdobePS 8.5.1	International English	1672K
01/12/98	AdobePS 8.5.1	Italian	1676K

Release date	Manufacturer	Language	File size
01/12/98	AdobePS 8.5.1	Korean	1669K
01/12/98	AdobePS 8.5.1	Spanish	1675K
12/24/97	AdobePS 8.5.1 U.S.	English	1665K
07/09/96	PSPrinter 8.3.1	U.S. English	1658K

Manufacturer PPD files for Macintosh Platforms

http://www.adobe.com/supportservice/custsupport/LIBRARY/pdrvmac.htm

Release date	Manufacturer	File size
09/08/97	Xerox	233K
05/30/97	Eastman Kodak	49K
05/30/97	Hewlett-Packard	347K
03/07/97	Dainippon	191K
03/07/97	EFI Fiery	138K
03/07/97	Fuji Film (LuxSetter)	12K
03/07/97	Linotype-Hell	141K
03/07/97	SofHa GmbH	41K
03/07/97	Sony	137K
03/07/97	XANTE Corporation	220K
02/24/97	Adobe	5K
02/01/97	AGFA	146K
02/01/97	Canon	159K
02/01/97	Crosfield Electronics	46K
02/01/97	Fargo Electronics	21K
02/01/97	GDT Softworks	34K
02/01/97	IBM	36K

Release date	Manufacturer	File size
02/01/97	Oki	121K
02/01/97	Pix Computer Systems (ColorLink)	6K
02/01/97	PrePRESS Solutions	222K
02/01/97	QMS	107K
02/01/97	Qume QumeScripTEN	5K
02/01/97	Seiko Epson	71K
02/01/97	Seiko Instruments	72K
02/01/97	Shinko	5K
02/01/97	Tektronix	361K
02/01/97	Unisys	17K
10/02/96	Birmy Graphics PowerRIP	18K
06/05/96	Apple LaserWriter	173K
06/05/96	AST PS-R4081	5K
06/05/96	Autologic	219K
06/05/96	Bull Italia PageMaster	13K
06/05/96	CalComp	29K
06/05/96	COLORBUS Software	58K
06/05/96	Colossal	33K
06/05/96	Compaq PageMarq	34K
06/05/96	Dainippon Printing Co. Ltd. (RIPStick)	7K
06/05/96	Dataproducts	90K
06/05/96	Digital	147K
06/05/96	DuPont	7K
06/05/96	Fujitsu	5K
06/05/96	Fuji Xerox	124K

Release date	Manufacturer	File size
06/05/96	Hitachi	39K
06/05/96	IDT	4K
06/05/96	Indigo	24K
06/05/96	Laser Graphics	16K
06/05/96	Laser Press	18K
06/05/96	Management Graphics	26K
06/05/96	Mannesmann Scangraphic	85K
06/05/96	Mitsubishi Electric	44K
06/05/96	Monotype	48K
06/05/96	NEC	87K
06/05/96	NeXT	3K
06/05/96	Oce Graphics	5K
06/05/96	Panasonic	27K
06/05/96	Radius	24K
06/05/96	Ricoh	26K
06/05/96	Schlumberger	5K
06/05/96	Scitex	76K
06/05/96	Sun Microsystems	7K
06/05/96	Texas Instruments	157K
06/05/96	Varityper	275K
06/05/96	VerTec Solutions	7K
04/04/95	3M	48K

Requesting Remote Output

In early versions of XPress, collecting all the files pertaining to your document file was a manual process. But, for complex documents this was often a time-consuming task, and the files required for remote output could easily be missed. QuarkXPress 4 now includes the *Collect for Output* command, which has the effect of locating and copying all the various elements needed for taking your file to a service bureau.

Before Collecting Your Files

Before you begin the process of collecting your files for output, there are a few things you may want to do before commencing the process. Since file size and complexity may be an issue when transferring your document files to the service bureau, you may streamline the document by eliminating unused resources such as stray items and stored attributes your file doesn't need in order to output. Performing the following steps may reduce your document file size, speed printing, or reduce the complexity of the document, but before you begin, be sure to make a copy of your document by choosing Save As (CTRL/CMD+ALT/OPTION+S).

- **Eliminate all unused items on your pasteboard** by selecting them and pressing DELETE/BACKSPACE. The Pasteboard is the area outside of your page borders on which items won't print.

TIP ⟶ *To find all pasteboard items, change the document view size to roughly 20 percent to view an entire spread and its pasteboard. Unlike with Thumbnails view, you can still use tools to select and delete items.*

- **Delete any unwanted or "spare" pages** in the document, including pages such as those found at the end of the document that aren't considered part of your finished document. It's also a good idea to delete unused master pages using the Document Layout palette.

- **Remove unused Style Sheets**   To do this, open your document and choose Edit | Style Sheets (SHIFT+F11), choose Style Sheets Not Used from the Show drop-down menu, select the unused style sheets that display in the list, and click Delete. To save your changes and exit the dialog box, click Save.

TIP   *When deleting style sheets, if an alert message appears asking you to replace one style sheet with another, don't panic. Although the style sheet isn't applied to text in the document, it may be specified as the* Based On *or* Next Style *for another style sheet. In this case, you may not want to delete the style sheet, especially if you expect to edit the document again later.*

- **Remove unused Colors**   Open your document and choose Edit | Colors (SHIFT+F12), choose Colors Not Used from the *Show* drop-down menu, select the unused colors that display in the list, and click Delete. Click Save to save your changes and close the dialog box.

- **Remove Dash & Stripe and Lists**   Perform the same operation as above by deleting unused dashes and stripes, together with unused Lists, in your document by choosing the appropriate command from the Edit menu. As with style sheets, you may get an alert when deleting a Dash & Stripe even though it's not actually in use. It might be specified as a Rule in an unused style sheet.

- **Remove any items that are completely obscured by other items**   Although this may be difficult—since you won't be able to see the items—doing so can significantly reduce your overall file size. Layered items can create complex documents and cause unnecessary printing delays. For example, you may have an automatic text box on each page that you never used. Or you may have a footer that's intentionally obscured by an advertisement that bleeds off the page.

- **Review the fonts used in the document**   Check Utilities | Usage | Fonts tab to make sure no unexpected fonts are listed. Occasionally an errant space is in a different font, and QuarkXPress 4 will require that font for output.

Using the Collect for Output Command

The Collect for Output command streamlines this process and copies your document file, all picture files (including TIFF and EPS), and a Report document in the form of an XPress tags (XTG) document to a specified folder or drive. The Report file may be used to review the fonts and XTensions used in your document, as well as details surrounding picture placements, paragraph and character style sheets, colors, and applied trapping methods.

TIP ──────▶ *Before you use the Collect for Output command, it may be wise to ensure that your system has a reasonable amount of free hard drive space available for copying these files, and to create a new separate folder for XPress to copy the files into. Copying the files into a folder that already contains other XPress documents may cause confusion as to which files belong to which output document.*

TIP ──────▶ *Before choosing Collect for Output, save your recent changes by choosing File | Save (CTRL/CMD+S)*

To use the Collect for Output command, follow these steps:

1. Choose File | Collect for Output. XPress immediately scans the picture files in your document to verify their location and modification dates. If any pictures are detected as missing or modified, the following dialog box will appear:

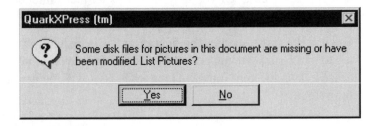

2. This dialog box enables you to review your picture status. Click *No* if you don't want to review the picture status. But, unless you're using OPI, in almost every case you'll want to check to ensure that no pictures have changed or are missing. If pictures are missing, they may not be included with the files collected for output.

3. Click *Yes* to review the status of pictures in your document. Doing this will cause the following dialog box to appear:

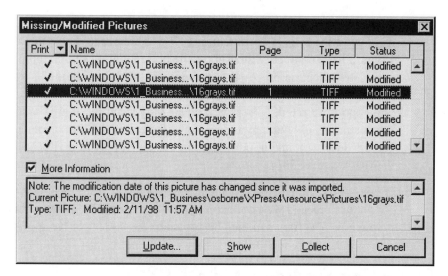

4. Use the *Update* command button to update any missing or modified pictures in your document. Click the *Show* button to locate and display selected pictures in your document. When completed, click the *Collect* button to enable XPress to proceed with the Collect to Output sequence and display the following dialog box:

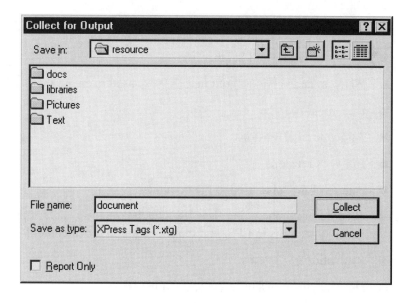

5. This dialog box enables you to set a location for the collected files. Enter a name for the Report document that XPress creates to describe your file. If you'd like create only the Report file before going through the complete collection process, click the Report Only option in this dialog box. Enter a name for your Report file in the Name field. With the Report Only option selected, XPress will create only a summary of your document, which you may then review. To review the file, open a new XPress document and import the report as an XPress Tags file, or open the file in a text editor.

6. If you have reviewed the file and are satisfied that your document is ready for output, proceed with collecting your files, by clicking OK in this dialog box. The files will then be copied to the folder you've specified.

Reviewing the Report File

When a report file is created, the following details about your document are summarized in an XPress Tags file:

- Document name

- Date of the file

- Total pages

- Document width and height

- Platform and version(s) of QuarkXPress used to create the file

- Document file size

- All required XTensions

- Active XTensions

- Names of the fonts used in the document

- Graphics used, including their file size, box/picture angle, skew, path name, type, fonts in EPS, and their location in the document

- Resolution of pictures

- H&J specifications used in the document

- Each color created and information to reproduce custom colors

- Trapping information including preference methods selected

- Color plates required for each page

The Report file is quite thorough—as is the entire Collect for Output command—in summarizing and copying all information related to your document output. However, this feature has taken heavy criticism from users because it doesn't collect the fonts used in your document.

Using the Output Template

As a convenience for sending a file for output, you may also use the Output template included with XPress for actually ordering your output. The purpose of this template is to enable you to print a hard copy and to hand-mark your output request. In most cases, you'll want to use the output request form provided by the service bureau, to get an idea of what you'll be charged for any services you request. But, where that isn't possible or where such a form doesn't exist, the output template may serve as a guide. Figure 16-1 shows the information included on the Output template. The template is named *Output.QXT* (Windows) or *Output Request Template* (Macintosh) and is located in your QuarkXPress program folder in the Documents folder.

In the case of the Output template, Macintosh users have an advantage over Windows users. Using the Macintosh version of XPress, you can import the Report file directly into the Output Request Template, selecting Include Style Sheets on import. The resulting document can then be included with the collected output files to be sent electronically to the service bureau.

Special-Needs Printing

It goes without saying that not all documents are created equal, and certain types of documents or circumstances may require special printing procedures. This section covers: cases where you may need to print oversized documents in tiles, a typical imagesetter printing session, and preparing a portable print file.

Printing Manually-tiled Pages

Tiled printing is often required when your document page size is significantly larger than the largest page size your printer is capable of generating, and when you ultimately need a proof printed to actual size. For example, if you're creating a

E L E C T R O N I C   O U T P U T   R E Q U E S T

CLIENT INFORMATION

Contact Person: _____

Company: _____

Address: _____

City, Province, Postal Code: _____

Office Phone: _____

Home Phone: _____

DELIVERY INFORMATION

__ Deliver   __ Hold For Pickup   __ Call When
Complete

Delivery Address: _____

City, Province, Postal Code: _____

TURNAROUND INFORMATION

__ Normal   __ Rush   __ Emergency

FONT INFORMATION

__ Adobe/Linotype __ Agfa   __ Bitstream

__ Monotype   __ _____   __ _____

COLOUR MANAGEMENT INFORMATION

__ Match colours according to assigned source profiles.
(Include necessary profiles with job.)

COPYRIGHT INFORMATION

All that appears on the enclosed medium (including, but not
limited to, floppy disk, modem transmission, removable media)
is unencumbered by copyrights. We, the customer, have full
rights to reproduce the supplied content.

Signature: _____

Date: _____

OUTPUT MEDIA (CHECK ALL THAT APPLY)

__ Film   __ RC Paper   __ Colour Proof

__ Laser Print   __ Colour Slides __

_____

__ Negative   -or-   __ Positive

__ Emulsion Down   -or-   __ Emulsion Up

OUTPUT SPECIFICATION

__ Output All Pages

__ Output The Following Specified Pages…

From: _____ To: _____

_____

CROP MARKS

__ Yes   __ No

RESOLUTION/DPI

__ 1200/1270   __ 2400/2540   __ 3000+

SCREEN RULING/LPI

__ 65   __ 85   __ 133

__ 150   __ 175   __ _____

COLOUR SEPARATION PLATES

__ Cyan   __ Magenta   __ Yellow   __ Black

__ _____   __ _____   __ _____   __

_____

COLOUR PROOF SPECIFICATION

__ Proof All Pages

__ Proof The Following Specified Pages…

From: _____ To: _____

_____

LASER PROOF PROVIDED WITH JOB?

__ Yes   __ No

OTHER INFORMATION

Type information about the job here.

FIGURE 16-1   Quark's supplied output order form

24-by-18-inch poster but your printer prints only to Legal-sized (8.5-by-14 inch) or Letter-sized (8.5-by-11 inch) pages, you'll need to tile print it.

XPress' Tiling option is found in the Print | Document tab dialog box and features two modes besides Off: Manual and Automatic. But the tiling exercise is actually a function of setting several options, including choosing the Printer, PPD, page size, and other options you may require. Choosing the Automatic tiling is perhaps the safest and easiest method to use, for it has the result of enabling XPress to determine the portion of your document page that appears on each tile and it centers the section on each page output page. Choosing *Automatic* also enables you to set Automatic Overlap and Absolute Overlap. For information on using these options, see *Setting Document Options* earlier in this chapter.

The automatic tiling method has little regard for the labor subsequently required in assembling the tiles, or for the amount of output material used in the process. Manual tiling—although it takes more thought—gives you full control over these two factors. Where the Automatic method enables you to use only a single page size and orientation, the manual method enables you to print each tile as you choose. In the example above, to print a 24-by-18 inch poster in tiles to a printer capable of printing Letter or Legal-sized pages, the Automatic method creates between 6 and 9 tiles, depending on how the output material is oriented (portrait or landscape). Using the Manual method, you may use only 5—4 legal plus 1 letter- sized tile as shown in Figure 16-2.

To begin your Manual tiling exercise, sketch out a tiling plan based on the size of your document page and your available output sizes. Keep in mind that since each tile will be printed individually, you may toggle the orientation of pages or even change page sizes. Figure 16-2 shows a typical planning sketch.

With this scenario in mind (a landscape-oriented 24-by-18-inch document page), follow these steps in the manual tiling of this page:

1. Open your document and display XPress' Rulers (CTRL/CMD+R). Double-click on the ruler origin (the point at which the vertical and horizontal ruler bars meet) to set them to exactly align with the upper-left corner of your page. Manual tiling has the effect of printing a tile of the area that falls below and to the right of the ruler origin.

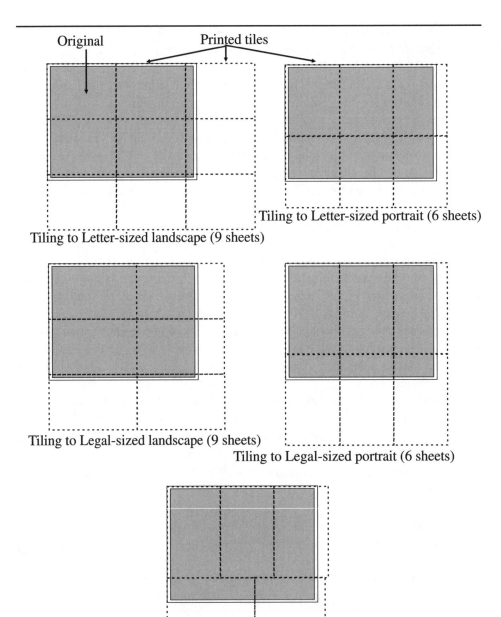

Manual tiling with 3 at Legal-sized portrait, 1 at Legal-sized landscape, and 1 at Letter-sized landscape (5 sheets)

FIGURE 16-2   Planning manually-tiled output

2. With your tiling sketch in hand, drag vertical and horizontal guidelines to the points at which your tiles will meet. In this case, set two vertical guidelines at **8.5** and **17** inches and a horizontal guideline at **14** inches as shown in the following illustration.

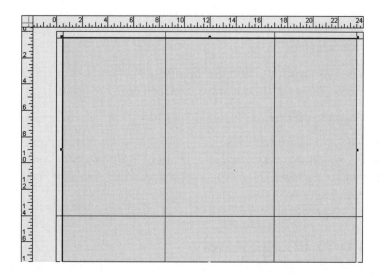

3. Choose File | Print (CTRL/CMD+P) to open the Print dialog box and select your printer, to select its corresponding PPD file from the Printer Description drop-down menu in the Setup tab, and to enter your page number and number of copies you'd like to print of your tiles.

4. Choose Legal as the Paper size, and Portrait as the orientation.

5. Click the Document tab and choose Manual from the Tiling drop-down menu. At this point, your first tile is in position, but you may want to choose other options from the Setup or Options tabs.

6. Click the Preview tab to verify that the position of the first tile is in the upper-left corner of your document page.

7. Click the Print button to simultaneously print the first tile and save your current settings, and then close the Print dialog box. The first tile prints.

8. Drag your ruler origin to print the next tile, in this case to a point at the upper edge and 8.5 inches to the right.

9. Choose File | Print (CTRL/CMD+P) and notice your settings are saved from the previous session. Click the Print button to print the second tile and close the dialog box. The second tile prints.

10. Repeat the above procedure to print the third tile, moving methodically left to right, top to bottom. When you reach the fourth tile, be sure to change the orientation of your output material to *Landscape* in the Document tab.

11. When you reach the fifth tile, be sure the page size is set to Letter and the orientation is set to Landscape, and then print the last tile.

12. Assemble the tiles as you would normally.

If your printer isn't capable of printing to the edges of your output pages, you'll need to make allowances when planning your tiling and subsequently positioning your ruler origin.

Printing to Imagesetters

Printing to an imagesetter can be a tricky matter, since most imagesetters are fed by rolls of film instead of precut sheets. The Setup tab features controls specifically for printing to imagesetters. As a practical exercise in printing to an imagesetter, follow these steps:

1. With your document open, choose File | Print to open the Print dialog box.

2. Choose the imagesetter you want to use from the Printer drop-down menu, and enter your page number(s) and copies to print.

3. Enter your specific printing specifications in the Document tab.

4. Click the Setup tab, and choose your imagesetter PPD from the Printer Description drop-down menu. Notice that the *Paper Size* is automatically set to *Custom* and the *Paper Height* is set to *Automatic*.

5. In the *Paper Width* field, enter the maximum image width your imagesetter supports.

6. In the Paper Height field, enter the width or height of your document (depending on whether you're printing in portrait or landscape orientation), and add enough space to accommodate Registration marks if this option is selected. An extra inch is usually enough.

7. Choose *Center* from the *Page Positioning* drop-down menu. This has the effect of centering your page vertically and horizontally within the image-able output material size you've specified. If you decide to choose any of the other options, you may want to specify a value in the *Paper Offset* field described in the next step.

8. For *Page Positioning* options other than *Center*, specify a Paper Offset value. The *Paper Offset* option enables you to control where the left edge of the document page begins from the left edge of the output material.

9. Enter a value in the *Page Gap* field. *Page Gap* enables you to control the space between printed pages when printing onto a continuous roll of output material. A gap of 6 points is often enough space to separate pages so that they can be cut apart.

10. Choose your orientation by selecting either *Portrait* (the default) or *Landscape*. If your document page is wider than the output material size you've chosen, Landscape is chosen automatically.

11. Click *Print* to print your pages to the imagesetter.

Creating a Print File

Print files are used as an alternative to printing to a connected printer. Normally when you print a file, a collection of data describing your document is sent directly to an online printer. By contrast, when a print file is created, the data used to print the document is temporarily stored in a data file, which may be stored indefinitely until downloaded to a printer. Print files enable you to create a complete and self-contained representation of your printed page that is usually transferred by some means to the destination, or "target," printer. Creating a print file—sometimes referred to as a PRN file—is not a complex operation and is very similar to printing to your desktop printer. As long as you have the correct drivers installed and a basic understanding of the way the target printer operates, creating the file is a relatively simple task.

Print files essentially contain text in the form of PostScript commands, which your target printer will interpret to reproduce the page. Having the correct printer driver installed on your system before you print to file is perhaps the only requirement—the rest of the setup may be done on your desktop. To install a printer driver, obtain the latest version from your hardware manufacturer or service bureau, and consult your system documentation for exact procedures on installing the driver.

With the correct driver is installed, create a print file from QuarkXPress for Windows by following these steps:

1. Open your QuarkXPress 4 file and choose File | Print. Select the correct printer in the Print dialog box and set your remaining parameters in the usual way or according to your target printer capabilities.

2. Under Windows 95, click the Start button and choose Setup | Printers to open the Printers window. Click once on the printer icon representing the printer you want to use to highlight it and choose File | Properties. The [*printer name*] Printer Properties dialog box opens.

3. Click the Details tab. This tab contains specific port communications options, including a drop-down menu with the label *Print to the Following Port*. Choose the option *FILE (creates a file on disk)* from the list and click OK to accept the changes.

4. The next time you print to this printer, it will create a print file; as the file is being created, the printer's driver will prompt you for a name and a location to save the file. Print files on the Windows platform are applied with the three-letter extension PRN.

NOTE *Once you've changed the printer to print to file, you'll need to change it back again to print normally. If you regularly create print files, you may want to create a specific printer just for this purpose.*

5. Name and save your print file in the Print to File dialog box.

6. With the correct driver is installed, create a print file from QuarkXPress 4 for Macintosh by following these steps:

1. From the Apple menu, select the Chooser. Locate and select the appropriate PostScript print driver.5.

2. Open your QuarkXPress 4 file and choose File | Print. Select the correct PPD from the Setup tab and set your remaining parameters in the usual way or according to your target printer capabilities.

3. Click the Printer button at the bottom of the dialog box. Click OK to bypass the alert that displays.

4. A dialog box displays for the printer selected in the Chooser. In the Destination area, click File instead of Printer. Click Print or Save (this is driver-specific).

5. A Save As dialog box will prompt you to name and specify a location for the file. In addition, depending on the selected driver, you'll need to specify several options such as format, data, PostScript level, and font inclusion. Click Save.

6. Click Print in the QuarkXPress Print dialog box.

After your computer has finished writing the file to disk, you may send it to the service bureau (or whoever will be printing it) in a number of different ways. Compressing the file before you send it is always a wise choice. A common Windows compression utility is PKZip, while StuffIt is popular on Macintosh platforms.

A Remote Output Checklist

When sending your document files and the files collected by the Collect for Output command to the service bureau, it may be wise, as a precaution, to review a checklist to ensure that you haven't left anything out. For example, you may want to include any fonts used in your document if your document uses fonts the service bureau may not already have. Or, if you deal regularly with the service bureau, you want to store commonly-used picture files for documents on their system. In any case, the following will serve as a checklist when purchasing output from a remote service.

- Provide all electronic files copied by the Collect for Output command.

- Include a printed hard-copy (or fax) summary of the document. For this you may want to simply print the Report created by the Collect for Output command.

■   Include a hard copy (or fax) of the pages you'd like to have output, so that the service bureau may cross-check against the output to ensure that the output is satisfactory. In the case of color separations, include a hard-copy proof of the separations along with a composite printout.

■   Include a hard copy (or fax) of your ordering information, by using either the Output template or an order form supplied by the service bureau.

■   In the case of requesting color output in film separation form or color matching, or both, include a color composite of the document pages to be printed. The color composite should be at least a reduction of the original document, clear enough to demonstrate reasonably accurate color and legible enough to identify fonts, font styles, and characters.

Conclusion

The printing functions in XPress 4 may be overwhelming at first, but if you take a step at a time, you'll eventually master them. The number of print engine features in XPress 4 has grown considerably, compared to past version features. In this chapter, you've explored many of the most common printing features in XPress. You've learned how to optimize and prepare your files for output, how imagesetters work, and how to print special-needs documents. While these topics have dealt specifically with printing for offset reproduction, there's still one area to explore in the next chapter, *Printing Color Separations*.

CHAPTER 17

Printing Digital Color Separations

If you work in a high-end desktop color publishing environment, if you want to prepare files for high-end offset reproduction using QuarkXPress, or if you're simply looking for better ways to work with digital color, look no further. This chapter will provide you with tips and techniques for preparing color picture files from other applications. And, you'll discover XPress 4's slightly hidden (and largely undocumented) features for creating color files to use within XPress as well as in other applications.

Printing Typical Digital Color

Under typical circumstances, importing a color picture file into XPress is a straightforward operation. You simply create a picture box and import the file using any of XPress' compatible picture formats, such as EPS or TIFF. What you see on your screen is merely a preview, while the data itself that *represents* the picture is linked to and stored externally, outside XPress. Wherever your XPress document file goes, the picture file is sure to follow.

Using typical picture color such as four-color process, the file you import must be prepared in a specific format—CMYK. While files will often originate in RGB color, this isn't compatible with printing your document to four-color process. All that's usually required for this is a simple color mode change from RGB to CMYK—often in TIFF because of its widespread compatibility. This may be done easily using most popular image-editing applications such as Photoshop or PhotoPaint. In fact, most color desktop applications used for specific purposes—such as graphic illustration or 3D modeling—feature export filters capable of creating TIFF files in CMYK color. So you may not need a dedicated image editor at all. When a CMYK picture is imported into XPress, the process colors required to reproduce it are already available. And when the file is printed, the process colors in the imported CMYK TIFF picture end up separating to the corresponding CMYK plates, along with the other color items in your document.

Not all digital separations are prepared in full color, though. Some may contain two or three colors—sometimes more—depending on the complexity of the picture and reproduction. If a digital photograph isn't process color, it has ultimately been edited and prepared using spot color. Two- and three-color digital photographs are referred to as *duotones* and *tri-tones*. These too are created using an image-editing application and saved to the PostScript EPS format. This is the most common format supporting multiple ink colors in a single file. When a duotone or tri-tone is imported into your document, the ink colors are imported as well.

Quark's DCS Publishing Technique

The scenario above describes importing a single file into your XPress document, eventually to be separated at the film separation stage. Although the resulting separations are often satisfactory, this may not be good use of the imagesetter's raster image processor (RIP) time. When an imagesetter's RIP separates a picture file into individual separations, it stops imaging the film while it performs the necessary separation calculations. For small picture files, this additional time may not even be noticed, but if your document includes multiple large-sized, high-resolution color picture files, the extra time can easily accumulate to hours—while the costs mount.

That's where Quark's DCS (desktop color separations) technique comes in. Introduced in Chapter 15, the DCS concept involves digitally separating the picture files into EPS format before they reach the imagesetter's RIP. Digitally separating a file may be done using a professional-style desktop image editor such as Photoshop or PHOTO-PAINT. It's a highly specific process for a specialized function, but the results are significant and the advantages can definitely be rewarding.

TIP *Using the DCS technique, digitally-separated picture files may be scanned, created, and stored at the service bureau location or wherever the document will be output.*

When the DCS technique is used, the digital separations for each color are substituted for a color "placeholder" preview on your document page. One separation file is required for each color plate being printed as described in Figure 1.

Separating Pictures Digitally for XPress

For any process or spot color picture to be eligible for this process, it must be in a condition ready to print. In short, all image editing changes such as image manipulation, filter effects, and image adjustments must be complete. Then, no matter which format the picture file is in, it may need to be converted to TIFF either in CMYK or spot color. Once the picture is in TIFF, the commands become fairly straightforward.

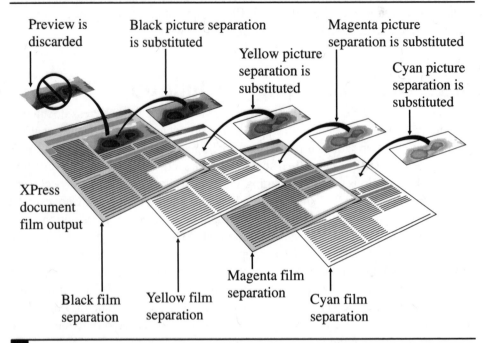

Preview is discarded

Black picture separation is substituted

Yellow picture separation is substituted

Magenta picture separation is substituted

Cyan picture separation is substituted

XPress document film output

Black film separation

Yellow film separation

Magenta film separation

Cyan film separation

FIGURE 17-1   Using digitally separated DCS files to print process color pictures

For example from Photoshop, follow these steps to create a digitally separated picture:

1. If you haven't already done so, complete your picture editing and save the file.

2. Convert color pictures destined for process color to CMYK (Image | Mode | CMYK Color).

3. Choose File | Save As, choose *TIFF* as the format, and provide a name. This file will serve as your *safe copy*. A safe copy is simply a second file which can be used if something unfortunate happens to your original.

4. Choose File | Save As, choose Photoshop *EPS* as the format, enter a name for the digitally-separated files, and click OK. An ancillary dialog box will appear with further EPS format options.

5. Choose *TIFF (8 bit/pixel)* from the Preview drop-down menu.

6. Choose *On (72 pixel/inch color)* or *On (72 pixel/inch color)* from the DCS drop-down menu for your preview preference.

7. Choose Binary from the Encoding drop-down menu. Click OK to create the separations.

The DCS file technique is also referred to as the "five file" technique since five files are created from a single color picture file, as shown next. One master EPS file is created for use as the picture preview for importing into your XPress document page; also created are four supporting EPS files representing cyan, magenta, yellow, and black. The preview file is the *only* file that may be used for importing into your XPress document. The resulting digitally-separated EPS files take the form of PostScript and do not contain any image to preview.

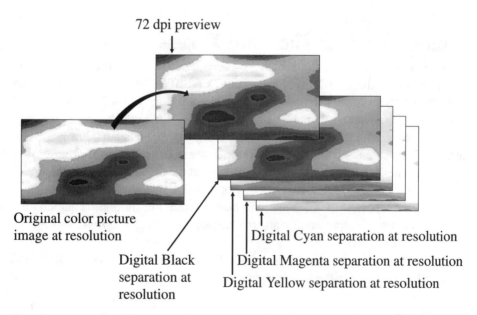

72 dpi preview

Original color picture image at resolution

Digital Black separation at resolution

Digital Cyan separation at resolution

Digital Magenta separation at resolution

Digital Yellow separation at resolution

Creating separation files from Photoshop will result in the following files:

Filename.EPS (the master preview file)
Filename.c (cyan EPS separation)
Filename.m (magenta EPS separation)

Filename.y (yellow EPS separation)
Filename.k (black EPS separation)

NOTE ➤ *The above example merely uses Photoshop as an example. Other image-editing applications may be used to create DCS files, although the specific commands may differ and the resulting EPS files may be named differently. For example, PHOTO-PAINT uses the file extensions 01, 02, 03, and 04 to represent the four process colors.*

TIP ➤ *When creating digital separations you may encounter two variations on DCS, which can be puzzling if you're not sure which is which. The DCS format is the original format developed by Quark and supports only process color, while DCS 2 supports both process and spot colors. Using DCS 2, additional PostScript separations are created for each additional spot color.*

Importing DCS Files into XPress

Once your digital separations have been created, the master preview EPS file may be imported into your XPress document as an EPS file, using options in the Get Picture (CTRL/CMD+E) dialog box. At this point only *you* will know it's a master preview representing a digital separation. Since the file is in EPS format, you won't be able to determine its color depth using the Usage | Pictures tab. However, when the Collect for Output command is used to prepare your document for transferring to a service bureau, XPress will automatically collect the required digital separations.

To verify this, use the Report Only option in the Collect for Output dialog box to create a report of the files that will be collected. For more information on using the Collect for Output command, see *Requesting Remote Output*, in *Chapter 16, Printing Your Pages*.

In the case of preparing a Photoshop DCS file, a typical report will identify the digital separations in the following way:

@picture items:
Driveletter:\folder\filename.eps
Cyan plate *filename*: *Driveletter:\folder\filename*.c
Magenta plate *filename*: *Driveletter:\folder\filename*.m
Yellow plate *filename*: *Driveletter:\folder\filename*.y
Black plate *filename*: *Driveletter:\folder\filename*.k

Screening Hazards for Duotones and Tri-tones

Regardless of whether or not you use the DCS technique for preparing your files, one hazard exists for users who may not be familiar with preparing duotones or tri-tones for printing. The hazard arises when printing the screens associated with the spot colors in a duotone. When a duotone is imported, the colors it contains are automatically appended to your XPress document colors list. And, when the document is printed to color separations, the duotone colors are automatically available for printing.

However, by default, all spot colors in a document are destined to print at the same angle as the black plate—which may not produce satisfactory results when your document is reproduced in offset printing. Since, by their nature, duotone inks print on top of each other, the screen angles for each color should be different in the same respect that process colors are angled differently. To improve the appearance of duotones—or indeed any multiple-color picture that includes spot colors—you may want to change the screening angles. One solution is to angle the screens to match those for process colors, but ultimately you'll need to contact your printing vendor for directions as to which angle to use for your duotone spot colors. Options for changing color screening angles may be accessed by choosing File | Print (CTRL/CMD+P) to open the Print dialog box, choosing Separations in the Document tab, and clicking the Output tab shown next.

Change screening angles for ink colors by choosing *Other* from the *Angle* drop-down

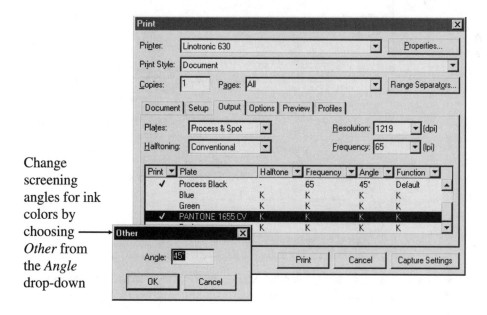

For more information on changing the screen angles for printed ink colors, see *Output Options* in *Chapter 16, Printing Your Pages*.

Preparing Digital Separations from XPress

If you've been following along in this chapter, you might already be aware that you may digitally separate picture files before they reach your XPress document using an image editor. But, you may also use XPress itself to digitally separate individual pages using the Save Page As EPS command (CTRL/CMD+ALT/OPTION+SHIFT+S). This command is useful for creating color-separated files of your XPress pages for use in XPress itself or in other applications.

The Save Page As EPS command (shown next) is capable of saving your page to either DCS or DCS 2. The format you choose will depend on whether your document contains simply process color, or spot and process combined.

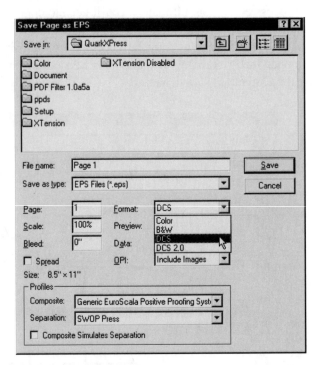

The files that XPress 4 creates while using the DCS option are similar to those created by other DCS-compatible applications, although with its own naming scheme for the digital separation files. In this case five files are created for process color (more if spot colors are involved), including the master preview EPS file and four process colors—cyan, magenta, yellow, and black. By default, the files are created in the same folder as your original document, and use the following naming scheme:

Filename.EPS (the master preview file)
*Filename*_C.EPS (cyan plate)
*Filename*_M.EPS (magenta plate)
*Filename*_Y.EPS (yellow plate)
*Filename*_K.EPS (black plate)

These files may then be reimported into XPress, or imported into other applications where they behave independently of XPress.

NOTE *The Save Page As EPS command doesn't include an option for embedding the fonts in an EPS file. If the file you're preparing is destined for use in another application, outputting at a service bureau, or use on a different user's system, be sure to include the necessary fonts with the file. If you fail to include the fonts, font substitution may occur when the EPS files are printed.*

For more information on using XPress' Save Page As EPS feature, see *Using Save Page as EPS* in *Chapter 18, Beyond QuarkXPress*.

Conclusion

This chapter has exposed you to a slightly higher-end focus on working in color with XPress. For basic color layout techniques, separating images for digital color may be slightly ahead of its time, but at some point you may find yourself considering using it. It's also not a technique you'll find very well documented, since it essentially falls somewhere between XPress and the other applications you may use.

When it comes to working with digital separations, QuarkXPress 4 *rules*. Although the practice of separating your picture into digital separations may not be a technique you use every day, it's comforting at least to know it's available to you should you need it.

CHAPTER 18

Beyond QuarkXpress

If you use XPress 4 in a relatively "closed" publishing environment, chances are that many of the issues covered in this chapter will be of little concern to you. But, in instances where you may be using XPress 4 to create layouts for special purposes, the topics discussed next will definitely interest you.

This chapter explores assorted issues that surround working with XPress in the real world. It explores cautions to note, and describes a few hazards to avoid, when you're moving files between platforms such as from Windows 95 to Macintosh platforms and vice versa. If you need to prepare your XPress layouts for use in *another* XPress layout or in another software application, you'll discover some interesting features for doing this. If you haven't already updated your version of XPress to 4.02, you'll also find a summary of all that's changed and the many problems that have been fixed.

Moving Files Between Versions and Platforms

As complex as it is, XPress 4 enables you to "port" files between platforms. *Porting* is the term used to describe moving a document file from one platform version to another. For example, you may port a QuarkXPress version 4.*x* file from Macintosh to version 4.*x* on the Windows platform and vice versa. You may also port files that have been created or saved in previous versions across platforms, whereby the file is ported and updated simultaneously.

When moving XPress document files between platforms in either direction, consider the following limitations of XPress' porting capabilities:

■ Perhaps the most significant anomaly you may encounter when porting files across platforms is the ever-present problem with font compatibility. Windows users often employ TrueType fonts while Macintosh users tend to avoid them. Contrariwise, Macintosh platform users often use Adobe Type 1 fonts, which may not be available on the Windows platform.

> *TIP*
>
> *When porting a file between platforms, be sure to also port all supporting files that may have been imported into your document file. In some cases, the file may need to be imported again to display or print properly. You don't need to create new picture boxes to accomplish this¤when the file is ported, XPress will retain all scaling, color, picture box specifications, and so on. Simply use the Pictures tab of the Utilities | Usage dialog box to reestablish the link between your XPress document and the imported file. If the picture doesn't display properly because it has a PICT preview, you may need to reopen the file in your image editor or illustration application and resave it with a TIFF preview, and then update the preview in your XPress document.*

- When moving files from Macintosh to Windows, you may also encounter problems associated with the use of ligatures. A ligature is a single character (such as X, Y, and Z) incorporating the shape of two joined characters and often used in certain instances by professional desktop publishers. In these cases, there simply is no equivalent on Windows. Character spacing and size may also differ slightly between platform versions of a certain font. If your document uses fonts where these differences exist, you may encounter text reflow problems due to the difference in spacing or size. Again, there's simply no workaround for this without closely examining text in the ported file against an original hard-copy proof of the document file being ported. Spacing and line breaks may then be corrected manually. If you're going to produce a variety of documents in a cross-platform environment, take the time to locate fonts that are available in the same version for both platforms, then test the fonts to see if they reflow.

- Certain picture file formats may not port between platforms, and even if successfully ported, some pictures may not appear or print as they should. For example, the popular PICT format on the Macintosh operating system may not properly port. Likewise, pictures prepared in Windows Metafile format on Windows versions of XPress may not display or print correctly when ported to the Macintosh. Instead, use the application used to create the picture to save the file in a Macintosh compatible format such as TIFF or EPS and reimport the picture after your document has been ported.

- Object linking and embedding (OLE) objects imported into Windows versions of XPress 4 won't be supported when the file is ported to a Macintosh version of XPress.

- Likewise, the Publish and Subscribe features unique to the Macintosh operating system aren't supported on Windows versions of XPress.

- Your XPress Preferences application file (located in your QuarkXPress folder) won't port successfully across platforms. The XPress Preferences file controls application preferences for your version of XPress and stores user settings, custom kerning and tracking information, hyphenation exceptions, other customized preferences, and so on. However, the preferences you've set in your document for such things as Style Sheets, Colors, H&Js, Lists, and dashes and stripes will open seamlessly on the platform to which your file is ported.

- When opening a ported XPress document on a different platform version, the file isn't automatically saved in the current platform state. To save the file, use the Save (CTRL/CMD+S) or Save As (CTRL/CMD+ALT/OPTION+S) commands. After being saved, the file becomes a current-platform version.

- Although more than one user on a network may open Book files, all users must be working on the same platform. Book files can't be opened on two different platforms at the same time.

- QuarkXPress 4 Library files and Auxiliary Dictionaries can't be ported across platforms.

If you *are* faced with the challenge of porting files, XPress may display a series of alert dialog boxes for you as the files are opened, depending on the contents of the document and how it's been prepared. For example, while opening a file that originated as a Macintosh XPress document, the first dialog box you may encounter is the ligatures warning shown next.

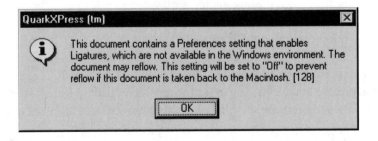

As noted earlier, ligature characters available to certain fonts on the Macintosh platform aren't supported by Windows. Hence, this warning simply informs you of this fact. When you see this warning, you may want to check your ported document against hard copies of the original document file to determine whether text reflow has occurred (and whether incorrect characters have been substituted for ligatures). Also note that if you subsequently reopen the document in the Macintosh version of XPress 4, the ligatures feature remains off. If you want ligatures, you'll need to turn the feature back on by checking Ligatures in the Character tab of the Document Preferences dialog box.

The next dialog box to appear during the porting process is likely to be the Preferences alert. A variety of preferences saved with the original document may not be compatible with the alternate platform version you're currently using to open the file. In the case of preference warnings, clicking the Keep Document Settings button is often the safest route to follow. The Preferences warning also displays details regarding the incompatibility of the preferences compared to the document and your program preference file, as shown next.

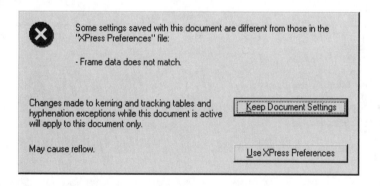

Following this Preferences warning, you'll likely encounter the most serious warning of all, and one that you often have little recourse to: the fonts warning dialog box. As mentioned earlier, unless the system being ported to has the same fonts installed, this warning will appear. If fonts aren't a concern to you, you may click the *Continue* button as shown next and your fonts will be substituted with your system's default font. Unfortunately, this usually results in overflowing text boxes, making it difficult—if not impossible—to read the text in the document.

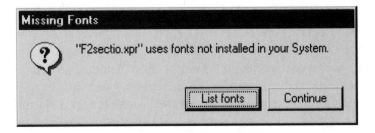

However, most electronic layout artists will likely find themselves feeling a little uneasy about seeing this message—and rightly so. Font substitution problems can often require hours of corrective work. To avoid that, if you have access to the missing fonts, close the file without saving any changes and install the font(s) on your system. To set substitutes for the missing font(s), click the List Fonts button to view a list and set the substitutes. For each missing font in the list, highlight the font and click Replace to set a replacement as shown in the following dialog box.

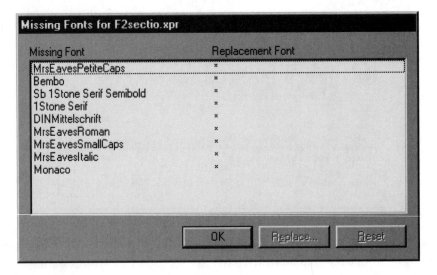

If you choose to open the document without setting replacements, you may still view the missing fonts by using the Usage command Fonts tab, which should perhaps be the first dialog box you visit after opening any ported file. Missing fonts are indicated in the list by curly braces—such as { and }—while the weight and style are indicated inside less than/greater than symbols, < and >. Clicking the More Information option will expand the dialog box to reveal further comments regarding the font. To open the Usage dialog box shown next, choose Utilities | Usage.

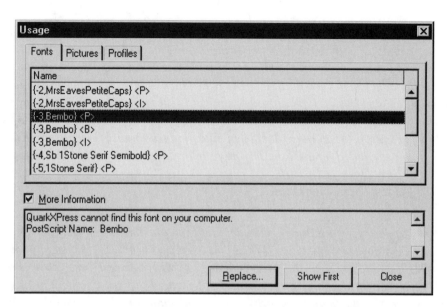

The Usage dialog box also enables you to view a list of the missing or modified pictures that the document requires in order to print properly. Clicking the Pictures tab of the Usage command will list all of the pictures in the document (as shown next) and will enable you to reimport them, a step that's always necessary to reestablish a picture's location and linking information.

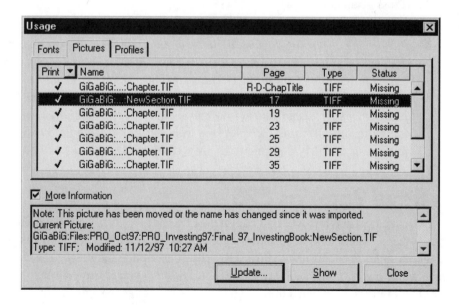

TIP *When porting XPress 4 document files from Macintosh to Windows program versions, adding the three-letter file extension .**QXD** (including the period) will make opening the file less problematic. Adding this extension will enable you to view the document in the Open dialog box, since the Windows default Files of Type drop-down menu is set to automatically display files with this extension. For QuarkXPress template documents, add the .**QXT** extension. Macintosh document files don't normally use file extensions, unless added by the user. For more information on opening files using the File | Open (CTRL/CMD+O) command, see* Opening Files *in Chapter 1, XPress Train Quickstart.*

NOTE *Updating your XPress document files from previous versions of XPress can be a complex operation. When you open a version 3.3 document in 4, the first time you save, the Save As dialog box will open and force you to choose a new format—3.3 or 4. Quark implemented this as a safeguard against users' accidentally converting all their documents to version 4 files. You'll need to rename the document and save it over your existing document file, to update it for version 4. To save your XPress 4 document as an XPress 3.3 document, use the Save As (CTRL/CMD+ALT/OPTION+S) command and choose 3.3 from the* Version *drop-down menu. For more information on using the Save As command, see* Using Save As Options *in Chapter 1, XPress Train Quickstart.*

TIP *When saving or porting document files to previous versions for use on older Windows 3.x platform versions of QuarkXPress, limit your file's name to the 8-and-3 file-naming convention (8 characters maximum for the name, 3 for the extension). The Windows 3.x operating system doesn't support long filenames or special characters in document names (such as spaces), unlike Macintosh and Windows 95 platform versions. For example, change a filename such as* **My document 1** *to* **my_doc1.QXD**.

Using Save Page as EPS

If you've ever searched for an export command of some kind in XPress, it was likely in vain—there is none. Instead, use the Save Page as EPS command, which lets you save whole pages in encapsulated PostScript page description language. The ability to save whole pages or page spreads as EPS files enables you to use your layouts in other QuarkXPress documents or to save them for use in other applications.

PostScript pages are much more versatile than bitmap images, since they may be infinitely resized and printed at the maximum resolution of the printer in use. When pages are saved, all of the information they contain—including object fills, Bezier lines, and so on—are self-contained in the EPS file, so that they may be transferred through networks, ported across platforms, or archived without the need for QuarkXPress to be loaded on a host system in order to be used. If the page contains high-resolution picture files linked to the document, the data representing these images may be included in the EPS file using OPI options.

CAUTION ➤ *The Save Page as EPS command doesn't embed fonts into the EPS file when it's created. For fonts used in the document being saved as EPS to print correctly, the same fonts must either be available on the host system being used to print the document or be resident in memory on the printer in use. Therefore, when using EPS files in a cross-platform environment, you may want to carefully test the fonts.*

18

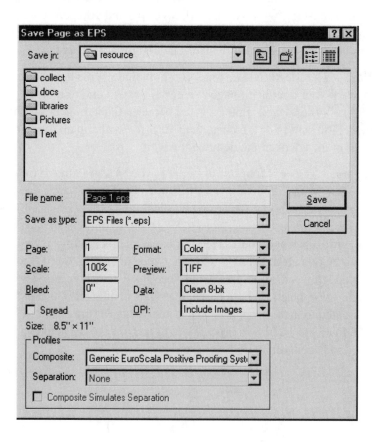

Options in the Save Page as EPS dialog box, shown on the previous page, are defined as follows:

- **Filename**   Enter a filename for XPress to assign to the new EPS file. By default, the filename is set to "Page X," where X represents the page number currently being displayed on your screen.

- **Save as Type**   This drop-down menu is specific to the Windows version of XPress 4 and is set to EPS by default, since this is the only option that exists.

- **Page**   In this field, enter the document page number you want to save in the EPS format. You may also enter an absolute page number—which corresponds to the page's actual sequence in your document—by entering a "+" (plus) before the number.

- **Scale**   Enter a scaling for the document page being saved to EPS. Scaling must fall within a range between 10 and 100 percent. In other words, the term *scale* is slightly misleading since you may only *reduce* the document page's overall size. The default is 100 percent.

- **Bleed**   The Bleed field enables you to include items that overlap the edges of your document page to a certain extent and to include them in your EPS file as well. Enter a value between 0 and 6 inches. While left at the default setting of 0 inches, your EPS file will clip all overlapping items at the edges of the document page.

- **Format**   The next four options enable you to set treatment of header, color, and data formats for your EPS file. The Format drop-down menu enables you to choose *Color, B&W* (black-and-white/grayscale), *DCS* (desktop color separations), or *DCS 2.0*. These options are vastly different in their formats and you'll need to choose them carefully for your EPS file to be prepared correctly. Choose *Color* to enable the EPS to be created with a color preview, or choose *B&W* to set the preview to a single color, black. In both cases, the items contained in the EPS will also be created to include color or black-and-white (or grayscale). Choose *DCS* to create an EPS in process color, or *DCS 2.0* to include process color and spot colors.

- **Preview**   The *Preview* drop-down menu enables you to include a preview header in the EPS file in *TIFF* format or *None*. Choosing *TIFF* (the default) sets the preview in tagged image file format (TIFF), and choosing *None* leaves the EPS without any preview at all. Omitting the preview is sometimes useful for reducing the resulting EPS file size.

- **Data**   Three choice are available from this drop-down menu: *ASCII*, *Binary*, and *Clean 8-bit*. The capability to choose the Data type that describes an EPS file gives you a certain degree of flexibility when printing a document containing the EPS file through a print spooler as well as to a wider range of printer types. *Clean 8-bit* (the default) is similar to *Binary*, but omits additional data strings that *Binary* adds to communicate with parallel port printers. The *ASCII* format is a more versatile format, compatible with a wide range of printers and print spooling software.

TIP *If you're saving an EPS file for use on QuarkXPress Windows versions, choose either Clean 8-bit or ASCII rather than Binary as the Data format. Using the binary EPS is problematic if you try to print it through a parallel port (which only Windows-based PCs have). It may also be problematic if you print a document to a Windows-based print spooler that doesn't support binary-format EPS files. Even if a given spooler* does *support binary EPS files, printing may be time-consuming when printing binary data. If you're printing from a Windows platform version of XPress using a parallel port, choose* ASCII *or* Clean 8-Bit. *Also, use* ASCII *or* Clean 8-bit *if you're employing a Windows-based print spooler, even if you're using nothing but Macintosh versions of XPress. In fact, Clean 8-bit is superior to using ASCII since it's designed to result in a smaller, faster print download to most printers.*

- **OPI**   This option enables you to determine whether picture information is included in the EPS file. OPI (open prepress interface) options enable you to print using only the preview contained in the EPS file or to substitute this with the original data file representing the picture. Before printing, the high-resolution images are substituted for lower-resolution placeholders. Choose *Include Images* (the default) to include all TIFF and EPS picture information in the EPS file being created. Choose *Omit TIFF* to leave out all TIFF picture data and insert OPI comments to link to these files externally when the EPS file is printed. Or, choose *Omit TIFF &*

18

EPS to leave out both TIFF and EPS data and insert OPI comments to link to these files externally. When choosing either of the latter two options, the omitted picture files will need to accompany the EPS file to print correctly.

■   **Spread**   Choose this option to create an EPS file of the complete spread. While selected, the *Spread* option will include whichever page is facing the page entered in the Page field.

■   **Profiles**   The Save Page as EPS command was revamped with the release of the XPress 4.02 Updater to include three new color profile options for choosing the *Composite Printer* and *Separation Printer* profile information to be inserted as comments in the EPS file. You may also choose the Composite Simulates Separation option. Profile information will apply only if the EPS file you're creating is destined to be imported into a QuarkXPress document supporting Quark's color management system, and profile information will only become useful if the destination document is actively using CMS. For more information on using Quark's CMS, see *Chapter 15, Using Quark's Color Management System.*

Quark's New PDF Export Filter

Shortly after the release of XPress 4, a new PDF export filter Xtension was released to enable QuarkXPress users to generate portable document files (PDFs) of their pages. The PDF filter has also been integrated into the release of the XPress 4.02 Updater. At the time of this writing, the feature was an "alpha" release, meaning that for the most part it was still mostly a gleam in the developers' eyes. For what it's worth, alpha software preempts "beta" software, which is more widely released for testing to a select group of users. And, following beta, the final product is shipped. The disclaimer here is that what you're about to explore is the alpha version of the filter, meaning that options or interface elements could easily change (and most likely *will* change).

If you're still using the original release of XPress 4, and would like simply to download the PDF filter, you may do so by visiting Quark's Web site at URL **http:\www.quark.com**. The last-known locations for Macintosh and Windows versions of the PDF filter are as follows:

Mac version, at URL:
ftp://ftp.quark.com/xpress/xtensions/mac/quark_xt40/PDFFilter10a5a.Hqx

Windows version, at URL:
ftp://ftp.quark.com/xpress/xtensions/win/quark_xt40/PDF_Filter10a5a.exe

The PDF Export Filter for QuarkXPress enables you to save one or more pages from your XPress 4 document as a PDF file. Adobe's PDF format has become popular for many applications because the files may be viewed with the Adobe Acrobat viewer, distributed free of charge. PDFs display and print independently of the host program used to create the document and need no supporting files such as pictures or fonts. The filter saves the pages in PostScript format and employs the use of Adobe Acrobat Distiller software to create the file. To successfully create a PDF file using the export filter, you must have at least the following:

- QuarkXPress 4.02

- Adobe Acrobat Distiller PPD (PostScript Printer Description)

- Adobe Acrobat Distiller 3 software

Once you've obtained the filter, you may install it by following these steps:

1. First, uncompress the downloaded file by double-clicking on it.

2. Quit XPress (CTRL/CMD+Q).

3. Place the PDF Export Filter in your QuarkXPress/XTension folder.

4. Launch QuarkXPress to access the features of the PDF Export Filter.

NOTE *You must have the Adobe Acrobat Distiller PPD in the list of PPDs shown in the PPD Manager. To make the PPD available, use the PPD Manager opened by choosing Utilities | PPD Manager.*

To successfully create a PDF using QuarkXPress Windows versions, you must set up a PostScript printer to print to a file, as opposed to an actual connected printer. To do this, follow these steps:

1. Click the Start button and choose Setup | Printers to open the Printers window. Click once on the printer icon representing the printer you want to use, highlight it, and choose File | Properties. The [*printer name*] Printer Properties dialog box opens.

2. Click the Details tab. The Details tab contains specific port communications options, including a drop-down menu with the label *Print to the Following Port*. Choose the option *FILE (creates a file on disk)* from the list and click OK to accept the changes.

Once the filter is successfully installed and you have opened both XPress and the document you want to export pages from, follow these steps to create a PDF:

1. Choose Utilities | Save as PDF to open the Save as PDF dialog box shown next.

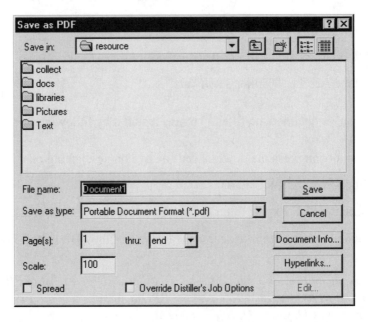

2. Enter a name for your new PDF. By default your XPress filename is used.

3. Enter the starting page number in the Page(s) field. By default, this is set to your currently-displayed page.

4. Enter the last page in the series of pages you want to create the PDF for, or choose End from the drop-down menu.

NOTE ➔ *You may not create a PDF of noncontinuous pages, as you're able to do in XPress' Print dialog box. Instead, the pages you use must be in sequence.*

5. Enter a reduction or enlargement for your PDF pages. All pages created will be applied with the scaling you enter here. Pages may be scaled within a range of between 0.1 and 800 percent.

6. To export one spread per page, click the *Spread* option.

7. If you want, click the Document Info button to open the Document Info dialog box shown next, to include Title, Subject, Author, or Keywords with the PDF.

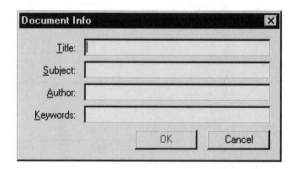

8. Click the Hyperlinks button to open the Hyperlinks dialog box and choose from *Maintain List Links, Create Bookmarks from Lists*, or *Maintain Index Links* (discussed later in this section).

You also change Adobe Acrobat Distiller's compression settings, by clicking the *Override Distiller's Job Options* option, which enables the adjacent *Edit* button. Click the *Edit* button to open the *Compression* tab of the PDF Filter Preferences dialog box shown next.

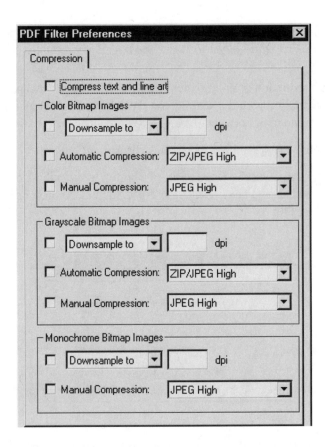

9. Once your options have been chosen, click OK to create the PDF and close the Save as PDF dialog box. Your PDF is created. To view the PDF, open it in Adobe Acrobat Reader to ensure that the file has been created according to your needs.

Setting PDF Hyperlink Options

Following the steps above, you'll encounter a series of Hyperlink options, which at the time of this writing were still in development. The term *hyperlink* describes the action of clicking on an item to navigate to a designated link location. According to Quark, these options are intended to have the following effects (once finalized):

■ **Maintain List Links** When this option is selected, the resulting PDF will include hyperlinks to pages that relate to each list item in your document: for example, a hyperlinked table of contents. For information on creating and working with lists in XPress, see *Working with Lists* in *Chapter 10, Laying Out Documents*.

- **Create Bookmarks from Lists**   When this option is selected, the resulting PDF will automatically include bookmarks to the pages to which each of the List items refers. Bookmarks is a built-in feature of Adobe Acrobat Reader 3.

- **Maintain Index Links**   When this option is selected, the resulting PDF will include hyperlinks to pages from an index of their contents. This feature operates in a similar way to XPress' Index palette feature. For more information on using the Index palette and creating indexes, see *Working with Indexes* in *Chapter 10, Laying Out Documents*.

TIP ➤ *The items in a list or index don't need to be in the same document. For example, you may have created a TOC or index for an entire book, in which case the PDF will find only list and index items in the same document.*

PDF Filter Preferences

Following the steps above, you may also want to customize the compression of your new PDF differently from the compression options set in the Adobe Acrobat Distiller software. Compression is always a big issue when it comes to portable files, since the smaller the files are, the more portable they become. Ultimately, you'll want to choose the options that offer the most compression without sacrificing the display or printing qualities of your new PDF.

The Compression tab of the PDF Filter Preferences dialog box enables you to select from a variety of compression methods for your PDF file. Choosing Compress Text and Line art enables you to reduce the information associated with displaying fonts, lines, and shapes created in your document. You may also set compression options independently for *Color*, *Grayscale*, and *Monochrome* bitmap images, roughly defined as follows:

- **Color and Grayscale Bitmap Images**   Both color and grayscale bitmap images offer identical options when it comes to choosing their compression methods. You may reduce the resolution of the bitmaps' downsampling or subsampling options and set automatic or manual image compression algorithms used in their compression, including five quality levels for each (ranging from high- to low-quality display). The higher the compression quality, the larger the file size.

■ **Monochrome Bitmap Images**   When choosing monochrome bitmap compression, the options are identical, except you have no automatic compression algorithm choice.

To view or change the Distiller or Compression options controlling your PDF Filter Preferences before you initiate use of the PDF Export Filter, choose Edit | Preferences | PDF filter to open the PDF Filter Preferences dialog box. This dialog box features the compression options described above, and Distiller preferences may be chosen from options shown next.

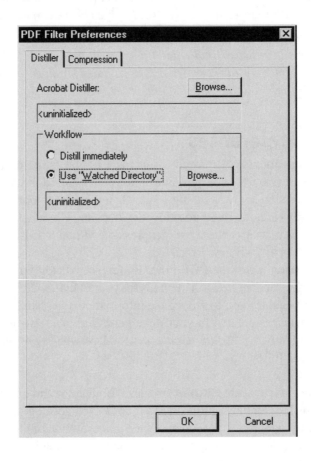

Options in the Distiller tab enable you to connect the PDF filter to your Adobe Acrobat Distiller software. Click the Browse button adjacent to the Acrobat Distiller heading to locate the folder containing your PDF distiller software.

Under the heading Workflow, choose either to distill the file immediately, or to postpone distillation of individual files by saving them (in PostScript format) to a folder that's periodically monitored by the Adobe Distiller. This folder is referred to as the "Watched" Folder. To define the Watched folder, click the *Use Watched Directory* option and click the Browse button to locate the folder. At the time of this writing, the Watched Folder preference had not been implemented. Instead, the Distill Immediately option is perpetually active no matter which option is chosen.

18

Updating to QuarkXPress 4.02

If you haven't already done so, you may want to get your hands on a copy of the QuarkXPress 4.02 Updater, which updates your XPress program to the most recent version and in turn fixes problems you may have encountered already or may encounter in the future. The "fixes" are extensive, and in some cases the Updater actually adds additional options to dialog boxes. This section details the procedures for installing the Updater and lists features or problems dealing with specific performance issues of XPress 4. The majority of this information comes directly from Quark, in an admirable customer-service effort.

Before You Update

Before updating your installed version of XPress, consider taking the following steps to ensure a successful installation:

- Make a copy of the QuarkXPress folder currently on your system. This will make sure that you have a working copy if the update is unsuccessful.

- Disable any virus protection software you may have running before launching the Updater. If you're concerned about viruses, it may be wise to run a virus check on the downloaded file. Following this, disable your virus detection before updating.

- Disable any screen savers you may have running, using your system tools.

Installing the Update

The Updater affects release version and versions 4.01 of QuarkXPress and updates them to version 4.02. To perform the update, follow these steps:

1. Decompress the downloaded Updater file by double-clicking on it. By default, the Updater creates a temporary folder on your system. Macintosh users should disable any nonessential extensions and control panels.

2. Locate the folder that has been created and double-click the Updater program. The updater will automatically locate the folder containing QuarkXPress 4. Macintosh users will need to select the version of QuarkXPress that's installed by choosing FAT, 68K, or PPC (that is, PowerPC).

3. Double-click the Updater file.

4. Locate the copy of the application you want to update.

5. Click *Update* to update your copy of XPress. After the updating procedure is complete, click the *OK* button to close the Updater. You may discard the folder and temporary files created when the Updater was uncompressed. It's also wise to store the Updater in a safe place, should you ever need to uninstall and subsequently reinstall and update your original version of QuarkXPress 4.

6. Launch XPress and notice the version number that appears in the splash screen as the program is loading, to verify that the update has actually taken place. Macintosh users should also take steps to reinitiate any extensions or control panels that were disabled.

7. Reactivate your virus protection software.

What the 4.02 Updater Does

After running the Updater, you may notice that some QuarkXPress XTensions have been replaced. If you're using the Quark CMS or Index XTensions in the XTension folder when you run the Updater, the Updater replaces them with newer version(s). Disabled XTensions are automatically replaced, and any disabled/enabled Xtensions are copied to their respective folders.

Updater Fixes for Save Commands

- You may now safely save a document in 3.3 format over a network to a Novell server *(Windows 95/NT versions only)*.

- When you save a document in 3.3 format, the application now correctly stores the *Last Modified* date for imported pictures *(Windows 95/NT versions only)*.

- Auto backup no longer produces erroneous *Duplicate filename* messages *(Windows 95/NT versions only)*.

- The message *File not found* is no longer displayed if you create a document in version 4, save it in 3.3 format, reopen it in version 4, and then try to resave it in version 4 format *(Windows 95/NT versions only)*.

- You can now use *Save As* to save a document over an existing file on a network volume *(Windows 95/NT versions only)*.

- A problem was fixed that caused version 3.*x* documents to take up the same amount of disk space even after much of their content had been removed. This fix can't, however, repair documents that have already been opened and saved in 4.0*x* *(Macintosh versions only)*.

Updater Fixes for Printing-Related Problems

- Program crash that occurs if you click Print in the Print dialog box while the Pages field is empty.

- Incorrect printing of hairlines.

- A problem occurring when choosing landscape orientation in the New Document dialog box and finding that it doesn't properly set the page orientation to landscape in the Setup tab of the Print dialog box.

- A PostScript error problem while printing a document with a LaserWriter version 7.*x* selected as the printer and a PostScript Printer Description (PPD) that uses a page size of *Custom*.

- Frame-trapping problems.

- Problems associated with drag-and-drop printing *(Windows 95/NT versions only)*.

- Problems when separating Canvas 3.5.1 Desktop Color Separation (DCS) files *(Macintosh versions only)*.

- Printing problems that occur when the *Paper Height* drop-down menu (File | Print | Setup tab) is set to *Automatic (Macintosh versions only)*.

- A printing problem that clips documents to 11.0 inches while the Generic Imagesetter printer type is selected *(Macintosh versions only)*.

- In versions 4.0 and 4.01 the only way to set a bleed was to enter a value in the *Bleed* field (File | Print | Document tab). Some users found this problematic because entering a value in the *Bleed* field would also outset the crop marks by that value (plus the default crop mark outset of 6 points). For this reason, the application has been updated as follows: A new feature, *Offset*, has been added to the *Document* tab of the *Print* dialog box (File | Print). To specify the distance between the edge of the page and the beginning of the crop marks, enter a value in the *Offset* field. The value in the *Offset* field is honored exactly, regardless of the value in the *Bleed* field.

    If a value is entered in the *Bleed* field (File | Print | Document tab), any element that's within the bleed area will print, even if doesn't touch the page.

- Ovals that display solid white or black within a Bezier object that has a wide frame will now print to a PostScript printer.

- The Arial font with *Bold* and *Underline* applied no longer prints as a black bar to the Lexmark Optra S and SC printers using the Lexmark 1.01 PS driver *(Windows 95/NT versions only)*.

- Text in certain rotated polygon text boxes of QuarkXPress 3.3*x* Macintosh platform version documents will now output properly from Windows 95/NT.

Updater Fixes for Text and Text Boxes

- A problem associated with text-display changes in linked text boxes while runaround and background properties are set to *None*.

- A clipboard-related problem associated with preserving the association between a block of text and its character style sheet whenever the text is copied and pasted.

- A problem associated with application crashes while trying to resize grouped text boxes.

- A problem associated with application crashes while trying to type text into a text box with the background set to *None* and a monitor setting of 1-bit (black-and-white) mode *(Macintosh platform versions only)*.

- Polygon-shaped text boxes will no longer display text outside the text box.

- Placing a right-aligned tab in a text box where the last character contains positive tracking or kerning will no longer cause the text to flow to the next line.

- Changing the *Endcap* style on a line in a version 3.*x* document will no longer cause text to run around the line incorrectly.

- Placing a right-indent tab (Windows: ALT+SHIFT+TAB, Macintosh: OPTION+TAB) in a text box where an italic font is being used will no longer cause the text to flow to the next line.

Updater Fixes for Pictures and Picture Boxes

- If you update picture files of different types in the *Pictures* tab of the *Usage* dialog box (*Utilities* menu), it will display the correct file type and will no longer revert to the file type of the first picture updated.

- Missing pictures located in a single folder will now update when a graphic from another folder is encountered in the *Usage* list (Utilities menu).

- Opening a QuarkXPress 3.*x* document containing an EPS file in a picture box with a background color of *None* will no longer download the *Non-White Areas* clipping path to the printer unless the path is modified.

- An Application Error no longer occurs when saving a page as an EPS with a filename that's longer than 100 characters *(Windows 95/NT versions only)*.

- When you choose File | Save Page as EPS with no printers installed, an "Unexpected end-of-file encountered" error will no longer occur when reimporting that EPS *(Windows 95/NT versions only)*.

- An Application Error no longer occurs when exporting a Print Style with a filename that's longer than 100 characters *(Windows 95/NT versions only)*.

- The application no longer displays Error Message [10000] when attempting to open a version 3.*x* document containing a complex picture.

- If a version 3.*x* document contains a vector EPS in a picture box with a background of *None*, the picture is given *Item* clipping when the document's opened in version 4.02.

- If you import a picture into a box that's the same size as that picture, fit to box (CTRL/CMD+SHIFT+F) now scales the picture to 100 percent.

- If you're updating pictures with a status of *Missing*, and the folder containing the first picture to be updated also contains other pictures that need updating, the application properly recognizes the other missing pictures.

- The application no longer crashes when you open the *Picture* tab of the *Usage* dialog box for a document containing more than 1,100 pictures.

- You can now move a polygon box using the arrow keys even after you delete a point from the box.

- The application no longer crashes when a *Merge* is performed on a group of objects that includes a line or text on a path with a runaround setting of *Manual (Windows 95/NT versions only)*.

- The application no longer crashes when you drag a picture from Microsoft Word to a document and then drag that picture to the desktop *(Windows 95/NT versions only)*.

- A white gap no longer prints between a frame whose width ends in 0.5 and a TIFF to which a *Non-White Areas* clipping path has been applied *(Macintosh versions only)*.

Updater Fixes for Bezier Items

- When Bezier boxes are created with fewer than three line segments, the boxes no longer fill with the frame color if the frame width is greater than 0 pt.

- A Bezier text box created with one corner point and one smooth or symmetrical point will no longer overflow. Also, it will now accept text if the box is converted to a text box from a picture box.

- The application will no longer crash when multiple Bezier point types are selected in the *Measurements* palette and the F9 key is used to close the palette *(Macintosh versions only)*.

- You can now split outside paths of a multiple-contour box containing a picture and move one of the elements *(Macintosh versions only)*.

Other Updater Fixes

- Switching the AppleTalk connection from *Printer Port* to *Ethernet* no longer results in a *Can't access network* alert message.

- A White box in front of a line of hairline width no longer defaults to *Overprint*; it now defaults to *Knockout*.

- Trapping settings applied to spot colors (*Edit | Colors | Edit Trap*) are now properly preserved for *Indeterminate* backgrounds.

- If certain XTensions software adds a tool to the Tool palette, that tool won't disappear if you close and reopen the palette.

- Vertical lines now correctly snap to guides.

- The application now properly handles paragraph style sheets when you import RTF files *(Windows 95/NT versions only)*.

- Box *Item Runaround* outset of zero is now properly preserved for square boxes when a document is saved in version 3.3 format *(Windows 95/NT versions only)*.

Conclusion

This chapter has discussed critical cross-platform issues when using both Macintosh and Windows platform versions of XPress. In it you have also explored saving your files in dependent and independent file formats, should the need ever arise—and it *will* someday. You've also seen a detailed summary of all that's changed for the QuarkXPress 4.02 update.

You've also reached the end of the last chapter in *Fundamental QuarkXPress 4*. Be sure to consult the appendices that follow this chapter, as they detail and summarize all the known keyboard shortcuts in XPress 4 and define the strange and unfamiliar terms used in this book.

PART V

Reference

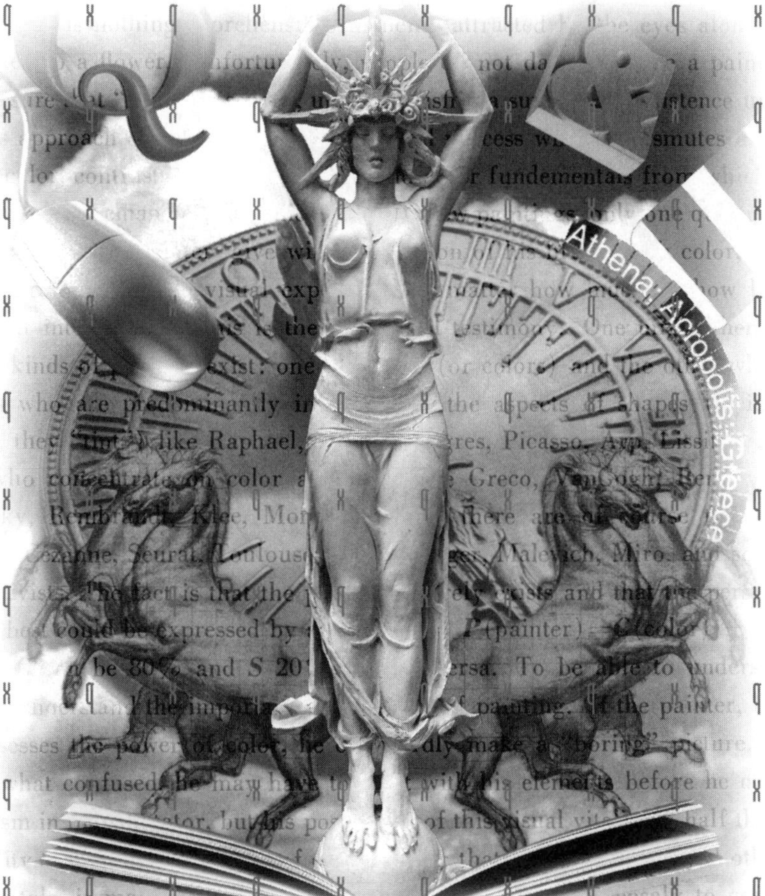

Glossary of Terms

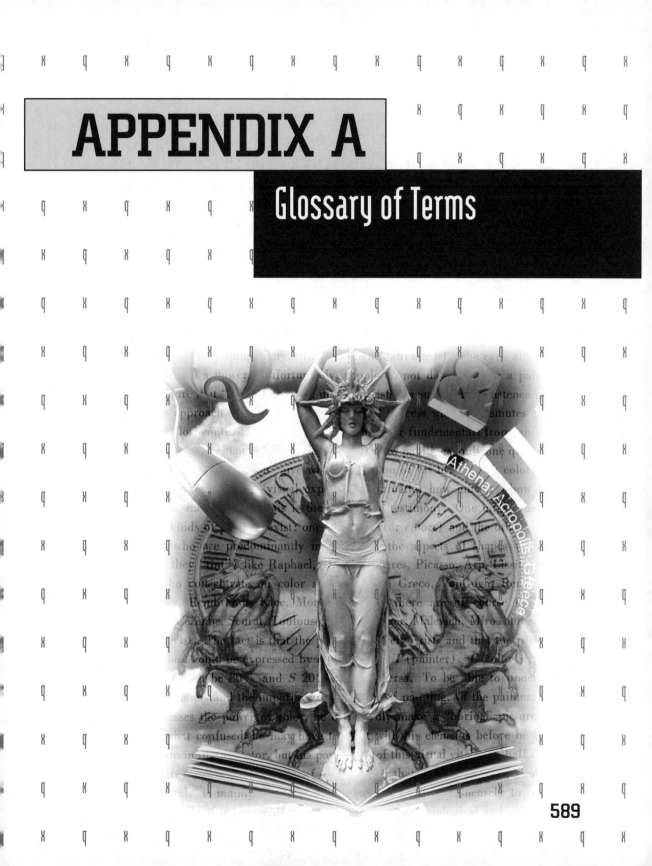

Athenai Acropolis Greece

Throughout the discussion of procedures and QuarkXPress-specific features in this book, you're undoubtedly going to encounter terms with which you may be unfamiliar. While a good portion of these mysterious terms stem from the use of XPress itself, many are specific industry terms that are referred to as you proceed through the book. The thrust of this alphabetical glossary is to define these terms in an easy-to-understand language. Although it is by no means a comprehensive dictionary of all terms you may encounter, it will provide you with an understanding of the most commonly-used ones.

Agate   A unit of measure used to describe vertical column length in advertising when calculating depth (and cost) of ad space used. XPress' ruler increments may be set to agates using the Horizontal and Vertical Measure drop-downs in the General tab of the Edit | Preferences | Document (CTRL/CMD+Y) command.

Alert   A dialog box that may appear if XPress (or your operating system) detects a problem with your application, your system, or your system drives. Alerts also appear when you're about to perform an operation that can't be undone using Edit commands. While using platform versions of QuarkXPress under Windows 95, Microsoft generally refers to these alerts as "warning messages."

Anchor   The term given to any item that's pasted between characters or paragraphs in a text box. Since anchored items become part of the text in your text box, they may move freely with the flow of text in your document.

Ascender   The portion of a text character that extends above the character's x-height.

ASCII   The acronym (rhymes with *pass-key*) for American Standard Code for Information Interchange and has long been a standard for data representing digital files (usually unformatted text).

Attribute   The generic term given to the characteristics of items or elements on your document page. Attributes include variables such as style, position, color, condition, and so on.

Auto leading   The term used to describe the vertical spacing between lines of text in your document while *Auto* is selected as the leading value. By default, XPress' Auto Leading feature is set to 20 percent of character height, but this value may be customized in the Paragraph tab of the Edit | Preferences | Document (CTRL+ALT/CMD+OPTION+Y) dialog box.

Baseline   The imaginary line on which all type rests.

Baseline grid   This term describes the vertical spacing measurement associated with your document's layout or design. When text and items in your document are made to align with the baseline grid, the result may often be a more professional-looking document. Baseline Grids in XPress underlie all items on your document page and are invisible and nonprinting. The spacing of the baseline grid may be set using the Paragraph tab of the Edit | Preferences | Document (CTRL+ALT/CMD+OPTION+Y) dialog box, and the display toggled using the View | Show/Hide Baseline Grid (CTRL/OPTION+F7) command.

Bezier   This term, named after mathematician Pierre Bézier, describes curves using two points, each controlled by a curve handle. The shape of a Bezier curve is defined by the relative position of the two points and the relative position of the curve handles associated with those points.

Bitmap   A term used to describe graphic images (XPress considers them pictures) that are composed of a pattern of pixels. The term bitmap is often interchangeable with the term *raster* image.

Bleed   The term bleed is used to describe the procedure by which images are intentionally left to overlap the document page edges, leaving the ink to figuratively bleed off the edge of the trimmed and finished page.

Blend   In XPress, the term blend refers to a smooth transition between two colors within the background of a box shape.

Body text   The term used to describe text characteristics or style of the main textual content of a document.

Book   In XPress, the term book refers to a specific type of file used in tracking, accessing, and managing the various sections (such as chapters) of a large publication. When these sections are part of a book file, their page numbers, styles, colors, and H&Js may be defined and managed globally.

A

Box   In XPress, a box may be any closed path that's capable of supporting pictures, text, or simply a colored background or frame.

Choke   In offset printing the term choke refers to the action or state caused by enlarging the edges of an item applied with a lighter color of ink to make it overlap the edges of an item applied with a darker color of ink. Choking is performed on different colored items to avoid registration problems when the document is reproduced in offset printing.

Comp   This is the short term for "comprehensive," which is essentially a sketched-out layout plan or design of a document. A comprehensive may be anything between a simply-drawn marker sketch to a full-color, exact duplicate of the finished printed document.

Composite   A printout of a document in which all of the document's colors and overlays are printed, rather than sketched or indicated.

Compound path   A shape composed of two or more open or closed paths. In the case of compound paths, the individual paths are referred to as *subpaths*.

Compression software   A program that compresses the size of a file, often used to make it easier to archive, transfer, or transmit.

Constrain   In XPress, this term is used to describe three states: moving, rotating, and drawing. When items are moved or rotated they may be constrained to vertical, horizontal, or angular rotational movement. While shapes are being drawn, the state of the various segments composing the shape may be constrained vertically, horizontally, or at given angles.

Content tool   This is perhaps one of the most critical tools to be aware of when creating or editing either pictures or text in XPress. When the Content tool is being used to edit text, it transforms to an I-beam cursor; when used for picture manipulation, it becomes a grabber hand.

Crop marks   A term for the corner marks that indicate the edges of a printed page.

Crosshairs   Used in ink and printing registration, crosshairs describe marks (also known as registration marks) that professional printers use to line up separate color film overlays for their presses.

Dash   In XPress, dashes are essentially the various on/off line patterns you may apply to the borders of boxes or lines.

Default   A predetermined setting for any attribute or property associated with newly-created documents and items. In XPress, nearly all default values or properties may be customized.

Density   Service bureaus refer to density as the value or measure given to the relative opaqueness of a developed film negative.

Descender   The portion of a character that falls below the baseline.

Deselect   For lack of a better term, deselect is used to describe the action of turning an option off, clearing a check box, deactivating a feature, or generally changing the state of an object to it's being *not selected.*

Device profile   A data file representing the color capabilities of a display, printing, or image-recording device.

DIC   Stands for Dainippon Ink and Chemicals, Inc., and refers to an enormous Japanese company responsible for producing (among other things) ink colors. The term DIC is often used to describe a specific cataloged ink color.

Didot   A didot is a European unit of measure subdivided into smaller units called *ciceros.*

Dot gain   This term refers to the phenomena of ink soaking into dry paper (absorption rate). The image becomes slightly larger and may be distorted. You can compensate for the gain at the film stage by adjusting the size of the dots.

Download   The action of transferring a file from a remote computer system to a local computer system.

Dpi   Dots per inch, which refers to a measure of dots in scanning resolution. Dpi also may refer to the detail an imagesetter renders on a film negative or positive.

Driver   A file, composed of machine programming commands, that communicates between software and hardware.

A

Drop cap   The term given to embuing the first letter in a paragraph, a dropped capital letter, with character properties larger and more pronounced than the text to follow.

Drum scanner   A type of scanner in which the original is mounted on a drum-style holder and spun at high speeds while a laser digitally records the image.

DTP   Service bureau language for desktop publishing.

Em dash   A dash the width of two zeros of a given font. Em dashes may be applied using the shortcut SHIFT+ALT/OPTION+- (hyphen).

Em space   Traditional typesetting defines an em space as a space whose width is equal to the point size of the text. Defaults in XPress set em space width equal to two zeros of a given font. This default may be changed by checking Standard Em Space in the Character tab of the Edit | Preferences | Document (CTRL/CMD+Y) command. Em spaces may be applied using the shortcut ALT/OPTION+SPACE X 2.

Emulsion   A photo-sensitive, silver-based coating applied to one side of a sheet of a polyester carrier. You can recognize the emulsion side of the film by its dull, nonreflective appearance.

En dash   The size of an en dash is exactly half the width of an em dash—and slightly larger than a hyphen. To create an en dash, enter the keyboard shortcut ALT/OPTION+- (hyphen).

En space   The size of an en space is exactly half the width of an em space. To enter an en space, use the keyboard shortcut ALT/OPTION+SPACE.

EPS   Stands for Encapsulated PostScript and refers to textual data representing a complete page or image. EPS files are based on PostScript—a page description language invented by the Adobe Corporation that has become a standard in the desktop industry for describing vector-based pages and images that may be printed independently of the resolution limitations of the device in use.

Extension   Refers to the three or fewer characters often following a file's name after a separating dot. The extension sometimes indicates which program the file originated from or which program is capable of editing it. On the Windows platform, all QuarkXPress documents—regardless of which version they are—are given the extension QXP. QuarkXPress uses different extensions for different types of files; for example QXT for templates, QXL for libraries, and QXB for books.

Flatbed   A type of scanner in which the original is placed face down on a flat document glass and a reflection-sensitive light bar passes below, recording the image data.

Flatness   Refers to the detail in which curves in your drawing are rendered to the printer or imagesetter.

Font   The digital description of a typeface. The term stems from early typesetting systems that, improving on font-cast metal type that dates back centuries, used large metal or nylon disks with images of letters cut out of them to represent typefaces. The term "font' comes from "found," meaning to pour, or done in a "foundry" and actually originates as far back as post-Gutenberg.

Font conflict   This is a state that occurs when one font has the same font identification number as another. This problem is essentially a thing of the past, but font conflict plagued service bureaus in the early days before font identification standards were set.

Frame   In XPress, this term is used to describe the properties of the outer border of a box.

Grayscale   A term from the realm of camera work, where a small strip of photographic paper, graduated in steps of gray, was photographed and developed along with artwork, acting as a benchmark for film density and image quality. Digitally speaking, a grayscale describes density values.

Greek   In XPress and other desktop typesetting systems, to greek a picture or text is to enable it to display without any detail. Instead, a gray color appears in picture boxes or gray stripes appear to roughly represent text size.

Halftone   The term given to a picture that will eventually be reproduced in dots of varying size to simulate varying degrees of gray or color.

A

Header In XPress this may actually be two different things. A header may be the text appearing at the top of a page to identify the subsection of the larger document. It may also be the information contained in a picture file used to describe the image it contains. Picture headers may be in various resolutions, color conditions, or color levels.

Highlight This may be either a state or an action. When an item or text is highlighted, it's immediately available for editing. To highlight text or an item is to *select* it, causing it to be available for editing.

I-beam This is the style of cursor used by XPress while working in text boxes using the Content tool.

Imagesetter A PostScript or non-PostScript printer that generates a high-resolution, hard-copy printout.

Insertion point The point at which your I-beam cursor has been or will be clicked, indicating a point for text entry.

Invisible [characters] In XPress, the term invisibles refers to nonprinting characters such as paragraph returns, spaces, line feeds, and tab characters. In XPress, you may control the display of invisibles in a text box by choosing View | Show/Hide Invisibles (CTRL/CMD+I).

Item This is a highly-generic term used to describe any element that may exist on your document page. In XPress, there are four basic types of items: lines, text boxes, picture boxes, and text paths.

Justified The state of a paragraph of text that aligns on both the right and left margins.

Kerning The action of editing or altering the space between specific combinations of characters in text with the aim of improving the text's readability.

Knockout A term that refers to eliminating the shape of a colored area below another shape on a higher layer. The term knockout is the opposite of *overprinting*.

Laminate Colored layers of a microthin carrier film-bonding process that produces a highly accurate color sample of the finished printed film.

Landscape   Represents page orientation and describes both document orientation and print orientation. Document orientation is set in the New Document dialog box when your document is first created; print orientation is set in the Setup tab of the Print dialog box. In XPress, landscape describes a page that has greater width than height. This term is used in *all* page layout systems or word-processing applicaitons as is Portrait (the opposite of Landscape).

Leading   The vertical space between lines of text in a paragraph. Leading (pronounced *ledding*) is often measured in points and, by default, measures the distance between baselines of text. Leading stems from the days when strips of lead were added to (or removed from) text spacing in order to adjust line spacing.

Library   In XPress, a library is a specific file format that may be used to store pictures, text, or items that make up entire QuarkXPress layouts independently of the documents from which the items originate. Library items may be moved between libraries or to document pages, and may be opened by multiple users and exchanged between users.

Ligature   A specialized character available in most Macintosh fonts that combines two characters into one. Ligatures are often used to increase legibility and to add flair and design to text in artistic documents.

Line art   Any artwork composed of a solid black or solid white image, digital or otherwise.

Linear   In XPress, the term linear refers to a style of color blending. When two color backgrounds are blended in a linear, the transitions occurs evenly between the colors.

Linen tester   A small magnifying glass used to closely examine film.

Linotronic   A line of imagesetters manufactured in Germany by Linotype-Hell.

LPI (lines per inch)   Refers to the number of rows of dots counted in one linear inch of a screen tint or halftone screen.

Master item   These items that automatically appear on your document pages originate—and are controlled by—master pages. Master page items may be manipulated like other items on your document page.

A

Master page   One of the key features of XPress is the capability to create and apply master pages with commonly-used page elements and properties. Master pages are nonprinting pages that automatically create page properties and items when applied.

Moiré   An undesirable effect, pronounced *more-aye*, that appears as a blurry checkerboard or tartan style when two or more pieces of screen film are aligned at improper angles.

Nudge   In XPress this term refers to the action of moving items or pictures in boxes in 1-point increments using the Left, Right, Up, and Down arrow keys on your keyboard. You may also nudge items or pictures in boxes 0.1 points by holding the ALT/OPTION key in combination with the ARROW keys.

Overprint   In offset printing, the term overprint refers to the action of layering the color of one item on top of another differently-colored item. An overprint is the opposite of a knockout.

Palette   In XPress, this is a term given to an interface element that may "float" over on your document window and represent a specific collection of properties or feature options. Palettes may be minimized or maximized by double-clicking their title bars.

PDF   Stands for Portable Document Format, a compressed-file format (developed by Adobe) used for creating document proofs and World Wide Web page documents that may be viewed independently of fonts and graphics necessary for printing.

Pica   A unit of measure unique to the printing industry and widely adopted by the desktop publishing industry to measure fonts, page coordinates, size, or distances. Six picas are roughly equivalent to one inch and are subdivided into a smaller measure called points. Each pica is subdivided into 12 points, so an inch is roughly equivalent to 72 points.

Picture   In XPress, this is the generic term for any image, graphic, etc., that's imported or pasted into a picture box. Whether it's a TIFF, an EPS, a pie chart, or a photograph of your grandma, XPress refers to it as a picture.

PKZip   Windows-based file compression program. PKZip is available from PKWare, Inc., 7545 N. Port Washington Road, Glemdale, WI 53217-7176, (414) 352-3670.

Plate   A term referring to paper or metal sheets installed onto a printing press. Service bureaus use this term to describe a color separation or film overlay that represents a color of ink.

Point   A unit of measure unique to the printing industry and widely adopted by the desktop publishing industry to measure fonts, page coordinates, size, or distances. One point is equal to 1/72 of an inch, and 12 points are equal to 1 pica.

Portrait   Represents page orientation and describes both document orientation and print orientation. Document orientation is set in the New Document dialog box when your document is first created, and print orientation is set in the Setup tab of the Print dialog box. In XPress 4, portrait describes a page that has greater height than width. As with Landscape orientation (the opposite of Portrait) this definition is true of *all* page layout systems or word-processing applications, and dates back to photographic studios of last century.

PPD   This is the acronym for PostScript Printer Description and is a file representing the specific properties of an output or printing device.

Preview   In XPress, this term refers to the low-resolution image XPress uses to represent picture files placed on your document page.

Print file   A PostScript text file created when printing a document. On the Windows platform, print files are usually recognized by the file extension PRN. A print file may contain all the information necessary for imaging a file to a particular printer.

Processing   This term means either film processing or image (data) processing. Film processing is the action of developing, fixing, and washing exposed film; data processing refers to computer calculations that the RIP of an imagesetter performs.

Processor   This term refers either to the machine that physically develops, stops, fixes, washes, and dries the film in an imagesetter, or to the main computer chip that drives your computer.

Proof   As a noun, the term given to a printed document used for reviewing the text, composition, and/or color of a document before it's reproduced in offset printing. "Proof" as a verb means to proofread, or carefully check all words, images, and alignment on a page.

A

Property   This is a generic term given to the characteristics of items or elements on your document page. Properties include variables such as style, position, color, condition, and so on.

Raster graphic   This term is used to describe graphic images (which XPress considers pictures) that are composed of a pattern of pixels. The term raster graphic is often interchangeable with the term *bitmap*.

Registration   The procedure of matching several film overlays by alignment markings imaged onto the film. The term also means to match overlays by viewing the alignment of images they contain.

Resident scans   Digital images stored at a service bureau for the convenience of imaging a client's linked files.

Resolution   The measure of detail contained in a displayed or printed image. Resolution refers to the level of detail an imagesetter records on film. The higher the resolution, the more detail displayed, printed, or recorded.

Reverse   The term reverse refers to the action of applying white to a darker area, to reproduce a shape such as a graphic picture or text.

Rich black   This is a formulated process color that appears and prints as black, but may appear more saturated and intense than simply printing 100 percent black alone. Rich black may be composed of 100 percent black ink, plus an additional color—or colors—such as cyan or magenta, or both.

RIP   Raster image processor is a term that refers to the data-crunching engine in many imagesetters. Commonly referred to as a "RIP," it can be used both as a verb and as a noun. For example, a file is RIPped (on a RIP) before it's imaged.

RRED   Stands for right-reading emulsion down, which describes the condition of imaged film. RRED describes film on which, when you hold it vertically with the emulsion side facing away from you, you can read the text and images from left to right.

RREU   Stands for right-reading emulsion up, which describes the condition of imaged film. RREU describes film on which, when you hold it vertically with the emulsion side toward you, you can read the text and images from left to right.

Runaround   This term describes text that's set to follow the contours of a picture or other item's shape. In XPress, you may apply runaround effects automatically by using the Runaround tab of the Modify dialog box (CTRL/CMD+T).

Screen frequency   Describes the LPI (lines per inch), or number of rows of dots measured in one linear inch.

Segment   This term refers to a line or curve created between two Bezier points.

SelectSet   A line of imagesetters developed by AGFA, Inc.

Separation   In XPress, the term separation refers to the dissection of various layers of ink color onto film for the purpose of printing multiple colors on an offset printing press.

Solid   When a color is solid, its shade has been set to 100 percent. When referring to leading, the term solid refers to a leading space of none, meaning no additional space (besides the vertical height of the characters) has been applied between lines of text.

Source file   The original or native file created by a program.

Spooler   A type of software program or dedicated computer that handles the print traffic between one or several computers and one or several imagesetters. Files may be held in the spooler indefinitely, or until it's necessary to image them.

Spread   Two or more pages positioned beside each other. In XPress, pages may be viewed, printed, or exported as spreads.

Text chain   This refers to text boxes that have been linked using linking tools. When text boxes are linked, text may flow from one text box in the chain to another as the text changes size, or as content is added or removed.

Tile   An individual section that's printed when the dimensions of a document exceed the maximum size of the output material.

Title bar   The portion of an interface element such as the XPress application window, a document window, or a palette that identifies the element. A title bar may also contain command buttons that offer control over the window or palette to which it belongs.

A

Track   The state of the spacing between words and characters in a string of text.

Trap   A condition where one color item has been expanded to overlap the edges of another differently-colored item, to compensate for press misregistration.

Uncheck   The state or action where a feature or option is deselected or *turned off* or a check box is cleared.

X-height   The height of a lowercase character minus the height of its ascenders and descenders.

APPENDIX B

Keyboard Shortcuts

s QuarkXPress evolves, the list of its available commands and functions continues to grow, as do the application shortcuts. Quark has gone to great lengths to accommodate the needs and desires of a wide cross section of users spanning two platforms. The sophistication and usefulness of these shortcuts will be of value to the expert-level user on down to the first-time beginner. When it comes to reference information, this is perhaps the most valuable section you'll ever read (although actually reading it may be more than a little tedious.) You may want to skim through it, see what it contains, and then check back for specific commands.

File Command Shortcuts

The following shortcuts apply when performing basic file, document, export, and print command functions in XPress 4:

Open existing document	CTRL/CMD+O
Create **new** document	CTRL/CMD+N
Create **new library**	CTRL/CMD+ALT/OPTION+N
Close document/template	Windows: CTRL+F4 Macintosh: CMD+W
Close all documents *(Macintosh only)*	OPTION+Click Close button or CMD+OPTION+W
Save	CTRL/CMD+S
Save As	CTRL/CMD+ALT/OPTION+S
Revert to last Auto Save	Hold ALT/OPTION while choosing File | Revert to Saved
Import text/picture	CTRL/CMD+E
Save Text	CTRL/CMD+ALT/OPTION+E

Append	CTRL/CMD+ALT/OPTION+A
Save Page as EPS file	CTRL/CMD+ALT/OPTION+SHIFT+S
Document Setup	CTRL/CMD+ALT/OPTION+SHIFT+P
Page Setup	CTRL/CMD+ALT/OPTION+P
Print	CTRL/CMD+P
Quit QuarkXPress	CTRL/CMD+Q
Help	F1/HELP

Edit Command Shortcuts

The following keyboard shortcuts apply when you're working with command functions for editing states for the clipboard and when you're accessing editing states for preferences or property sheets.

B

Clipboard Commands

Undo	CTRL/CMD+Z (or F1 on Macintosh)
Copy	CTRL/CMD+C (or F3 on Macintosh)
Cut	CTRL/CMD+X (or F2 on Macintosh)
Paste	CTRL/CMD+V (or F4 on Macintosh)
Select All	CTRL/CMD+A
Copy attributes from one paragraph to another	ALT/OPTION+SHIFT+click
Drag-copy text (with interactive preference on)	SHIFT+drag
Drag text (with interactive preference off)	CMD+CTRL+drag *(Macintosh only)*
Drag text (with interactive preference off)	CMND+CTRL+SHIFT+drag *(Macintosh only)*

Preference Commands

Open **Application** preferences	CTRL/CMD+ALT/OPTION+SHIFT+Y
Open **Document** preferences	CTRL/CMD+Y
Open **Paragraph** preferences	CTRL/CMD+ALT/OPTION+Y
Open **Trapping** preferences	CTRL/OPTION+SHIFT+F12
Open **Tool** preferences	Double-click item creation or Zoom tool

Property Sheets

Open **Style Sheets**	SHIFT+F11
Open **Colors**	SHIFT+F12
Open **H&Js**	Windows: CTRL+SHIFT+F11
	Macintosh: OPTION+SHIFT+F11
	or CMD+OPTION+H

TIP *To change document property sheets, choose the above with a document open. To change application default property sheets, open the property sheets while no documents are open.*

Style Command Shortcuts

The following shortcuts apply when you're formatting text styles using the Content tool in Text boxes, and when you're applying line styles or properties using either the Item or Content tool.

Apply Text Styles

**Size	Other** (dialog box)	CTRL/CMD+SHIFT+\
Plain	CTRL/CMD+SHIFT+P
Bold	CTRL/CMD+SHIFT+B

Italic	CTRL/CMD+SHIFT+I
Underline	CTRL/CMD+SHIFT+U
Word Underline (underscore)	CTRL/CMD+SHIFT+W
Strikethrough	CTRL/CMD+SHIFT+/
Outline	CTRL/CMD+SHIFT+O
Shadow	CTRL/CMD+SHIFT+S
All Caps	CTRL/CMD+SHIFT+K
Small Caps	CTRL/CMD+SHIFT+H
Superscript	Windows: CTRL+SHIFT+0 (zero) Macintosh: CMD+SHIFT++ (plus)
Subscript	Windows: CTRL+SHIFT+9 Macintosh: CMD+SHIFT+- (hyphen)
Superior	CTRL/CMD+SHIFT+V
Align **Left**	CTRL/CMD+SHIFT+L
Align **Centered**	CTRL/CMD+SHIFT+C
Align **Right**	CTRL/CMD+SHIFT+R
Align **Justified**	CTRL/CMD+SHIFT+J
Align **Forced**	CTRL/CMD+ALT/OPTION+SHIFT+J
Increase **character** size by preset value	CTRL/CMD+SHIFT+>
Increase **character** size by 1 point	CTRL/CMD+ALT/OPTION+SHIFT+>
Decrease **character** size by preset value	CTRL/CMD+SHIFT+<
Decrease **character** size by 1 point	CTRL/CMD+ALT/OPTION+SHIFT+<
Resize character **proportionally** (with mouse)	CTRL/CMD+ALT/OPTION+SHIFT+drag sizing handle
Resize character **nonproportionally** (with mouse)	CTRL/CMD+drag sizing handle

B

Resize character **constrained** (with mouse)	CTRL/CMD+SHIFT+drag sizing handle
Apply **next** font in list to highlighted characters	CTRL/OPTION+SHIFT+F9
Apply **previous** font in list to highlighted characters	CTRL/OPTION+F9

Line Styles

Open Line Width | Other dialog box	CTRL/CMD+SHIFT+\
Increase Line Width by preset value	CTRL/CMD+SHIFT+>
Decrease Line Width by preset value	CTRL/CMD+SHIFT+<
Increase Line Width by 1 point	CTRL/CMD+ALT/OPTION+SHIFT+>
Decrease Line Width by 1 point	CTRL/CMD+ALT/OPTION+SHIFT+<

Picture Command Shortcuts

The following shortcuts apply when you're working with pictures in picture boxes. While you're working with pictures inside boxes, the Content tool must be the tool in use; while you're working with the picture boxes themselves, the Item tool must be in use:

Increase picture size 5 percent	CTRL/CMD+ALT/OPTION+SHIFT+>
Decrease picture size 5 percent	CTRL/CMD+ALT/OPTION+SHIFT+<
Center picture in box	CTRL/CMD+SHIFT+M
Fit picture to box	CTRL/CMD+SHIFT+F
Fit picture to box **proportionally**	CTRL/CMD+ALT/OPTION+SHIFT+F
Open **Picture Contrast** Specifications dialog box	CTRL/CMD+SHIFT+C
Open **Halftone** Specifications dialog box	CTRL/CMD+SHIFT+H
Toggle **Negative/Positive** picture	CTRL/CMD+SHIFT+- (hyphen)

Nudge picture in box 1 point (Content tool)	LEFT, RIGHT, UP, DOWN arrow keys
Nudge picture in box 0.1 point (Content tool)	ALT/OPTION+LEFT, RIGHT, UP, DOWN ARROW keys
Import picture at **36 dpi**	SHIFT+click Open button in Get Picture
Import color **TIFF as grayscale**	CTRL/CMD+click Open in Get Picture
Import grayscale **TIFF as black-and-white**	CTRL/CMD+click Open in Get Picture
Import EPS *without loading spot colors*	CTRL/CMD+Click Open in Get Picture
Reimport *all pictures* in document	CTRL/CMD+Click Open in Open dialog box
Resize box *and* scale picture	CTRL/CMD+drag
Resize box, scale picture **constraining** box shape	CTRL/CMD+SHIFT+drag
Resize box and picture, **maintaining** picture ratio	CTRL/CMD+ALT/OPTION+SHIFT+drag

Text, Font, and Spacing Command Shortcuts

The following shortcuts apply when you're formatting text, font, and spacing properties using the Content tool in text boxes.

Text

Access **Leading** field	CTRL/CMD+SHIFT+E
Open Paragraph **Formats** tab	CTRL/CMD+SHIFT+F
Open Paragraph **Tabs** tab	CTRL/CMD+SHIFT+T
Open Paragraph **Rules** tab	CTRL/CMD+SHIFT+N

Spacing: Kerning, Leading

Access Leading field	CTRL/CMD+SHIFT+E
Increase **leading** 1 point	CTRL/CMD+SHIFT+"
Increase **leading** 0.1 point	CTRL/CMD+ALT/OPTION+SHIFT+"
Decrease **leading** 1 point	CTRL/CMD+SHIFT+:
Decrease **leading** 0.1 point	CTRL/CMD+ALT/OPTION+SHIFT+:
Increase **kern/track** 1/20 em	CTRL/CMD+SHIFT+}
Increase **kern/track** 1/200 em	CTRL/CMD+ALT/OPTION+SHIFT+}
Decrease **kern/track** 1/20 em	CTRL/CMD+SHIFT+{
Decrease **kern/track** 1/200 em	CTRL/CMD+ALT/OPTION+SHIFT+{
Increase **baseline shift** 1 point	Windows: CTRL+ALT+SHIFT+) Macintosh: CMD+OPTION+SHIFT++ (plus)
Decrease **baseline shift** 1 point	Windows: CTRL+ALT+SHIFT+(Macintosh: CMD+OPTION+SHIFT+ - (minus)
Increase vertical/horizontal scaling 5 percent	CTRL/CMD+]
Increase vertical/horizontal scaling 1 percent	CTRL/CMD+ALT/OPTION+]
Decrease vertical/horizontal scaling 5 percent	CTRL/CMD+[
Decrease vertical/horizontal scaling 1 percent	CTRL/CMD+ALT/OPTION+[

Selection, Edit, Modify, and Move Command Shortcuts

The following shortcuts apply when you're editing text with the Content tool and modifying or moving items using the Item tool.

Selecting Items

Select item	Click with Item tool
Select **hidden** item	CTRL/CMD+ALT/OPTION+SHIFT+click where items overlap
Select multiple items or points	Hold SHIFT while clicking items
Deselect all items (Item tool selected)	TAB
Select items in specific area	Drag around/across items

Selecting, Highlighting, and Deleting text

When you're selecting text using the Content tool *I-beam* cursor in text boxes, the following shortcuts apply:

Select *specific* characters	Drag cursor vertically and/or horizontally across characters or lines
Select a **word**	Double-click the word
Select a **word** and its period or comma	Double-click between word and punctuation
Select entire **line**	Triple-click anywhere in the line
Select entire **paragraph**	Quadruple-click anywhere in the paragraph
Select **all text** in story	Five clicks anywhere in story, or CTRL/CMD+A
Highlight between insertion points	SHIFT+click insertion points

When you're moving the I-beam cursor using the Content tool in text boxes, the following shortcuts apply:

One **character**	Left or RIGHT ARROW keys
One **line** (vertically)	UP or DOWN ARROW keys
One **word**	CTRL/CMD+LEFT or RIGHT ARROW keys
One **paragraph**	CTRL/CMD+UP or DOWN ARROW keys
Start of line	CTRL/CMD+ALT/OPTION+LEFT (or HOME in Windows)
End of line	CTRL/CMD+ALT/OPTION+RIGHT (or END in Windows)
Start of story	CTRL/CMD+ALT/OPTION+UP (or CTRL+HOME in Windows)
End of story	CTRL/CMD+ALT/OPTION+DOWN (or CTRL+END in Windows)

When deleting text, the following shortcuts apply:

	Windows	Mac
Delete previous character	BACKSPACE	DELETE
Delete next character	SHIFT+BACKSPACE or DELETE	SHIFT+DELETE
Delete previous word	CTRL+BACKSPACE	CMD+DELETE
Delete next word	CTRL+DELETE or CTRL+SHIFT+BACKSPACE	CTRL+SHIFT+DELETE
Delete highlighted text	BACKSPACE or DELETE	DELETE

Edit Items

Edit **Shape**	Windows: F10 Macintosh: SHIFT+F4
Edit **Runaround**	Windows: CTRL+F10 Macintosh: OPTION+F4
Edit **Clipping** Path	Windows: CTRL+SHIFT+F10 Macintosh: OPTION+SHIFT+F4

Change point to **Corner** Point	CTRL/OPTION+F1
Change point to **Smooth** Point	CTRL/OPTION+F2
Change point to **Symmetrical** point	CTRL/OPTION+F3
Change segment to **Straight** line	CTRL/OPTION+SHIFT+F1
Change segment to **Curve** line	CTRL/OPTION+SHIFT+F2

Modify Items

Open **Modify** dialog box	CTRL/CMD+M or double-click with Item tool
Open **Frame** dialog box	CTRL/CMD+B
Open **Colors** dialog box	CTRL/CMD+CLICK color in **Colors** palette
Open **Clipping** dialog box	CTRL/CMD+ALT/OPTION+T
Open **Runaround** dialog box	CTRL/CMD+T
Open **Step and Repeat** dialog box	CTRL/CMD+ALT/OPTION+D
Duplicate selected item	CTRL/CMD+D
Group items	CTRL/CMD+G
Ungroup grouped items	CTRL/CMD+U
Toggle **Lock/Unlock** item	F6
Bring to **Front**	F5
Bring **Forward** (one layer)	Windows: CTRL+F5 Macintosh: OPTION+F5 or hold OPTION while choosing ITEM | BRING TO FRONT
Send to **Back**	SHIFT+F5
Send **Backward** (one layer)	Windows: CTRL+SHIFT+F5 Macintosh: OPTION+SHIFT+F5 or hold OPTION while choosing ITEM | SEND TO BACK
Open **Space/Align** dialog box	CTRL/CMD+, (comma)

B

Constrain rectangle to square, or oval to circle	Hold SHIFT while drawing or sizing
Constrain **rotation** to 0, 45, 90 degree increments	Hold SHIFT while rotating
Constrain **line** to 0, 45, 90 degree increments	Hold SHIFT while drawing, sizing, or rotating

Move Items

Nudge item by **1 point**	LEFT, RIGHT, UP, DOWN ARROW keys
Nudge item by **0.1 point**	ALT/OPTION+LEFT, RIGHT, UP, DOWN ARROW keys
Move item *without constraining*	Drag item
Constrain item movement to vertical/horizontal	Hold SHIFT while dragging

Drawing Tool and Path-Creation Command Shortcuts

When you're drawing or editing Bezier shapes, the following shortcuts apply:

Delete Bézier point	ALT/OPTION+click or BACKSPACE/DELETE
Delete Bezier point *while drawing*	BACKSPACE/DELETE
Add Bezier point	ALT/OPTION+click segment
Change **Smooth to Corner** point (or vice versa)	Windows: CTRL+SHIFT+drag curve handle Macintosh: CTRL+drag curve handle
Change **Smooth to Corner** point *while drawing*	Windows: CTRL+click, and then press CTRL+F1 Macintosh: CMD+CTRL+click.
Edit Bezier shape *while drawing*	Hold CTRL/CMD while creating point

Retract curve handles	Windows: CTRL+SHIFT+click point Macintosh: CTRL+CLICK point
Expose curve handles	Windows: CTRL+SHIFT+drag point Macintosh: CTRL+click point
Select all points in selected item	CTRL/CMD+SHIFT+A or triple-click a point
Select all points on active subpath	Double-click point
Convert **Bezier line** to filled-center **Bezier box**	ALT/OPTION while choosing Item I Shape I Bezier
Constrain **Point** to 45 degrees of movement	Hold SHIFT while dragging point
Constrain **Curve Handle** to 45 degrees of movement	Hold SHIFT while dragging handle

B

View and Page Command Shortcuts

When you're changing page display states, page item display, or document view display, the following shortcuts apply:

Fit in Window	CTRL/CMD+0 (zero)
Fit **largest spread** in Window	ALT/OPTION+Fit in Window, or CTRL/CMD+ALT/OPTION+0 (zero)
Actual size	CTRL/CMD+1 (one)
Thumbnails	SHIFT+F6
Access **Page View** field	Windows: CTRL+ALT+V Macintosh: CTRL+V
Toggle view between 200 percent and Actual	CTRL/CMD+ALT/OPTION+click
Any view to Actual size (*Macintosh only*)	OPTION+click with Caps Lock on
Actual size to Fit in Window (*Macintosh only*)	OPTION+click with Caps Lock on

Zoom **In**	Windows: CTRL+SPACE+click or drag Macintosh: CTRL+click or drag
Zoom **Out**	Windows: CTRL+ALT+SPACE+click or drag Macintosh: CTRL+OPTION+click or drag
Toggle Show/Hide **Guides**	F7
Toggle Show/Hide **Baseline Grid**	CTRL/OPTION+F7
Toggle Show/Hide **Rulers**	CTRL/CMD+R
Delete all **horizontal** *ruler guides*	ALT/OPTION+click horizontal ruler
Delete all **vertical** *ruler guides*	ALT/OPTION+click vertical ruler
Toggle **Snap to Guides** on/off	SHIFT+F7
Toggle Show/Hide **Invisibles**	CTRL/CMD+I
Toggle Show/Hide **Tool** palette	F8
Toggle Show/Hide **Measurements** palette	F9
Toggle Show/Hide **Document Layout** palette	Windows: F4 Macintosh: F10
Toggle Show/Hide **Style Sheets** palette	F11
Toggle Show/Hide **Colors** palette	F12
Toggle Show/Hide **Trap Information** palette	CTRL/OPTION+F12
Toggle Show/Hide **Lists** palette	CTRL/OPTION+F11
Show Font Usage	F13 *(Macintosh only)*
Show Picture Usage	Windows: SHIFT+F2 Macintosh: OPTION+F13
Show **Index** palette	CTRL/CMD+ALT/OPTION+I

Open **Go to Page** dialog box	CTRL/CMD+J	
Toggle Master Pages/Document Pages display	Windows: SHIFT+F4 Macintosh: SHIFT+F10	
Display next Master Page	Windows: CTRL+SHIFT+F4 Macintosh: OPTION+F10	
Display previous Master Page	Windows: CTRL+SHIFT+F3 Macintosh: OPTION+SHIFT+F10	

The following keyboard shortcuts apply when you're navigating or scrolling your document pages:

	Windows	**Macintosh**
Toggle Enable/Disable live scrolling	None	OPTION+drag scroll box
Scroll view with grabber hand	ALT+drag	OPTION+DRAG
Go to **start** of document	CTRL+HOME	CTRL+A
Go to **end** of document	CTRL+END	CTRL+D or END
Up one screen	PAGE UP	CTRL+K
Down one screen	PAGE DOWN	CTRL+L
Up one page	SHIFT+PAGE UP key	CTRL+SHIFT+K
Down one page	SHIFT+PAGE DOWN key	CTRL+SHIFT+L
View **first** page	CTRL+PAGE UP	SHIFT+HOME
View **last** page	CTRL+PAGE DOWN	CTRL+SHIFT+D or SHIFT+END
View **next** spread	ALT+PAGE DOWN	NONE
View **previous** spread	ALT+PAGE UP	NONE

The following shortcuts apply when you're scrolling a document using the Macintosh extended keyboard *only:*

B

Start of document	HOME
End of document	END
Up one screen	PAGE UP
Down one screen	PAGE DOWN
To **first** page	SHIFT+HOME
To **last** page	SHIFT+END
To **previous** page	SHIFT+PAGE UP
To **next** page	SHIFT+PAGE DOWN

Document Window Tiling and Stacking Shortcuts

The following shortcuts apply when you're tiling and stacking document windows on Macintosh versions of XPress 4 *only:*

Tile/Stack document windows at Actual size	CTRL+Tile/Stack
Tile/Stack document windows at Fit in Window	CMD+Tile/Stack
Tile/Stack document windows at Thumbnails	OPTION+Tile/Stack
Tile/Stack document windows at Actual size from title bar	CTRL+SHIFT+Tile/Stack
Tile/Stack document windows at Fit in Window from title bar	CMD+SHIFT+Tile/Stack
Tile/Stack document windows at Thumbnails from title bar	OPTION+SHIFT+Tile/Stack
Show next document in stack *(Windows only)*	CTRL+F6

Find/Change and Search Character Shortcuts

The following shortcuts apply when you're working with the Find/Change palette:

Open Find/Change palette	CTRL/CMD+F
Close Find/Change palette	CTRL/CMD+ALT/OPTION+F
Change **Find Next** button to *Find First*	Hold ALT/OPTION while clicking Find Next

The following shortcuts apply when you're searching for specific or generic characters using the Find/Change palette:

Search/change character	Press shortcut	Result/code
Any character (wildcard, Find only)	CTRL/CMD+?	\?
Tab	CTRL/CMD+TAB	\t
New paragraph	CTRL/CMD+RETURN	\p
New line	CTRL/CMD+SHIFT+RETURN	\n
New column	CTRL/CMD+ENTER	\c
New text box	CTRL/CMD+SHIFT+ENTER	\b
Previous box page # (number)	CTRL/CMD+2	\2
Current box page #	CTRL/CMD+3	\3
Next box page #	CTRL/CMD+4	\4
Punctuation space	CTRL/CMD+.	\.
Flex space	CTRL/CMD+SHIFT+F	\f
Backslash	CTRL/CMD+\	\\

B

Spell-Check Shortcuts

The following shortcuts apply when you're spell checking your word, story, or document using Spell Check and the Check Word, Check Story, and Check Document dialog boxes:

Check spelling of **word**	Windows: CTRL+W Macintosh: CMD+L
Check spelling of **story**	Windows: CTRL+ALT+W Macintosh: CMD+OPTION+L
Check spelling of **document**	Windows: CTRL+ALT+SHIFT+W Macintosh: CMD+OPTION+SHIFT+L
Suggest hyphenation	CTRL/CMD+H

When you're spell checking text using Check Story or Check Document dialog box commands, the following shortcuts apply while suspect words are highlighted in the list:

To Lookup a suspect word	ALT/CMD+L
To Skip a suspect word	ALT/CMD+S
To Add a suspect word to your auxiliary dictionary	ALT/CMD+A
To add all suspect words to the auxiliary dictionary	ALT/OPTION+SHIFT+Close/Done button

Dialog Box Commands Shortcuts

The following shortcuts apply in general while you're entering values or selecting command buttons in dialog boxes:

Display next tab in tabbed dialog box	CTRL/CMD+TAB
Display previous tab in tabbed dialog box	CTRL/CMD+SHIFT+TAB
Cursor/selection to next field	TAB

Cursor/selection to previous field	SHIFT+TAB
Highlight field with text cursor	Double-click in field
Clipboard functions	Same as for text
Perform calculations in field	Use add (+), subtract (-), multiply (*), divide (/) operators between values
Select OK (or currently bordered button)	RETURN or ENTER
Cancel	ESC/CMD+. (Period)
Apply	ALT/CMD+A
Keep Apply state selected (except Space/Align)	CTRL/CMD+OPTION+click Apply button
Select **Yes** as dialog box response (Windows only)	Y
Select **No** as dialog box response (Windows only)	N

Palette Command Shortcuts

The following shortcuts apply when you're working in XPress' floating palettes:

Minimize/maximize any floating palette	Double-click palette title bar
Select **next** tool in Tool palette	CTRL/CMD+ALT/+TAB
Select **previous** tool in Tool palette	CTRL/CMD+ALT/+SHIFT+TAB
Keep Tool palette tool **selected** after use	ALT/OPTION+click tool button in palette
Highlight **first field** of Measurements	CTRL/CMD+ALT/OPTION+M
Apply values and/or **Exit** palette	ENTER
Cancel values and/or **Exit** palette	Windows or Macintosh: ESC Macintosh: CMD+. (period)

Open **Section dialog box** for page in Document Layout	Click lower-left corner of palette
Open **Insert Pages** dialog box in Document Layout	ALT/OPTION+drag master page onto document page area
Open **Style Sheet pop-out** in palette	RIGHT/CTRL+click name in Style Sheet palette
Open **Style Sheets** dialog box	CTRL/CMD+click style sheet name in palette
Apply **No Style**, and then *selected style*	ALT/OPTION+click style sheet name in palette

Shortcuts for Specialized Characters

The following shortcuts and keyboard combinations apply when you're working in text boxes and entering specialized characters:

Automatic in-text page number tag for previous text box in chain	CTRL/CMD+2
Automatic in-text page number tag for current text box in chain	CTRL/CMD+3
Automatic in-text page number tag for next text box in chain	CTRL/CMD+4
Add automatic page number on master page	CTRL/CMD+3
Insert one symbol font character	CTRL/CMD+SHIFT+Q, and then type character
Insert one Zapf Dingbat font character	CTRL/CMD+SHIFT+Z, and then type character

	Windows	**Mac**
Discretionary hyphen	CTRL+HYPHEN	CMD+HYPHEN
Discretionary new line	CTRL+ENTER	CMD+RETURN
Force Indent	CTRL+\	CMD+\
New box	SHIFT+ENTER (on keypad)	SHIFT+ENTER (on keypad)
New column	ENTER (on keypad)	ENTER (on keypad)
Nonbreaking em dash	CTRL+ALT+SHIFT+=	CMD+OPTION+=
Em dash	CTRL+SHIFT+=	OPTION+SHIFT+- (hyphen)
Non-breaking em dash	CTRL+ALT+SHIFT+=	CMD+OPTION+=
En dash	CTRL+ALT+SHIFT+- (hyphen)	OPTION+- (hyphen)
Nonbreaking en dash	CTRL+ALT+SHIFT+- (hyphen)	OPTION+- (hyphen)
En space	CTRL+SHIFT+CTRL+SHIFT+6	OPTION+SPACE
Nonbreaking hyphen	CTRL+=	CMD+=
Right indent tab	SHIFT+TAB	OPTION+TAB
Nonbreaking space	CTRL+5	CMD+5
Breaking en space	CTRL+SHIFT+6	OPTION+SPACE
Nonbreaking en space	CTRL+ALT+SHIFT+6	CMD+OPTION+SPACE
Breaking flexible space	CTRL+SHIFT+5	OPTION+SHIFT+SPACE
Nonbreaking flexible space	CTRL+ALT+SHIFT+5	CMD+OPTION+ SHIFT+SPACE
Breaking punctuation space	SHIFT+SPACE, or CTRL+6	SHIFT+SPACE
Nonbreaking punctuation space	CTRL+SHIFT+SPACE or CTRL+ALT+6	CMD+SHIFT+SPACE

B

Inserting Tag Characters

The following is a listing of QuarkXPress 4's style tags:

Character attributes	Code
Plain	<P>
Bold	<B>
Italic	<I>
Outline	<O>
Shadow	<S>
Underline	<U>
Word underline	<W>
Strikethrough	</>
All caps	<K>
Small caps	<H>
Superscript	<+>
Subscript	<->
Superior	<V>
Type style of current style sheet	<$>
Change font	<f"*fontname*">
Change font size	<z###.##> measured in points
Change color	<c"*colorname*"> or <cC###,M###,Y###,K###,cW###>
Change shade	<s###>
Horizontal scale	<h###>
Kern the next two characters	<k###.##>
Track	<t###.##>
Set baseline shift	<b###.##>
Vertical scale	<y###.##>

Paragraph attributes	Code
Left-align paragraph	<*L>
Center-align paragraph	<*C>
Right-align paragraph	<*R>
Justify paragraph	<*J>
Force justify	<*F>
Set tab stops	<*t(##.#, #,*"fillcharacter"*> where *t* sets the tab stop, and information in parentheses indicates tab stop, tab type (0=left, 1=center, 2=right, 3=decimal, 4=comma or align on character), and leader character
Set paragraph attributes	<*p##.#,##.#,##.#,##.#,##.#,##.#,g or G> where the first 7 values set left, first, right, leading, space before, space after, and lock to baseline to on (G) or off (g)
H&J	<*h*"H&Jstylename"*>
Rule above	<*ra(##,#,*"colorname"*,#,##,##,##> where items in parentheses represent line width, line style, color, shade, from left, from right, and offset values. The style number corresponds to the order in which line styles appear in the rules Style drop-down menu beginning at 1. The rule offset value may be specified in points, or a percentage as in ##%; including a *T* before the left indent sets the option to the width of actual characters in the first line of text of the paragraph text to follow.
Rule below	Same as above, only preceded by <*rb
Drop cap	<*d(*charactercount,linecount*)>

B

| Keep with next | <*kn1> turns the feature on, <*kn0> turns it off |
| Keep together | <kt(A)> set the feature to Keep All lines together, and <kt(#,#)> sets it to begin and end on specific lines |

Style sheet definition	**Code**
Apply normal style sheet	@$:*paragraph text*
Apply no style sheet	@:*paragraph text*
Define a style sheet	@*stylesheetname=*<*paragraphattributes*>
Base a style sheet on another	@*stylesheetname=*[s*"based-onname"*]<*paragraphattributes*>
Apply a defined style sheet	@*stylesheetname:paragraph text*
Style definition	@*stylesheetname [s]*<*paragraphattributes*>

Special characters	**Code**
New line (soft return)	<\n>
Discretionary return	<\d>
Hyphen	<\->
Indent here	<\i>
Right indent tab	<\t>
Standard space	<\s>
Figure space	<\f>
Punctuation space	<\p>
1/4-em space	<\q>
Discretionary hyphen	<\h>
Previous text box number character	<\2>
Current text box number character	<\3>

Next page text box number character	<\4>
New column	<\c>
New box	<\b>
Decimal ASCII code for character	<\#*decimalvalue*>
Indicator for Mac OS character set	<e0>
Indicator for Windows character set	<e1>
ISO Latin 1 character set	<e2>
@ symbol	<\@>
< symbol	<\<>
\ symbol	<\\>

B

In the 16-page color insert of this book you've seen a variety of full-color layout and design examples demonstrating certain features of XPress. While some of the examples demonstrate complex text formatting to achieve a desired layout effect, others are highly complex and involve integrating pictures with text and use unique program features available in XPress. Thanks and credit go to the following companies and/or individuals who lent their time, energy, and resources in providing these examples.

Rebecca Rees, Design Associate
Fast Company Magazine
Boston, Massachusetts

Jake Widman, **Publisher**
Jean Zambelli, **Art Director**
Publish Magazine
San Francisco, California

Elaine Chu
Elaine Chu Graphic Design
Oakland, California

Malcolm Frouman, Art Director
Business Week
New York, New York

Mary Power Patton, Director of Public Relations
Vantage One Communications Group
Cleveland, Ohio

Thomas and Constance Puckett
Intelligent Design Enforcement Agency (I.D.E.A.)
Portsmouth, New Hampshire

Wendy Cotie
Cotie Communications
Ottawa, Canada

The following descriptions correspond directly to the pages in the color insert and will help provide more detail about the images.

PAGE 1

Description: *Business Week*, Cover Design "*The Best Mutual Funds*"
February 3, 1997 issue

Designer: Francesca Messina

Firm: *Business Week*

Format: Letter size, portrait, process color

Contact: *Business Week*, The McGraw-Hill Companies,
1221 Avenue of the Americas, New York, NY 10021-1095

This first of a series of cover design and layout examples shown in *Fundamental QuarkXPress 4* demonstrates XPress' strengths in manipulating text in order to mold characters to guide the reader's eye. A background texture-style graphic picture is used to add interest and color to what would otherwise be a stark, flat background.

PAGES 2, 3, 4, and 5

Description: *Macworld,* 1996-97 editorial calendars

Design: Elaine Chu

Illustrations: Gordon Studer, Chris Lensch, John Ritter, Ron Chan,
Riccardo Stampatori, Larry Goode, Stuart Bradford,
Richard Downs, LeVan/Barbee Studio, James Yang, Hank Osuna

Firm:	Elaine Chu Graphic Design
Client:	*Macworld Magazine*, IDG
Format:	All examples are 21.5 inches by 11 inches horizontal gatefold with a finished size of 11 by 7.25 inches printed with full-bleed on all sides in full process color.
Contact:	Elaine Chu Graphic Design 302-748 Oakland Avenue, #302 Oakland CA 94611 Phone (510) 597-1087 Fax (510) 597-1087 egchu@aol.com. Contact Richard Doans at (510) 470-0435 Contact Hank Osuna at **www.hankosuna.com**

Created for Macworld magazine, these quarterly calendars were mailed out to advertisers to remind them of the close dates for specific issues and to preview upcoming editorial highlights. The client's request was to have all the copy incorporated into a visually striking, legible, and functional calendar format. With this in mind, a hierarchy of information was worked out the list the days of the week and numerals were chosen in a straightforward manner. The typography was played with in the way each of the names of the months were "interwoven" into the calendar grid. A bit of kerning was required, and color trapping too. Both were easily done in Quark.

The EPS illustrations were imported into the Quark layouts. The piece was printed in process colors. Custom Quark color palettes were made using CMYK screen builds which supported the illustrators' palettes. Color also served as a connecting element for content. The tined box of each of the close dates linked up with the same color tint in the respective month's end editorial highlights. The size of these calendars is 11" x 22" and they function both as direct mail pieces and as mini-posters. Response was positive both at Macworld and among their advertisers.

PAGE 6

Description: *Brochure design*

Designer: Thomas S. Puckett

Firm: Intelligent Design Enforcement Agency (I.D.E.A.)

Format: Letter size, portrait, process color

Contact: Thomas S. Puckett, Intelligent Design Enforcement Agency (I.D.E.A.)
               55 Miller Avenue, #5, Portsmouth, New Hampshire 03801
               Phone (603) 433-9334
               Fax (603) 436-3821
               www.intelligentdesign.com

This brochure features bright colors and a bold simple design. As part of a direct mail campaign to introduce a new company, it was designed to capture immediate attention. Quark XPress and Adobe Photoshop were used in the design.

PAGE 7

Description: Direct mail brochure design

Designer: Thomas S. Puckett

Firm: Intelligent Design Enforcement Agency (I.D.E.A.)

Format: Letter size, portrait, process color

Contact: Thomas S. Puckett, Intelligent Design Enforcement Agency (I.D.E.A.)
               55 Miller Avenue, #5, Portsmouth, New Hampshire 03801
               Phone (603) 433-9334
               Fax (603) 436-3821
               www.intelligentdesign.com

EVOLV is a company that provides Web technology for the building industry. The firm's business image called for a slick, modern design. Different computer screen montages were photographed and used as small details throughout the brochure. QuarkXPress 4 and Adobe Photoshop were used to create the brochure.

C

PAGES 8 and 9

Firm: Vantage One Communications Group

Client: Cleveland-Cliffs, Inc.

Format: Oversized 9 by 12 inches, portrait, process and spot color

Description: Custom corporate publication

Design/Art Direction: Molly Markey/Mario Rini
Vantage One Communications Group, Inc.

Photography: Trepal Photography, Cleveland & Western Reserve
Historical Society Archives, Cleveland, Ohio

Author: Richard J. Osborne

Editors: Jeanne A. Weitman, Cleveland-Cliffs, Inc., and Edward J. Walsh,
Custom Publishing Group

Printing: The Perlmuter Printing Company, Cleveland, Ohio

Contact: Mary Power Patton, Director of Public Relations
Vantage One Communications Group
850-812 Huron Road
Cleveland, Ohio 44115-1126
Phone (216) 479-7788
www.vantageone.com.

Celebrating 150 Years is an anniversary book that Cleveland-Cliffs, Inc. produced for internal use as a corporate gift to be distributed to its past and present employees (13,000 circulation). In serving the client's needs, Vantage One Communications Group was in charge of designing and developing this book to showcase Cleveland-Cliffs' 150 years as a celebration, rather than as a history book. The designers' extensive Quark experience, and their knowledge of Adobe Photoshop and Macromedia Freehand came into play in creating this work.

The cover image, the large red letter C, and a diamond-shaped field of color is a distinctive corporate identity for Cleveland-Cliffs, and worked well in the cover design.

The goal of the first two-page spread was to show in full color what a mine looks like. The aerial, panoramic view helps the reader picture the enormous size of the mine.

The second two-page spread uses Freehand EPS files that were imported into the Quark layout and a number overlays were added. The clear image quality of the EPS files assured that the final work would be attractive and readable.

PAGE 10

Description: *Publish Magazine*, April 1998 cover

Art Director: Jean Zambelli

Photo Mosaic: Robert Silvers

Base Photo: Adobe Image Library

Mosaic Photos: Creative Americans

Portraits: Carl Van Vechten, 1932-1964

Format: Letter size, process color

The cover story for April was the annual stock photo directory. A mosaic was a perfect way to convey the idea of the overwhelming quantity of stock images covered. The base photo shows a young woman with an excited expression. This added a warm, friendly feeling to the vintage black and white photos used to make up the mosaic. Black and white was used for drama and simplicity, but to add depth to the Photoshop file, the images were saved as a tiff and "colorized" it in Quark with a four-color navy blue. We added a fifth plate to the Quark file to make our cover lines stand out in fluorescent yellow. All of the trapping was set in Quark using overprint and auto amount (+).

Description: *Publish Magazine*, May Feature: Managing the Mix

Art Director: Jean Zambelli

Designer: Natalie Jeday

Illustration: Stephanie Power

It is increasingly common to find Macintoshes, PCs, and Unix Worstations all under one roof. The design challenge was how to present this information in a provocative manner. The solution was to bring life to the subject by illustrating three types of computer characters: one for the Macintosh representing its artistic uses, one for the PC, representing its business uses, and one for the Unix workstation, emphasizing its heftier mathematical abilities. They were all brought together under the happily content figure of the system manager.

Stephanie Power was picked as illustrator because we felt her whimsical approach would attract readers and balance out the dryness of the piece. The dilemma in choosing a typefact was to either pick one reflecting the playfulness of the illustration or go the other direction and choose a more sedate face reflecting the serious content of the story. Gill Sans was finally chosen for its ability to straddle that line. The typeface and elements from the illustration carry on the theme throughout the story. All the irregular shapes and ornamental drop caps were created in QuarkXPress.

Description: *Publish Magazine*, May Feature: Give Yourself a Big Promotion

Art Director: Jean Zambelli

Photographer: Jim Hildreth

Contact: Publish Magazine
501 Second Street, 6th floor
San Francisco, CA 94107
Phone (415) 978-3280
Fax (415) 975-2613
www.publish.com

We wanted the featured self-promotion campaigns to be the stars of the show so we kept the layout as clean and open as possible. The headline type "Give yourself a..." was arranged in QuarkXPress using baseline shift and tracking. All graphic elements (other than the word "Promotion" and the matching drop caps) were created in QuarkXPress.

PAGES 11, 12, and 13

Description: *Fast Company,* Cover design *"Free Agent Nation"*
December/January 1998 issue.

Cover Designer: Patrick Miller, Fast Company Art Director

Page 42: *Report from the Future* Designed by Gretchen Smelter, Senior Designer;
Photography by Everard Williams Jr.;
Written by Katharine Mieszowski

Page 78: *Work Rites* Designed by Gretchen Smelter, Senior Designer;
Photography by Katrina Dickson; Written by Eric Ransdell

Page 100: *Unit of One Holiday Guide/Travel* Designed by Gretchen Smelter,
Senior Designer; Photography by Furnald/Gray;
Styling by Rich Holben

Page 113: Designed by Gretchen Smelter, Senior Designer

Page 151: *Free Agent Almanac* Designed by Patrick Mitchell, Art Director;
Illustrations by Harry Campbell

Format: Oversized 8.75 by 11.25 inches, process color with full bleed

Contact: Rebecca Rees, Design Associate, *Fast Company Magazine,*
77 North Washington Street, Boston, Massachusetts, 02114-1927
Phone (617) 973-0300
www.fastcompany.com

Fast Company magazine provides information on the new economy and workplace for people who believe in fusing tough-minded performance with sane human values. The magazine's two fundamental propositions: there is a new world of business evolving, and there is a community committed to new ways of working, competing, and living and growing, are reflected in the cutting-edge design work found in the magazine's layout and design. Contact **www.fastcompany.com** for more information and subscription details.

PAGE 14

Description: Corporate Advertising supplement

Designer: Wendy Cotie

Firm: Cotie Communications

Format: Letter size, portrait, process color

Contact: Wendy Cotie, Cotie Communications
                   15 Cherrywood Drive
                   Nepean, Ontario K2H 6H1
                   Phone (613) 820-2060
                   Fax (613) 820-8675

This four-page advertorial from *Canadian Business* magazine was produced for Prospectus, Inc. and their client KMPG Ltd. The ad was produced using Photoshop and Illustrator for all scans and graphics, and QuarkXPress for typography and the composition.

PAGE 15

Description: *Business Week*, feature spread "*Special Report: Internet Communities*," May 5, 1997 issue

Art Director: Andrée Kahlmorgan

Illustrations: Dave Jonason

Format: Letter size, two-page spread, full bleed process color

Contact: *Business Week*, The McGraw-Hill Companies,
                   1221 Avenue of the Americas, New York, NY 10021-1095

The full-color two-page spread at the top of page 15 in the color insert demonstrates XPress' extensive picture-handling capabilities with picture-masking and text runaround features in use. This particular example uses a variety of XPress-defined process colors applied to the background and various text boxes.

Page 15

Description: *Business Week*, Cover story "*Hey Kid, Buy This!*," June 30, 1997 issue

Art Director: Francesca Messina

Photographs: Elizabeth Hathon

Format: Letter size, two-page spread, full bleed process color

Contact: *Business Week*, The McGraw-Hill Companies, 1221 Avenue of the Americas, New York, NY 10021-1095

The full-color two-page spread at the bottom of page 15 of the color insert demonstrates full use of XPress' picture-clipping and text runaround capabilities.

Page 16

Description: *Business Week*, Cover design "*How to Play This Market*," June 16 1997 issue

Design: Molly Leach

Illustrations: Gary Hallgren

Format: Letter size, portrait, process color

Contact: *Business Week*, The McGraw-Hill Companies, 1221 Avenue of the Americas, New York, NY 10021-1095

This cover design uses the strengths of XPress' text control to format and manipulate text and integrate graphic pictures in a layout which effectively guides the reader's eye.

A

B

C

G

H

I

N

Q

T